ADVANCE PRAISE FOR
MASTERING MEDITATION

"Rinpoché's teachings are genuine manifestations of Lama Tsongkhapa's tradition. It is wonderful to see that more of his clear, practical, and precious instructions are now available in English."
—Geshé Tenzin Namdak, senior Western student of Rinpoché and resident teacher at Jamyang Buddhist Centre, London

"Although typically associated with the Kagyü tradition of Tibetan Buddhism, the profound meditation on the nature of mind known as mahāmudrā (the great seal) is also important among the Geluk, whose masters have studied, practiced, and taught the technique for many centuries. In this accurate, scholarly, and highly readable translation, Ven. Tenzin Gache brings to light two important texts by the beloved modern Geluk master Chöden Rinpoché (1930–2015): a clear exposition of how to attain calm abiding (*śamatha*), which is an essential part of mahāmudrā meditation, and a detailed commentary on the root verses on mahāmudrā composed by the First/Fourth Panchen Lama, Losang Chökyi Gyaltsen (1570–1662). Chöden Rinpoché's discussion of mahāmudrā is among the most thorough and practical of any written by a modern Gelukpa—including lucid discussions of the philosophical analysis required to perfect sūtra-level mahāmudrā and of procedures for great-seal tantric practice, while Ven. Gache's introduction, notes, and supplementary sections provide a helpful window onto Rinpoché's incisive and inspiring writings. *Mastering Meditation* is a superlative book, which should be on the bookshelf of anyone interested in mahāmudrā, its place in Geluk tradition, and its power to reveal to us the true nature of our mind."
—Roger R. Jackson, author of *Mind Seeing Mind: Mahāmudrā and the Geluk Tradition of Tibetan Buddhism*

"Embodying the scholarship of a *lharampa* geshe and the insights of a realized yogi, Chöden Rinpoché is the perfect master to explain how to meditate on the ultimate nature of the mind, and does so in this wonderful book, made accessible by Venerable Gache's excellent introduction and translation. Highly recommended."
—Dr. Nicholas Ribush, director, Lama Yeshe Wisdom Archive

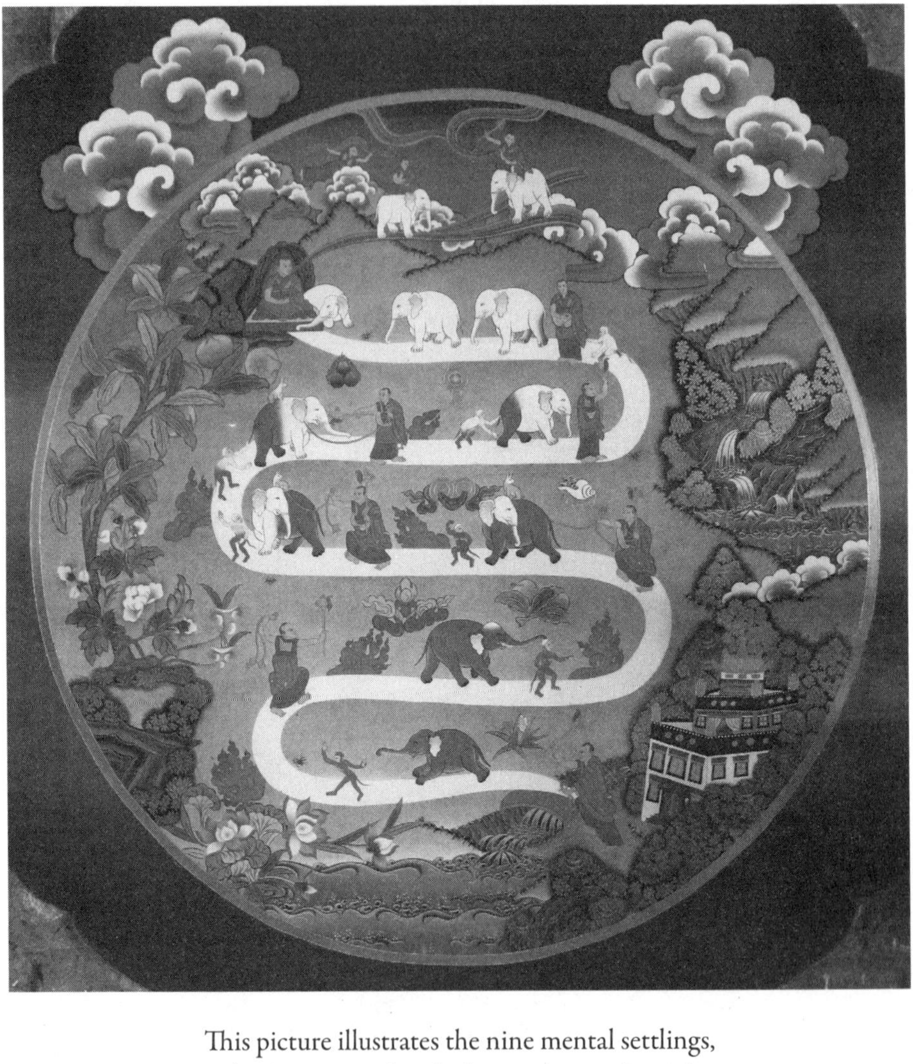

This picture illustrates the nine mental settlings, culminating in calm abiding and special insight.

Mastering Meditation

Instructions on Calm Abiding and Mahāmudrā

His Eminence Chöden Rinpoché

FOREWORD BY

His Holiness the Dalai Lama

TRANSLATED, INTRODUCED,
AND ANNOTATED BY

Ven. Tenzin Gache

Wisdom

Wisdom Publications
199 Elm Street
Somerville, MA 02144 USA
wisdomexperience.org

Library of Congress Cataloging-in-Publication Data
Names: Chöden Rinpoché, 1930–2015, author. | Gache, Tenzin, translator.
Title: Mastering meditation: instructions on calm abiding and mahāmudrā / His Eminence Chöden Rinpoché; translated, introduced, and annotated by Tenzin Gache.
Description: First. | Somerville: Wisdom Publications, 2020. | Includes bibliographical references and index.
Identifiers: LCCN 2019025467 (print) | LCCN 2019025468 (ebook) | ISBN 9781614296188 (hardcover) | ISBN 9781614296294 (ebook)
Subjects: LCSH: Meditation—Buddhism. | Meditation—Buddhism—Early works to 1800.
Classification: LCC BQ5612 .C47 2020 (print) | LCC BQ5612 (ebook) | DDC 294.3/4435—dc23
LC record available at https://lccn.loc.gov/2019025467
LC ebook record available at https://lccn.loc.gov/2019025468

ISBN 978-1-61429-618-8 ebook ISBN 978-1-61429-629-4

24 23 22 21 20 5 4 3 2 1

Cover design by Jim Zaccaria. Interior design by Gopa & Ted2, Inc.
Cover image courtesy of Kurty Wong.
Diligent efforts were made in every case to identify copyright holders of the photographs. The author and the publisher are grateful for the use of this material.
Permission to use the image on page ii is courtesy of Mr. Tsering Phuntsok and Norbulingka Institute. The illustration of the dissolution on page 163 and the illustration of the channels and chakras on page 171 are courtesy of Yamantaka.org. The illustration of Paṇchen Losang Chökyi Gyaltsen on page 254 is courtesy of Andy Weber.

Printed on acid-free paper that meets the guidelines for permanence and durability of the Production Guidelines for Book Longevity of the Council on Library Resources.

Printed in Canada.

Contents

A Lamp Clarifying the Path to Liberation:
The Manner of Actualizing Calm Abiding and Instructions
on Gendenpa Mahāmudrā

Foreword

BY HIS HOLINESS THE DALAI LAMA

MEDITATION PRACTICE is essential for the development of spiritual qualities such as loving-kindness, compassion, and wisdom to reach their fullest potential. Without training our mind through meditation, our mind wanders and our ability to focus and apply our mind in a disciplined manner remains weak.

There are two broad categories of meditation practice, one belonging to calm abiding (*shamatha*) that focuses on training attention, stability, and awareness, and the other belonging to special insight (*vipashyana*), which is focused on cultivating insight through analysis. The purpose of achieving calm abiding is not just for the sake of gaining higher levels of concentration. Rather it is to serve as the basis for achieving special insight realizing emptiness through which afflictive emotions can be removed completely. Mahāmudrā is a highly advanced form of practice of special insight, and the transmission of its instruction exists also in the Gelug Tradition.

I am glad that Chöden Rinpoché's teachings on these two topics are now compiled into this book, *Mastering Meditation*. I commend the translator and all those who have worked hard in making these teachings available in English.

Publisher's Acknowledgment

The Publisher gratefully acknowledges the generous help of Awakening Tara Singapore and donors and Neo Kok Theng in sponsoring the production of this book.

Gyalten Translation Group's Preface

The Gyalten Translation Group of Awakening Vajra International gratefully wishes to acknowledge the extensive efforts of Venerable Tenzin Gache in producing this lucid translation of His Eminence Chöden Rinpoché's profound guide to mahāmudrā and calm abiding.

As movingly recounted in Venerable Gache's preface, Chöden Rinpoché had and continues to have a profound effect on all with whom he came into contact. Not only was he an accomplished scholar who held and transmitted rare oral traditions, untiringly teaching the Dharma in the East and West at the behest of His Holiness the Dalai Lama, but he was also a legendary yogi who accomplished a near twenty-year solitary retreat under the direst of circumstances. Anyone who ever had the good fortune to experience Rinpoché's presence will have little doubt that Rinpoché himself embodied, at the highest level, the realization of the practices described in this book.

This skillful translation constitutes what will hopefully be the first in a series of works edited by the Gyalten Translation Group and published by Wisdom Publications. Initiated by Geshe Gyalten Kungka, principal disciple of His Eminence Chöden Rinpoché, the series will focus on preserving and spreading Rinpoché's intellectual and spiritual legacy, while also presenting works by Geshe Gyalten and other close disciples of Rinpoché. The Gyalten Translation Group (Jeff Seipel, Gyalten Tsondue, Sue Bartfield, Timothy Brown, and Gyalten Jigdrel) offers its sincere thanks to Venerable Gache, to Laura Cunningham at Wisdom Publications, and to all the students of Chöden Rinpoché around the world who have shown great devotion to Rinpoché and steadily supported the work of Awakening Vajra International. We also wish to thank Geshe Gyalten Kungka for his vital role as an indispensable communicator of Rinpoché's teachings and, most of all, Rinpoché himself—now reincarnated as Tenzin Gyalten Rinpoché—without whom none of these activities would have been possible.

Gyalten Translation Group

A rare photo of Chöden Rinpoché at Sera in Tibet, circa 1950s.

Translator's Preface

Chöden Rinpoché, through his presence in this world, substantiated the veracity of the Buddha's teachings and the inconceivable potential of the human mind. From his purposeful, serene movements to his delicate but compassionate smile, from the confident humility with which he depicted the path to liberation to his almost otherworldly aura of wisdom and peace, the timeless Dharma was the spark breathing vitality and care into Rinpoché's most mundane actions, and he made it his life's work to convey to others, lucidly but gently, the fathomless depths of his insight.

Rinpoché lived a quiet, unassuming lifestyle, eschewing the normal measures of success, such as wealth, family life, and prestige. But that does not mean that Rinpoché did not have his own treasured goals or that he did not pursue them with a passionate ambition. From a very young age, Rinpoché assiduously devoted all of his time and energy to cultivating his mind, first through study and monastic training from childhood through early adulthood and subsequently through nearly twenty years of solitary retreat in austere conditions, all amid a time of great social upheaval in Tibet. He did so with unbending inner confidence gained through judicious scrutiny of the Buddha's teachings and with strength of conviction developed through observing the outstanding examples of countless past and current practitioners in his country.

I first had the unbelievably good fortune to meet Chöden Rinpoché when he visited Kurukulla Center for Tibetan Buddhist Studies in Medford, Massachusetts, in the fall of 2004, as I was beginning my final year of college just a mile away at Tufts University. Having found intellectual and personal solace in the Buddha's teachings, I had already determined to ordain as a monk upon completing my studies. But meeting Rinpoché added a new level of inspiration and conviction, as though one of the wise elders one reads about in the ancient sūtras had leapt off the page and appeared in the modern world. Spending only two precious weeks attending Rinpoché's talks drove home the recognition that the Buddhist teachings were more than just philosophical speculation. Suddenly the mundane world with its everyday concerns seemed hopelessly dull, and its inhabitants appeared as little children in the presence of this mature yet unremittingly pragmatic master.

During those weeks I made it my task to introduce friends, family, and teachers to Rinpoché's teachings. Even though many of them completely lacked a paradigm for comprehending who Rinpoché was or the extent to which he had developed his mind, all of them expressed gratitude, even awe, at the opportunity to be in his presence. One of my college professors expressed succinctly what most of us likely felt: "I don't know what he has done, but all I can say is, *I want what he's having!*"

Rinpoché extended a kind invitation to me to come live and study at Lhopa Khangtsen, his regional house group within Sera Jé Monastic University in South India, after completing my degree. Thus began my second process of maturation and education in a new world and culture. What I soon observed was that even among Tibetan monks, who possessed more of a context for Rinpoché's soaring heights of realization than did my Western friends, the presence of such a living master still provided an indispensable affirmation that the discipline we followed and the texts espousing it were not just arcane relics of an embellished past. Perhaps epithets for Buddha like "knower of all aspects" and "supreme guide of those to be tamed" referred to something concrete and even attainable with sustained focus and effort.

Tibetan society, especially monastic society, is in many regards a premodern culture struggling to integrate into the modern world. Through my years as a participant-observer in this context, I have gradually lost the starry-eyed enthusiasm with which I began and actually gained a deep appreciation for the achievements of Western culture, with its standards of education, technology, and access to information, medical care, and social support, which I would have taken for granted had I remained in my home country. Nonetheless, through semester after semester of Buddhist study and prolonged exposure to Rinpoché and other such rare masters, my initial intuition has grown into a deep conviction that we in the West are missing something extraordinary. Ancient Indian society followed a different trajectory of evolution and produced methods of mental cultivation that challenge basic paradigms of modern science regarding the nature and potential of the mind, and this knowledge was passed on to inheritors scattered around the Asian continent. Following a Mind and Life dialogue between Tibetan monks and Western scientists at Drepung Monastery in Mundgod, India, in January 2013, Christof Koch, chief scientific officer at the Allen Institute for Brain Sciences in Seattle, offered these reflections:

> What passed between these representatives of two distinct intellectual modes of thinking about the world were facts, data—knowledge. That is, knowledge about the more than two-millennia-old Eastern tradition of investigating the mind from the inside, from an interior, subjective point of view, and the much more recent insights provided by empirical Western ways to probe the brain and its behavior using a third-person, reductionist framework. What the former brings to the table are scores of meditation techniques to develop mindfulness, concentration, insight, serenity, wisdom and, it is hoped, in the end, enlightenment. . . . After years of daily contemplative exercise—nothing comes easily in meditation—practitioners can achieve considerable control over their mind.
>
> Twelve years of schooling, four years of college and an even longer time spent in advanced graduate training fail to familiarize our future doctors, soldiers, engineers, scientists, accountants and politicians with such techniques. Western universities do not teach methods to enable the developing or the mature mind to become quiet and to focus its considerable powers on a single object, event or train of thought. There is no introductory class on "Focusing the Mind." And this is to our loss![1]

In the developing milieu of Buddhism in the West, the existence of enlightenment in the full, traditional sense of the term remains an open topic of debate. Such debate is a positive step toward understanding, and those interested in these topics should not feel that they have no option but to take one teacher's word over another's. As aspiring practitioners did in traditional Buddhist cultures, we today can study, reflect, debate, and discuss with our teachers and other students. To some extent we can also test our own experience in meditation, but because advanced states like those described in this book require an enormous investment of time and energy to actualize, it is important to lay a groundwork of understanding through more inferential means. Otherwise, if one does not experience results after some time—and it is likely that one will not—one might give up the endeavor.

1. Koch 2013, 29. For an in-depth exploration of Western science's growing forays into traditional meditation, see especially Goleman and Davidson 2017.

Without individuals and communities dedicated to long-term study, reflection, and meditation, we will never know whether the refined states of consciousness the Buddha described—and that Rinpoché clarifies in this book—may become a reality. Fortunately, the Buddha's approach of reasoning and investigation is fully compatible with the approach of science, even if many of his claims challenge the current mainstream scientific worldview. Those with open minds and genuine interest must seriously consider these ideas.

When Rinpoché passed away in 2015, his close student and longtime attendant Geshé Gyalten asked if I would take on the task of translating many of Rinpoché's teachings into English. Although I was still less than halfway through the long process of full-time study, debate, and accumulation of merit that is life at Sera, I agreed with the consideration that this work would become a part of my own education. *Zhi gnas sgrub tshul dang dge ldan pa'i phyag chen gyi bka' khrid thar lam gsal sgron* (*A Lamp Clarifying the Path to Liberation: The Manner of Actualizing Calm Abiding and Instructions on Gendenpa Mahāmudrā*), Rinpoché's articulate and concise instructions on developing the mind all the way to full enlightenment, had not yet been translated and seemed a good place to start; that has become the book you're now holding in your hands.

The first part of this book contains instructions for developing calm abiding, an unshakable single-pointedness of mind. The second part offers advanced instructions on using calm abiding as a platform to develop mahāmudrā, a specialized meditation that uncovers subtle, hidden levels of mind and utilizes them to pierce into the ultimate nature of self and reality, leading finally to complete enlightenment.

It is my sincere hope that this translation of Rinpoché's instructions for developing concentration and insight will offer a coherent picture for those interested in examining the mind's potential and serve as accessible instruction for those wishing to make steps toward actualizing that potential.

I dedicate this translation to the long life of His Holiness the Fourteenth Dalai Lama, in loving memory of Chöden Rinpoché, Losang Gyalten Jikdrel Wangchuk, and to the long life and success of Tenzin Gyalten Rinpoché. May he bring the profound message of his predecessor to the world at large.

Gelong Tenzin Gache
Sera IMI House, Sera Jé

Translator's Introduction

THIS BOOK OFFERS practical instructions on developing the latter two of the three higher trainings of ethical discipline, concentration, and wisdom. The first part of the book, "Calm Abiding," teaches a method for developing single-pointed concentration. The structure of the teaching is roughly based on the celebrated *Liberation in the Palm of Your Hand* (Tib. *Lam rim rnam grol lag bcangs*), by Chöden Rinpoché's own teacher, Phabongkha Rinpoché, though Chöden Rinpoché does not quote this text directly and often diverges from its outlines into useful tangential explanations. The second part, "Mahāmudrā," is Rinpoché's direct commentary on the *Highway of the Conquerors: The Root Text of Mahāmudrā of the Precious Genden Instruction Lineage* (Tib. *Dge ldan bka' rgyud rin po che'i phyag chen rtsa ba rgyal ba'i gzhung lam*), by Losang Chökyi Gyaltsen, the Fourth Paṇchen Lama.[2] The root text and Rinpoché's commentary teach methods for developing insight into the nature of the self, the mind, and reality, through both the exoteric sūtra system and the more advanced system of secret mantra.

The Buddha's teachings offer a complete method for freeing the mind from all suffering and pain forever and fully developing one's potential to be of everlasting benefit to all sentient beings. Those who examine his teachings and gain authentic faith and interest in this extraordinary possibility engage in the practice of the three higher trainings. Although Buddhist practice can involve ritual aspects such as prostrations, mantra recitation, and altar offerings, these practices are meant to support—never to supersede—the three higher trainings.

The higher training of ethical discipline primarily involves refraining from harming others and limiting one's needs and desires to what is minimally required to sustain continued practice. Although this first training is not the principal subject of this book, Rinpoché does begin by emphasizing its importance, and readers should understand that without this basis, one cannot hope to advance further in the practice. Harming others creates

2. For a short biography and explanation of why Paṇchen Losang Chökyi Gyaltsen is alternatively considered the First or Fourth Paṇchen Lama, see appendix 1.

heavy imprints on the mind that will obstruct any significant progress in meditation, and having many desires leads to worry and distraction, hampering the development of concentration.

The higher training of concentration involves gaining mastery over the mind through developing its natural potential for focus, acuity, and dexterity, much as an athlete trains his or her body. Buddhist tradition maintains that the most effective tool for examining the nature of the mind is the mind itself but that most people's minds are too uncontrolled and unrefined to undertake such work. This second higher training turns the mind into a precise instrument, laying the groundwork for the development of insight.

The higher training of wisdom is twofold: it involves insight into the conventional nature of cause and effect and insight into the ultimate nature of reality. Through studying and contemplating cause and effect, a practitioner comes to see that experiences of happiness and suffering do not arise randomly. Although external circumstances can act as conditions for inner experiences, they do not act as the substantial cause, much like water and sunlight nourish a seed but are not the substantial cause of a sprout. Without a seed, water and sunlight alone cannot produce a sprout, and similarly without an imprint on the mind from past actions, external circumstances will not give rise to happiness or suffering in the mind. Positive, constructive actions and ways of thinking lead to happiness in the future, while harmful, destructive actions and thoughts lead to suffering. Although this process is logical and definite, because it occurs in a complex way, at a subtle level, and over a great length of time, usually we fail to notice its intricacies. For example, while a person who has become depressed might ascribe the cause to stress or to chemical processes in the brain, the primary cause could be the ripening of imprints he sowed many years earlier through angry behavior. Stress and biological factors only serve as conditions allowing this mental state to become manifest, but because the mind is coarse and murky, one fails to notice the ripening of imprints and blames the experience entirely on external factors. Further complicating this process, Buddhist psychology asserts that any effect is rarely traceable to a single cause but arises from a network of past causes, and this network can extend over many past lifetimes that are completely hidden to one's present mind.

By using the concentration that was developed in the second higher training, however, a practitioner can gradually gain insight into this subtle process and discern more correctly the nature of inner cause and effect. Such insight naturally leads to insight into the ultimate nature of self and phenomena: their lack of substantial, independent existence. One begins to recognize how the mind makes false imputations—exaggerating the qualities of things and over-reifying their status as good or bad, beautiful or ugly, friend or foe. By meditating in this way over a great length of time, one progressively frees the mind of false impositions and gains the wisdom that sees things as they really are, not how one presupposes or would like them to be.

Calm Abiding

"Calm abiding" translates the Tibetan term *zhiné* (Tib. *zhi gnas*; Skt. *śamatha*). *Zhi*—"calming" or "pacifying"—refers to pacifying distractions toward external objects. *Né*—"abiding"—means the mind abides focused on an internally cultivated object. With calm abiding, a meditator can remain focused on an object of meditation for as long as she wishes—hours, even days—without the slightest distraction. At the same time, a subtle, calming energy—the bliss of pliancy—pervades her body and mind, making it easy to remain comfortably seated and preventing worry and agitation. Although a meditator who has reached this stage might experience the arising of sensual desire, worry, or occasional anger during postmeditation sessions, if she recognizes these states arising and focuses her mind, they will rapidly subside in most cases. Calm abiding is a mental state far surpassing our ordinary conception of sound mental health, and it is only attainable with sustained effort over a long period of time.

How to Achieve Calm Abiding

Just as somebody who wishes eventually to run a marathon proceeds incrementally, running a bit more each day, and maintains sound health through proper diet and sleep, likewise somebody who trains to actualize calm abiding must take measured steps and forsake pursuits that do not support a sound, stable mind. On page 47, Rinpoché outlines the sixfold collection of causes that one must assemble to establish a basis for the actual practice of meditation. These causes are (1) staying in a conducive place, (2) having few wants, (3) having contentment, (4) thoroughly abandoning the bustle of many activities, (5) maintaining ethical discipline, and (6) thoroughly abandoning discursive thoughts.

Having laid a stable foundation, a practitioner chooses an objective support—a visualized object or quality of mind on which he will focus.

Some Buddhist traditions emphasize focusing on the breath, on sensations in the body, or on particular antidotes, like a decomposing corpse for one who tends toward desire. While some Tibetan practitioners do make use of these objects, the most common practice is to visualize the body of the Buddha and develop concentration by focusing on this visualization. Rinpoché chooses this method for his instructions, explaining on page 61 that it has certain advantages, such as creating positive potential in the mind and preparing a meditator for the more advanced visualization practices of the generation stage of tantra.

Visualizing this object to the best of one's ability (which initially might mean simply visualizing a thumbprint-sized shaft of golden light), a practitioner now attempts to maintain concentration. A beginner will be unable to hold the object in awareness for more than a few seconds. With practice, one is eventually able to hold the object in awareness for the duration of twenty-one respirations. At this point, one achieves the first of nine mental settlings, which are stages of concentration that culminate in actual calm abiding.

The second stage is reached when one can hold the object for the time it takes to recite the mantra *oṃ maṇi padme hūṃ* 108 times (about two minutes). At the third mental settling, one still loses the object periodically, but overall the time spent in concentration exceeds that spent in distraction.

When a practitioner can maintain the visualized object in mind for an entire meditation session without losing it, he has reached the fourth mental settling. However, he is still far from single-pointed concentration for two reasons: (1) the object lacks clarity and (2) distracting thoughts still cycle through the mind, even though they do not completely disrupt concentration. At this point, a practitioner begins to work with the two main obstacles to concentration: laxity and excitement.

Laxity is somewhat similar to the mental affliction of lethargy, but with two important distinctions. For one, ordinary people experience lethargy frequently but never experience laxity in the sense intended here. This mental formation only arises when one has achieved the stable concentration of the fourth mental settling. Secondly, lethargy is a nonvirtuous mind, as it leads to negative, self-defeating thought patterns and excessive sleep. Laxity can be either neutral or virtuous depending on what mind it accompanies, and abiding in laxity, especially subtle laxity, can be pleasant and feel like genuine concentration, when in actuality the mind is slightly dull. Gross laxity occurs at the fourth mental settling and means that the object lacks clarity. From the fifth mental settling, the object is clear, but with subtle laxity the clarity lacks intensity or sharpness.

Excitement, the other main obstacle, is a form of mental scattering. Mental scattering can have various causes, such as anger and even virtue—as when we are meditating, and we start thinking about practicing generosity—but the most common and most pernicious cause is desire-attachment. Thus excitement, a subtle form of desire, is singled out as a primary obstacle. Excitement could take the form of preconscious trains of thought that reveal themselves when the mind is focused, or it might simply manifest as flightiness or mental noise. Gross excitement is when the mind goes to another object, and one loses the object of meditation entirely. By the fourth mental settling this gross excitement has ceased, but one still deals with subtle excitement, the stir of conceptual thoughts just outside conscious awareness. Excitement at this point is subtle in the sense that it does not entirely overtake the mind, but it can still be forceful in the sense that it disturbs mental tranquility.

During the next four stages, the practitioner mainly focuses on the visualized object but occasionally applies antidotes to laxity and excitement when they become strong. If laxity is only mild, she may merely focus on brightening the visualized object, but if it is stronger, she may temporarily meditate on something uplifting, like compassion. If excitement is mild, the practitioner can imagine the object becoming heavier, but if excitement is strong—for example, if sensual desires arise continuously—she may address it more directly, by meditating on an antidote such as the foulness of the body.

By the seventh stage, laxity and excitement only arise weakly, and finally, at the eighth stage, if the practitioner makes effort at the beginning of the session, he can comfortably maintain the object in awareness without laxity and excitement. At the ninth stage, even this initial effort becomes unnecessary. Anytime he wishes to focus his mind, he can immediately and effortlessly enter into prolonged concentration. At this point, applying antidotes becomes superfluous, and the meditator simply relaxes into absorption. This stage is called a "simulacrum of calm abiding," but it is still not fully qualified calm abiding because the blissful pliancy of body and mind has yet to arise. By maintaining this state, soon such pliancy arises naturally in the meditator, and he achieves calm abiding.

Rinpoché also speaks of achieving calm abiding through the eight applications that are antidotes to the five faults. This presentation, drawn from the text *Differentiating the Middle from Extremes* (Skt. *Madhyāntavibhāga*; Tib. *Dbus mtha' rnam 'byed*), is another way of describing the same process of the mental settlings—it is not as though it is an entirely different method. The five faults are laziness, forgetting the instructions, laxity and excitement, not applying the antidote, and unnecessary application of the antidote. The eight applications are faith, aspiration, enthusiasm, pliancy, recollection, introspection, intention, and equanimity.

Among the faults to overcome, laziness is primarily an obstacle before beginning practice. One overcomes laziness through faith in the method, an aspiration to achieve calm abiding, and enthusiasm. "Faith" here is not blind faith, but a personal certainty gained through examining the possibility of attaining the outstanding qualities of calm abiding. Such faith leads to an aspiration to achieve calm abiding, and that aspiration leads to enthusiasm. When one actually achieves calm abiding, pliancy becomes an unshakable antidote to laziness, but until that time, one must rely on the other three antidotes.

During the first three mental settlings, the main obstacle is forgetting the instructions. This does not mean that if somebody asked, the practitioner would be unable to recall what her teacher had said. Rather it means that during the meditation session, the mind wanders off and loses the object. In other words, the object must be kept in active memory. The antidote here is recollection.[3]

From the fourth stage, one no longer completely forgets or loses the object, so laxity and excitement become the primary obstacles to overcome. As

3. I have chosen to translate the Tibetan *dran pa* (Skt. *smṛti*) as "recollection" throughout the text rather than the more familiar term "mindfulness." There is a long story behind the use of "mindfulness" to translate this term from traditional texts, which began with T. W. Rhys Davids in the nineteenth century. Although the original connotation of the term—"memory applied to purposeful activity in the present"—correctly conveyed the sense of recollection that the Sanskrit and Tibetan do, the term has taken on such varied associations in our modern Western culture that it often is taken to mean "awareness" or "equanimity." These associations distort the original meaning, which is clearly related to active memory—keeping some important understanding in mind and not being distracted rather than simply being open to whatever might appear to the mind. Especially in this context of calm abiding, the term specifically means keeping the object of meditation in mind, and so "recollection" seems a less ambiguous term. For an excellent presentation of the issues surrounding translation of this term, see Thanissaro 2012.

an antidote, one cultivates introspection, an internal awareness of whether these obstacles are affecting the mind.[4] When one actually recognizes laxity and excitement, it is a fault to not apply an antidote, so one cultivates the antidote of intention (Skt. *cetanā*; Tib. *sems pa*) to apply an antidote. While intention is the antidote to not applying an antidote, it is not the specific antidote to laxity and excitement. Based on intention, one must apply specific antidotes to these (as mentioned above on page 5). Although the specific antidotes to laxity and excitement are important, they are not actually included in the eight applications that are antidotes. But one should understand that their importance is implied and that it is not sufficient merely to cultivate introspection and intention, just as merely sending spies and planning an attack are not sufficient means to repel an approaching army.

Finally, at the ninth stage, laxity and excitement no longer arise, so (unnecessarily) applying an antidote itself becomes an obstacle. One simply rests in equanimity and waits patiently for the bliss of pliancy to arise naturally.

Two more ways of viewing this same process, drawn from Ārya Asaṅga's Five Treatises on the Grounds (Skt. *Yogācārabhūmi*[*śāstra*]; Tib. *Sa sde lnga*), are by means of the six powers and the four mental applications. These again correspond to specific stages. During the first mental settling, a practitioner relies on the power of hearing—that is, she attempts to apply the instructions she has heard. During the second mental settling, she relies on the power of reflection, meaning she has gained some slight personal experience and in light of that can reflect on the meaning of what she has heard. During the third and fourth settlings, she relies on the power of recollection, because she makes continuous effort to keep the object in mind. During the fifth and sixth settlings, because she is still struggling with laxity and excitement, she relies on the power of introspection. During the seventh and eighth settlings, she has almost completely overcome laxity and excitement, and so she relies on the power of zeal to overcome their last traces. Finally at the ninth settling, she no longer needs to make such effort, and she can relax

4. I have chosen to translate the Tibetan *shes bzhin* (Skt. *saṃprajanya*) as "introspection." Often this term is translated as "awareness" or "alertness," but I think "introspection" more precisely captures the specific meaning, which is to be aware of the state or contents of one's mind.

into the momentum built over the previous stages, relying on the power of thorough familiarization.

Again, during the first two settlings, a practitioner applies the mental application of focused engagement: strongly focusing so as not to lose the object. From the third to the seventh settlings, because laxity and excitement still arise, one applies interrupted engagement. Since at the eighth settling these obstacles will not arise so long as one makes effort, one applies uninterrupted engagement. Finally, at the ninth stage, one no longer needs to make effort, and so the mental application is spontaneous achievement.

Actualizing Calm Abiding

As a practitioner abides single-pointedly in the ninth mental settling, eventually he will experience a pleasant sensation "like somebody placing a warm palm on his freshly shaved head," as Rinpoché describes on page 89. This sensation indicates that agitated "winds," or subtle energies, are leaving the body. At this point one achieves physical pliancy, leaving the body suitable to engage in virtue, especially to sit comfortably for long periods of meditation. Physical pliancy is an actual physical phenomenon, as the subtle energy channels of the body are physical in nature but exist at a more refined level than the gross matter we experience with our sense organs. Next arises the bliss of physical pliancy, the corresponding bodily sensation. One feels comfortable and blissful and finds it easy to stay in meditation and not seek out sense pleasures, which now seem very coarse and unsatisfying. Soon one also experiences a corresponding bliss of mental pliancy, and at first this bliss is so strong that it temporarily disturbs mental stability. But after a short time, the mind stabilizes and integrates the new burst of energy, and this bliss becomes a strong support for prolonged, effortless concentration. This mind no longer belongs to the desire realm that encompasses all the mental states ordinary people experience but is instead an access concentration of the first dhyāna.[5]

5. I have left the Sanskrit term *dhyāna* (Tib. *bsam gtan*; literally "stable mind") untranslated throughout this text. The standard English translation would be "concentration," but that term I have reserved for translating *samādhi* (Tib. *ting nge 'dzin*). Samādhi denotes concentration in a general sense, while a dhyāna is a specific refined state of mind that a practitioner achieves through intense concentration meditation. Especially because Tibetan tantric practitioners cultivate samādhi but intentionally forgo cultivating dhyāna, translating both terms as "concentration" would lead to the self-contradictory statement "Tibetan practitioners cultivate concentration but forgo concentration." Because the dhyānas are

	Stage of Mental Settling	Main Fault to Overcome	Antidote to That Fault	Power to Cultivate	Stage of Mental Engagement
	Preliminary stages	Laziness	Faith, aspiration, enthusiasm, and pliancy*		
1.	Setting the mind	Forgetting the instruction	Recollection	Hearing	Focused engagement
2.	Continuous setting			Reflection	
3.	Fixing and setting			Recollection	Interrupted engagement
4.	Close setting	Laxity and excitement, and not applying the antidote	Introspection and intention		
5.	Disciplining			Introspection	
6.	Pacifying				
7.	Thoroughly pacifying			Zeal	
8.	Making one-pointed				Uninterrupted engagement
9.	Setting in equipoise	Applying the antidote	Equanimity	Thorough familiarization	Spontaneous achievement
	CALM ABIDING				

* Note that pliancy is listed here because it is an antidote to laziness, but it is not actually achieved at this point. One only achieves pliancy along with actual calm abiding, at which point one easily overcomes laziness.

If a practitioner has been using the body of the Buddha as a meditative object, up until this point that visualized object, a mental image, has been a meaning-generality—a general picture without the fine details of a real physical object and lacking the physical qualities of moment-to-moment change. Due to the intense concentration of calm abiding, the image now takes on a superbly vivid quality that surpasses any mental visualization one could create before.[6] On pages 93–94, Rinpoché describes how a meditator now feels as though the object is so vivid and stable that he could count the individual atoms. On page 94, Rinpoché even questions whether one might now be observing an actual Buddha.

Nevertheless, a practitioner who has just achieved calm abiding still has a great deal of work to do in developing the mind, even though he will be able to do so without the laziness and fatigue that plague beginners.

What to Do with Calm Abiding

A practitioner who has newly achieved calm abiding can abide comfortably in single-pointed concentration on her chosen object for hours, even days. However, if she changes the object or tries to analyze the object within the space of calm abiding, laxity and excitement will reemerge, temporarily disturbing her calm abiding. So the next step is to work with just these two skills—changing the object and analyzing it. Initially analysis, such as considering the object's impermanent nature, will slightly unsettle the mind, but gradually it will not do so, and eventually analysis will actually enhance concentration. When the practitioner reaches a point where analyzing the

---

strongly emphasized in Theravāda practice, they are often known in the West by their Pāli name: *jhāna*.

6. As an interesting point of comparison, Buddhaghosa's famous meditation manual *The Path of Purification* (Pāli *Visuddhimagga*), which has been highly influential in Burma and other Theravādin countries, describes how with the attainment of access concentration, a meditation object becomes a "counterpart sign," which is far more vivid than the original visualized object. From Bhikkhu Ñāṇamoli's translation (Buddhaghosa 1991): "The difference between the earlier learning sign and the counterpart sign is this. In the learning sign any fault in the kasina is apparent. But the counterpart sign appears as if breaking out from the learning sign, and a hundred times, a thousand times more purified . . . but it has neither colour nor shape; for if it had, it would be cognizable by the eye, gross . . . But it is not like that. For it is born only of perception in one who has obtained concentration, being a mere mode of appearance. But as soon as it arises the hindrances are quite suppressed, the defilements subside, and the mind becomes concentrated in access concentration." A comparative study of that tradition with this Tibetan system would likely bear fruitful insights.

object actually *increases* the blissful pliancy she experiences, she has achieved special insight,[7] also known as the union of calm abiding and special insight.

Calm Abiding in Hīnayāna Practice[8]

Having achieved special insight, a practitioner can now choose between a variety of different paths for further developing his mind. If he wishes, he can further develop concentration into the four dhyānas and four formless absorptions. These are increasingly refined states of consciousness that lead to progressively stronger concentration and physical and mental bliss and peace. Especially with the fourth dhyāna, which is considered the most effective for meditating on the stages of the path, a practitioner can develop the six clairvoyances (Skt. *abhijñā*; Tib. *mngon shes*), although the first three dhyānas are also adequate for this task. With continued meditation, the experienced image may eventually transform into what is called a "mental-object form" (Skt. **dharmāyatanarūpa*; Tib. *chos kyi skye mched kyi gzugs*). It is no longer a static, undetailed mental image but a functioning thing, experienced not by a conceptual consciousness but by a mental direct perception.

For ordinary people, waking mental consciousness is only conceptual, and its appearing objects are necessarily meaning-generalities. Only in dreams do we have nonconceptual mental activity, and only then do we experience these mental-object forms. As a result, most of us consider that the function of mental consciousness is to think, not to perceive directly like sense consciousness does. But with the intense concentration achieved through calm abiding and the dhyānas, a practitioner can develop heretofore unexperienced abilities.

The first of these is the clairvoyance of magical emanation (Skt. *ṛddhy-abhijñā*; Tib. *rdzu 'phrul gyi mngon shes*). Here a practitioner learns to work

7. Because the term "special insight" (Tib. *lhag mthong*—literally "superior vision"; Skt. *vipaśyanā*—literally "diligent viewing") is so often used in relation to meditation on emptiness, some people misunderstand it to refer only to meditation on emptiness. However, special insight simply means the ability to analyze within the space of calm abiding with that analysis actually enhancing bliss and concentration. In that regard, it is not even a uniquely Buddhist practice and is actually a necessary prerequisite for achieving the dhyānas.

8. I hesitate to use the term *Hīnayāna* (literally "lesser vehicle") for its derogatory connotation. However, the alternative *Theravāda* would be unsuitable, because I am describing Hīnayāna practice according to the Tibetan presentation rather than the Theravādin's own, although there likely is significant congruity.

with and enhance the mental-object form that appears to her mind. For example, she might visualize a disk of fire in such detail that it seems as bright and hot as an actual fire. During the first stage of this process, called the "path of emanation" (Skt. *nirmāṇamārga*; Tib. *sprul lam*), she gains the ability to emanate this fiery disk with her mind and keep it in awareness. In the second stage, called the "source of overpowering" (Skt. *abhibhvāyatana*; Tib. *zil gnon gyi skye mched*), she learns to control this appearance, much like a skilled puppeteer can manipulate a puppet as easily as he moves his own body. In the third stage, called the "meditative stabilization of totality" (Skt. *kṛtsnasamādhi*; Tib. *zad par gyi ting nge 'dzin*), she increases the fire such that it seems to cover more and more of the physical plane. Although this appearance of fire is still only a mental one and is only perceptible to other beings who have access to mental direct perception, through prolonged concentration one gains the ability to impact the material plane as well.[9] Such visionary experiences appearing to one's mental consciousness is a less advanced stage, while their appearing to one's sense consciousness happens at more advanced levels.

With the clairvoyance of the divine eye (Skt. *divyacakṣurabhijñā*; Tib. *lha'i mig gi mngon shes*), a practitioner can observe distant events and the transmigration of other sentient beings between death and rebirth. With the divine ear (Skt. *divyaśrotrābhijñā*; Tib. *lha'i rna ba'i mngon shes*), he can hear distant sounds and listen to Dharma teachings in other realms. With the clairvoyance of knowing others' minds (Skt. *paracittābhijñā*; Tib. *gzhan sems shes pa'i mngon shes*), he can see deeply into the minds of others. With the clairvoyance of recalling past existences (Skt. *pūrvanivāsānusmṛtyabhi-*

9. The idea of focusing on a mental image until it transforms into an actual physical experience may resonate with those who have some understanding of the generation and completion stages of tantra. In the generation stage, one mentally creates a detailed, visualized maṇḍala, holding it in concentration. In the completion stage, one actually generates one's subtle energies in the form of this maṇḍala. However, Geshé Ngawang Sangyé explains that there is an important distinction to understand here. In the case of the meditative stabilization of totality, which is a less advanced practice, one directs intense concentration to the mental image until it gradually develops physicality, thereby acting as the substantial cause for the resulting physical object. In tantra, the visualized maṇḍala of the deity does *not* become the substantial cause for the actual deity one manifests in the completion stage. Rather, visualizing the deity in the generation stage is like a rehearsal session, such that a practitioner can easily recreate that same experience from within the subtle wind mind that he manifests in the completion stage. Here, the subtle wind mind itself, rather than the previously visualized object, becomes the substantial cause of the physically real (at a subtle level) maṇḍala of the completion stage. (Personal communication, November 2017.)

jñā; Tib. *sngon gnas rjes su dran pa'i mngon shes*), he can trace his consciousness into progressively more distant past lives.

Although these first five clairvoyances can be useful aides on the path, the most important for a Buddhist practitioner is the clairvoyance of extinction of contamination (Skt. *āsravakṣayābhijñā*; Tib. *zag zad kyi mngon shes*)—that is, the attainment of nirvāṇa, the cessation of afflictions. To achieve this state, a practitioner directs her concentration toward the stages of the Buddhist path: meditation on impermanence, the four noble truths, the twelve links of dependent arising, selflessness, and so on. With such strong concentration, one can much more easily develop deep insight into these topics and can eventually develop direct perception of them, thereby gaining an antidote that cuts ignorance at the root. With a correct perception of the nature of self and reality and of karmic cause and effect, one eliminates the basis for craving and anger to arise, just like poisoning the root of a tree will stop its sprouting new branches and leaves.

Calm Abiding in Mahāyāna Practice

A Mahāyāna practitioner, wishing to achieve not only personal liberation from saṃsāra but also full enlightenment in order to most effectively benefit others, seeks not only to uproot the afflictions but also to purify the mind thoroughly of all stains that obstruct its potential to see all existence clearly. Abandoning these knowledge obscurations requires not only much more prolonged meditation but also even more profound levels of concentration than a Hīnayāna practitioner develops. The (nontantric) Mahāyāna sūtras describe the meditative stabilization of leaping over (Skt. *avaskandhasamāpatti*; Tib. *thod rgal gyi ting nge 'dzin*).[10] Here a bodhisattva not only develops the dhyānas and formless absorptions mentioned above but also trains in rapidly shifting between these subtle states of consciousness, moving up and down and "leaping" between them. For example, he might shift directly from the highest formless absorption back to an ordinary coarse desire-realm mind, and then into a special refined state called "absorption of cessation" (Skt. *nirodhasamāpatti*; Tib. *'gog pa'i snyoms 'jug*)—the absorption of cessation of manifest conscious experience.

10. See Conze 1975, 501ff. Conze translates "leaping over" as "the crowning assault." Hīnayāna texts also describe a leaping-over style of meditation, but the key difference is that the Hīnayāna practice does not utilize either the desire realm mind or the absorption of cessation, and so is much less difficult than the practice described in the Mahāyāna sūtras.

Through prolonged training in this method, he gains an extraordinary "purified dexterity" (Skt. *viśuddhikara*; Tib. *rtsal byang*) such that every mind, even ordinary nonmeditative experience, becomes a powerful concentration. Using this level of concentration to meditate on emptiness, he can gradually purify even the subtlest stains of obscuration in the mind, ultimately attaining the state of a buddha.

Calm Abiding in Tibetan Buddhism and Tantra

Given the apparent centrality of the dhyānas and formless absorptions in Buddhist practice in general and Mahāyāna practice in particular, many readers may be surprised to see hardly any mention of them in Tibetan practice texts. For instance, Tsongkhapa does not describe them in the *Great Treatise on the Stages of the Path to Enlightenment* (Tib. *Lam rim chen mo*), nor does Rinpoché touch upon them in this book.

Scholarly Tibetan works, such as Tsongkhapa's *Golden Garland of Eloquence*,[11] do in fact cover these topics in depth, but they are absent from practical meditation manuals because Tibetan practitioners rarely make the effort to actualize them. Phabongkha Rinpoché explicitly states "it is possible to go on to achieve the dhyānas and formless absorptions, but because there is little need to do so, we do not generate them."[12] All Tibetan schools consider tantric techniques of meditation to be the most expedient path toward complete buddhahood, and for the more advanced levels of tantric practice, having achieved the dhyānas is actually considered a major obstacle. A practitioner certainly must have superb concentration, meaning the calm abiding and special insight described above are indispensable. But further developing calm abiding into an actual dhyāna will temporarily suppress all desire for sense pleasure, including sexual desire.[13] So long as this

11. Tib. *Legs bshad gser phreng*. For an English translation of this work, see Tsongkhapa and Sparham 2008–13.

12. See Pabongka 1991, 674.

13. According to the strict Geluk interpretation, somebody who has achieved an actual dhyāna will still have that absorption state present in his continuum at a subtle level even during postmeditation. That absorption, though nonmanifest, will nonetheless inhibit the arising of sense desire. Other traditions, such as the Theravāda, seem to maintain that although sense desire will not arise during the actual meditation period, it may still arise in postmeditation, though it will be weak and unlikely to disturb the practitioner. Despite this minor discrepancy, both traditions agree that dhyāna merely suppresses the afflictions and that it is a conditioned state that, if not conjoined with insight, will eventually decline in this

dhyāna does not degenerate, the practitioner will not experience the arising of such desire. For certain tantric practices, a meditator can make use of the energy of desire in his body, and so achieving a dhyāna would temporarily disqualify him from engaging in such profound practices. Because this point could lead to certain misunderstandings, let us briefly touch upon these.

The first question that may arise is this: by putting aside the nontantric Mahāyāna meditations, such as leaping over meditative stabilization, in favor of tantric meditations, does one forsake the Mahāyāna path? The Tibetan tradition considers that tantric practice is still within the scope of Mahāyāna practice. Mahāyāna (that is, "greater vehicle") practice is distinguished from Hīnayāna ("lesser vehicle") practice by the goal for which a practitioner strives. A Hīnayāna practitioner seeks personal liberation from saṃsāra, while a Mahāyāna practitioner seeks the complete enlightenment of a buddha. Within the context of Mahāyāna, one can utilize the Pāramitāyāna (nontantric "perfection vehicle") or the Vajrayāna (tantric or "vajra vehicle"). These two are not distinguished by the goal, because both are aimed at buddhahood. Rather, they differ in terms of the style of meditation. Furthermore, a serious mistake would be to think that a Mahāyāna practitioner discards Hīnayāna practice and a Vajrayāna practitioner discards Pāramitāyāna practice. A Mahāyāna practitioner must also engage in the more basic Hīnayāna meditations, such as meditation on impermanence, the four noble truths, and so on, both to diminish her own mental afflictions and to be able to guide others on that path. However, she would stop short of actualizing the final goal of Hīnayāna practice (personal liberation), because that would be an obstacle to certain Mahāyāna practices, such as generating great compassion. Generating compassion for the suffering of others is easier when one can reflect on one's own suffering. Similarly, a Vajrayāna practitioner must still engage in the Pāramitāyāna practices of giving, ethical discipline, patience, and so on. But regarding certain specific styles of advanced meditation, he will put them aside in order to engage

---

or future lives, allowing the afflictions to arise again in full force. Again, a comparative study of these two traditions could help to resolve apparent contradictions.

Some modern presentations also suggest that beginners, or intermittent meditators, may occasionally "glimpse" dhyāna concentration. In the Geluk presentation, a practitioner can only achieve these states after a prolonged process that begins with cultivating calm abiding, and once achieved they are relatively stable, not something that one experiences sporadically. I am not sure if there is a source for such an assertion in other traditions.

in tantric meditations. Nevertheless, an advanced tantric practitioner will eventually actualize the dhyānas anyway, without having to make special effort to do so.

The other common misunderstanding that can naturally arise when hearing that tantric practice makes use of sexual desire is to think that tantra authorizes licentiousness. To the contrary, great tantric masters like Tsongkhapa still strongly emphasize the Buddha's teachings that unrestrained pursuit of sensual gratification will lead to one's own ruin and that to pursue sense pleasures in the name of spiritual enhancement is even more damaging to one's long-term psychological health. In the context of affirming that sexual desire is normally entangled with delusion and an unhealthy exaggeration of the positive qualities of objects, Tsongkhapa and others also recognize that the arousal of sexual energy, much like anger, sets off powerful physiological reactions that temporarily keep the mind intensely focused on the object of desire or the object of anger. It is indeed this very intense focus itself that usually prevents a person under the sway of desire or anger from seeing the bigger picture and leads them to act in ways they later regret. Furthermore, this intense focus temporarily suppresses worry and other unpleasant thoughts, which is why we may experience it as pleasant and why it can be so dangerously addictive. But for an advanced meditator—one who has already achieved the superb concentration of calm abiding and special insight and ideally has mastered the generation stage practices described below—it is possible to disentangle this physiological reaction from the deluded thought patterns that give rise to it and from the object it apprehends. In other words, when sexual desire arises, rather than following through in fulfilling the desire, one turns that energy toward meditation on the nature of the mind. Such a possibility leads us to the second part of Rinpoché's book.

Mahāmudrā

In a general sense, *mahāmudrā*, or "great seal," refers to the emptiness of all phenomena and also to the subtle mind of great bliss that realizes this emptiness. Whether or not a particular set of practices labels that mind "mahāmudrā," the ultimate goal is the same. His Holiness the Dalai Lama often emphasizes that mahāmudrā meditation should not be taken as an alternative to the graduated path that culminates in the completion stages of tantra. Rather, the example clear light that is included in the stage of isolation of mind according to the Guhyasamāja system (see below) is itself the basis for the name *mahāmudrā*.

But in a specific sense, certain texts and cycles of teachings explicitly use the term *mahāmudrā* and describe meditation in this context. These teachings originated in India with the great adept Saraha, who is said to have received them directly from the bodhisattva Vajrapāṇi. His lineage later split into two streams, both of which the Tibetan translator Marpa received and brought to Tibet, transmitting them into the Kagyü lineage. The Geluk oral lineage of mahāmudrā traces back to Tsongkhapa, who, though indeed exposed to and influenced by this Indian lineage, eventually received these teachings directly from the buddha Mañjuśrī. During the early stages of his life, Tsongkhapa communicated with Mañjuśrī through the medium of his instructor, the Kagyü Lama Umapa Pawo Dorjé (Tib. Dbu ma pa dpa' bo rdo rje), but eventually gained the ability to perceive Mañjuśrī directly with his eye sense consciousness. Thus in the lineage prayer, we see that Tsongkhapa follows Mañjuśrī directly without an intermediary. Tsongkhapa did not commit these teachings to writing; he only passed them orally to certain select disciples, beginning with Tokden Jampal Gyatso. For several centuries it remained a secret practice, only passed on orally, but in the seventeenth century Losang Chökyi Gyaltsen (the Fourth Paṇchen Lama) composed the first written account of mahāmudrā within the Geluk school. Rinpoché chooses this classic text, *Highway of the Conquerors*, as his basis for explication of this style of meditation.

Rinpoché frequently mentions the distinction between sūtra-system mahāmudrā and secret-mantra-system mahāmudrā. These two practices are complementary, with the latter utilizing tantric levels of meditation to deepen one's concentration and insight. The Paṇchen Lama's text deals mainly with the sūtra system, with only a brief initial reference to the secret mantra system, but in his commentary, Rinpoché makes a substantial digression to explain the secret mantra system as well.

Sūtra-System Mahāmudrā

In the sūtra system, the "great seal" refers to the *object* of meditation, the emptiness of all phenomena. All phenomena are "sealed" by the emptiness of inherent existence, or the absence of existing in a fixed, independent way that would preclude dependence on causes, dependence on parts, and dependence on mental labels and constructs. This seal is "great" because by realizing it, one can be free of all misfortune and hardship. One who meditates on emptiness applies lines of reasoning to deconstruct the normal ways we assemble a map of reality. Although most of our normal conceptual frameworks come from innate tendencies and patterns of thought rather than intentionally contrived philosophical systems, still by applying intentional reasoned analysis, we can begin to challenge these innate tendencies. For example, a child who looks in the sky will likely come to the conclusion that the sun is revolving around the Earth. However, through learning about science, his view will change, and even though the sun will still appear to be spinning around the Earth, his habituation to analysis will preclude his assenting to that appearance.

One can begin meditation on emptiness with any object—a pot, a house, or a forest. In the context of mahāmudrā, one takes the mind itself as the object. "Mind" here means the mere quality of awareness and clarity, and so the first step is to identify this "mind" through personal experience. Although recognizing this conventional nature of the mind is a major step in the right direction, Rinpoché, commenting on the Paṇchen Lama's root text, explains on page 214 that it is a mistake to view this vivid wakefulness as the mind's final nature. To identify that final nature, one must look deeper, applying reasoning by relying on the teachings of great past masters. In that context, Rinpoché gives a brief description of emptiness as it is understood by various schools of Buddhist thought, and also describes emptiness in relation to the person, explaining that it is necessary first to recognize emptiness on the basis of the person before moving on to a more difficult basis like the mind.

Once one identifies the ultimate nature of the mind, one abides observing this nature. If a meditator has not already achieved calm abiding, he can use this very object—emptiness—to do so. If he has already achieved it, he applies calm abiding and special insight to meditate continuously on emptiness.

Mantra-System Mahāmudrā

In the sixth verse of his root text, the Paṇchen Lama briefly mentions the mantra system of mahāmudrā. Rinpoché comments extensively on this terse verse, giving a lucid explication of this system. In tantric practice, the object of meditation—emptiness—is no different from the object in the sūtra system. What is different is that the object-possessor—the mind meditating on emptiness—is more refined. As such, "mahāmudrā" in this context does not refer to the object—emptiness—but to the very subtle mind of great bliss that meditates on emptiness, also called the "wisdom of inseparable bliss and emptiness." In this context, the wisdom of emptiness is "sealed" by subjective bliss and objective emptiness in the sense of not going beyond them; no coarse minds are manifest, and emptiness and bliss seem to pervade all experience. Alternatively, at more advanced stages this wisdom is "sealed" in being liberated from saṃsāra. All of the practices of tantra are steps toward this final realization, and so Rinpoché begins by describing these initial stages.

While in sūtra, meditation on emptiness involves focusing on a pure vacuity that is the lack of findability of inherent existence, in tantra one takes a more advanced step. Within the very space of this meditation on emptiness, the meditator imagines forms, thereby manifesting conventional appearances without losing the apprehension of emptiness. Tantric practice consists of four classes—action, performance, yoga, and unsurpassed yoga tantra—which involve progressively more complex visualizations and associated meditations. Unsurpassed yoga tantra (Skt. *anuttarayogatantra*; Tib. *bla na med pa'i rnyal byor*) is further divided into the generation stage (Skt. *utpattikrama*; Tib. *bskyed rim*) and completion stage (Skt. *sampannakrama*; Tib. *rdzogs rim*).

During the generation stage, a practitioner meditates on taking the three bodies into the path. One first imagines dissolving all appearances into emptiness, simulating the experience of death, and imagines that one experiences the wisdom truth body (Skt. *jñānadharmakāya*; Tib. *ye shes chos sku*) of the Buddha. From within that space, one visualizes a seed syllable, representing the complete enjoyment body (Skt. *saṃbhogakāya*; Tib. *longs spyod rdzogs pa'i sku*), which corresponds to the ordinary experience of arising in the bardo between lives. That syllable transforms into the body of a deity, representing the emanation body (Skt. *nirmāṇakāya*; Tib. *sprul sku*), which corresponds to the ordinary experience of rebirth. One trains continuously in these visualizations, with the aim of eventually being able to transform the actual experiences of death, bardo, and rebirth into a swift path to enlightenment.

One can also use the generation stage as a means of actualizing calm abiding. Rather than using an object like the Buddha's body, as described above, one visualizes oneself as the deity and one's surroundings as the maṇḍala, or pure environment, of the deity. These visualizations are intricate and extremely difficult to manifest, much less sustain in focused awareness. Nevertheless, if one is able to do so, the strength of calm abiding achieved will be far superior to the one attained by meditating on a simpler object. A practitioner who attains calm abiding focused on the deity in this manner actualizes the gross generation stage.

One who wishes to actualize the subtle generation stage visualizes the entire maṇḍala of the deity in a space the size of a mustard seed. Although visualizing a complex scene in such a small space and holding it in focused awareness for hours at a time might seem impossible to many of us, it is helpful to reflect that through prolonged training, things that once seemed difficult may become easy, and those that once seemed impossible might seem at least within reach. Furthermore, while training the body will inevitably encounter limits, the mind is not bound by such limits, according to Buddhist philosophy. It is up to the individual to investigate these claims, through reflection and personal experience.

The necessity of training in such refined mental acrobatics is that in the next stage, the completion stage, one uses this extraordinary concentration and mental dexterity to manipulate the subtle energies of the body. To attempt to do so *without* such a foundation of mental training could be disastrous. But in order to manifest the very subtle mind that will engage in the final practice of mahāmudrā, an advanced practitioner must work with these energies.

As Rinpoché explains on page 169, the completion stage is further subdivided into six stages: (1) isolation of body, (2) isolation of speech, (3) isolation of mind, (4) illusory body, (5) meaning clear light, and (6) unification. (Rinpoché follows a common tradition of condensing these stages into five.) During the first stage, a practitioner begins to dissolve the energies of the body, or winds, into the central channel. This central channel flows from the forehead over the crown and down the back of the spine, ending at the tip of the genitals. The very subtle mind resides at the center of the heart channel wheel, but to immediately open the central channel here would be dangerous, even if one has already completed the subtle generation stage. So in the stage of isolation of body, one starts by drawing the winds into the central channel at the navel.

Readers who have stayed in solitary meditation retreat may have experience of the efficacy of temporarily segregating one's body and mind from ordinary thoughts and activities as a means of gaining deeper insight into ordinarily obscure internal processes. This retreat experience can be invaluable as a means of identifying and transforming dysfunctional patterns of thought, speech, and behavior. During the three stages of isolation in the context of the completion stage, a practitioner enhances this segregation at a profound, internal level, *isolating* the wind energies from their ordinary flow patterns in order to purify them.

In the next stage, isolation of speech, one begins to dissolve the winds at the heart. During isolation of mind, one dissolves all of the winds into the indestructible drop at the center of the heart, thereby accessing the clear light, or very subtle mind, that resides there. Among the five primary winds flowing through the body,[14] the pervasive wind, which is spread throughout the body and particularly concentrated in the joints, is considered the most difficult one to dissolve, and it is especially in this context that a practitioner may utilize sexual desire in order to dissolve this wind into the heart.[15]

Having dissolved all the winds into the heart, a practitioner now experiences the subtlest level of mind—the clear light (Skt. *prabhāsvara*; Tib. *'od gsal*). Because she has prepared through sūtra meditations and the generation stage meditations, she now uses this very subtle mind to meditate on emptiness. Meditation on emptiness with this subtle, blissful level of

14. The five primary winds are life-bearing wind, upward-moving wind, pervasive wind, fire-accompanying wind, and downward-voiding wind.

15. Because in this context a qualified practitioner may practice with a partner, and because there is widespread misunderstanding of the presence of such a practice in Buddhism, some comments are in order. First of all, based on Tsongkhapa's interpretation of the Indian tantric texts, in the Geluk school it is strictly forbidden for monastics to engage in tantric practice with a consort. Anybody who engages in such practices and still claims to hold monastic vows is not practicing in accordance with Tsongkhapa's instructions. In the extremely rare case that a monk has reached the stage of isolation of mind, where such practice could actually be useful, he has three options: (1) give back his monastic vows and practice with a consort, (2) arouse the energy of desire merely through creative visualization, or (3) wait until death to actualize the clear light. It is useful to note that Tsongkhapa himself is said to have chosen the third option, recognizing that by giving back his monastic vows to practice with a consort, he would set an undesirable precedent for the pure monastic lineage he had initiated. Some commentators, such as Khedrup Norsang Gyatso (*mkhas grub nor bzang rgya mtsho*), assert that a superior practitioner does not need to make use of any of these three methods and can simply manifest the clear light through intense concentration in a dream state. As for how one can tell whether one is ready for practice with a consort, the oral tradition mentions that one needs full control over the elements, which is described as being able to balance in vajra posture on a single blade of grass or through concentration to cause all the fruit to fall from a tree and then bring it back up to hang on the branches as before. In his *Book of Three Inspirations* (*Zab lam na ro'i chos drug gi sgo nas 'khrid pa'i rim pa yid ches gsum ldan*), Tsongkhapa warns ". . . there are those, of course, who claim that all the characteristics need not be present, and that still the practice will be profound . . . I can only say that to practice on that basis is exceedingly unwise, and easily opens the door to the lower realms" (Tsongkhapa 1996, 165).

mind is mantra-system mahāmudrā. Although the primary objective here is to meditate on emptiness and abandon obscurations, a practitioner who meditates utilizing the clear light in this way is said to achieve levels of clairvoyance, such as recollection of past lives and knowledge of faraway objects and events, that are much sharper and more penetrating than those achieved through the dhyānas described earlier.

Initially, this realization of emptiness is still conceptual—accessing emptiness via a mental image rather than through direct experience. As such, this stage is still the example clear light and not the meaning clear light, which is the fourth stage of the completion stage. Based on his training in imaginatively taking the three bodies into the path, a practitioner arises from this very subtle meditation in a subtle energetic body in the form of the deity and maṇḍala. This comprises the third stage—the illusory body (Skt. *māyādeha*; Tib. *sgyu lus*)—here called the "impure illusory body" because a practitioner still has afflictions in his continuum, even though they are relatively weak. When his clear light meditation on emptiness leads to a direct perception, he achieves the fourth stage—meaning clear light. Arising from this stage, he achieves the pure illusory body, commences the fifth stage with the unification of abandonment, and simultaneously abandons all afflictive obscurations. Entering again into meditation on emptiness, he achieves the unification of realization. Because he has yet to abandon the subtler knowledge obscurations, this stage is called "learner's unification." When he abandons these, he achieves the unification of no more learning, the stage of buddhahood.

How to Use This Book

This book is intended to serve as a supplement, but not a replacement, for the hands-on personal instruction that comes from work with a qualified teacher and the supportive context of a community of practitioners mutually committed to abiding in the Buddha's discipline. The practices outlined here are far from easy, the means of engaging in them is far from obvious or familiar, and engaging in them wrongly or too quickly can lead to serious imbalances of mind and body. The misapplication of physical yogas may lead to bodily injury, but the misapplication of these mental yogas can be devastating.

Suffice it to say, most readers will not actually be at a level where they are prepared to engage in these practices. However, that should not discourage

Five Paths Shared with Sūtra System	Uncommon Tantric Stage	Special Features	Obscurations Abandoned
Path of accumulation	Gross generation stage Subtle generation stage		
Path of preparation Heat Peak Patience Supreme mundane qualities	Completion stage: 1. Isolation of body 2. Isolation of speech 3. Isolation of mind, ending with example clear light 4. Impure illusory body	Union of calm abiding and special insight focused on emptiness	Ordinary appearance and adherence to ordinary appearance
Path of seeing	5. Meaning clear light	Direct perception of emptiness	
Path of meditation	6. Learner's unification of abandonment, along with pure illusory body Learner's unification of realization	Arising from equipoise on emptiness; path of release Again entering into meditation on emptiness	Afflictive obscurations
Path of no-more-learning	Unification of no-more-learning	Full buddhahood	Knowledge obscurations

them from reading this book, because in so doing they may more clearly understand the goal of Buddhist practice, generate enthusiasm for it, and set about building a foundation that will act as a cause to achieve it in the future. On pages 96 and 97, Rinpoché himself explains,

> Beginners like us have a great variety of non-Dharmic projects, while Dharma practice only arises occasionally. Even if we meditate on something like calm abiding, it will be difficult to achieve on account of not completing the collection of causes. If instead for the time being we train well in going for refuge, contemplating

> on karmic cause and result, and so forth, guarding well the ethical discipline of abandoning the ten nonvirtues and so forth, and if we do so emphatically, the reward for us will be greater.

The first step on the Buddhist path is to reflect on the Buddha's core teachings of karmic cause and effect, the pervasiveness of suffering, and the precious opportunity afforded by being born as a human being. If we gain some experiential understanding of these points, then we can keep coming back to that understanding as we progress along the path. Again, on page 71, Rinpoché describes the importance of these preliminary steps:

> In order to elevate the mental state, initially as a means of bringing joy to the mind we can do as described in the *Great Treatise on the Stages of the Path to Enlightenment* in the section on how to actualize calm abiding within the context of the being of great capacity, where Tsongkhapa explains the advice on the six perfections for one engaging in the bodhisattva's conduct. If we do what is described there, then even before we practice calm abiding, we would have had some experience of the great meaning of and difficulty in finding the leisure and fortune of a perfect human rebirth and the benefits of the mind of enlightenment. In that case, then when the mind becomes depressed, if we reflect on the benefits of relying on a spiritual friend, the great meaning of and difficulty in finding the leisure and fortune of a perfect human rebirth, the benefits of the mind of enlightenment, and so forth, then a vibrant mental joy will arise, and the mind's abiding low in depression will lift, so we should do that. If we don't have a great deal of familiarity with those virtuous minds, it will be difficult for that joy to arise. If we have adequate familiarity, then when we recollect those benefits, like freshening up by throwing or sprinkling cold water on our face, the mind will become clear and bright.

As Rinpoché makes clear, if we lack these fundamentals, then we will face obstacles when striving for calm abiding. Actualizing calm abiding is extremely difficult and requires intense focus in solitude over a long period of time, conjoined with a substantial accumulation of merit. If our motivation is merely to have some kind of blissful experience or to gain something of which we can boast to others, we will be unable to sustain our resolve when obstacles inevitably arise. Even with the right motivation, if we haven't sufficiently prepared our minds, we will be unable to lift ourselves out of depression when it arises, and we will be overwhelmed with thoughts like "This retreat is a waste of time" and "I could better use my energies doing Dharma service rather than meditation." Therefore, before entering retreat for calm abiding, we must gain personal certainty that actualizing calm abiding is really the most worthwhile goal if we want to achieve benefit for ourselves and others. Rinpoché always advised his students to take a long view, gradually building a solid foundation through study and reflection before entering into single-pointed retreat.

As Rinpoché explains on page 62, "a yogi has to infer these things mainly from his or her own experience; others' words cannot describe it exactly as it is." Those who undertake such intensive practice will recognize that each person's experience in retreat will be highly personal and often difficult to express. The instructions in this book provide a guideline, expressed in a common language that Buddhist meditators have developed over the centuries. No matter how refined, no language can adequately express the experiential quality of these states of mind. In the process of developing single-pointed concentration, a practitioner will inevitably run up against all kinds of emotional and psychophysical stuck points that she has accumulated, and she must learn to deal skillfully with them. Calm abiding is equilibrium of body and mind, a state of pristine mental health developed through a prolonged process. The nine mental settlings are not just "nine simple steps." The process will be unique to each person, who will have to learn to attune to her body and mind and be patient. Meditation is, ultimately, a process of befriending one's own mind, even though it requires strict discipline. Each person must come to understand this process through experiential trial and error, not simply by reading about it in a book.

Some forms of meditation involve intentional focus on sensations in the body, and while the method Rinpoché outlines here instead emphasizes focusing on a visual image, a meditator cannot just ignore his bodily sensations in the initial stages. A stable visualized object reflects a stable, balanced, peaceful body and mind. At first, as we try to visualize an object, we will find that it jumps around, constantly changes size, and appears at awkward angles, if it appears at all. If the inside of one's mind is chaotic and turbulent, the object of observation will reflect that. Sometimes it will be necessary to let go of the visualized object and address disturbances in one's own mind, as these will become more manifest as the mind gains some concentration. As the mind gradually settles down, the visualized object will become stable. Just as you cannot muscle your way to good health by exercising furiously in a short period, you must develop meditative stabilization gradually through prolonged practice. Concentration will naturally arise when the mind is balanced. The Tibetan word for a realized being, "drang song" (*drang srong*)—which is roughly equivalent to the Sanskrit *ṛṣi*, or "seer," and is often translated as "sage" in English—literally means "one who has straightened body and mind." The methods in this book may appear esoteric and foreign, but in actuality they are progressively deeper means of coming home to the natural well-being and poise that is available to us all.

May Rinpoché's invaluable instructions, drawn from his vast learning and personal experience, provide a gateway for those who genuinely wish to investigate and discover this remarkable state of lucidity and peace, which overflows with compassion and understanding. May those who read them be inspired to set out on the long but fruitful path of mental cultivation, bringing peace and harmony to themselves and the whole world.

A Note on the Translation

THIS BOOK IS a translation of the Tibetan edition *Zhi gnas sgrub tshul dang dge ldan pa'i phyag chen gyi bka' khrid thar lam gsal sgron*, or *A Lamp Clarifying the Path to Liberation: The Manner of Actualizing Calm Abiding and Instructions on Gendenpa Mahāmudrā*, the fourth book in a series of Chöden Rinpoché's teachings published by Jamyang Publication, Lhopa Khangtsen, House No. 4, Sera Jé Monastery. A committee of senior students from the Khangtsen transcribed a collection of Rinpoché's oral teachings on calm abiding and mahāmudrā and then consulted closely with Rinpoché himself regarding details in the final version. Special mention should go to Gen Namgyal Chöphel, who found time in his busy schedule of geshé studies to work meticulously with this text and check many fine details with Rinpoché. In this translation, numbers in brackets throughout indicate the page numbers of the Tibetan original.

I have done my best to translate Rinpoché's teachings as precisely as possible, without addition or omission. At the same time, I have tried to convey the phraseology in colloquial English without being too overtly literal. On occasions where the translation alone does not fully capture the meaning, either because of discrepancies between connotations of Tibetan and English words or because Rinpoché himself assumes a certain level of background understanding on the part of listeners (who often were traditionally educated monks), I have either added terms in brackets or given explanation in the footnotes.

The second half of this text also includes Paṇchen Losang Chökyi Gyaltsen's *Dge ldan bka' brgyud rin po che'i phyag chen rtsa ba rgyal ba'i gzhung lam*, or *Highway of the Conquerors: The Root Text of Mahāmudrā of the Precious Genden Instruction Lineage*: the root text of Geluk mahāmudrā. Readers will notice that I have rendered the translation in metered verse. Having myself been educated in the traditional Tibetan context, it is my strong conviction that keeping root texts in verse is essential for conveying the original style and pedagogical approach of the Buddhist tradition. Tibetan translators from Sanskrit went to great lengths to maintain metered verse throughout the hundreds of volumes of translations of scripture and commentary, but English translators have overwhelmingly opted to translate into prose, likely because the versified texts are often terse and ambiguous. Although I deeply admire the efforts that have been made so far, I believe that a next step in building upon these efforts going forward will be to maintain the verse, even if the meaning is not immediately clear, based on three interrelated sentiments within the Buddhist textual tradition:

1. Many texts of realized masters contain multiple levels of meaning that gradually unfold as a reader's own understanding deepens. If the apparent meaning of a text is immediately evident on a first reading, a reader will tend to gloss over it quickly without considering it more closely. When the meaning is terse and ambiguous, a reader is forced to contemplate its meaning carefully.
2. Root texts in verse are usually accompanied by explanatory commentary, as is the case in this book. Thus, as the concise, condensed verse is gradually unpacked, the hidden meaning naturally reveals itself, leading to a shift in perception. After that, when one reads the verse, its meaning seems starkly obvious, like a hidden image embedded in a collage of dots.
3. In a traditional context, a student would memorize the root verses before understanding their meaning. In that way, the full effect of points 1 and 2 above would be experienced. While readers may not choose to memorize the root text before reading Rinpoché's commentary (though certainly they are encouraged to do so if they can!), the simple impact of the language in verse is likely to leave an imprint on the mind at an unconscious level. We are all familiar with the phenomenon of having a song in your head—it is much more common than having a prose passage in your head, perhaps because metered verse resonates with innate patterns in the human mind.

That being said, I have tried to render the meaning as clearly as possible within the constraints of the poetic meter. I have followed Geshé Graham Woodhouse's style in his excellent translations of Tsongkhapa's "Praise for Dependent Relativity" and "The Essence of the Vinaya Ocean." Whereas Tibetan meter usually follows seven or nine syllables per line, such a style is awkward in English, and so Geshé Graham chose the English style of eight syllables, or four beats, per line (iambic tetrameter). Geshé Graham advises, "One way to chant it is simply to raise the pitch of the voice slightly on the sixth syllable of each line."[16] Iambic tetrameter contains four beats per line. Normally each beat is two syllables, for a total of eight per line, as for instance in:

> To SEE mind's NAture FURtherMORE . . .

When a beat contains two syllables, the second is stressed. On occasion, a single beat might only contain one syllable, such as in:

> SO does CHÖkyi GYALtsen SAY . . .

wherein the first beat is simply the syllable "so." Also on occasion, a beat can contain three syllables, as in:

> To END, whatEVer WHOLEsomeness COMES . . .

Here the last beat contains three syllables: "-someness comes." In this case the last syllable, "comes," is stressed.

On a few occasions when four English beats simply could not accommodate the density of the Tibetan verse, I have increased the syllables per line within a stanza, such as:

> The GENden GREAT Seal LIneAGE (pause) conDENSes
> AND imPARTS well THE . . .

In such a case, one line can simply be read as two lines.

Literary Tibetan contains a special feature whereby a two-syllable word can be contracted into a single syllable, a feature unavailable in English except with the occasional use of apostrophes (for instance, rendering "inseparable" as "insep'rable").

Because Rinpoché refers to it repeatedly in the text, I have also included a translation of the Geluk Mahāmudrā Lineage Prayer (Tib. *Phyag chen brgyud pa'i gsol 'debs*). This prayer also I have rendered in meter. Likewise, I have translated into meter all quotations Rinpoché cites from various Indian and Tibetan metered texts.

16. Gyatso and Woodhouse 2011, xi To assist readers in reading the meter, I have made a recording of a recitation that reflects the rhythm as I intended. To access this recording, please visit wisdomexperience.org/mastering-meditation-recitation.

In the question-and-answer chapters that come at the end of the both parts of this book, I've supplemented the original text with some material from the latter part of Rinpoché's *Thun drug bla ma'i rnal 'byor gyi 'grel pa dang / zhi lhag gi nyams len gyi skor bcas* (2018). The latter part of that new book is a condensed presentation of the topics in this present book, but a few of the quotations seemed to enrich the present discussion. The first part of that book, Rinpoché's commentary on the Six-Session Guru Yoga, I hope to translate separately at a later date.

Tibetan names and terms have been rendered phonetically throughout, with a Wylie transcription included in the first instance for those who read Tibetan. Names of Indian masters I have rendered in Sanskrit or occasionally in English, if the meaning of the name is important for understanding. Ven. Gyalten Jigdrel, a PhD student in Buddhist studies (classical Indology) at the University of Hamburg who was also a close student of Chöden Rinpoché, has kindly added the Sanskrit diacritics throughout. A Sanskrit word marked with an asterisk indicates that the Sanskrit was conjecturally back-translated from the Tibetan with a fair, though by no means uncontestable, degree of plausibility.

One final point bears mentioning. The Tibetan language expresses general statements without the use of a pronoun. For example, the phrase "if you meditate, you must make preparations" would simply be "if meditate, must make preparations." Thus a translator into English is left with the option of translating it alternatively as "if you meditate . . . ," "if we meditate . . . ," "if one meditates . . . ," "if he meditates . . . ," or "if he or she meditates . . ." Depending on the context, I have shifted between these various options. Because English does not contain a suitable non-gender-specific third-person-singular pronoun, I have opted to switch between "he" and "she," even though that does not reflect any explicit expression in the Tibetan. Although Tibetan Buddhist texts are heavily oriented toward male practitioners, as Buddhism takes root in the more egalitarian West, more and more women are entering into these profound practices, and so rather than simply using the traditional "he" for general reference, I have tried to reflect a more inclusive approach.

Pronunciation of Tibetan Phonetics

ph and *th* are aspirated *p* and *t*, as in *pet* and *tip*.

ä is similar to the *e* in *fell*.

ö is similar to the *eu* in French *seul.*
ü is similar to the *ü* in the German *füllen.*
é is similar to the *e* in *prey.*

Pronunciation of Sanskrit
Palatal *ś* and retroflex *ṣ* are similar to the English unvoiced *sh.*
c is an unaspirated *ch* similar to the *ch* in *chill.*
The vowel *ṛ* is similar to the American *r* in *pretty.*
ñ is somewhat similar to a nasalized *ny* in *canyon.*
ṅ is similar to the *ng* in *sing* or *anger.*

A Lamp Clarifying the Path to Liberation

The Manner of Actualizing Calm Abiding and Instructions on Gendenpa Mahāmudrā

Zhi gnas sgrub tshul dang dge ldan pa'i phyag chen gyi bka' khrid thar lam gsal sgron zhes bya ba bzhugs so

༄༅། །ཞི་གནས་སྒྲུབ་ཚུལ་དང་། དགེ་ལྡན་པའི་ཕྱག་ཆེན་གྱི་བཀའ་ཁྲིད
་ཐར་ལམ་གསལ་སྒྲོན་ཞེས་བྱ་བ་བཞུགས་སོ། །

Part 1
Calm Abiding

A TRANSLATION OF

Bsam gtan gyi ngo bo zhi gnas la bslab tshul gyi bka' khrid
Instructions on How to Train in Calm Abiding,
the Essence of Concentration

༄༅། །བསམ་གཏན་གྱི་ངོ་བོ་ཞི་གནས་ལ་བསླབ་ཚུལ་གྱི་
བཀའ་ཁྲིད་ཅེས་བྱ་བ་བཞུགས་སོ། །

ONE

The Importance of the Union of Calm Abiding and Special Insight

IN ORDER TO ACHIEVE the state of a buddha, we must train in a path that unifies calm abiding and special insight and thereby become a buddha. We may be able to place our mind in equipoise until the end of the eon in a calm abiding that is devoid of the special insight that realizes selflessness. But by not seeing as incorrect the determined object of the apprehension of a self,[17] this meditation will only become a cause for further cycling in saṃsāra, not a cause for liberation. Likewise, devoid of calm abiding, the wisdom that realizes selflessness cannot by itself do much to harm the ignorance that apprehends a self, the root of saṃsāra. Therefore, we definitely must rely on a meditation that is the unification of calm abiding and special insight. As the victor's child Śāntideva has said in his *Engaging in the Bodhisattva Deeds*:

> Know special insight well-conjoined
> with calm abiding quells the taints.
> Seek calm abiding at the start.[18]

[2] As I said, the root of our circling in saṃsāra since beginningless time is none other than the ignorance that apprehends a self. Thus, as an antidote to subdue this ignorance that apprehends a self, we must generate the wisdom that realizes emptiness. Furthermore, if we don't have calm abiding, this wisdom that realizes emptiness cannot alone subdue ignorance; since we must mount the wisdom that realizes emptiness on the horse of calm

17. The apprehension of a self observes an existent object—the person—and apprehends it in an incorrect way—as existing inherently. Thus the "determined" or "apprehended" object, the inherently existent self, is incorrect.

18. Śāntideva, *Engaging in the Bodhisattva Deeds*, 8.4. For an English translation of this text, see Śāntideva 1997.

abiding and thereby subdue confusion, we must meditate by unifying calm abiding and special insight.

As for "calm abiding," because it is mainly (1) the pacification of the mind's distraction toward external objects and (2) a stable abiding on a single object of observation, it is called "peaceful" or "calm abiding." Within a secure factor of stability on the object of observation, one maintains not a loose but a firm manner of apprehension. If one maintains this tight manner of apprehension with an intense factor of clarity, it becomes the practice of calm abiding. Otherwise, without the factor of stability, calm abiding's obstacle of excitement arises. Without the intense factor of clarity, laxity arises. Thus, for calm abiding, we definitely need to be free of these two faults. But that alone is not enough: we also need to be able to elicit the mental and physical bliss of pliancy that comes through the force of meditating free of these two faults.

[3] Well then, what is this thing called "eliciting the bliss of pliancy"? Having pacified the assumption of bad states of body and mind[19] that make the body and mind unserviceable for virtue, one gains pliancy—the serviceability or ability to utilize the body and mind as much as one likes for virtue. If through that force comes a strong blissful experience, we have elicited bliss,[20] and a meditative concentration supported by that special kind of bliss is called "calm abiding."

As for calm abiding itself, it is a common practice of both Buddhists and non-Buddhists. Thus a stable calm abiding does arise even in the continuum of non-Buddhists. Non-Buddhists meditate on calm abiding and actualize the four dhyāna absorptions and the four formless absorptions.[21] When

19. Skt. *(kāyacitta)dauṣṭhulya*; Tib. *lus sems kyi gnas ngan len*. These "bad states of body and mind" are said to be residual effects of conditioning to afflictions, even though they themselves are not afflictions. Bad states of body might include tightness and poor posture, and bad states of mind might include mental heaviness and lack of clarity.

20. Note that "bliss" (Skt. *sukha*; Tib. *bde ba*) here does not literally mean, as it usually does, a pleasant sensation, which has a very specific meaning in Buddhist psychology. Here the term "bliss" is used more loosely. "Bliss of pliancy" is simply the ease and freedom from worry that comes with freedom from bad states of body and mind. In very deep states of concentration (such as the fourth dhyāna), as well as in times of making effort to achieve more advanced concentration, one may experience a neutral rather than a pleasant sensation, but the "bliss of pliancy" is still present.

21. These are progressively more refined states of concentration that one can achieve on the basis of calm abiding. The "four dhyāna absorptions" are simply the "first, second, third, and fourth dhyānas." The first one is free of desire for sense pleasures, the second is free of any

they achieve the absorption of the peak of cyclic existence,[22] they think, "I've achieved liberation!" In each meditative session, they may be able to stay in absorption for many hundreds of thousands of years, or even until the end of the eon. However, without the support of the thought of definite emergence,[23] their meditation does not become a cause of liberation. For example, when our teacher (Buddha) came to this world, a forder[24] named Udraka Rāmaputra, on achieving the absorption of the peak of cyclic existence, thought "Now I have achieved liberation!" and placed his mind in the equipoise of calm abiding for a long time. [4] Upon arising from his

---

gross conceptual motivation, the third is free of joy—which the meditator experiences as an unsettling of mind—and the fourth is free of bliss, which again is experienced as a hamper to concentration. The "four formless absorptions" are further refinements of concentration. Unlike the four dhyānas, they are distinguished not by progressively subtler mental factors but by progressively subtler objects of concentration. During the absorption of the sphere of limitless space, the meditator no longer perceives forms but only a vast vacuity. During the absorption of the sphere of limitless consciousness, he no longer experiences space but only pervasive consciousness. During the absorption of nothing at all, there is the experience as though nothing at all is appearing to the mind. During the absorption of neither discrimination nor nondiscrimination, gross discrimination is suspended, and only a very subtle level of discriminating awareness remains.

The Buddha explained that there is a danger that those who achieve these levels of concentration will mistakenly believe that they are liberated from saṃsāra because they will no longer experience manifest suffering. However, afflictions still lurk in the depths of the mind, and they will eventually become manifest and cause the dhyāna to decline. Nevertheless, the Buddha did strongly encourage his followers to make use of the dhyānas, especially the fourth one, for meditating on the stages of the path. In the Tibetan tradition, a practitioner of tantra intentionally forsakes attaining them (see introduction).

22. This is an alternative name for the absorption of neither discrimination nor nondiscrimination. It is called "peak of cyclic existence" because it is the most refined state of consciousness still included within cyclic existence.

23. Skt. **niḥsaraṇa(citta)*; Tib. *nges 'byung gi bsam pa*. This term, which literally means "the thought of definite emergence," is often translated as "renunciation." In this context, "definite emergence" means liberation from saṃsāra, and "the thought" means the strong intention to achieve definite emergence. In other words, this mind *observes* liberation and *wishes* to achieve it. "Renunciation," on the other hand, though a related mind, would *observe* objects of attachment and *wish* to abstain from pursuing them. "Thought of definite emergence" emphasizes the positive intention to achieve something, whereas "renunciation" emphasizes the corresponding negative intention to give something up.

24. "Forder" (Skt. *tīrthika*; Tib. *mu stegs pa*) is a common way to refer to non-Buddhist religious practitioners. Rather than being derogatory, this epithet is actually meant to be encouraging. It implies that these practitioners are making efforts to cross the stream of cyclic existence and reach nirvāṇa, even if they are not on exactly the right path according to the Buddhist understanding.

absorption and seeing a rat gnawing on his dreadlock, he became angry, causing his absorption to degenerate. He generated the wrong view, thinking, "There is no liberation!" and was subsequently born in hell.[25]

Also, some forders place their minds in absorption into calm abiding and stay until the end of the eon. By enjoying the bliss of absorption and staying for a long time in that state, they exhaust all of the merit they previously accumulated. Although at first they had thought, "I've achieved liberation!" later when they arise from concentration and see with clairvoyance that they will again be born in saṃsāra by the force of karma and afflictions, they generate the wrong view, thinking, "There is no liberation!" By the force of that they are born in the unfortunate migrations. Because this is a common occurrence, we can conclude that in order to achieve our ultimate aim, calm abiding alone is of no benefit.

Calm Abiding Needs to Be Supported by the Mind of Refuge

When we are practicing to actualize calm abiding, we must do so in conjunction with generating a pure mind of refuge in our continuum. That refuge in turn must be based upon (1) fear of all of the suffering of cyclic existence and (2) belief that one's lama and the Three Jewels have the power to save us from this suffering. If we actualize calm abiding in conjunction with this mind of refuge, it will become a practice of Buddhadharma. If we do not aim merely for the next life but conjoin our practice of calm abiding with a thought of definite emergence that sees all the wonders of saṃsāra as like a pit of fire and wishes to attain liberation from that, it will become a cause for liberation. [5] If we conjoin it with bodhicitta, thinking, "For the

25. Phabongkha Rinpoché mentions this story in *Liberation in the Palm of Your Hand* (Pabongka 1991, 675). Udraka Rāmaputra was also the name of one of the two teachers that Prince Siddhārtha met before he became the Buddha. According to the sūtras, the Rāmaputra who taught the Buddha died with his meditative stabilization intact and was reborn in the formless realm. Geshé Ngawang Thokmé suggests that the Rāmaputra referred to here, whose meditative stabilization declined, was a student of the one who taught the Buddha. It was a common practice in ancient India for students to take the name of their teacher.

Certain sūtras, such as the perfection of wisdom sūtras, describe how practitioners sometimes achieve deep states of concentration and mistake these states for liberation. Although they may as a result experience rebirth in a peaceful higher realm, when the state eventually exhausts itself, they lose faith in the possibility of liberation, and their subsequent anger and frustration can be strong enough to cast them into a hell realm.

purpose of all mother sentient beings, I must achieve the state of a perfectly completed buddha. For that reason, I am actualizing calm abiding," it will become a cause of complete buddhahood.

The difficulty we face in generating the realization of calm abiding in our continuum is not like that of non-Buddhists, who meditate on calm abiding in order to progressively actualize the four dhyānas and four formless absorptions.[26] Because our mind is under the power of afflictions, we tend to recall all sorts of useless, meaningless things, so whatever we meditate on does not became a path to liberation, and we do not make great strides. If and when we achieve calm abiding, we can use that as the mental basis[27] for meditating on death and impermanence, bodhicitta, the path that realizes naturelessness, and so forth. Then it will be easy to generate in our continuum a realization of whatever we meditate on, we will make great strides on the path, we will swiftly achieve yogic accomplishments, and so forth. In light of such a great difference, we meditate on calm abiding for that reason and not in the non-Buddhist manner described above.

Without calm abiding, we will be unable to generate clairvoyance, bodhicitta, the paths of accumulation, preparation, seeing, and meditation,[28] and so forth. [6] If we have calm abiding, we will quickly generate them, so we

26. The point Rinpoché seems to be making here is that although Buddhists and non-Buddhists alike undergo hardship to attain calm abiding, they do so for different reasons. The non-Buddhist does so merely to attain the dhyānas and formless absorptions, considering the attainment of one of these to constitute liberation, while the Buddhist does so to abandon the root of afflictions.

27. Skt. **cittāśraya*; Tib. *sems rten*. "Using calm abiding as a mental basis" does not mean that on the one hand there is calm abiding while another mind meditates on impermanence. Rather, it means that the mind meditating on impermanence is itself in the nature of calm abiding.

28. The path to buddhahood is marked by five stages. During the first stage, the "path of accumulation," a practitioner mainly focuses on learning and contemplation. During the next stage, the "path of preparation," one prepares for a direct realization of emptiness by focusing mainly on meditation, gradually diminishing the dualistic appearance of emptiness in meditative equipoise. Finally, on the "path of seeing," one "breaks through," experiencing emptiness directly, unmediated by a meaning-generality. During the "path of meditation," one cultivates this direct experience of emptiness, continuing to accumulate merit to enhance its force. At the end of this path, one achieves the "path of no-more-learning," or complete buddhahood. Although there is some controversy over whether one can enter the path of accumulation before achieving calm abiding, all traditional texts are clear that one would need to achieve it soon thereafter and that it would be an absolute necessity for the latter four paths.

must meditate on calm abiding. If we achieve calm abiding, we will achieve control over our own mind.

Jé Tsongkhapa said,

> King concentration, mind control.
> When placed, immobile mountain lord.
> When sent, it meets all wholesome things.
> Prompts useful bliss of body, mind.[29]

At the moment, because we have not gained control over our mind, we are under the control of the afflictions. If someone achieves calm abiding, he achieves control over his mind, and because such a person can control his mind such that it stays wherever he places it, Tsongkhapa said, "King concentration, mind control." That is, calm abiding is like a king who controls the mind. Tsongkhapa continued, "When placed, immobile mountain lord." That is, whatever object of observation you place your mind on, like the lord of mountains it remains firmly without moving. For example, if you place it on a thought such as "May I achieve buddhahood for the benefit of all sentient beings," you can stay on that thought for a long period of time. Also, if you spread out your focus—that is, send your mind to various objects—whatever virtuous object you place your mind on, your calm abiding will engage just that object. [7] Thus, Tsongkhapa then said, "When sent, it meets all wholesome things." He continues, "Prompts useful bliss of body, mind." Having achieved calm abiding, if you meditate or engage in any other virtuous activity, your physical and mental bliss will only increase; weariness and fatigue will not arise. If you achieve calm abiding, such abilities will come.

As I said before, no matter how much you meditate on calm abiding alone, you will be unable to cut the root of cyclic existence and thus will not be liberated from saṃsāra. But if on top of having calm abiding, you are able to generate the special insight that realizes emptiness, by unifying those two you will achieve liberation from saṃsāra.

29. Tsongkhapa, *Song of Experience*, v. 19. This text is often called the condensed lamrim because it is Tsongkhapa's shortest exposition of the stages of the path. For a translation, see Tenzin Gyatso 2002.

Special Insight

You might wonder, "Well then, what is this thing called 'special insight'?"

You analyze an object from within the space of equipoise in calm abiding. A wisdom conjoined with bliss elicited by the force of such analysis is called "special insight." If you achieve a stable calm abiding, from the space of equipoise in calm abiding you will be able to perform analysis with a wisdom that individually investigates objects. When we haven't attained a stable calm abiding, if we engage in analysis, the factor of stability degenerates. [8] If our calm abiding achieves a secure factor of mental stability, it does not degenerate when we engage in analysis. For example, if under a deep body of water, fish swim back and forth, they are unable to disturb the surface. Likewise, from a space of secure mental settling on an observed object, although we analyze, the intensity of our factor of clarity only becomes stronger, and through the force of that we generate an even greater bliss than before. Bliss elicited by the power of analysis is the bliss of special insight. Bliss at the time of mere calm abiding is bliss born through the force of the stability factor.[30]

Calm abiding is an indispensable tool. From the point of view of sūtra, there are the five paths and ten grounds, and during mantric practice there are realizations of the path of completion.[31] Without calm abiding we will be unable to correctly generate any of these. If we are to actualize calm abiding, we must actualize it in conjunction with the minds of refuge, renunciation, and bodhicitta. If we are able (1) to generate bodhicitta and a calm abiding that abides stably on an observed object and (2) to analyze, from the space of calm abiding, the meaning of emptiness and thus be able to generate the special insight that realizes emptiness, then on the basis of a path that unifies those two—calm abiding and special insight—the attainments of liberation and the state of buddhahood will arise. [9] For example, if at nighttime there is a fresco on the wall in a house, to view that painting we need a bright torch. That torch also must not be disturbed by the wind. If

30. The point here is that before achieving special insight, using calm abiding to engage in analysis causes the stability of mind to temporarily waver. When one achieves special insight, then engaging in analysis not only does not harm concentration, but it actually enhances it.

31. The "five paths" are explained in note 9 above. The "ten grounds" are further subdivisions of the fourth path, the "path of meditation": ten stages marked by progressively greater realization and powers of mind. The "realizations of the path of completion" are the isolation of body, isolation of speech, isolation of mind, illusory body, clear light, and unification (see introduction).

the wind disturbs the torch, we will be unable to see the painting clearly, and even if there is no wind, if the torch is not bright, we will likewise be unable to see the painting well. Special insight is like the bright torch, and calm abiding that is a secure mental settling on an observed object is like being unmoved by the wind.

This manner of actualizing calm abiding is explained in many great texts like protector Maitreya's Five Religious Treatises,[32] Ārya Asaṅga's Five Treatises on the Grounds,[33] and so forth. Jé the Great [Tsongkhapa] unerringly delineated the meaning of those texts. Likewise, the holy lamas like His Holiness the Fifth Dalai Lama, Paṇchen Losang Chökyi Gyaltsen, Paṇchen Losang Yeshé, and so forth took those great texts as a basis and clarified their meaning.[34] The very essence of all of those is what I am explaining now.

32. These are (1) *Ornament for Clear Realization* (Skt. *Abhisamayālaṃkāra*; Tib. *Mngon par rtogs pa'i rgyan*), (2) *Ornament for the Mahāyāna Sūtras* (Skt. *Mahāyānasūtrālaṃkāra*; Tib. *Theg pa chen po mdo sde'i rgyan*), (3) *Differentiating the Middle from Extremes* (Skt. *Madhyāntavibhāga*; Tib. *Dbus dang mtha' rnam par 'byed pa*), (4) *Distinguishing Dharma and Dharmatā* (Skt. *Dharmadharmatāvibhaṅga*; Tib. *Chos dang chos nyid rnam par 'byed pa*), and (5) *Sublime Continuum* (Skt. *Mahāyānottaratantraśāstra*; Tib. *Theg pa chen po rgyud bla ma'i bstan bcos*). Various translations are available: for example, (1) Brunnhölzl 2010, (2) Maitreya 2014, (3) Maitreya 2006, (4) Maitreya 2004, and (5) Maitreya 2000.

Ornament for the Mahāyāna Sūtras explains the practice of calm abiding in relation to the nine mental settlings, while *Differentiating the Middle from Extremes* explains it in terms of the five faults and eight mental applications.

33. These are (1) *Grounds of Yogic Practice* (Skt. *Yogācārabhūmi[śāstra]*; Tib. *Rnal 'byor spyod pa'i sa* [or alternatively, Skt. *Maulī Bhūmiḥ*; Tib. *Sa'i dngos gzhi*]), (2) *Compendium of Grounds* (Skt. *Vastusaṃgrahaṇī*; Tib. *Sa gzhi bsdu ba*), (3) *Compendium of Enumeration* (Skt. *Paryāyasaṃgrahaṇī*; Tib. *Rnam grangs bsdu ba*), (4) *Compendium of Doors of Explanation* (Skt. **Vivaraṇasaṃgrahaṇī / *Vyākhyā(na)saṃgrahaṇī*; Tib. *Rnam par bshad pa'i sgo bsdu ba*), and (5) *Compendium of Ascertainments* (Skt. *Viniścayasaṃgrahaṇī*; Tib. *Gtan la dbab pa bsdu ba*). Part of the first is available in translation in Ārya Asaṅga 2016.

34. These authors all composed important lamrim (stages of the path) texts. These texts are not direct commentaries on Maitreya's and Asaṅga's texts, but they elucidate the central themes. These texts are the following:

1. By Tsongkhapa, *The Great Treatise on the Stages of the Path to Enlightenment* (Tib. *Byang chub kyi lam rim chen mo*) (Tsongkhapa 2000). Tsongkhapa also composed a *Middle-Length Stages of the Path* (Tib. *Byang chub lam rim bring 'ba*) (Tsongkhapa 2012).
2. By Gyalwang Ngawang Losang Gyatso, the Fifth Dalai Lama, *Sacred Words of Mañjuśrī* (Tib. *'Jam dpal zhal lung*). A partial translation is available at https://www.jangchuplamrim.org/wp-content/uploads/Archive-Texts/JCLR-ENGLISH-07-20130912-SacredWordsManjushri-Durovic-PartialDraft.pdf.
3. By Losang Chökyi Gyaltsen, the Fourth Paṇchen Lama, *The Easy Path to All-Knowing* (Tib. *Thams cad mkhyen par bgrod pa'i bde lam*) (First Paṇchen Lama 2013).

To actualize calm abiding, stable recollection and introspection are very important prerequisites. For example, we may recognize that when people with stable recollection and introspection practice for calm abiding, they achieve it easily, while those without stable recollection and introspection have a hard time actualizing it when they practice.

4. By the Fifth Paṇchen Lama, Losang Yeshé, *The Swift Path to All-Knowing* (Tib. *Thams cad mkhyen par bgrod pa'i myur lam*). A partial translation is available at https://www.jangchuplamrim.org/wp-content/uploads/Archive-Texts/JCLR-ENGLISH-08-20130913-SwiftPath-Durovic-PartialDraft-v02.pdf.

TWO

Assembling the Preconditions for Calm Abiding

[10] IN ORDER to actualize calm abiding, in the beginning it is important to rely on its preconditions. Relying on the preconditions for calm abiding means that in order to actualize calm abiding, there is a particular collection of causes that we definitely need to assemble. If we do not assemble these conducive conditions, then even if we practice for thousands of years we will not achieve calm abiding. Thus Atiśa said in his *Lamp for the Path*,

> When calm abiding's branches rot,
> then though you meditate with zeal
> a thousand years, still you will not
> accomplish concentration here.[35]

It is said that if you assemble the collection of causes for calm abiding—that is, if you assemble the necessary conducive conditions for actualizing calm abiding—then if for six months you engage in the actual practice of maintaining an object of concentration, you will achieve calm abiding.

The assembly of causes is sixfold:

1. Staying in a conducive place.
2. Having few wants.
3. Having contentment.
4. Thoroughly abandoning the bustle of many activities.
5. Maintaining pure ethical discipline.
6. Thoroughly abandoning discursive thoughts of desire and so forth.[36]

35. Atīśa Dīpaṃkaraśrījñāna, *Lamp for the Path to Enlightenment* (Skt. *Bodhipathapradīpa*; Tib. *Byang chub lam gyi sgron ma*), v. 39. For a translation, see Tenzin Gyatso 2002.

36. The Tibetan term *rnam rtog*, which I have rendered here as "discursive thought," is difficult to translate into English. Because *rnam rtog* implies exaggerating the importance of

You definitely need to assemble all of these.

[11] First, staying in a conducive place: In order to actualize calm abiding, the site of achievement—that is, the residence where you abide—must be as explained in *Ornament for the Mahāyāna Sūtras*:

> The place where wise ones practice is
> found well, a pleasant dwelling, and
> a pleasant land, with pleasant friends,
> with easy yoga's assets complete.[37]

You need "an abode possessing the five characteristics": (1) found well, (2) pleasant, (3) in a pleasant environment, (4) with pleasant friends, and (5) possessing pleasing requisites. Mainly, it needs to be an isolated place in accordance with the mind of the practitioner and where she feels at ease.

1. *Found well.* One can obtain the means of subsistence without relying on sinful means or wrong livelihood; thus "subsistence is found well." Since we need to rely on subsistence in order to live, for that purpose in some places we may have to leave our hermitage and go down to the town. By contrast, in a place that is "found well," subsistence is easy to come by. Also, that subsistence definitely must be unmixed with acquisition through sinful means or wrong livelihood, such as marketing the holy speech of the Buddha.[38]

2. *A pleasant dwelling.* An important point is that if previous lamas have practiced in a place and thereby blessed it, by virtue of those blessings a beginner who stays there will easily generate realizations. [12] Even if we can't find such a place, a place where there are not many people and such moving about during the day and that is without loud sounds such as water and dogs at nighttime is called "pleasant." In short, we need a place free of noise and commotion, which are irritants to concentration.

---

things or distorting situations with our habitual projections, another translation might be "superstitious thoughts." The connotation here is excessive rumination, stirred up by afflictions of desire, anger, jealousy and pride. This term might be translated literally as "conceptual thought," but that translation could be misleading. Conceptual thought, guided by learning and wisdom, is indispensable for any Buddhist practice—even single-pointed concentration. What one abandons here is not thinking altogether but unnecessary deliberation and worry over objects of attachment and aversion.

37. Maitreya, *Ornament for the Mahāyāna Sūtras*, 14.7.

38. This means selling Dharma texts for profit.

If the place we stay has people whose *samaya* with their lama has degenerated, this will create obstacles to our generating realizations. Thus we need a place free of such samaya degenerates. Likewise, if the place is one that has experienced a split in the saṅgha and subsequent disturbance in the community, it will be like, for example, grass not growing on earth burned by fire: through the force of the degeneration of samaya, all classes of qualities of abandonment and realization will not arise. So we need a place unlike that one. Furthermore, we need a place without the kinds of beings who will harm us, such as ferocious animals, thieves, nonhuman elemental spirits, and so forth. If it is a place where nonhumans stay and we stay anyway, thinking, "I'm not afraid of nonhumans. I won't be unable to stay here," then later there will be a danger of these nonhumans delivering harm to us. So if it is a place inhabited by nonhumans, we must be gentle to them and offer *tormas* and the like. [13] If we get to know them, they might help us, but if we use wrathful means, while there may be some limited benefit in the short run, they will wait for an appropriate time and then harm us. For example, once a retreatant was staying in a cave inhabited by a *tsen* spirit.[39] Because the retreatant employed wrathful means to expel the demon, the demon was not able to harm him right away. However, the demon subsequently waited for an appropriate time to deliver harm. One day the retreatant's two benefactors fell into a quarrel. When the retreatant came to act as a mediator, the demon seized the opportunity to harm him, striking his head with a stone and killing him. Since such things happen, we shouldn't inspire hostility in nonhuman beings. If instead we meditate on love and compassion for them, it will purify their continuum, and they won't harm us.

3. *In a pleasant environment.* Some retreatants develop bodily illness due to not tolerating the environment where they stay. Then they say to themselves, "Now my practice of meditation won't come about," and in the end they must stay and recover, working for a living. Since these things happen, instead we need a pleasant environment that won't cause us illness.

[14] 4. *With pleasant companions.* Bad companions are those with views and behavior at odds with our own, those who enjoy distractions, or carefree people who act without restraint. Rather, we need harmonious Dharma friends who share our view and behavior. Furthermore, they must be friends to whom you will abide showing respect and will keep "looming heavily

39. This is a kind of violent, territorial spirit.

in the corner of your eye."[40] For example, if you are about to engage in an unwholesome activity, you might hesitate, thinking, "Mightn't it upset them?" It is good if we have such people to whom we afford such respect, and generally there is no fault in having many such harmonious Dharma friends.

5. *Possesses requisites that are conducive to yoga.* This doesn't mean that one stocks up all kinds of conducive conditions in terms of external things and that everything goes smoothly. For example, if you are a practitioner of meditation, when you are actually going to meditate, you acquire the requisite texts and essential instructions in the way of empowerments, oral transmissions, commentaries, and the like. Before entering retreat, you engage in hearing and contemplation on the object of meditation in order to clarify uncertainties. In such a way, when you are ready to meditate, this is called "possessing requisites that are conducive to yoga."

The protector Maitreya [in the *Ornament of the Mahāyāna Sūtras*] has said that we need such a place with the five qualities of being found well, a pleasant abode, a pleasant environment, with pleasant companions, and possessing requisites conducive to yoga.

[15] The second out of the collection of six causes is having few wants: Having few wants, along with having contentment, is one of the two most important things for actualizing the Dharma. If we lack the qualities of few wants and contentment, then we won't be satisfied with merely having food, clothes, and a place to stay. Instead, we will put great effort into achieving all the perfect conditions. In the course of achieving that, lots of work will come about, leading to the greatest obstacle—not having time to actualize the Dharma. So, it is said that we need few wants and contentment.

The opposite of few wants is avarice (Skt. *mahecchatā*; Tib. *'dod pa che ba*; literally "having great wants"). Avarice is when we see things we don't have and think, "I need something like this. I need something like that." Such great need and desire is called "avarice." The opposite of that, like an antidote to it, is not craving for excellent or excessive food, clothing, residences, and such, but considering just what is needed to be adequate; it is called "few wants."

40. In Tibetan culture, one does not look directly at somebody one holds in authority but rather bows down and glances sideward at them, even when speaking to him or her. The connotation here is having a companion in whose presence we would be ashamed to engage in nonvirtue.

Third, contentment: [16] When you have one thing, but you aren't satisfied with it and think, "I still need something else," this is called "discontentment." The antidote to that is abiding with the thought "If I have food, clothes, and shelter and such just enough to sustain me—if it's just able to sustain my body—that's okay." This is called "contentment." If we have contentment, even if we don't have a lot of things, our desires will be satisfied, we will think, "Now I'm okay," and our mind will become rich and won't have any problems. If we don't have contentment, then no matter how many things we have or how good they are, our mind will be like a beggar's, and we will still be thinking, "I have nothing."

For example, when our teacher Buddha came to this world, there was a beggar named Poor Peaceful (Tib. Dbul po des pa). Since he had a kind heart and a pacified, subdued manner, he got the name Peaceful. One day Poor Peaceful found a priceless jewel. When he found this jewel, somebody asked, "What do you plan to do with that jewel?" He said, "I want to give it to the poorest, most destitute person in this land."

[17] One day he carried the jewel and gave it to the country's king, Victorious.[41] The king asked, "You said you were going to give this to the poorest person, so why are you giving it to me?"

Poor Peaceful replied, "Since your lack of contentment is the worst, you are the poorest person in this land!" and gave him the jewel.

There is a history to this story. Earlier, in India, King Victorious invited the Buddha and his hearer disciples for alms offerings. For three days the king respectfully made offerings, and Poor Peaceful meditated on rejoicing in that. When we meditate on rejoicing, if our realization is greater than the person in whose actions we rejoice, we achieve greater merit than they do. So when Poor Peaceful meditated on rejoicing, he achieved greater merit than the king.

After receiving his alms, the Blessed One asked King Victorious, "Today, to whom shall I dedicate the virtue? To the one with the strongest roots of virtue or to somebody else?"

Thinking that, as sponsor, he himself had achieved the most extensive roots of virtue, the king replied, "Please dedicate to the one with the

41. Tib. Gsal rgyal; Skt. Prasenajit; literally "Clearly Victorious over Armies." This king was a longtime student of the Buddha. Although he is often referred to by his Sanskrit name in Western literature, I have chosen to translate the meaning of his name into English, because it adds an important effect to the story Rinpoché tells.

strongest roots of virtue." [18] Because the king replied like that, the Blessed One dedicated the merit to Poor Peaceful.

On the second day, the Blessed One again asked the same question, but the king, unable to say "Please dedicate to me," replied, "Please dedicate to whomever has achieved the greatest virtue." Again, the Buddha dedicated to Poor Peaceful.

On the third day, the king conferred with his servants, saying, "Today, we must find a way to make it so Poor Peaceful will not secure the roots of virtue but rather that they will be dedicated to the king." The servants beat Poor Peaceful. Having been beaten, on that day Poor Peaceful didn't meditate on rejoicing. Consequently, the Buddha had to dedicate the virtue to the king. This is just a tangential point.

For these reasons, having few wants and contentment are extremely important qualities, and so those seeking liberation definitely must rely on them. Without contentment, a king will in actuality be no different from a beggar, as the story above illustrates.

[Fifth,] for one out of the collection of six causes, we need what is called "pure ethical discipline."[42] Ethical discipline is the foundation for all good qualities. [19] For example, it is like the ground where we plant crops, and it is like the root of a tree. If we have pure ethical discipline, on that basis good qualities will arise, while if we don't have pure ethical discipline, there will be no foundation for good qualities to grow, so we definitely need pure ethics. Also, if we have pure ethical discipline, we will be able to cast away gross external distractions. The Buddha explained to his hearer Saṅgha that while they definitely required the most basic requisites of living and the three monastic robes,[43] they were not allowed to keep more than that. So if we have pure ethics, we will come to see the faults of objects of desire, and since we won't require many external things, distraction toward external objects will stop of its own accord. Thus, we need pure ethical discipline.

42. Rinpoché has reversed the order of the fourth and fifth out of the collection of causes.

43. Fully ordained monks and nuns carry three robes with them at all times: the lower robe (Skt. *nivāsana*; Tib. *sham thabs*) and the two upper robes (Skt. *cīvara* and *saṃghāṭi*; Tib. *chos gos* and *snam sbyar*). The Buddha also allowed his monastic followers to carry certain requisites, like a begging bowl and water filter.

[Fourth,] on top of that, we must avoid the bustle of many activities. "Bustle" refers to things like the commotion of many people gathering or attachment to trifling activities, which leads to a lack of leisure time and lots of work.[44] We definitely must abandon such bustle. If we don't, many meaningless activities will come our way, [20] and through things like excessive conversation our time will go to waste. So we need few goals and few activities without a lot of frantic bustle. If we have few wants and contentment, we will come to have fewer goals and activities, gross distraction will subside, and it will be easier to achieve concentration.

When practicing single-pointedly, if our body and mind abide in isolation, realizations will arise in our continuum, and from that vast benefits for many beings will follow. Other activities like astrology, medicine, divination, and performing rituals or pūjās in the homes of lay people generally do benefit others, but when we are practicing to achieve calm abiding, they become causes for our mind to be distracted externally, so we should forsake them.

Sixth, thoroughly abandoning discursive thoughts like desire and so forth: Through the force of attachment to the enticing objects of the five senses and so forth, many discursive thoughts arise, so we must let go of attachment. To do so, we need to think about the faults of objects of desire and meditate on impermanence and so forth.

If you assemble well such a collection of causes, it will be easy to achieve calm abiding.

44. The Tibetan *phal pa* (Skt. *prākṛta*), which I have translated here as "trifling," is often used in contradistinction to Dharma activities. So even ordinarily important activities like working a job and taking care of a family would fall into the category of *phal pa* here, in contrast to time spent studying and meditating on Dharma.

THREE

The Actual Method of Achieving Calm Abiding

[21] WELL THEN, what is the actual method for achieving calm abiding? This is from Maitreya's *Differentiating the Middle from Extremes*:

> [Concentration] arises from relying on
> formations eight, which halt five faults.[45]

The lord Maitreya explains that calm abiding is a concentration that arises from meditating by relying on the eight applications [translated in the verse as "formations"], which are antidotes for the purpose of abandoning the five faults.

As for the five faults, the same text says,

> Inertia, to forget advice,
> excitement, laxity, not to
> apply an antidote, and to
> apply one: we accept five faults.[46]

When preparing to develop concentration, the laziness [translated in the verse as "inertia"] that doesn't want to engage in virtuous activities like calm abiding and so forth arises. That is the first fault.

As for the second fault, at the actual time of practicing concentration, we need to choose a particular object of observation and abide on it with a stable mind. On top of that, having identified that objective support,[47] we need to familiarize our mind with it. We need recollection to keep such

45. Maitreya, *Differentiating the Middle from Extremes*, 4.3cd. See also Maitreya 2006.

46. Maitreya, *Differentiating the Middle from Extremes*, 4.4.

47. Skt. *viṣayālambana*; Tib. *dmigs rten*. This term refers to the object on which the mind meditates. It is called a "support" or "base" because it grounds the mind and because by focusing on it, the mind becomes concentrated.

an objective support immediately[48] in the space of mind without losing it; lacking recollection and losing the objective support in our space of mind is called "forgetting the instructions."[49]

The third fault is as follows: When actually meditating on concentration, if laxity and excitement arise, they will obstruct concentration, [22] so during the actual session of concentration we reckon these two—laxity and excitement together—as a single fault.

When laxity and excitement arise, not relying on the antidote to them is called "not applying the antidote." When laxity and excitement arise, we need to apply the antidote. "Not applying" means that we do not apply the antidote even when they arise; this is the fourth fault.

The fifth fault: When we are free of laxity and excitement [at the ninth mental settling],[50] if we strongly apply an antidote it will actually harm the factor of stability, so at that time, rather than applying an antidote we need to place our mind in equanimity. If we don't place our mind in equanimity but instead apply an antidote, it becomes a fault.

Among the eight applications to counter the five faults, four are said to be antidotes to laziness. "Laziness" is not wishing to achieve roots of virtue or is a mind that does not delight in virtue. The actual antidote for such laziness is called "pliancy."[51] There are two kinds of pliancy: physical pliancy and mental pliancy. When our body and mind become suitable to put to use in whatever way we wish, it is called "physical and mental pliancy." [23] Before achieving such pliancy, as a basis we begin by making effort and meditating, so we need effort as a cause for pliancy. In order to generate such forceful effort, as a basis we need a strong aspiration that aims to achieve concentration. For example, in any worldly activity or other virtuous practice, if we

48. Tib. *thur re*. Gen Namgyal Chöphel explains that in this context, "immediate" implies that the object appears as though it were "right in front of you, right now," as opposed to being simply something you are abstractly thinking about.

49. Here "forgetting" means that one loses the object in concentration because the mind is distracted elsewhere, not that one cannot recall the object when asked. See Rinpoché's comments on page 57.

50. Tsongkhapa explains in the *Great Treatise on the Stages of the Path to Enlightenment*, "The 'equanimity' that is explained within the eight applications that abandon, in *Differentiating the Middle from Extremes*, is equivalent to the ninth mental [settling explained in other texts]." Translation mine; see also Tsongkhapa 2000, 3:81.

51. Pliancy is the actual antidote to laziness, because when one achieves it one overcomes laziness completely. However, one does not achieve pliancy until one actually achieves calm abiding, so in the initial stages, one relies on the other three antidotes.

have an aspiration aiming for it, we will be able to bear hardship for the sake of it. So we need a great aspiration to seek after concentration. In order for such an aspiration to arise, we need a faith from thinking over the various benefits of concentration. If such faith arises in our mind, through the force of that, there is no way we will not achieve concentration; the aspiration to strive that thinks, "I definitely must achieve concentration," will naturally induce it. These four—faith, aspiration, effort, and pliancy—are the antidotes to laziness.

The antidote to laxity and excitement checks whether or not laxity and excitement are arising in the mind, like a scout who reconnoiters an army. We need the sentry of introspection to check whether laxity and excitement are arising or not. Although introspection is not literally the antidote to laxity and excitement, since it is a like a spy watching over whether laxity and excitement arise or not, we call it "introspection."[52] [24]

In this context, forgetting the objective support or letting it slip from our active memory is called "forgetting the instructions." It is said that before even beginning to prepare for meditative stabilization, laziness is a fault, while forgetting the instruction is a fault at the actual time of making preparations for stabilization [that is, during the initial stages of meditation]. So the reason for positing "forgetting the instructions" as a fault is that when meditating on stabilization, we definitely need an objective support, and if we forget this basis, we will not achieve stabilization. Thus, at the time of preparing for meditative stabilization, forgetting the instructions is a fault.

Regarding the antidote to that fault, it's not merely that, if somebody else asks, "What is your objective support?" or if we try to remember the support ourselves, we are unable to recall it. Rather, through remembering the objective support, we don't forget it and are able to hold it vibrantly in our active memory. Also, merely to achieve calm abiding, any objective

52. The point here is that introspection lets us know when we need to apply an antidote, but mere introspection is not itself sufficient as an antidote. Following Rinpoché's example, a scout might tell us that enemy troops are approaching, but the scout does not himself repel these troops. Having recognized laxity and excitement, a practitioner must apply the actual antidotes. For laxity, the most basic antidote is to sharpen the object of apprehension, a stronger antidote is to uplift the mind by meditating on faith and compassion, and the strongest antidote is to break the session entirely. For excitement, the first step is to imagine the object becoming heavier or to focus on the breath. If this method fails, one might meditate on suffering and other topics that settle the excitement. Rinpoché describes these methods in greater detail on pages 64 through 77.

support will do. [25] For example, some non-Buddhists take rocks, sticks, and so forth as a basis and manage to achieve calm abiding.

The Means of Taking the Buddha as the Objective Support

Generally speaking, we can take anything as an objective support and, through practice, actualize calm abiding, but for us Buddhists it is more meaningful when actualizing calm abiding if we can take as a support the holy body of a buddha, the holy body of our teacher Śākyamuni, or the holy body of our *yidam* deity and practice with that. In addition to actualizing calm abiding, if we rely on the Buddha as our object, we will remember the Buddha and so forth. In light of such a significant difference, we take the holy body of the Buddha as an objective support and achieve calm abiding.

When actualizing calm abiding, if we keep changing from one object to another, we will not succeed, so whatever object we take from the start, we should focus on that very one and actualize calm abiding. When taking the holy body of our teacher Buddha as the objective support, if when our lama describes it to us we can ascertain his holy body with a golden hue, endowed with a crown protrusion, with his right hand pressing the earth and his left displaying the mudrā of equipoise, and with the three monastic robes[53] adorning his holy body, and if such a complete form can appear to our mind, that will do. [26] Otherwise, we can take a good look at a picture or relief carving of the holy body and bring it to mind. Even just before the time of meditating, it is permissible to observe that very representation and meditate.[54]

Regarding the preparations: when we first practice to actualize calm abiding, we practice the complete six preparatory practices.[55] Then, having with-

53. See note 43.

54. Gen Namgyal Chöphel clarifies this point: at the *start* of the meditation session one looks at the image and then holds it in mind during meditation. One should not actually look at the image with one's eyes *during* the meditation session.

55. The "six preparatory practices" to complete before meditation are as follows:

1. Cleaning the place and arranging representations of the Buddha's body, speech, and mind (that is, an image, a text, and a stūpa or vajra and bell). This is said to have five benefits: (1) clarifying one's mind, (2) clarifying others' minds, (3) giving joy to the minds of the gods, (4) accumulating roots of virtue to be beautiful [in future lives], and (5) establishing that, at the dissolution of the body, one will achieve high status in happy migrations as a god.

drawn the preparatory-practice merit field,[56] we imagine that it dissolves into the lama Thupwang[57] at our crown. If we mentally shrink the holy body of the lama Thupwang and take that as our objective support, a firm stability factor of mind will arise, so we reduce the size of the lama Thupwang at our crown to a mere finger width. If that mere finger width is too high in front of us, excitement will arise, and if it is too low, laxity will arise, so imagine it in the space in front at the level of one's navel[58] and meditate. Take as an objective support an image that is merely half the length of a thumb. When observing this object, at the beginning we won't be able to cause a clear image with complete facial features and hands to appear. Since at first we

---

2. Arranging offerings that were achieved through right livelihood.
3. Sitting comfortably in the sevenfold posture of Vairocana, and from the space of a special virtuous mind, going for refuge, generating bodhicitta, and so forth.
4. Visualizing the merit field.
5. Performing the seven-limbed prayer along with a maṇḍala offering for the purpose of accumulating merit and purifying negativities.
6. Making requests in line with the traditional instructions and definitely mixing one's continuum [with the lineage and one's teacher].

(Source: Samdrup, *Sgom sde tshig mdzod chen mo*, vol. 3.) For a clear English language presentation of these practices, see Chos-'byor 2001.

56. This assembly of lineage lamas and meditational deities is visualized in the context of the Lama Chöpa practice. For an excellent guide to the figures in this merit field, see Pabongka Rinpoche 1990–2001, part 1, appendix B.

57. Tib. *thub dbang*; Skt. *munīndra*; literally "powerfully able one." This is an epithet for Śākyamuni Buddha. It takes the *muni* ("capable one" or "sage") from his name and affixes an emphatic to distinguish him from ordinary sages.

58. One should not visualize the Buddha immediately in front of one's navel, but a foot or two in front. Rinpoché has said elsewhere:

> The reason for placing the objective support in the space in front of your navel is that it is easier to dispel laxity and excitement. However small you can visualize the objective support, it is said that to that degree your factor of stability will be stronger.
>
> If you have a problem of being unable to visualize it that small, you should make it the size of a mere finger, or merely half the length of a thumb. At first it won't come clearly. If at first you think of the holy body of the Buddha as the size of merely half the length of a thumb, then if after that the image gets bigger or smaller, or if other colors appear to your mind, you shouldn't follow those changes . . . Even if he appears clearly with all the [thirty-two] marks and eighty signs, still you shouldn't follow that. Once you get a good factor of stability, you can clarify the image and meditate on that. (Chöden Rinpoché 2018, 100–101).

Visualizing him at the navel level is one possibility, but depending on one's disposition, it might be better to visualize him at the level of one's forehead or the tip of the nose. One's personal teacher should advise the most suitable practice.

need an objective support for the mind to abide on beyond just remembering the appearance of Śākyamuni's golden-hued holy body as our object, if we try to cause all the features like hands, feet, eyes, and so forth to appear, there is a danger that we will lose the object. [27] If we lose the objective support, we won't achieve calm abiding, so it's very important not to lose it. As for the objective support, we need something obstructive to ground the mind, so if we find just that, we can be content with it. Even if at first all the parts of the holy body, such as head, hands, feet, and so forth, do not individually appear to the mind—and whether the color of the holy body of our teacher Buddha is clear or not—if something like an upright yellow form appears, we can be satisfied and observe just that. We need to hold it in mind with a firm mode of apprehension and an intense awareness, without our mind being distracted to various other objects.

Furthermore, while observing just that object that we first observed, we need to meditate with a firm mode of apprehension, without being distracted toward other objects. Since the holy body of the Buddha on which we are meditating is of a golden hue, we think, "I must meditate on a golden holy body," and if other colors like blue and so forth appear, it is inappropriate to follow after them.

As for the size, in the beginning, we should meditate on the body merely the size of half the length of a thumb and shouldn't try to cause a larger one to appear. If an object that grounds the mind arises, if we go beyond just observing that and first check "Is it appearing clearly?" that will harm our factor of stability, so in the beginning we can be content with merely that grounding appearance. [28] Later, if we get a slight factor of stability toward the object, it is good if we can slowly imagine in succession the hands, feet, wheel marks on the palms and soles, face, hair tuft on the forebrow, and so forth and gradually clarify the appearance. If we achieve calm abiding in this way, as described in the great texts, on the basis of that we will be able to advance to the higher and higher paths. In the past some people, relying on so-called "pith advice" that does not accord with the great texts, have said, "Don't engage in any conceptual thought at all. Don't direct the mind anywhere. Relax and abide: that is calm abiding. That is meditative stabilization." Even today, there are those who say such things. It is our own fault if we don't understand this important point. We need to practice and actualize calm abiding as it is described in the great texts.

When actually tending to the object we use to achieve calm abiding and staying in a fully qualified abode for actualizing calm abiding, first we need to do the six preparatory practices such as cleaning the place, arranging a representation of the Buddha's holy body, speech, and mind, and so forth. Generally speaking, whether we are meditating on calm abiding or engaging in some other practice, initially it is very important to prepare well by means of these six preparatory practices. [29] Preceded by a good preparation, the actual session will also go well. However poorly the preparation is done, to that same degree the actual session will go poorly.

Having done the six preparatory practices, withdraw the merit field. Having withdrawn the merit field, imagine that guru Śākyamuni Buddha comes to the crown of your head. Make the request to him: "Please bless me, in general, to cleanse and purify all wrongdoing and obscurations and to quickly achieve the state of a guru buddha. In particular, please bless me to generate easily the realization of calm abiding." Through our requesting in this way, from the holy body of the guru will flow a stream of nectar-light rays, which enter into your crown, cleansing and purifying all wrongdoing and obscurations that create hindrances to actualizing calm abiding. Imagine that you are blessed to achieve quickly the realization of calm abiding.

There are non-Buddhists who, for an object of calm abiding, take "stones and sticks"—small rocks and small twigs—and actualize calm abiding. Mainly, calm abiding arises more easily if one observes the object with which one has the greatest familiarity. [30] However, if we observe the holy body of the Buddha, while abiding in calm abiding we will accumulate merit and cleanse obscurations. We will be reminded of a special objective basis of prostration and offering. The great difference from merely observing stones and sticks is that, by observing the holy body of the Buddha, we will remember the Buddha, and on the way we will easily accumulate vast stores of merit and virtue, will be reminded of the objects of refuge and field of merit, and so forth.

Where to Meditate on the Objective Support

Imagine that, because you have made requests to the guru Śākyamuni at your crown, a mere half-thumb-sized replica of his holy body separates from his heart and comes to rest in front of the space between your eyebrows or at the level of your navel. If you place it in front of your navel, a firm factor of stability will arise, and if you place it in front of your eyebrows, it is good for the factor of clarity. Imagine in the space of your mind whatever aspect of observation, with its various characteristics and so forth, on which your lama has clearly instructed you.

When meditating, place in the space in front of your navel the holy body of the Buddha, the size of a mere half a thumb, that has separated from the heart of guru victor Śākyamuni at your crown. By placing your mind single-pointedly on that, you must actualize the factor of stability. [31] It is important to secure to that object a tight manner of apprehension that does not wander to other objects. If from the very first session you make the duration especially long, laxity and excitement will arrive and you will lose the object, so at first it is best to practice in short sessions. If we break during a period of the session when the factor of stability, an intense factor of clarity, and so forth are going well, afterward we will think, "It will go well again next time," and will want to engage in concentration again. If instead we hold out hope for a clear object right away and make the session very long, after a while we will lose the object we are trying to sustain, and we will become exhausted. Thus we won't want to engage in the practice again. So at first, we are better off not mainly focusing on trying to attain a tight mode of apprehension and clear object of observation but rather making many short sessions. Later, when we do get a firm factor of stability to the object, we can lengthen the session and focus on trying to get an intense factor of clarity. However, whenever a factor of stability arises, we must be cautious about laxity, and whenever a factor of clarity arises, we must be cautious about excitement. Furthermore, when the state of mind gets especially low, there is a danger of laxity, and when it gets especially high, there is danger of excitement. [32] A yogi has to infer these things mainly from his or her own experience; others' words cannot describe it exactly as it is.

When observing an object in that way and actually practicing to achieve calm abiding, if one meditates uninterruptedly—not taking breaks except to sleep, eat, and use the bathroom—calm abiding will quickly arise. For example, there is a kind of stick that, if we keep rubbing two of them together, we will get fire. If we keep taking break after break in rubbing, they will become cold and we won't get fire, but if we rub without break until fire arises, soon the fire will blaze. Likewise when we meditate on calm abiding, it is said that if we place our mind just on that object we have chosen and meditate without break for a day, a month, or a year, as long as the collections of causes for calm abiding are complete, we will achieve it in six months [at minimum].[59]

59. Those of sharpest faculties who apply strong effort can achieve calm abiding in six months. For most people it takes longer—often several years. Rinpoché has said elsewhere:

> If you assemble such a collection of causes, it is even possible to be able to actualize calm abiding alone in six months. In the past there were some practitioners who achieved it in six months, and even in recent times there are those who

As for "forgetting the objective support" or "forgetting the instructions": if we lose recollection of the objective support and can't hold it in mind, this is called "forgetting the instructions." As an antidote to that, we need strong recollection; [33] we need to rely on a forceful recollection that can hold the objective support immediately[60] without losing it. Some people naturally have stable recollection and introspection and do not forget things. Others are forgetful and immediately forget things. Therefore, it is important to rely on recollection and introspection without forgetting. For somebody with unstable recollection, it is difficult to achieve calm abiding, while for somebody with stable recollection, it is easier.

Teaching on Recollection with Three Characteristics

Well then, what kind of thing is this that we call "recollection"? Just like worldly people usually say "I remember that" and "I don't remember that," "recollection" is a mental factor possessing three characteristics:

1. Object: It observes an object that one has seen and known and with which one has familiarity.
2. Mode of apprehension: It holds immediately in its mode of apprehension that very object with which one is familiar.
3. Function: During that time, it does not scatter from that object to others.

Considering such recollection as very important, by continuously relying on recollection one should make effort not to forget the object. [34] It is said that if one knows the manner of nurturing concentration, it is just that manner of nurturing recollection.

If you are going to meditate taking the holy body of our teacher Buddha as an object, before that you yourself must observe a drawing or carving of

claim to have done so. Then there are those who practice for seven years and can't actualize it, and those who are able to get to the sixth mental settling but say that are unable to move to the seventh. Among those, it is possible that some of them didn't assemble all the causes, or that they assembled them at first but in the meantime they degenerated. I think it could be on account of that. (Chöden Rinpoché 2018, 92.)

60. See note 48.

his holy body and ascertain its characteristics, or you can become familiar with it through the explanations of your lama. Through these methods, the object becomes a "familiar thing." Because recollection observes the object single-pointedly, generating a tight or forceful manner of apprehending and holding it, it is called a "tenacious manner of apprehension." By causing just that object to appear to the mind without scattering to other objects, recollection becomes endowed with three characteristics.

Similarly, the fault of "forgetting the instructions" that I explained above is losing the objective support. The antidote to losing the objective support is the forceful recollection that holds tightly without losing the objective support.

How to Identify Laxity

The third fault obstructing calm abiding is called "laxity and excitement." Laxity and excitement create obstacles during the actual session of cultivating meditative stabilization, so we need to stop laxity and excitement. [35] If at first we don't identify laxity and excitement, we won't be able to stop them and won't know how to do so, so it is said that we must identify laxity and excitement.

Generally among the different mental factors spoken of such as laxity, lethargy, and excitement, there is a difference between laxity and lethargy. Lethargy is like a looming heaviness of body and mind just before falling asleep that initiates the onset of sleep. A mental factor that causes a lack of mental clarity is called "lethargy." There is no virtuous mind that is in the nature of lethargy; whatever is lethargy is necessarily not virtuous. Lethargy must be either nonvirtuous or be a defiled neutral mind.[61] There *can* be a virtuous mind that is of the nature of laxity. Laxity is when, because one does not maintain a tight manner of apprehension, the factor of clarity lacks intensity, and the mind sinks and becomes loose. Like procrastination, "laxity" is one of the greatest obstacles to concentration.

There are two kinds of laxity: gross laxity and subtle laxity. Gross laxity is when, as we observe the holy body of the Buddha, recollection maintains the objective support and the mind stays on the object, but consciousness

61. Skt. **nivṛtāvyākṛta*; Tib. *sgrib lung ma bstan*; literally "obscuring and ethically neutral." "Obscuring" or "defiled" means that lethargy is an afflictive mental state. Afflictive mental states are not necessarily nonvirtuous, but they necessarily steer the mind toward nonvirtue.

has no factor of clarity or factor of lucidity[62] at all. [36] Although one has a mere factor of stability toward the object, there is no factor of clarity, as though something else were obscuring it; this is called "gross laxity." Alternatively, one does not lose the mode of apprehension of the object, maintaining both a factor of stability and also a factor of clarity. Although there is a factor of clarity, there is no tight mode of apprehension, and the force of the mode of apprehension loosens slightly. If that happens, there is no intensity of the factor of clarity, so we call it "subtle laxity." For example, if we are holding an object with our hand, there is a difference between holding without a tight grip versus gripping tightly and holding the object. Likewise, the kind of apprehension of the object of observation that lacks a tight mode of apprehension lacks an intensity of the factor of clarity, whereas if we focus and tighten the mode of apprehension and then hold the object in mind, that holding has an "intensity of the factor of clarity."

Although subtle laxity has a factor of clarity and firmly holds on to the objective support, its mode of apprehension stays as though relaxing. Since subtle laxity is a fault of not holding the objective support by tightening the mode of apprehension, we need to tighten the mode of apprehension and hold the object. If we tighten it, there is a risk of excitement and a risk of scattering to another object. Generally speaking, if one relaxes the mind, it is good for the factor of stability. [37] Since one then has a good factor of stability, many earlier Tibetans mistook subtle laxity for meditative stabilization.

We definitely need to understand this so-called "subtle laxity." For example, if there is an obvious enemy intent on harming us from afar, it is relatively easy to stop him. But with somebody who acts like our close friend and pretends to benefit us, we don't know when he will turn around and harm us, so this is our most serious threat. Likewise this subtle laxity, which has a factor of stability and a factor of clarity, is similar to meditative stabilization, so we are apt to mistake it for meditative stabilization. Thus it is the greatest obstacle. When it comes to identifying subtle laxity, although somebody may say, "You need a factor of stability. You need a factor of clarity,"

62. Gen Namgyal Chöphel explains that "factor of lucidity" (Tib. *dwangs cha*) and "factor of clarity" (Tib. *gsal cha*) differ in terms of degree; first one develops the factor of lucidity, and when this strengthens, it becomes the factor of clarity. According the *Great Treatise on the Stages of the Path to Enlightenment*, during gross laxity one *does* have the factor of lucidity, but Rinpoché is using the term in a slightly different manner. See Tsongkhapa 2000, 3:59 ("factor of lucidity" is there translated as "limpid").

these words cannot adequately describe to another person what is clear and what is good. So through our own experience, while meditating we should occasionally check whether our mode of apprehension is tight or not. If a focused, tight mode of apprehension is there, "intensity of the factor of clarity" has arisen. [38] If we have the factors of stability and clarity but the mode of apprehension lacks tightness and is slackening, then it is turning into laxity.

These are things that we need to analyze based on our own experiences. If subtle laxity builds up and we think that this subtle laxity is actual meditative stabilization, then air may even cease to flow through our nostrils and we may abide for many days with a stable mind. At the beginning, our mind might experience a pleasant sensation. However, that is an obstacle to meditative stabilization. For example, yesterday when I returned to Sera I met a Sera monk. He has a very good understanding of scripture and a clear ascertainment in his mind of all scriptural explanations of the manner of actualizing calm abiding. However, he said that he had gone to a solitary place to practice meditation and meditated on calm abiding for eight months. During those eight months, while meditating he had a secure factor of stability capable of inducing some level of bliss. Because of that, he thought, "Ah, now I have achieved actual calm abiding." However, there was a geshé of one of the new sects[63] who had [39] previously stayed in Bhutan and had practiced and attained calm abiding. The Sera monk said he asked the geshé for advice, and the geshé replied, "The intensity of your mode of apprehension is a little too weak. You still need to meditate a bit."

So he had a good understanding of scripture and knew based on scripture all about the manner of actualizing calm abiding, the objects of abandonment, and the antidotes, and yet still slight laxity and mental scattering arose for him.[64] For those of us who do not even have such familiarity with the great texts, such scattering will surely be prone to arise, so at that time we need to be careful. If we mistake the subtle laxity that is not actual meditative stabilization for actual meditative stabilization and meditate for a long time, because our recollection's mode of apprehension lacks a forceful intensity, it has no benefit; it will become a cause in this life for forgetfulness

63. Tib. *gsar ma*. These "new sects" include the Geluk, Kagyü, and Sakya schools, in contradistinction to the Nyingma or "old sect."

64. Rinpoché shared privately with Gen Namgyal Chöphel that this particular meditator was indeed eventually successful in actualizing calm abiding.

to increase and for lack of mental clarity to worsen, and it will be a cause in future lives for stupidity as an animal and so forth.[65]

These are important points that are not made completely clear in the great texts, so let me repeat: "gross laxity" is when there is a factor of stability but no factors of clarity or lucidity. [40] "Subtle laxity" is when there are both factors of stability and clarity, but a tight mode of apprehension or the intensity of the clarity factor is lost.

How to Identify Excitement

What is this excitement that is spoken of in "laxity and excitement"? Excitement belongs in the category of the mental affliction of desire-attachment [that is, it is a specific kind of desire-attachment]. A mental factor that scatters the mind to another object through the force of attachment is what we call "excitement." Generally speaking, meditative stabilization is something that needs a factor of stability, so if the mind scatters to another object, that is an obstacle to meditative stabilization. In this context, however, not all manners of scattering are discussed as obstacles, whereas excitement is said to be the greatest obstacle. When we distinguish scattering from excitement, scattering can be of three types: (1) Excitement is a scattering to another object through the force of attachment. Distraction to another object through the force of (2) hatred or (3) a virtuous mind is also scattering but is not excitement. In actuality, these latter two also create obstacles to meditative stabilization, but in this context excitement, which is scattering through the force of attachment, is spoken of as an obstacle, [41] while the other two are not mentioned as obstacles here. If other kinds of scattering cause obstacles to meditative stabilization, why are they not posited as obstacles here? Scattering to objects through virtuous minds or hatred is less frequent, while scattering to objects through attachment is much more common. Also, from the point of view of duration, scattering to objects through virtuous minds or hatred is of a short duration, while scattering to objects through attachment is of a long duration, so the former two are not spoken of as obstacles here.[66]

65. Meditating with subtle laxity, because it is not nonvirtuous, will not literally create the cause for animal rebirth. However, it will lead to a dullness of mind and may help to ripen previous imprints for such birth or, at the very least, waste one's precious human rebirth.

66. In addition to scattering through excitement being (1) more common and (2) of a longer

Why is it that scattering to objects through attachment is of a longer duration? Attachment is like soaking a piece of paper with oil. If a piece of paper is soaked in oil, it is extremely difficult to clean off the oil. Excitement, which scatters to objects through the force of attachment, is said to be an obstacle to meditative stabilization in a similar manner to that oil. When meditating on calm abiding, the mind needs to stay only on the objective support, so any scattering to other objects is an obstacle. For that reason, when meditating on calm abiding, if other thoughts about practicing generosity, making prostrations, or even love and compassion arise and cause distraction, [42] for the time being these are obstacles to meditative stabilization, so one should not follow these thoughts. If we follow them we will lose the object of calm abiding, so scattering to objects through virtuous minds is also, at the time of cultivating meditative stabilization, an obstacle, which we must stop.

Excitement also has both gross and subtle kinds. At the time of observing an objective support like the holy body of the Buddha, if the mind scatters to another object and we lose the objective support, that is called "gross excitement." In the case of subtle excitement, the mind does not get drawn away and lose the objective support, but from within the space of holding the objective support an enticing object is on the verge of arising in a corner of the mind. Subtle excitement is like, for example, water flowing under ice.

As an antidote to such laxity and excitement, one must rely on introspection, the sixth of the eight antidotes to apply to the five faults. Introspection is not the actual antidote that cuts laxity and excitement, but it recognizes laxity and excitement: it is the sentry that inspects whether or not laxity and excitement are arising. By keeping watch when laxity or excitement is about to arise, if introspection is able to be aware of them, it is best.

[43] Well then, what is this thing called "introspection"? An observing consciousness that stands guard or spies to see whether or not the object held by recollection is being lost or not is called "introspection." However, if we continuously use this introspection to check what is happening, it will harm our factor of stability, so we should prepare an investigating introspection and occasionally check just a bit. For example, if we hold in our hands a vessel full of water, we need to grip it tightly while also checking whether

---

duration than other forms of scattering, Phabongkha Rinpoché also mentions a third reason: it arises more easily. See Pabongka 1991, 660.

or not it is spilling out. Holding with the hands is like the factor of stability, and gripping tightly is like the intensity of the mode of apprehension. If the water starts to churn, it will spill out, so in order for it not to spill, one corner of the mind has to check whether or not it is churning: that is introspection.

Now, the fourth fault: when laxity and excitement arise, if we fail to make recourse to an antidote, it becomes the fault of not applying the antidote. [44] Before laxity and excitement arise, introspection stands guard. If it sees that laxity is about to arise, one tightens the object of observation, and if it sees that excitement is about to arise, one settles down the mind. Since we need to apply these methods to stop laxity and excitement, if they arise we definitely must make use of an antidote.

Introspection investigates whether or not the enemies of laxity and excitement are approaching, like a spy. If a spy sees an enemy approaching from a distance, he will send word and somebody else will come to do the actual work of stopping the enemy. Likewise, introspection is the mere sentry to check whether or not laxity and excitement are approaching. If laxity and excitement arise, the actual thing that stops them is the application of the antidote, an associated compounding factor.[67]

Well then, how do we actually apply the antidote? From the two laxities explained above, subtle laxity is the one that has the factors of stability and clarity, but due to lacking a tight mode of apprehension, it has lost the intensity of the factor of clarity. If subtle laxity arises, to stop it we do not need to break the session [45] nor do we need to let go of the object of observation. If we try to generate an intensity of the factor of clarity by tightening the mode of apprehension, when such an intensity arises, we have succeeded in stopping subtle laxity.

Furthermore, if we concentrate intensely on the object and it becomes *too* tight, there is a risk that the mind will slip into excitement. If instead we

67. Skt. *saṃskāra*; Tib. *'du byed*. Compounding factors are the fourth among the five aggregates that constitute a person. This aggregate includes a variety of constituents that are not included in the other four aggregates, such as all mental factors besides feeling and discrimination, as well as imprints on the mind, impermanence, and so forth. These various constituents are subdivided into "associated compounding factors"—that is, mental factors, which are "associated" with main minds—and "nonassociated compounding factors"—that is, all compounding factors that are not mental factors, such as imprints. The word *'du byed* can function in several ways, and here it is also translated as "application" and can be understood to mean "volition"—the will to do something (in this case, to apply an antidote). Because many of the mental factors included in the fourth aggregate are forms of volition, this aggregate takes that name.

make the object too loose, laxity will arise, so we need to put effort into a technique that brings about a balance between tightness and looseness. One needs to confirm this through personal experience. If you concentrate too strongly and you think your mind is starting to scatter, you should loosen the object, and if you're too relaxed and you think that laxity is arising, you should tighten your concentration, and so forth: these are things you need to know from experience. The Blessed One also explained that we need to have a balance between tightness and looseness. He himself explained, "If the strings of a sitar are too tight, one won't get a sweet sound, and also if they are too loose, one won't get a sweet sound, so by finding a balance between tight and loose, a sweet sound will arise. Likewise, by holding the mind not too tightly focused and not too loose, in a balanced state, meditative stabilization will arise." [46]

In addition, we have the story of Ācārya Candragomin:[68] Candragomin possessed the signs of one who has directly seen Ārya Avalokiteśvara and others, and proceeded to high levels of accomplishment. Nevertheless, early on when he was practicing calm abiding, he applied fierce effort and over-tightened his mind, leading to excitement. When he subsequently relaxed too much, laxity arrived, so he asked, "What should I do?"[69]

Subtle laxity is a condition that has factors of clarity and subjective clarity but lacks intensity of the factor of clarity. When subtle laxity arises, one must tighten the object. During subtle laxity, although there are factors of clarity and subjective clarity, an experience of an unclear mode of apprehension arises followed by subtle laxity, which has lost the intensity of the factor of clarity. To counter this loss of intensity, one needn't end the meditation session, but by tightening the object of observation it is said that one can counter it. At that time, if even by tightening the mode of apprehension one does not manage to counter it and if having lost the intensity of the factor

68. Candragomin, a renowned lay scholar of the Mind Only school, flourished at Nālandā Monastery in the seventh century.

69. This quote, from Candragomin's *Praise of Confession* (Skt. *Deśanāstava*; Tib. *Gshags bstod*) appears in full on page 83 of the Paṇchen Lama's Mahāmudrā autocommentary, *The Lamp That Further Clarifies*:

> When effort's made, excitement comes;
> I throw that out and slackness comes!
> So hard to find right equipoise:
> What to do with my troubled mind?

See also Tsongkhapa 2002, 3:51.

of clarity it is like the mind is deteriorating, or if there is no intensity, the mind is slack, the mode of apprehension is unclear, and it is as though one is about to forget the object, then gross laxity has arrived. [47] When gross laxity comes about, what method should we employ to counter it?

Laxity is not the mind gone into scattering but a case of the mind being too withdrawn inward, so through a fault that is like a slight sinking of the mental state, laxity comes about. Therefore, when gross laxity arrives, as a method to pacify it one needs to elevate the mental state. In order to elevate the mental state, initially as a means of bringing joy to the mind we can do as described in the *Great Treatise on the Stages of the Path to Enlightenment* in the section on how to actualize calm abiding within the context of the being of great capacity, where Tsongkhapa explains the advice on the six perfections for one engaging in the bodhisattva's conduct. If we do what is described there, then even before we practice calm abiding, we would have had some experience of the great meaning of and difficulty in finding the leisure and fortune of a perfect human rebirth and the benefits of the mind of enlightenment. In that case, then when the mind becomes depressed, if we reflect on the benefits of relying on a spiritual friend, the great meaning of and difficulty in finding the leisure and fortune of a perfect human rebirth, the benefits of the mind of enlightenment, and so forth, then a vibrant mental joy will arise, and the mind's abiding low in depression will lift, so we should do that. If we don't have a great deal of familiarity with those virtuous minds, it will be difficult for that joy to arise. If we have adequate familiarity, then when we recollect those benefits, like freshening up by throwing or sprinkling cold water on our face, [48] the mind will become clear and bright.[70]

Once there was a retreatant staying on Chakpori Hill (in Lhasa). That Chakpori retreatant was practicing and meditating well on the mind of enlightenment. Also at that time was one called Phurbuchok Jampa Gyatso,[71]

70. Rinpoché is making the point that we should train in these analytical meditations on the stages of the path *before* practicing for calm abiding. In that case, then when we are in retreat to actualize calm abiding, we can remember the experience we have previously generated. If instead we attempt to do these reflections for the first time while practicing calm abiding, we will be unable to generate sufficient strength of experience to overcome obstacles.

71. Phurbuchok Jampa Gyatso (Tib. Phur bu lcog Byams pa rgya mtsho, 1825–1901) was a renowned scholar from Sera Jé Monastery. He was the tutor to the Thirteenth Dalai Lama and composed an introductory text on debate that has become a standard textbook at Sera Jé and some other major monastic colleges. See Perdue 1992.

a master of the lamrim teachings, who would always give lamrim teachings in the summer and autumn. When Phurbuchok arrived in the presence of the Chakpori retreatant, they spoke about the mind of enlightenment. While they were speaking together, the retreatant remarked, "When you arrived, like once again lightening the load of my pack, we fell into a talk about the mind of enlightenment. If you were to talk about this to others, they wouldn't take to it. When we spoke about the mind of enlightenment, I remembered its benefits, and faith and respect arose in my mind. On the basis of that, my pack has become light again."

If we meditate recollecting the benefits of the mind of enlightenment and so forth but still are unable to pacify laxity, there is an oral instruction on a forceful method for cutting laxity. [49] What is it? Imagine your mind in the aspect of a white light at your heart. Reciting "Phat!" imagine that with the sound of "Phat" your mind emerges from the crown of your head and merges with the sky. If you do that, it can help to pacify laxity. Also, if you think in this way when you have wind disease or an unhappy mind, it can benefit. You need to imagine that your mind merges with the sky above. Alternatively, if you say "Ha!" and exhale outward and then imagine that that air pervades all of space, it can also benefit an unhappy mind.

If even by thinking in this way you still can't clear away laxity, then you should break the meditation session and go to a high place or a place where wind blows. Staying in a high, distant place where you can see into the distance, look around. If by looking around your mind becomes spacious and relaxed, then return to your meditation. These are manners of relying on the antidotes for laxity.

Subtle excitement is when, without losing the objective support, the mind is on the verge of distraction to a familiar object. That subtle excitement arises because the mind is a little too tight. [50] Since that onset of excitement is due to the fault of the mind being excessively tight, one should loosen the mode of apprehension slightly. If one loosens a bit, it will help with the mental distraction. If it doesn't help, it means gross excitement has arrived. What is that onset of gross excitement? It is a fault of the mind being too elevated. If we have a vibrant mental joy, we shouldn't increase the joy too much. With excessive joy, there will be the fault of excitement arising, and it will also be an obstacle to generating good qualities. For example, Śuddhodhana, the father of our teacher the unequaled king of the Śakyas, was excessively joyful because his son was the teacher Buddha Bhagavān. No matter how much the Buddha explained the Dharma to him, he couldn't attain the results of stream entry and so forth.[72] That is the fault of the mind being excessively joyful.

One day the Buddha employed skillful means such that when Śuddhodhana was coming to meet the Buddha, the four great kings[73] guarded the doors of the east, south, west, and north, and when they saw him coming they said to him, "You aren't allowed to go into the presence of the Buddha." On account of that his pride diminished slightly. [51] Even though he was the Buddha's father, since he was unable to ascend into the Buddha's presence, his spirits dropped. Later when the Buddha taught the Dharma the king's mind descended to the right place and by listening to the Dharma in the end he achieved stream entry.

For that reason, if we have excessive mental joy, excitement will arise, so we need to bring down the mental state. As a method for bringing down the mental state, if we reflect again and again on death and impermanence, the suffering of the unfortunate migrations, the faults of saṃsāra, and so forth, a distinct mental sorrow will arise and excitement will in turn become weaker. As I mentioned above, when we haven't meditated much before on these subjects, it is a bit difficult, whereas once we have meditated, when we think of death and impermanence, if we are sitting we will soon need to stand. Having stood and gone about, if we remember death and impermanence, we will soon need to sit down—such is the terror that will arise in our mind. If that arises, the mind of sorrow with saṃsāra is definite to arise.

Even having practiced like that, if you are still unable to dispel excitement, there is a forceful method for cutting excitement. Observing the rising and sinking of the breath, act as if you are deceiving your mind on it[74];

72. According to the Hīnayāna system of progress toward liberation, there are four stages to attain: (1) stream enterer, at which one first has a direct experience of selflessness; (2) once returner, at which one who has already directly experienced selflessness abandons most of the afflictions related to the desire realm such that one can only be born once more in the desire realm; (3) nonreturner, at which one abandons all of the desire realm afflictions and can only be reborn in the form or formless realms; and (4) arhat, at which one abandons all afflictions of the three realms and cannot again be reborn by the power of affliction and karma.

73. In traditional Indian Buddhist cosmology, the "four great kings"—gods of the desire realm—guard the four cardinal directions of the world. They are Dhṛtarāṣṭra (Tib. Yul 'khor srung) in the east, Virūḍhaka (Tib. 'Phags skyes po) in the south, Virūpākṣa (Tib. Spyan mi bzang) in the west, and Vaiśravaṇa (Tib. Rnam thos sras) in the north.

74. Gen Namgyal Chöphel clarifies the meaning of "deceiving the mind" in this context. If one has a rambunctious child, then one gives him a toy to play with to stop him running

exhale one breath, then inhale one. Then again should you should exhale one and inhale one. [52] Not merely counting the coming and going of that breath but also keeping your mind from wandering to another object, think "exhale . . . inhale . . . ," counting "one . . . two . . ." When you are able to count about twenty-eight breaths, you are said to have achieved the first among the nine mental settlings, called "placing the mind." If by thinking in this way you are able to dispel excitement, then again you can continue meditating.

Initially, without falling under the power of laxity and excitement, meditate in a relaxed manner for a short while. Then, when the meditation improves slightly, slowly and carefully increase the length of the session. Otherwise, if you instead insist on meditating for a long time right from the start, laxity, excitement, and so forth will cause obstacles and thoughts like "My mind is a mess!" "Now, this isn't working!" and "This is too hard!" will arise. So in accordance with the advice "leave off when the meditation is enjoyable," if you manage to get a clear object of observation, break the session right there. If you do that, then later when it is time to meditate again, you will want to meditate. Otherwise, if even without a clear object of observation, you insist and continue meditating anyway, you will lose what slight clarity of the object you have. [53] When you see the meditation seat on which you have practiced, you will feel anguish and revulsion. So at first, you should break the session when the meditation is clear.

If you break the session when the meditation is clear, it's like, for example, two close and mutually comfortable friends who part ways: later, if they see each other, both will feel distinct joy. Likewise with meditation, if you break the session when you have clear concentration, when you're about to sit for your next session you will have a clear object and will want to meditate. Thus, you should definitely break the session in a state of clarity.

Otherwise, if you break the session after your mind has become unclear, then when it is time to sit again for the next session, the object will be unclear and you won't want to meditate. For example, once there was a great accomplished practitioner named Druptop Losang Namgyal.[75] While he was giving an oral transmission of the *Assorted Sayings of the Kadampa Mas-*

---

around wildly. Likewise here, one occupies the mind with a mildly challenging task to stop it from wandering to various other objects.

75. Druptop Losang Namgyal (1640–1741), who spent most of his life in solitary retreat, was a teacher to Yongdzin Yeshé Gyaltsen and many others. He appears in the fifteenth verse of the Mahāmudrā Lineage Prayer.

ters,[76] he saw the words "these days, during the degenerate era, is the time to subdue your own mind, not the time to subdue somebody else's mind." Seeing these words, he started to cry, and after crying it was time to finish the teaching session for the day. [54] The next day when he began teaching, he started right from those very words, so having spoken them, again he started crying. In that way, he was unable to complete the teaching. Likewise, if you stop the session while the meditation is unclear, you will stay in that lack of clarity, so from the beginning, without sitting for a long time, if you can have a short session free of the obstacles of laxity and excitement, you should stop right there. It is okay even if you need to complete eighteen short sessions in one day. Then in a relaxed manner, through your own power, you will be able to stay in meditation, and you can increase the length of the session. At first, beyond having many short sessions with relaxed exertion, it is unskillful to apply great, forceful effort.

The fifth fault, applying the antidote when laxity and excitement are absent, arises when laxity and excitement have ceased through your relying on an antidote. Even after laxity and excitement have ceased, if through a great exertion of introspection you still rely on intention [the seventh application], considering it an antidote, it will harm your ability to abide in a firm meditative stabilization, so without applying an antidote, you should just leave your mind as it is. At that time, if even though you are free of laxity and excitement you still apply an antidote, it will harm your mental settling, so such an application of an antidote is itself a fault. [55] As an antidote to *over*-application, there is what is called "desisting from application."[77] Leaving aside the application of an antidote, you must rely on desisting from application, such that you do not apply an antidote.

How It Becomes a Fault if You Let Go during or before the Eighth Mental Settling

It is said that "on the basis of the nine means of settling the mind, one actualizes calm abiding"; I will now explain the last two of these. During

76. Tib. *Bka' gdams pa'i gsung bgros thor bu*, a text compiled Chegom Sherap Dorjé (Lce sgom pa Shes rab rdo rje). See Jinpa 2008, 559–610.

77. Skt. *saṃskāropekṣā*; Tib. *'du byed btang snyoms*; literally "equanimity [with regard to] application." This is one of the three distinct meanings of "equanimity" in Buddhist psychology and should not be confused with the other two, which are limitless equanimity—the wish for all beings to abide in equanimity free of attachment and hatred—and equanimous feeling—a neutral sensation that is neither pleasant nor painful.

the eighth of the nine mental settlings that constitute the method for actualizing calm abiding, if at the beginning of the session a practitioner exerts a slight effort, then until the session is completed laxity and excitement will not create obstacles. At that stage one does not need a great effort of guarding introspection to check whether or not laxity and excitement are arising, so there is said to be at that time a "mere effort of introspection." With a firmness of mind certain that laxity and excitement will not arise, although a person may place their mind in equipoise in meditative stabilization for a long period of time, laxity and excitement will not arise. Furthermore, since this person doesn't need to rely on introspection that checks whether or not these two arise, they are said to "let go of the effort of introspection."[78]

The two—(1) the ability to let go of the effort of introspection and (2) a more general need for effort—are not mutually contradictory. Although it is said that one should not let go of effort until the ninth mental settling, in the context of the eighth mental settling it is said that it is *like* being able to let go. [56] Thus these two statements are not contradictory. In this context, because a person is able to complete the session without laxity and excitement creating obstacles, it is said that "one needn't rely on strong effort like before." Not needing to rely on even a slight effort comes about during the ninth mental settling. Although one lets go of effort during the *ninth* mental settling, it is said to be inappropriate to let go of it before arriving at the *eighth* mental settling. Many earlier Tibetans, saying, "Supreme letting go is supreme meditation" and not correctly apprehending the stage at which one should let go of effort, would let go before that eighth stage: that was inappropriate. According to the great texts, one must definitely continue with effort until reaching the eighth mental settling. Until Jé Tsongkhapa arrived on the scene, what these people spoke of in saying, "Supreme letting go is supreme meditation," was that very lack of intensity of the factor of clarity, which though having a slight factor of stability has turned to subtle dullness. Because it has a slight factor of stability, they would err thinking that subtle dullness was actual meditation.

Jé the Great, in accordance with the great texts and relying on the per-

78. In his text *Mañjuśrī's Oral Instruction*, the Fifth Dalai Lama explains: "At this point, being able to let go means letting go of effort, *not* discarding the intensity of the manner of apprehension." Ngawang Losang Gyatso 2012, 269.

sonal instructions of Mañjuśrī, said, "That is nothing but dullness. It is not an actual meditative stabilization of calm abiding. To achieve actual calm abiding, you need to practice according to the great texts." [57] Because Jé the Great thwarted such faults entering into the teachings of the Buddha and the teachings' sliding into degeneration and so forth—all of which are stains of lack of understanding or of holding opposing views—he was indeed extremely benevolent toward Tibet.

If, saying that "supreme letting go is supreme meditation," somebody mistakes that subtle dullness without an intensity of the factor of clarity for actual meditation and meditates for a long time, they will end up farther away from meditative stabilization.

The Actual Manner of Sustaining the Object of Observation

So, how should one sustain the object of observation? If you have fulfilled all the necessary conditions for calm abiding, such as an abode with five characteristics[79] and so forth, sit down on a comfortable seat. If you elevate your back slightly, there is the advantage of not causing pain to the rear, so arrange a seat like that. Your body should be arranged in "the sevenfold posture of Vairocana"—so called because it is similar to the sitting style of Buddha Vairocana. The seven characteristics of Vairocana's posture are (1) the legs arranged in the vajra position, (2) the hands placed in the mudrā of equipoise, (3) the hips [or lower back] straight, (4) the teeth and lips even and the tip of the tongue lightly pressed against the roof of the mouth, (5) the head slightly bent forward, (6) the eyes cast toward the tip of the nose, and (7) the shoulders straight.[80] By sitting in

79. See page 48.

80. Although there are in fact eight points here and Rinpoché does not clarify how they condense to seven, I have combined "keeping the teeth and lips even" and "pressing the tongue against the roof of the mouth" to make seven. This manner of enumeration is based on that of Gyalwa Ensapa. Ensapa adds an eighth point—counting the breath—but in regard to the first seven, he combines the two as I have done:

> The legs, the hands, the hips: that's three.
> Teeth, lips, and tongue together make four.
> Head, shoulders, eyes, and breath: four more.
> Eight points of Vairocana, these.

(Translation mine; see also Pabongka 1991, 149.) The "vajra position" means that each foot is placed on the opposite thigh. This position is often known in the West as the "lotus pos-

the sevenfold posture of Vairocana, the body will be straight, causing the energy channels to be straight. [58] If the channels are straight, the energy winds will flow directly through them, making it easier for one to develop realizations.

Tradition has it that once upon a time in India, there was a monkey who would regularly see the hearer disciples[81] of the Buddha sitting in the vajra position to practice meditation nearby to where he stayed. Later, when the hearers moved to another place, a group of forders came to meditate in that place. These forders engaged in practice as though lying down and would sit with their legs outstretched. When the monkey came and saw them sitting with their legs outstretched, he arranged their legs in a folded position and lifted those lying down into the vajra position. When he had done that, the forders wondered, "What is this way of sitting? If we sit in this way, there appears to be some difference." Because they sat in the vajra position, they quickly achieved meditative stabilization.

Still, some people are different than others. Another story holds that in old times there was a hearer arhat named Ox Lord (Skt. Gavāṃpati; Tib. Ba glang bdag). [59] This Ox Lord, no matter how much he meditated in the vajra position, was unable to generate realizations. Since he wasn't generating realizations, the Blessed One said to him, "The makeup of your body's energy channels is not like that of most men. Rather, it is like the makeup of the energy channels of an ox, so lie down like an ox and meditate." By lying down and meditating, he quickly achieved meditative stabilization.

Placing your body in the sevenfold posture of Vairocana, in accordance with the lamrim, do the preparatory practices.[82] Withdraw the preparatory-practice merit field and imagine that your lama in the emanation body

ture," likely based on the Sanskrit term *padmāsana* used in Hindu yoga traditions. In the Tibetan system, the "lotus position" actually refers to the position adopted by a female deity in union with a male.

81. Hearer disciples (Skt. *śrāvaka*; Tib. *nyan thos*) are Hīnayāna practitioners who have heard the teachings directly from the Buddha or from other hearers. Note that the Sanskrit term *śrāvaka* is derived from the stem of the causative form (*śrāv*[*ayati*], literally meaning "one who has heard and causes others to hear") of the verbal root √*śru*. The Tibetan *nyan thos* (literally, "listens and causes to hear") reflects this meaning as well. The commentarial literature makes it clear that the connotation is somebody who hears the teachings, internalizes them to achieve liberation, and subsequently expresses that experience to others, but does not initiate any new elaborations beyond what the Buddha taught.

82. See note 55.

aspect[83] sits at the crown of your head. From your lama seated at your crown comes a replica said to be "merely a *tson*"[84]—that is, merely half the length of the thumb. That mere half-thumb-sized replica separates from the lama: now place it in the space in front of your navel and meditate observing it. Although at first all the features like hands and feet will not appear clearly, if you have an appearance to your mind like a clear, upright shaft of yellow, focus merely on that and hold it in memory without forgetting it. If you maintain a tight mode of apprehension without letting your mind wander, you will be able to generate a faultless meditative stabilization. If you intend to actualize calm abiding by observing the body of Mahācakra Vajrapāṇi, a form of Vajrapāṇi, [60] visualize his body in front of you. Although at first a body complete with three faces and six arms will not clearly appear, if an upright blue shaft appears to your mind, it is adequate at the start just to be able to maintain that appearance without your mind wandering to other objects. For calm abiding one needs a single-pointed abiding free of laxity and excitement. Through your holding a tight mode of apprehension, laxity will be unable to intrude, and through your mind not wandering to other objects, excitement will be unable to intrude. So, you must meditate like that. As for the clear appearance of the hands, arms, and so forth, if a stability factor has arisen, one needs gradually to clarify the appearance, but at the beginning one will be unable to have clear appearance or abide for a long time.

When the factor of stability arises, you must prepare for the tarnish of laxity. If the factor of stability arises, laxity draws near,[85] so as a method for dispelling laxity you must tighten the factor of clarity and the mode of apprehension. Again, if by your having tightened the mode of apprehension the factor of clarity becomes very strong, excitement will draw near. If excitement draws near, loosen that taut mode of apprehension a bit and seek again a steadier factor of stability. [61] Doing that, as the factor of stability gradually arises, one must be cautious about laxity, and as a strong factor of clarity gradually arises, cautious about excitement. On top of that, establish a spy of introspection to check whether or not laxity and excitement are arising. Since introspection is like an examiner or a spy, when laxity or excite-

83. That is, in the aspect of Śākyamuni Buddha.

84. A tson (Tib. *tshon*) is the distance from central knuckle to tip of the thumb.

85. Laxity as a mental factor does not arise in ordinary people but only in meditators who have achieved a factor of stability. See introduction.

ment are on the verge of arriving, you must notice right away. If you notice at that time, it will be easier to stop them, whereas it will be more difficult to stop them once they have actually arrived.

FOUR

A Step-by-Step Explanation of the Nine Mental Settlings

WITH REGARD TO the nine mental settlings spoken of in the statement "to actualize calm abiding requires the nine mental settlings," the first mental settling is called "setting the mind." The second is called "continuous setting." The third is "fixing and setting." The fourth is "close setting." The fifth is "disciplining." The sixth is "pacifying." The seventh is "thorough pacifying." The eighth is "making one-pointed," and the ninth is "setting in equipoise."

The first mental settling, setting the mind, holds the objective support in mind, but it does not have a significant mental factor of stability in addition to that, so at this point it is called merely "setting the mind." During that setting, apart from merely setting the mind on the objective support, [62] one is unable to abide there for a long time, so it is called "setting." In the process of actualizing such a concentration, one seeks an objective support. When the mind is set on that objective support, it will seem as though your conceptual thoughts have increased. But if you ask, "Have my conceptual thoughts increased?" it is not that they have increased. Whereas before you didn't analyze how many conceptual thoughts arose over time, now that you have to put a stop to the various conceptions, you are analyzing how many of them arise, and so it seems to be more. Therefore, that is indicative of recognizing conceptual thoughts. For example, if there are many people coming and going from a checkpoint in the road, when you don't check how many people there are, you don't get a clear idea of the amount. If one day you count how many there actually are coming and going, it will seem as though there are more than usual. So in that way, you must identify conceptual thoughts. As we discussed yesterday, while counting your in and out breaths, if for a period of twenty-one breaths you are able to stay on the objective support without your mind wandering, you have achieved the first stage, "setting the mind."

[63] The mere setting of the mind on the objective support in the first

mental settling is achieved through the power of hearing. The manner of achieving through the power of hearing is to sustain the object of observation on the basis of an explanation by one's lama: "As a part of achieving calm abiding, you need an objective support such as the holy body of the Buddha. He has one face and two hands, with the right pressing the earth and the left in equipoise. He has a crown protrusion and his holy body is golden in color." Thus it is called "achieving through the power of hearing."

The second mental settling is continuous setting. This is slightly longer in duration than the first stage. That is, sometimes you are able to slightly extend your sustaining concentration without distracting thoughts, so there is a slightly longer duration of the factor of stability than before. Your mind is able to abide for the duration of, for example, the counting of one rosary of the *maṇi* mantra.[86] At this stage, sometimes thoughts arise, and sometimes it is like being without thoughts, as though thoughts have taken a rest.

These nine methods of settling the mind contain all six powers and also all four mental applications.[87] First of all, the first mental settling correlates with the first of the six powers, the power of hearing. As described above, [64] you listen to the instructions from a lama. You place your mind on the object of observation just as he or she explains, so it fulfills the power of hearing. Because at the second stage you continuously think on the meaning of what you have heard, this stage is achieved through the power of reflection. During the first two mental settlings, when concentration is newly established, laxity and excitement are frequent and a factor of stability only arises a little bit, so among the four mental applications it is the stage of the mental application of focused engagement (or, focusing and engaging). At this stage, between the two, the factor of stability and distraction, distraction lasts longer and it is as though there is no factor of stability.

The third stage is called "fixing and setting." What is that? If, for example, you tear a hole in your clothes, you will quickly fix it with a patch. Likewise here if the mind wanders from the objective support, when you recognize the distraction, you apply a method to place the mind on the basis again. Since you do that, it is called "fixing and setting." As the duration of meditation becomes longer, distractions become less. Even if you occasionally lose the objective support, again you goad the mind onto the objective sup-

86. This is *oṃ maṇi padme hūṃ*, the mantra of Avalokiteśvara, the buddha of compassion. One rosary would mean 108 recitations of the mantra.

87. See introduction.

port like patching your clothes. [65] That is fixing and setting. At this stage, you must rely on strong recollection. At the time of actual calm abiding, thoughts will exhaust themselves, like a man who becomes exhausted from working a lot. If you are free from laxity and excitement, you must continuously place the mind, and if you are able to place it for slightly longer, you should extend the session.

The fourth mental settling is called "close setting." At this stage if, relying on strong recollection, you start by placing the mind on the objective support, you will not forget or lose the objective support so long as you maintain that recollection.[88] Since one establishes the previous stage of fixing and setting and this present stage of close setting by relying on strong recollection, they are achieved through the power of recollection among the six powers.

The fifth stage is called "disciplining." Since at the fourth stage of close setting one withdraws the mind inward by relying on strong recollection, now at the stage of disciplining there is a danger of laxity arising by virtue of drawing the mind too strongly inward, so one must make recourse to the antidote for laxity. For that purpose, initially one must generate a powerful introspection that checks whether laxity is coming. [66] Since laxity is a low state of mind that arises on account of being too loose, as an antidote one must heighten the state of mind and so forth. Although at the fourth mental settling gross laxity arose, during this fifth settling, by relying on the power of recollection and a strong power of introspection, one is able to block gross laxity. However, since there is a danger of subtle laxity, as a means of dispelling that one must be on guard for subtle laxity and, if it arises, meditate on mental joy, faith, happiness, and so forth. You must encourage and uplift the mental state.

The sixth mental settling is called "pacifying." During the fifth mental settling you encouraged and uplifted the mind, so there is a danger of excitement. Since there is a danger of subtle excitement on account of too much encouragement, one generates a forceful introspection in order to block that danger of subtle excitement. When introspection brings awareness and blocks excitement, it is calling "pacifying."

The seventh mental settling is called "thorough pacifying." During the

88. The Tibetan *de'i bar du* ("so long as") is ambiguous here. I have translated it as "so long as you maintain that recollection," but it could also mean "until you complete the meditation session."

fifth and sixth mental settlings, one needed to generate a forceful introspection and, taking precautions against the dangers of subtle laxity and subtle excitement, block them. [67] From among the six powers, those two stages were achieved through the power of introspection. From this seventh stage on, one is said "to be endowed with the powers of recollection and introspection" or "to have fully matured the powers of recollection and introspection." It is like, for example, a person growing up and reaching adulthood. During the seventh mental settling of thorough pacifying, since the powers of recollection and introspection have fully matured, it is difficult for laxity and excitement to arise. Although it is difficult for them to arise, they are not abandoned, so one must generate the power of zeal and, seeing even subtle laxity and excitement as faults, abandon them.

During this seventh stage, since one relies on forceful effort and stops laxity and excitement as soon as they arise, laxity and excitement are unable to respond with significant harm. When laxity and excitement do arise, forceful effort harms them. During the first two mental settlings, among the four mental applications, one practiced the mental application of focused engagement. From the third to the seventh stage, one practices the mental application of interrupted engagement. What is the meaning of calling the mental application practiced up to this point "interrupted engagement"? Although one has a factor of stability, still occasionally distractions will come. Since the obstacle is slight, here the mental application is called "interrupted engagement."

[68] The eighth mental settling is called "making one-pointed." When you reach this stage of making one-pointed, at the beginning of a session you place the mind in meditative stabilization, thinking, "I must not allow laxity and excitement to arise," and relying on strong effort. Subsequently if you are in equipoise, laxity and excitement will not arise until you break the session.

Laxity and excitement are the main obstacles when actualizing calm abiding. Although at first when stopping laxity and excitement one must apply strong effort, later when the force of laxity and excitement becomes minimal, it is sufficient to rely on an antidote occasionally and ever so slightly. When the force of laxity and excitement has thoroughly waned, then to stop them one needn't apply effort. For example, in a war, when the enemy has power, one must rely on ferocious effort to stop them. If that power wanes a bit, one can relax slightly, and if that power completely wanes, one becomes totally relaxed. Likewise, we rely on effort in meditation in that way.

During the eighth mental settling, if one first relies on a slight effort, he will be able to stay until the end of the session without distractions creating obstacles, [69] so among the four mental applications, this is the mental application of uninterrupted engagement. Since during the seventh and eighth mental settling a practitioner must rely on effort, these two are achieved through the power of zeal.

The ninth mental settling is called "setting in equipoise." During this stage, concentration is achieved spontaneously without requiring effort. For example, if you have practiced a recitation like Tārā well, then having mentally placed Tārā on your crown, even if you do some other activity, Tārā will stay with you until you complete the practice; likewise here since concentration arises spontaneously without relying on effort, it is said to be "achieved spontaneously without effort." At this stage, since the mind has a secure factor of stability, one gains the ability to engage in the activities of walking, lying down, and sitting while keeping the mind placed in equipoise on the objective support.

This ninth mental settling is also called "a single-pointed concentration mind of the desire realm."[89] During the ninth mental settling, one does not achieve actual calm abiding. Although it is not actual calm abiding, it is posited as a simulacrum of calm abiding. At the stage of the ninth mental settling, one needn't apply the slightest effort, so among the four mental applications, [70] the mental application of spontaneous achievement is fulfilled. Among the six powers, this mental settling is achieved through the power of thorough familiarization.

89. Buddhist cosmology divides existence into "three realms": the desire, form, and formless realms. These realms refer both to particular states of mind and also to external worlds that reflect the state of mind of those born into them. Our human world is included within the desire realm. Except for the rare human beings who have achieved calm abiding, all of the minds we experience—such as sense consciousness, thought consciousness, and dreams—are desire realm minds. As such, the realm we are born into reflects these states of mind. Objects are physically dense and naturally give rise to desire and craving. When one achieves calm abiding, the mind of calm abiding is no longer included within the desire realm but becomes an access concentration of the form realm. One has not yet achieved the actual first dhyāna of the form realm but has achieved a preparatory level of it. If one deepens concentration and achieves this first dhyāna, then at death one may be reborn in the form realm, a subtle realm of light that reflects the mental state of beings who have achieved this tranquil and blissful concentration. (See introduction.)

This ninth mental settling is still included within the desire realm, but because it is single-pointedly focused and not unsettled like most desire realm minds, it is called "single-pointed concentration of the desire realm."

The Differences between the Nine Mental Settlings

What is the difference between the first and second mental settlings? Although neither of these two has a secure factor of stability, compared to the first mental settling, the second mental settling has a slightly longer-lasting factor of stability. Thus, these two are different in terms of the duration of the factor of stability.

What is the difference between the second stage (continuous setting) and the third stage (fixing and setting)? During fixing and setting, if a distracting thought arises, then immediately you recognize the distraction as a fault and stop it, as though patching up clothing, so the duration of distraction is shorter. During the second stage distraction lasts a little longer, so these two are different in the duration of distracting thoughts.

What is the difference between the third stage (fixing and setting) and the fourth stage (close setting)? During the third stage of fixing and setting it is possible to lose the objective support, but during the fourth stage of close setting one generates a powerful recollection and completes the power of recollection, so the difference is that one cannot lose the objective support in the fourth stage.

What is the difference between the fourth stage (close setting) and the fifth stage (disciplining)? [71] The difference is that during the fourth stage, gross laxity can arise, while from the fifth stage onward gross laxity cannot arise. At this stage, although there is no gross laxity, still one must take great caution in regard to subtle laxity.

What is the difference between the fifth and sixth stages? During the fifth mental settling, one must take great caution regarding subtle laxity, while during the sixth mental settling, one does not need to take great caution for subtle laxity. Thus there is a difference in needing or not needing to take great caution. Not only that, but also at the sixth stage subtle excitement arises less than before.

What is the difference between the sixth and seventh mental settlings? During the sixth stage, one must take significant precautions against harm from laxity and excitement.[90] At the seventh stage, if distraction arises, then

90. This statement would seem to contradict the earlier statement that at the sixth stage one does not need to take great precautions for laxity. Gen Namgyal Chöphel says that this latter statement is probably mainly concerning subtle excitement, for which one *does* need to take great caution at the sixth stage but not at the seventh.

immediately one generates zeal and is able to stop it. On account of that, since one doesn't need great caution regarding the harm from subtle laxity and excitement at the seventh stage, there is a difference in terms of whether or not it is necessary to take great caution to avoid the danger of falling prey to subtle laxity and excitement. When I say it is not necessary to take great caution for the danger of falling prey to subtle laxity and excitement, it's like, for example, when fighting with an enemy you cause the power of the enemy to completely decline. From then on there is no great danger, [72] so it is adequate just to take marginal means to stop him.

What is the difference between the seventh and the eighth stage? During the seventh stage, although the faults of subtle laxity and excitement arise, one can stop them with zeal. During the eighth stage, by merely relying on zeal at the outset of the meditation session, laxity and excitement will not arise until the session is complete. Thus there is a difference in terms of laxity and excitement arising at all.

What is the difference between the eighth and ninth stages? During the eighth stage one exerts a slight effort at the outset of the session, while at the ninth stage no effort is required at all. So there is a difference regarding relying or not relying on effort.

How the Nine Mental Settlings Fulfill the Six Powers and Four Mental Applications

The fourth topic[91] is this: how does one actualize the nine mental settlings by means of the six powers? As I explained before, the first mental settling is achieved by means of the power of hearing. The second is achieved through the power of reflection. The third and fourth are achieved through the power of recollection. The fifth and sixth are achieved through the power of introspection. The seventh and eighth are achieved through the power of zeal. The ninth is achieved through the power of thorough familiarization.

91. Calling this section "the fourth topic" is based on the outline of Phabongkha Rinpoché's *Liberation in the Palm of Your Hand*. Because Chöden Rinpoché is basing his teaching on that text, he is proceeding based on the outline of its section on calm abiding, and the first part of this book roughly follows Phabongkha's outline. That section is divided into six subsections: (1) relying on the collection of causes for calm abiding; (2) the actual manner of actualizing calm abiding; (3) on that basis, the manner of actualizing the nine mental settlings; (4) the way of achieving that through the six powers; (5) how that includes the four mental applications; and (6) from that, the means of generating actual calm abiding.

These nine mental settlings also fulfill the four mental applications. During the first and second mental settlings, [73] a practitioner is endowed with [that is, relies upon] the mental application of focused engagement. From the third to the seventh stage, he is endowed with the mental application of interrupted engagement. During the eighth stage he is endowed with the mental application of uninterrupted engagement and during the ninth with that of spontaneous achievement.

During the first two stages, there is no more than just a short-lived factor of stability, so although we don't call it "interrupted engagement" at this point, there is interruption and re-engagement. We do not call it that, however, because the factor of stability is so slight that there is not even a basis for talking about whether laxity and excitement do or do not create obstacles. So it's not as though we take there to be no interruption and therefore don't call it "interrupted engagement." [In other words, it's not that there is uninterrupted engagement but rather that there is no genuine engagement at all.] From the third to the seventh stage, the meditation acquires an increasingly strong factor of stability, and one engages in meditation with laxity and excitement occasionally creating obstacles, so we call it "interrupted engagement." During the eighth stage, if at the outset of the session a practitioner relies on a slight effort, she will successfully complete the session without laxity and excitement creating obstacles, so at this point we call it "uninterrupted engagement." As I explained before, just as somebody who has practiced recitation can begin reciting and, even if their mind is distracted elsewhere, keep reciting from memory, likewise at the ninth stage one does not rely on effort. [74] A practitioner engages effortlessly and naturally from the state of meditative stabilization, so we posit the "mental engagement of spontaneous achievement."

FIVE

The Means of Achieving Actual Calm Abiding

THE SIXTH TOPIC[92] is the means of achieving actual calm abiding. The ninth mental settling has stable concentration, but it is not actual calm abiding, so at this point one has not achieved actual calm abiding. What, then, do we need for actual calm abiding? A practitioner meditates again and again on concentration, becoming intensely familiar with it. Relying on this intense familiarity, the power of the factor of stability gradually induces pliancy of body and mind and the bliss of pliancy.[93] First pliancy of body and mind arises, and then the bliss of physical and mental pliancy is induced. A meditative stabilization supported by such a bliss of pliancy is called "calm abiding."

With regard to physical pliancy and mental pliancy: the state achieved at this point is called "physical pliancy" because, having pacified all assumptions of bad physical states in which the body is not serviceable for virtuous practices, the body becomes as serviceable as one desires for virtuous practices. Likewise mental pliancy is a state wherein, having pacified all assumptions of bad mental states in which the mind is not serviceable for virtuous practices, the mind becomes as serviceable as one desires for virtuous practices. [75] Regarding assumptions of bad physical states, these include jumping around like a monkey, while the assumptions of bad verbal states include calling others *mangmo* and so forth.[94] In short, it is suitable to say that all vulgar behavior of body and speech is an assumption of bad states.

92. See previous note.

93. The *Great Treatise on the Stages of the Path to Enlightenment* explains that in one meditative session, one sequentially achieves mental pliancy, physical pliancy, the bliss of physical pliancy, and finally the bliss of mental pliancy. See Tsongkhapa 2000, 3:82–85.

94. Jumping around like a monkey and calling women *mangmo* are traditional examples of coarse behavior that arises not from afflictions like desire and anger but simply due to imprints of past habituation. (*Mangmo*—Tib. *dmangs mo*—is a term used to refer to low-caste women.) Usually these examples are used to describe the behavior of arhats who have abandoned the afflictive obscurations but not the knowledge obscurations that a buddha

What is the sign preceding the generation of mental pliancy? One has pacified away the assumption of bad physical states, and as a sign of having pacified that, one experiences a pleasant physical sensation as though somebody were placing the palm of his or her hand on your freshly shaved head, causing a sensation of [warm] heaviness in the brain. That is a pleasant sensation, not an unpleasant one. First the mental pliancy in which the mind is serviceable just as one desires for virtuous practices arises, and then the force of that induces physical pliancy. A wind energy that induces physical pliancy pervades all parts of the body. Through that wind pervading all parts of the body, one is freed of the assumption of bad physical states, and there arises a distinctive, pleasing tactile sensory object that is physical pliancy, which makes the body light, free of discomfort, and as serviceable as one desires for virtuous practices; physical pliancy, a pleasant tactile object, arises. This is an especially pleasing inner object of tactile experience. [76] There arises immediately thereafter a great bliss called the bliss of physical pliancy, which is what experiences that tactile object. On account of that bliss of physical pliancy there arises in the mind a great experience of joyful bliss. That experience is called "the joy of mental pliancy" or "the bliss of mental pliancy." This great experience of joyful bliss elates the mind such that one is temporarily unable to stay on the object of observation. During that experience, one does not have steady meditative stabilization. Afterward, as the overly joyful experience subsides a bit and the joy becomes more stable, one attains "the meditative stabilization supported by the bliss of pliancy."

Does the joy become less intense? Although the joy does not actually become less intense, it no longer unsettles the mind, and as it stabilizes, we call this state "the mind supported by unwavering joyful bliss." When that arises, one has actualized calm abiding and is also at the same time said to have actualized the access level of the first dhyāna. This first access level is called "not unable."[95] On the basis of this [mental] path, whatever

---

abandons. As such, these arhats have a pure motivation but may still on occasion accidentally make clumsy bodily movements or use uncouth speech. The point here is that by achieving calm abiding, one eliminates the gross levels of the obstructions in the energy channels that give rise to brash or uncoordinated movements and speech. On achieving calm abiding, one achieves much greater control over one's body and speech, although one does not completely eliminate the possibility of these behaviors until achieving buddhahood.

95. The access level of the first dhyāna is traditionally called "not unable" because with it one is able to meditate on the Hīnayāna and Mahāyāna paths. The point is that while achieving any of the four actual dhyānas is preferable, a practitioner with great skill can also make use

realizations there may be, both mundane and supramundane, one is able to generate them, so it is called "not unable." It's like, for example, in worldly parlance when somebody is not unable to do work, whatever it may be, so we say "he is able."

of just this access concentration to achieve realizations. Some traditions consider that one can even use this access concentration to achieve the level of an arhat, though to achieve buddhahood one definitely needs the actual dhyānas.

SIX

Questions and Answers

[77] What is access concentration?

"Access of the first dhyāna" is a preparation for the actual absorption. On the basis of that, one is able to achieve an actual absorption of the first dhyāna and so forth [that is, on the basis of the access for the second dhyāna, one achieves the second, and so on]. If the practitioner is a non-Buddhist, he actualizes the "eight dhyāna/formlesses"—that is, the four actual dhyānas and the four actual formless absorptions. When he achieves those, the thought arises, "Now I have attained liberation." There are even those who subsequently get angry, whereby their meditative stabilization degenerates, and they are born in hell. In the Buddhist tradition, even without achieving the actual first dhyāna, if one can actualize the access concentration, it is possible on that basis to achieve the state of arhatship, which has abandoned all afflictions without exception.[96]

If one can actualize such a state of calm abiding, then while making requests to the object of refuge, one can have a clear appearance to the mind of the refuge object; also when meditating on bodhicitta, because the observed object is stable, one can quickly generate realizations. In these and other ways, there is a great distinction between having achieved and not having achieved calm abiding.

Furthermore, with such a strong factor of clarity secured in the mind, if one analyzes microscopic particles[97] from within that clarity, she will even

96. Primarily based on the explanation in Asaṅga's *Compendium of Higher Knowledge* (Skt. *Abhidharmasamuccaya*; Tib. *Chos mngon pa kun las btus pa*), the Tibetan tradition asserts that it is possible to achieve arhatship based on only this access concentration. In Theravāda traditions, where many practitioners actually work to achieve the state of arhat, there is disagreement on whether or not it is possible to do so only with access concentration. For an illuminating discussion of this issue that presents arguments from both sides, see Shankman 2008.

97. In this context, the practitioner is examining the subtle details of the image appearing to the mental consciousness. At this point, the image takes on an especially vivid appearance,

be able to count, "one, two . . ." [78] Even if she continuously sees objects of desire that are the bases for the arising of afflictions, by remembering the drawbacks of afflictions, her mind will not be distracted. By drawing the mind inward into the space of meditative stabilization, even sleep can become meditative stabilization; such benefits will develop.

In a similar way the roots of virtue of observing the body of the Buddha, even if not supported by a pure motivation, can become a cause for liberation.[98] Perhaps if one is meditating on the generation stage of tantra, then through meditating on deity yoga, one observes the Buddha—we should consider this possibility.[99] When meditating on the self-generation of the deity, one does not meditate on the deity in the space in front but must generate oneself as the deity and meditate on that. Saying "all becomes emptiness," remember the meaning: one's aggregates, oneself at present, and the self that abides when you say "I" are all empty of inherent existence. Remembering that, purify into emptiness of inherent existence. Imagine that this mind you have generated that realizes emptiness and the wisdom truth body of a buddha that you will achieve in the future are inseparable, and on that basis generate a new body as a deity. Imagine that the new body is a buddha's body, and meditate observing that.

Must one necessarily observe that object as being outside, or is it appropriate to observe the *hūṃ* syllable at one's heart?

[79] If one generates oneself as a deity, then it is acceptable to observe oneself. There are also some who check inwardly how the mind is doing and meditate observing the mind. During the generation and completion stages of tantra, there are many objects of observation like the syllable *hūṃ*, the short *āḥ*, the drops, and so forth.[100] From among those, if a practitioner

---

substantially different than the static, generic mental image that one generated during the nine mental settlings. See introduction.

98. The comparison being made here is that just as through the power of meditative stabilization, sleep, which is not normally virtuous, can become virtuous, likewise through the power of the Buddha's blessing, an otherwise neutral mind observing the Buddha can become virtuous.

99. The point being made here is that during the nine mental settlings, the appearance of the body of the Buddha was a mere generic image, but here—and also in the generation stage—perhaps this vivid appearance is actually the Buddha. Rinpoché is not saying this is necessarily so but only that we should analyze and consider the possibility.

100. During tantric practice, one can take a variety of different objects as the objective support. One might take the seed syllable of a deity—*hūṃ*, or another syllable, depending on

observes the one with which he has the greatest familiarity, it will be easier to actualize calm abiding.

If one takes the holy body of the Buddha as an objective support, then by making requests to the object of refuge, the holy body of the Buddha will clearly appear as requested. If one continuously remembers the Buddha, bad behavior will gradually stop, and by remembering the Buddha at the time of death, one will not be born in unfortunate migrations. On account of such useful effects, observing the body of the Buddha is said to be an excellent method. Other than that, merely to actualize calm abiding, it is acceptable to take any object of observation. Once there was a cattle herder who was actualizing calm abiding. He was unable to achieve calm abiding practicing with other objects. Since he was a cattle herdsman who usually went around with cows, he was always seeing cow horns. [80] For that reason his master said to him, "Observe the horn of a cow, and practice!" By practicing in that way, he quickly actualized calm abiding.

For one of inferior faculties is it all right to initially actualize calm abiding as explained in the perfection vehicle before practicing tantra and then subsequently combine that with the practice of tantra? And when meditating on the generation stage of tantra, since one practices in six sessions per day, how does one go about beginning to apply a method for actualizing calm abiding?

If one initially intends to actualize calm abiding in accordance with the perfection vehicle, it is said that if one does not assemble the collection of causes for calm abiding, then even practicing for a thousand years one will not achieve it. Since we don't know how long this human life will last, by getting caught up in just that practice, one incurs a loss. Thus it is better if one doesn't just merely do that but also meditates on the higher and higher paths, trying to make an imprint.[101] If one gains familiarity with the lamrim and the generation and completion stages, she will be able to plant a firm

---

the deity—or one might meditate on the "short *āḥ*," meaning a shorthand representation of the Tibetan letter *ah* (see illustration on page 171). One may also meditate on the drops, which are energies within the subtle channels.

101. Gen Namgyal Chöphel points out that this answer is directed to a particular person. Rinpoché is emphasizing that for most people, getting preoccupied with achieving calm abiding can become an obstacle to meditating on the stages of the path. Without these more basic meditations, meditation on calm abiding could simply become a distraction. Rinpoché is of course not intending to deny that in certain cases a person might actually be ready to practice for calm abiding.

imprint on the mind. If somebody of sharp faculties thinks over the entire path, it becomes a supreme practice. When meditating on the generation stage, one generates the celestial mansion of the deity, his hand symbols, and so forth. [81] That meditation is meditation on the coarse generation stage. If one is able to have a clear appearance of all of that at one time, she should meditate on calm abiding. If one willfully actualizes calm abiding during the generation stage, she should then complete the gross generation stage and during the subtle generation stage meditate observing the maṇḍala of the deity on a subtle drop.

When meditating on the generation stage of tantra, is it necessary to actualize calm abiding separately, or can one actualize calm abiding together with the generation stage meditations?

[One can actualize it along with the generation stage meditations.] In order to generate the realization of the [coarse] generation stage, it is not necessary to actualize calm abiding. There are even those who first have the realizations of the generation stage and then achieve calm abiding during the completion stage. As it is explained in great texts, if one is to actualize it during the [subtle] generation stage, one does *not* actualize it when first generating the inestimable mansion and the deity visualization. Meditating on the supporting and supported maṇḍala [the mansion and the deities], one achieves the ability to cause this all to appear as an object of mind. After that, one meditates on the subtle drop—that is, a small drop [that contains miniature supporting and supported maṇḍalas]. One must observe that drop and meditate to actualize calm abiding.[102]

What is this thing called "the sixfold collection of causes"? How should one identify each of these individually?

[Rinpoché went on to give a long explanation similar to the discussion on pages 47–53. At the end he added an important point:]

Beginners like us have a great variety of non-Dharmic projects, while Dharma practice only arises occasionally. Even if we meditate on something

102. Rinpoché is describing the manner of actualizing calm abiding with the *subtle* generation stage. It is also possible to actualize calm abiding with the coarse generation stage, meaning one visualizes the deities in a normal size, not in a subtle drop. The advantage of actualizing calm abiding with the subtle generation stage is that through the force of such a subtle visualization, a practitioner actualizes both calm abiding and special insight simultaneously.

like calm abiding, it will be difficult to achieve on account of not completing the collection of causes. If instead, for the time being, we train well in going for refuge, [85] contemplating on karmic cause and result and so forth, guarding well the ethical discipline of abandoning the ten nonvirtues[103] and so forth, and if we do so emphatically, the reward for us will be greater.[104]

How should one meditate on the lamrim? When meditating on special insight,[105] since one is engaging in analysis, does meditation on the lamrim become analytical meditation or not? Is such analysis special insight or not? Does it have some relation to special insight or not?

When you first meditate on the lamrim, you need to engage in analysis. For example, even when you meditate on the freedoms and endowments[106] or whatever else, you need to sustain a forceful mind for a long time, and it is said that a forceful mind over a long period of time will not come about unless you engage in analysis. As such, you can understand the need for analysis. When meditating on the lamrim, while it is unsuitable to engage in analysis at the time of practicing calm abiding, you need to engage in analysis on the other topics. Having analyzed, if a thought arises that "it is just like that," then hold it there for a bit. Such analysis is also considered meditation. Meditation includes both analytical and placement meditation.

103. The "ten nonvirtuous actions" include three of body, four of speech, and three of mind: (1) killing, (2) stealing, (3) sexual misconduct, (4) lying, (5) harsh speech, (6) divisive speech or slander, (7) idle speech or gossip, (8) covetousness, (9) harmful intent, and (10) wrong views (especially denying the existence of karmic cause and effect or the existence of the Three Jewels of Refuge).

104. See note 101.

105. For a description of special insight, see introduction.

106. These are the eight leisures and ten endowments that characterize a precious human rebirth. The eight leisures are freedom from birth (1) as a hell being, (2) as a hungry ghost, (3) as an animal, (4) as a long-life god (who mistakes his meditative absorption for liberation), (5) as a barbarian (that is, in a place where the Dharma is not available), (6) as one holding wrong views, (7) in a time when a buddha has not taught, and (8) with imperfect faculties (that is, with mental or physical handicaps). The ten endowments include five in relation to oneself: (1) birth as a human, (2) birth in a central country (where Buddhism has spread), (3) birth with sound faculties, (4) not having committed one of the five actions of immediate retribution, and (5) having faith in the Three Jewels. And they include five in relation to others: birth in a place and time in which (6) the Buddha has come, (7) he has taught the Dharma, (8) the teachings have not died out, (9) people still follow the teachings, and (10) people treat each other with kindness and concern.

Calm abiding is called "placement meditation," while analyzing impermanence and so forth is called "analytical meditation."

[86] When meditating on the lamrim, although one should engage in analysis on all topics except calm abiding, such analysis is not itself special insight. For it to become special insight, one first needs to achieve calm abiding. First one actualizes calm abiding. Having actualized it, if one is able from that space of calm abiding to induce bliss supported by pliancy through the force of analyzing an object, one has actualized special insight. Therefore, analysis when one has not achieved calm abiding is not called special insight.

To achieve calm abiding, will it take one's entire lifetime?

This is said to differ depending on whether or not one has stable recollection and introspection. If one has stable recollection, it is a little easier to achieve. Mainly, as I explained previously, one must assemble the collection of causes. As I quoted before, "If you assemble the causes, you will actualize it in six months; if you don't assemble the causes, you will not actualize it in a thousand eons."

To actualize calm abiding, since you need to abandon all distractions, how can you possibly actualize it while living as a householder?

As I explained above in terms of the collection of causes for calm abiding, if you are able to abide with a stable mind, and not be distracted toward other objects, then you will be able to achieve calm abiding. Without that, since you haven't assembled the causes, it will be difficult. There have been many bodhisattvas who were kings or ministers and achieved liberation as householders. They were all able to actualize calm abiding as householders, and on that basis many of them meditated on special insight.[107]

Which is better: first to settle on the view of emptiness and then to actualize calm abiding, or first to actualize calm abiding and then to settle on the view?

That depends on your degree of familiarity with these two topics. If you have greater familiarity with emptiness, it is better first to meditate on emptiness [87] and then to actualize calm abiding. If you have greater familiarity with calm abiding, then you should actualize that first.

107. This question was inserted from Chöden Rinpoché 2018, 107–8.

What can I do to know whether I have a stronger propensity due to past imprints for emptiness or calm abiding?
Merely through hearing about the subject, you develop strong interest in it. For example, Candrakīrti says in his *Supplement to the Middle Way*,

> When even as a common being, this person hears of emptiness
> from deep within a fervent joy repetitively does arise.
> Arising from this fervent joy come tears that make his eyes
> moist and
> his body hairs all stand on end. A being like this possesses the
> mind's seed of total buddhahood.[108]

People who, when they hear the words "profound emptiness," experience a joyous feeling in their hearts and think, "Wouldn't it be wonderful if I could realize that?" have a deep-seated imprint for emptiness. Those who on hearing the words "calm abiding" think, "Since that is extremely marvelous, how wonderful it would be if it arose in me?" have a stronger imprint for that.

[88] **It is explained that when actualizing calm abiding, one should not change whichever object one has initially selected until achieving calm abiding. That being the case, if one is staying in a retreat for calm abiding and is reciting a practice like self-generation for which one has a commitment, since one must take the deity as an object of observation, does this constitute changing the object?**
When one is meditating on the self-generation, the generated deity is not the observed object of calm abiding. Beyond explaining that one should not change the observed object of calm abiding, there is no mention that one is not allowed to observe other objects when doing different meditations.

Regarding the holy body of the Buddha mentioned in the phrase "one must meditate on a holy body the size of a mere half a thumb as the observed object of calm abiding"—should one meditate on a lifeless holy body [that is, a statue] or meditate on an actual holy body of the Buddha?
One should meditate on an actual holy body of Buddha. Normally when we meditate, we should meditate on an actual holy body of Buddha, not on a statue.

108. Candrakīrti, *Supplement to the Middle Way*, 6.4–5.

Since we have never seen directly the holy body of our teacher Buddha, regarding this "half-thumb-sized holy body of the teacher, the observed object of calm abiding" that is spoken of, how exactly should we imagine that it is the actual Buddha?

[89] It is explained as being unlike a statue that you place in front of you, but as a holy body in the shape of a man with light rays and blazing flames. Although the fire flickers and blazes, the shape is said to be like a human form, but without the heaviness of flesh and blood. Instead, it is the holy wisdom truth body appearing in the form of the Buddha's form body—a Buddha Bhagavān in the nature of light. Furthermore, one should think that he is in the process of enacting deeds [for the welfare of sentient beings, even while seated in the space in front].[109] As for the shape, after taking a good look at a statue, you should imagine that it is just like that.

Calm abiding does not analyze the object but is placed on it single-pointedly. As for the object of observation, if you create something with your mind and then abide observing it with your eyes, will you be able to actualize calm abiding?[110]

You won't achieve calm abiding. Calm abiding must be actualized in the mind, not in the eye consciousness. In previous times, there were some who practiced like that, but it is said that they did not understand the method for actualization. Mainly you should take a good look at the object with your eyes, then cause that image to appear to your mind. Meditating on that very object with your mind, you should actualize calm abiding in your mind.

[90] Since the holy body of our teacher Buddha is a mass of light with complete sense faculties, do we not see the five vital organs and the six hollow organs?[111]

There is no need to think like that. Since the Buddha is a holy body estab-

109. A special quality of the Buddha is said to be his ability to have multiple streams of consciousness occurring simultaneously, whereby he is able to enact deeds elsewhere, through magical emanation, even while sitting in meditation on emptiness.

110. The questioner here appears to be confused about the nature of visualized objects. He or she is asking whether one should create a physical appearance with the mind and then observe that appearance with the eyes. Except in very unusual cases, such a feat is not possible, and even if it were, one should not meditate by observing an object with the eyes.

111. The five vital organs are the heart, lungs, liver, spleen, and kidneys. The six hollow organs are the stomach, large and small intestines, testes, gallbladder, and bladder.

lished by the appearance of wisdom itself, what need is there for such things as the inner organs? The need for the five vital organs and the six hollow organs is for cases where you need a basis for the mind to abide. Since the Buddha is established by the appearance of wisdom itself, there is no such need. When you are establishing for yourself that such things are not needed, it is sufficient to think that "this is the actual teacher, in the nature of light."

When actualizing calm abiding by observing the deity's holy body, is it better to observe oneself in the form of the deity or to generate a front generation deity and then do calm abiding meditation on that?
If it is during the generation stage of tantra, then since you need to generate yourself as a deity, it is better to observe that. Otherwise, if it is during a front generation practice, then you should generate the deity in front and observe that in the manner of observing the Buddha's body explained above.

Can one achieve buddhahood without relying on tantra?
One cannot achieve buddhahood without relying on tantra.

[91] **Can the continuity of saṃsāra be severed for all beings without exception?**
It is said that it can be. We can understand that to be so from the statement, "Saṃsāra does not have a beginning, but there can be an end."

Is it so that, without relying on tantra, one is not a Mahāyānist, and sentient beings who do not practice tantra can never become buddhas?
One can be a Mahāyānist without relying on tantra. Such a one can traverse the path as far as the tenth bodhisattva ground,[112] but then in order to become a buddha he or she definitely must enter the tantric path. One must meet a virtuous friend teaching the path of secret mantra in this or another lifetime and enter the tantric path to become a buddha. Without entering the tantric path, one will not become a buddha.

112. The bodhisattva path includes five paths and ten grounds. The five paths are the path of accumulation, the path of preparation, the path of seeing, the path of meditation, and the path of no-more-learning (buddhahood). The path of meditation is further divided into the ten grounds. The tenth ground is the highest stage just before buddhahood.

Yesterday when Rinpoché was teaching on the *Heart Sūtra*, he mentioned achieving the state of buddhahood by relying on the three principal aspects of the path: renunciation, bodhicitta, and the correct view of emptiness. Today he has explained that without relying on tantra, one will not become a buddha. Aren't these two statements slightly contradictory?

Yesterday when I explained that by relying on the three principal aspects of the path one becomes a buddha, I was speaking from the point of view of sūtra. In that context, there is no talk of not becoming a buddha without relying on tantra, so there is no fault of contradiction.[113]

[92] Don't bodhicitta and the view realizing emptiness, without relying on tantra, have the strong potential that is able to achieve the state of buddhahood?

Without relying on tantra, they don't have such potential. The reason is that in order to achieve buddhahood one must realize emptiness with a subtle mind, and that realization must arise in the nature of bliss.[114] Such a thing does not exist except in the tantric path.

Is it not possible to achieve the five paths—the paths of accumulation, preparation, and so forth—without achieving calm abiding?

It is said that one cannot achieve them without calm abiding. There are some who accept that one can achieve a mere path of accumulation without calm abiding, but in accordance with Gyaltsap Rinpoché's explanation in *Clarifying the Path of Liberation*,[115] we say that in order to achieve a path, one must achieve calm abiding.

113. The point here is that the sūtra presentation of the path makes no mention of the need for incorporating tantra. The implication is not that one does not need these three principal aspects of the path for buddhahood according to tantra. One who practices tantra incorporates that practice within the context of these three principal aspects.

114. See introduction and the second half of this book. In tantra, while one still meditates on the object of emptiness, one meditates on it with a much subtler level of mind than is utilized in the sūtra path.

115. Gyaltsap Darma Rinchen, *Clarifying the Path to Liberation* (*Thar lam gsal byed*). This is Gyaltsap Jé's extensive commentary on Dharmakīrti's *Commentary on Valid Cognition* (Skt. *Pramāṇavārttika*; Tib. *Tshad ma rnam 'grel*). This is the primary text on valid cognition studied in Geluk monasteries. However, I have not located such a quotation anywhere in that text, and Geshés Ngawang Thokmé and Ngawang Rabga both suggest that Rinpoché was referring to another text by Gyaltsap Jé, *Ornament of the Essence*. In chapter 4 of this latter text, Gyaltsap clearly states that "'application' [in the context of 'application to full

If one is staying in a retreat for calm abiding, do one's usual recitations and virtuous practices not create obstacles for calm abiding?
Generally engaging in many activities will create many obstacles to calm abiding, but if you break the continuity of the recitations for which you have a commitment, you will incur a fault, so you should do them without fail. Other than that, if you have many other recitations for which you do not have a commitment, it's okay to put them aside.

[93] **It is possible to actualize calm abiding during the practices of the generation and completion stages of tantra?**
It is.

Since you said that it is possible to achieve calm abiding during the two stages of tantra, does meditation on calm abiding naturally go along with the two stages? [That is, does it come naturally without special effort just by meditating on the two stages?]
Since at first it does not come in that way, initially you must actualize calm abiding intentionally. If it is during the generation stage, you observe the holy body of the deity and actualize calm abiding. When meditating by generating yourself as the deity, if initially you observe a rather large body of the deity, it will be difficult to get a factor of stability. However small you can make the objective support, to that degree the factor of stability will lengthen in duration, so first you should imagine a small holy body of the deity. However, there are also some people who achieve the mental settlings by observing a large deity's body. [94] During the completion stage, there are also some people who achieve calm abiding by observing drops and letters.[116]

In order to cut the root of saṃsāra, one needs both calm abiding and

---

awakening in all aspects'] implies the union of calm abiding and special insight." Because "application to full awakening in all aspects" is synonymous with a bodhisattva path, most textbooks, including those used at Sera Jé, take this statement to mean that in order to enter a sūtra path, one must first generate the union of calm abiding and special insight. Nevertheless, readers should understand that this is a debatable point—for example, at the beginning of his exposition of calm abiding in the *Great Treatise on the Stages of the Path to Enlightenment*, Tsongkhapa seems to imply that one does not need calm abiding to enter the path, and most Geluk authors agree that one can enter the tantric path before generating calm abiding, because calm abiding comes at the end of the coarse generation stage or, for some people, during the completion stage.

116. See note 100.

special insight. For example, if you want to cut down a tree, you need a sharp axe that will cut it directly, but it is not sufficient just to have the axe. You also need a strong, steady shoulder to swing the axe. Likewise, special insight is like the axe that directly cuts the root of saṃsāra, and calm abiding is like the steady shoulder that swings it. Another example is if you want to look at a detailed painting at nighttime. You need a bright lamp, but even if it is bright as lightning, if it is flickering, it will not allow you to see clearly. Another lamp may be fluttering in the wind, and you won't see clearly. So you need a clear, steady lamp. The special insight of realizing emptiness is like the brightness of the lamp, and calm abiding is like the quality of abiding steadily and not being blown in the wind. If you have a lamp like that, you can see even the fine details of any painting. Likewise, combining calm abiding and special insight, [95] seekers of liberation achieve all their desired aims; the example is explained in that way.

Also, in the *Three-Part Continuity*[117] it says the Buddha is "endowed with knowledge and holy legs." (In some versions of the text, it says "endowed with knowledge and legs." In any case, "holy legs" and "legs" have the same meaning.[118]) What does this statement signify? Here, legs are an example for calm abiding. For example, if a person has great qualities and strong

117. Skt. *Tridaṇḍaka*; Tib. *Rgyun chags gsum pa*. This is a prayer often recited by Buddhist practitioners, composed by the Indian paṇḍit Aśvaghoṣa (Tib. *Rta dbyangs*). The term "continuity" implies that it is something one must recite regularly. "Three-Part" indicates the three sections of the prayer. The first section, prostration, is the longest, and includes verses of praise to the Buddha. The middle section is the recitation of passages from sūtra—usually only the following two passages:

> Do not commit the slightest sin.
> Perform all marv'lous virtu'us deeds.
> Subdue your mind most thoroughly.
> This the Buddha's teaching is!
>
> A star, trick of the eye, a lamp,
> illusion, dewdrop, bubble or
> a dream, lightning, or as a cloud:
> view all phenomena like that!

In the extensive version, one recites the *Heart Sūtra*. The third section is a verse of dedication. For an English version of this prayer, see for example FPMT 2006, 73, in which the prayer is entitled "Praise to Shakyamuni Buddha" and is included in the section "Mahayana Prayers for Teaching Occasions."

118. The point here is that some Tibetan texts use *zhabs* for legs, while others use *rkang pa*. Both of these terms mean "legs," but the former is the honorific while the latter is the common term.

arms but no legs, he won't be able to accomplish all his purposes. If on top of great qualities and power he has stable legs, he will be able to accomplish any endeavor. Likewise, "knowledge" is special insight and "legs" are calm abiding. Furthermore, to get calm abiding you need pure morality, so both of these—morality and calm abiding—are similar to legs.

In a general sense, a Buddhist has as an object of practice the three higher trainings. "Endowed with knowledge" signifies the higher training in wisdom, while "endowed with legs" signifies the higher training in concentration and also the cause of that: the higher training in pure morality.

[96] I have spoken with a number of monks and nuns who have practiced to achieve calm abiding. However, I have only met one person who actually said, "I have actualized calm abiding." Someone said, "I have reached the fifth of the nine mental settlings." Another one said "I have reached the seventh level." This one said that when he sat focusing his mind, he could stay without any fault of laxity or excitement at all. For that reason he said he had reached the seventh level, and it seems to me he was correct in saying that.

The one who claimed to have reached the fifth level had been unable to abandon the laxity and excitement that I explained earlier are obstacles to calm abiding. However, he had been able to stop the gross manifestations of them, so he had reached the fifth level. He said, "I have reached just that level, but no matter how much I meditate, I can't advance further."

Those are cases of not having assembled the collection of causes or perhaps of having a slight deficiency of conducive conditions.

It also seems that the one who claimed to have achieved calm abiding had not assembled the collection of causes well. It is said that one who assembles the causes well will actualize it in six months. [97] He also said, "The bliss of pliancy also comes for me; I'm all right just where I am." However, when he asked another lama, the lama replied, "You still need an intensity of the clarity factor—that is, a tight manner of apprehension; aren't you a bit too loose?"

He then came to me and asked, "Now what should I do? Is it a good idea to meditate a little more, or should I stay just as I am?" He had thought he had achieved calm abiding, but I told him, "Perhaps it would be good if you could meditate a bit more." He then said, "If now I meditate again, I won't need more than three months' time." Such is the confidence that arose in him.

Part 2
Mahāmudrā

A TRANSLATION OF

Shes rab kyi ngo bo lhag mthong la bslab tshul dge ldan pa'i phyag chen gyi bka' khrid

The Manner of Training in Special Insight, the Essence of Wisdom: Instruction on Gendenpa[119] Mahāmudrā

༄༅། །ཤེས་རབ་ཀྱི་ངོ་བོ་ལྷག་མཐོང་ལ་བསླབ་ཚུལ་དགེ་ལྡན་པའི་ཕྱག་ཆེན་གྱི་
བཀའ་ཁྲིད་ཅེས་བྱ་བ་བཞུགས་སོ། །

119. Gendenpa (Tib. *Dge ldan pa*; literally "one endowed with virtue") is an early name for the followers of Tsongkhapa, who are more frequently referred to as Gelukpa.

SEVEN

Requesting Prayer to the Mahāmudrā Lineage

This prayer (verses 1–8, 37–38) was originally composed by Paṇchen Losang Chökyi Gyaltsen. Additional verses (9–15) were added by Kachen Yeshé Gyaltsen, tutor to the Eighth Dalai Lama. Subsequent verses were added by Phabongkha Dechen Nyingpo (16–32), Trijang Rinpoché (34), and Lama Zopa Rinpoché (36). Verses 33 and 35 may have been composed by Dampa Lodrö of Tsawarong, and verse 39 may have been composed by Kachen Yeshé Gyaltsen.

Namo Mahāmudrāya!

1. Spontan'ous palace, bodies three,
grand primal buddha, fam'ly's chief,
pervasive master, Holder of
the Vajra great[120]—I make requests.
To cut self-grasping's snare in my mind,
in love, compassion, bodhi mind train;
great seal's supreme path unified
to swiftly gain, send blessings forth.

2. This father three times' victors bears
in ten rimmed worlds, a bill'on fields:
wise Ārya Mañjuśrī—requests.
To cut self-grasping's snare in my mind,
in love, compassion, bodhi mind train;
great seal's supreme path unified
to swiftly gain, send blessings forth.

3. In this north snow land, second sage
lord master, sage's teachings of:
to Jetsün Losang Drakpa[121]—requests.

120. This refers to Vajradhara, who is Śākyamuni Buddha in complete enjoyment body aspect.

121. Tib. Rje btsun Blo bzang grags pa. This is the ordination name of Tsongkhapa (1357–1419).

To cut self-grasping's snare in my mind,
in love, compassion, bodhi mind train;
great seal's supreme path unified
to swiftly gain, send blessings forth.

4. Tsongkhapa, son of Mañjughoṣ,
attained line's teachings' holder chief:
to Tokden Jampal Gyatso[122]—requests.
To cut self-grasping's snare in my mind,
in love, compassion, bodhi mind train;
great seal's supreme path unified
to swiftly gain, send blessings forth.

5. You open oral line's cache of
advice, rear trainees fortunate:
to Baso Chökyi Gyaltsen[123]—requests.
To cut self-grasping's snare in my mind,
in love, compassion, bodhi mind train;
great seal's supreme path unified
to swiftly gain, send blessings forth.

6. Two yoga steps complete, you found
the deathless knowledge held in form:
to Drupchok Dharmavajra[124]—requests.
To cut self-grasping's snare in my mind,
in love, compassion, bodhi mind train;
great seal's supreme path unified
to swiftly gain, send blessings forth.

7. Unstained by bonds of eight concerns,
holds def'nite teaching's vict'ry flag:
to Losang Dönyö Drupa[125]—requests.

122. Tib. 'Jam dpal rgya mtsho (1356–1428).

123. Tib. Ba so chos kyi rgyal mtshan (1402–73).

124. This refers to Drupchen Chökyi Dorjé (Tib. Grub chen Chos kyi rdo rje, born 1457).

125. Losang Dönyö Drupa (Tib. Blo bzang don yod grub pa, 1505–66) is also known as Gyalwa Ensapa. He was posthumously recognized as the Third Paṇchen Lama.

To cut self-grasping's snare in my mind,
in love, compassion, bodhi mind train;
great seal's supreme path unified
to swiftly gain, send blessings forth.

8. Your saffron dance guides wander'rs to
three bodies' palace of delight:
to Khedrup Sangyé Yeshé[126]—requests.
To cut self-grasping's snare in my mind,
in love, compassion, bodhi mind train;
great seal's supreme path unified
to swiftly gain, send blessings forth.

9. From Victor Losang's teachings' lord
protector sep'rate not, knows all:
to Jetsün Losang Chögyen[127]—requests.
To cut self-grasping's snare in my mind,
in love, compassion, bodhi mind train;
great seal's supreme path unified
to swiftly gain, send blessings forth.

10. Texts—sūtra, tantra—barring none,
applied as one, gone to the end:
to Drupchen Gendün Gyaltsen[128]—requests.
To cut self-grasping's snare in my mind,
in love, compassion, bodhi mind train;
great seal's supreme path unified
to swiftly gain, send blessings forth.

11. Lord Losang's teachings' quintessence
with great zeal tasted, found the supreme,

126. Tib. Mkhas grub Sangs rgyas ye shes (1525–1591).

127. This is Paṇchen Losang Chökyi Gyaltsen (Tib. Blo bzang chos kyi rgyal mtshan, 1570–1662). "Lord protector" means Tsongkhapa himself.

128. Drupchen Gendün Gyaltsen (Tib. Grub chen Dge 'dun rgyal mtshan, 1532–1607) was a tutor to and student of Paṇchen Losang Chökyi Gyaltsen.

holds siddhi's vict'ry flag[129]—requests.
To cut self-grasping's snare in my mind,
in love, compassion, bodhi mind train;
great seal's supreme path unified
to swiftly gain, send blessings forth.

[Lineage of the autocommentary][130]

12. Deep Dharma nectar's essence vast
to trainees fortunate taught well:
to Gyüchen Könchok Gyaltsen[131]—requests.
To cut self-grasping's snare in my mind,
in love, compassion, bodhi mind train;
great seal's supreme path unified
to swiftly gain, send blessings forth.

13. Lord Losang Chögyen come again
as glory—teachings', wanderers'—
to Jetsün Losang Yeshé[132]—requests.
To cut self-grasping's snare in my mind,
in love, compassion, bodhi mind train;
great seal's supreme path unified
to swiftly gain, send blessings forth.

14. Lord Buddha blessed directly you
who mastered oral line's deep path:
to Jetsün Losang Trinlé[133]—requests.

129. This refers to Drungpa Tsöndrü Gyaltsen (Tib. Drung ba brtson 'grus rgyal mtshan, 1557–1650), a direct disciple of Paṇchen Losang Chökyi Gyaltsen. He was also known by the name Dorjé Dzinpa Könchok Gyaltsen (Rdo rje 'dzin pa dkon mchog rgyal mtshan), and this verse plays on that name—"holds" is 'dzin pa, and "victory flag" is rgyal mtshan.

130. Verses 12–22 trace the lineage of experiential explanation based on *The Lamp That Further Clarifies*, which Gyüchen Könchok Gyaltsen received directly from its author Paṇchen Losang Chökyi Gyaltsen.

131. Gyüchen Könchok Gyaltsen (Tib. Rgyud chen dkon mchog rgyal mtshan, 1612–1687) was a mantra master of Tashi Lhunpo.

132. Tib. Rje btsun Blo bzang ye shes, 1663–1737. He was the Fifth Paṇchen Lama.

133. Jetsün Losang Trinlé (1642–1708/1715) was a Shapdrung Lhasa tülku. Mongolian by

To cut self-grasping's snare in my mind,
in love, compassion, bodhi mind train;
great seal's supreme path unified
to swiftly gain, send blessings forth.

15. Lord Losang Victor's oral line's
heart-meaning's practice, gone to the end:
to Drupchok Losang Namgyal[134]—requests.
To cut self-grasping's snare in my mind,
in love, compassion, bodhi mind train;
great seal's supreme path unified
to swiftly gain, send blessings forth.

16. With love unerringly you taught
Jé Lama's oral line advice:
to most kind one named Yeshé[135]—requests.
To cut self-grasping's snare in my mind,
in love, compassion, bodhi mind train;
great seal's supreme path unified
to swiftly gain, send blessings forth.

17. Whole path's unerring teaching's heart,
you spread in all lands, near and far:
to Jetsun Ngawang Jampa[136]—requests.
To cut self-grasping's snare in my mind,
in love, compassion, bodhi mind train;
great seal's supreme path unified
to swiftly gain, send blessings forth.

18. Superb first Buddha's saffron dance;

---

birth, he was a late but close student of Paṇchen Losang Chökyi Gyaltsen and also of the Fifth Dalai Lama.

134. This master is also known as Drupwang Losang Namgyal (Tib. Grub dbang blo bzang rnam rgyal, 1640–1741).

135. This refers to Kachen Yeshé Gyaltsen (Tib. Dka' chen ye shes rgyal mtshan, 1713–1793), the First Ling Rinpoché and tutor (Yongdzin) to the Eighth Dalai Lama.

136. Ngawang Jampa (Tib. Ngags dbang byams pa, 1682–1762) was the First Phurbuchok.

Tibet and China, Dharma tends:
to Paṇchen Palden Yeshé[137]—requests.
To cut self-grasping's snare in my mind,
in love, compassion, bodhi mind train;
great seal's supreme path unified
to swiftly gain, send blessings forth.

19. Complete fine sūtra, mantra path
achieved with one mind, gone to the end:
to Khedrup Ngawang Dorjé[138]—requests.
To cut self-grasping's snare in my mind,
in love, compassion, bodhi mind train;
great seal's supreme path unified
to swiftly gain, send blessings forth.

20. Like second Thupwang, mast'ry firm,
guards teachings, clears with lectures, texts:
to Jetsün Dharmabhadra[139]—requests.
To cut self-grasping's snare in my mind,
in love, compassion, bodhi mind train;
great seal's supreme path unified
to swiftly gain, send blessings forth.

21. Objectless great love, eyes don't close,
deep knowing vast, Mañjuśrī-like:
to Yangchen Drupai Dorjé[140]—requests.
To cut self-grasping's snare in my mind,
in love, compassion, bodhi mind train;
great seal's supreme path unified
to swiftly gain, send blessings forth.

22. Bliss-empty yoga, gone to the end;

137. Palden Yeshé (Tib. Dpal ldan ye shes, 1737–80) was the Sixth Paṇchen Lama.

138. Tib. Mkhas grub Nga dbang rdo rje (1720–1803).

139. This refers to Ngülchu Dharmabhadra (Tib. Dngul chu Dharma Bha dra, 1772–1851).

140. Tib. Dbyangs can grub pa'i rdo rje (1809–87).

arrived at union's city straight:
to Khedrup Tenzin Tsöndrü[141]—requests.
To cut self-grasping's snare in my mind,
in love, compassion, bodhi mind train;
great seal's supreme path unified
to swiftly gain, send blessings forth.

Again . . . [Lineage of the root text][142]

23. Deep path's cognition, gone to the end.
Preached, realized teaching's vict'ry flag holds:
to Losang Tsöndrü Gyaltsen[143]—requests.
To cut self-grasping's snare in my mind,
in love, compassion, bodhi mind train;
great seal's supreme path unified
to swiftly gain, send blessings forth.

24. Not stained by faults or downfalls, holds
the heart of teachings' trainings three:
to Losang Dönyo Drupa[144]—requests.
To cut self-grasping's snare in my mind,
in love, compassion, bodhi mind train;
great seal's supreme path unified
to swiftly gain, send blessings forth.

25. Lord second victor Losang Drak
again sports as a saffron dance:

141. Tenzin Tsöndrü (Tib. Bstan 'dzin brtson 'grus, nineteenth century) was an abbot of Sera Mantric College and a direct teacher of Phabongkha Rinpoché, to whom he gave this lineage.

142. Here in verses 23–32, Phabongkha Dechen Nyingpo traces a second lineage he has received: the explanatory commentary based on the root text, whose author Paṇchen Losang Chökyi Gyaltsen gave this teaching to both Drupchen Gendün Gyaltsen and Drungpa Tsöndrü Gyaltsen. From these two it then descended separately from the earlier lineage.

143. Also known as Drungpa Tsöndrü Gyaltsen.

144. Tib. Blo bzang don yod grub pa (1602–78). This was Drungpa Tsöndrü Gyaltsen's student, who served as Jangtsé Chojé late in his life.

to Jetsün Gelek Gyatso[145]—requests.
To cut self-grasping's snare in my mind,
in love, compassion, bodhi mind train;
great seal's supreme path unified
to swiftly gain, send blessings forth.

26. The treasure—vast deep Dharma's path—
to those of fort'nate mind made clear:
to most kind Ngawang Jampa[146]—requests.
To cut self-grasping's snare in my mind,
in love, compassion, bodhi mind train;
great seal's supreme path unified
to swiftly gain, send blessings forth.

27. Makes clear the fine path free of extremes
with stainless reason's laughing roar:
to most wise Jikmé Wangpo[147]—requests.
To cut self-grasping's snare in my mind,
in love, compassion, bodhi mind train;
great seal's supreme path unified
to swiftly gain, send blessings forth.

28. Lord Losang victor's sect supreme
by teaching, practice, peerlessly spread:
to Jetsün Tenpai Drönmé[148]—requests.
To cut self-grasping's snare in my mind,
in love, compassion, bodhi mind train;
great seal's supreme path unified
to swiftly gain, send blessings forth.

29. Jé Jamgön's oral line's nectar's

145. Also known as Drupkhang Gelek Gyatso (Tib. Sgrub khang dge legs rgya mtsho, 1641–1713).

146. Ngawang Jampa (Tib. Ngag dbang byams pa, 1682–1762) was the First Phurbuchok.

147. This is Könchok Jikmé Wangpo (Tib. Dkon mchog 'jigs med dbang po, 1728–1791), the incarnation of Jamyang Shepa.

148. Tenpai Drönmé (Tib. Bstan pa'i sgron me, 1762–1823) was the Third Gungtang.

taste swelled exper'ence, insight's strength:
to Jetsun Könchok Gyaltsen[149]—requests.
To cut self-grasping's snare in my mind,
in love, compassion, bodhi mind train;
great seal's supreme path unified
to swiftly gain, send blessings forth.

30. In sites unknown, one-pointedly
attained line's teaching's vict'ry flag holds:
to Drupchen Ngödrup Rapten[150]—requests.
To cut self-grasping's snare in my mind,
in love, compassion, bodhi mind train;
great seal's supreme path unified
to swiftly gain, send blessings forth.

31. Purged, realized virtues gone to the end,
rains well-spoke Dharma, all that's wished:
to Tutor Gendün Gyatso[151]—requests.
To cut self-grasping's snare in my mind,
in love, compassion, bodhi mind train;
great seal's supreme path unified
to swiftly gain, send blessings forth.

32. Sports on peak of best scholars wise,
soars on two-staged attainment's rank:
to splendid Tenpai Nyima[152]—requests.

149. Könchok Gyaltsen (Tib. Dkon mchog rgyal mtshan, 1764–1853) was the Second Belmang. "Jamgön" (*'jam mgon*, literally, "Gentle Protector") is an epithet for Tsongkhapa.

150. Regarding Drupchen Ngödrup Rapten (Dngos grub rab brtan), the text notes, "A hidden yogi who gave up worldly affairs." "Sites unknown" (Tib. *nges med kyi gnas*, literally "uncertain abodes") suggests that he was an itinerant.

151. Yongdzin Gendün Gyatso (Yongs 'dzin dge 'dun rgya mtsho) was known as "Yongdzin" ("Tutor") because he was a tutor of the Tenth Tatsak Jedrung, Ngawang Palden Chökyi Gyaltsen (Ngag dbang dpal ldan chos kyi rgyal mtshan, 1850–86). This Tatsak went on to become a tutor of the Thirteenth Dalai Lama, and served for a time as regent of Tibet.

152. This refers to Khyenrap Pelden Tenpai Nyima (Mkhyen rab dpal ldan bstan pa'i nyi ma) of Gungru Gyatso Ling Monastery (Gung ru rgya mtsho gling), from whom Phabongkha Rinpoché received this lineage.

To cut self-grasping's snare in my mind,
in love, compassion, bodhi mind train;
great seal's supreme path unified
to swiftly gain, send blessings forth.

33. By love for all migrators forced,
holds sūtra, mantra's vict'ry flag:
to Jetsün Trinlé Gyatso[153]—requests.
To cut self-grasping's snare in my mind,
in love, compassion, bodhi mind train;
great seal's supreme path unified
to swiftly gain, send blessings forth.

34. In line with many victor's aims,
whole Sage's Dharma, insight, words,
unmatched works spreading all[154]—requests.
To cut self-grasping's snare in my mind,
in love, compassion, bodhi mind train;
great seal's supreme path unified
to swiftly gain, send blessings forth.

35. Friend spreading second victor lord's
heart essence, fort'nate trainees to:
kind Losang Yeshé[155]—to you, requests.
To cut self-grasping's snare in my mind,
in love, compassion, bodhi mind train;
great seal's supreme path unified
to swiftly gain, send blessings forth.

36. All refuge victors' gem of love
dawns as all trainees' guardian:

153. Trinlé Gyatso (Tib. 'Phrin las rgya mtsho, 1878–1941), also known as Dechen Nyingpo, was the Second Phabongkha.

154. This verse is a request to the Sixth Ling Rinpoché, Thupten Lungtok Tenzin Trinlé (Tib. Thub bstan lung rtogs bstan 'dzin 'phrin las, 1903–83), senior tutor to His Holiness the Fourteenth Dalai Lama. "Works" translates "Trinlé," so the third line is a play on his name.

155. This is the Third Trijang Rinpoché, Losang Yeshé Tenzin Gyatso (1901–81), junior tutor to His Holiness the Fourteenth Dalai Lama.

to Jetsun Tenzin Gyatso[156]—requests.
To cut self-grasping's snare in my mind,
in love, compassion, bodhi mind train;
great seal's supreme path unified
to swiftly gain, send blessings forth.

37. On past lord mahāsiddhas' seat
you, faithful trainee's glory, dawn:
my kind root lama, I request.
To cut self-grasping's snare in my mind,
in love, compassion, bodhi mind train;
great seal's supreme path unified
to swiftly gain, send blessings forth.

38. To see lord lama as a buddha;
to loathe this place, saṃsāra's wheel;
take load to free all motherly beings;
the glory of paths common and
uncommon—great seal's union state—
to swiftly gain, send blessings forth.

39. Your holy form and, father, my form;
Your holy speech and, father, my speech;
Your holy mind and, father, my mind:
Bless that insep'rably one in fact.

156. This is His Holiness the Fourteenth Dalai Lama (born 1935).

EIGHT

Highway of the Conquerors: The Root Text of Mahāmudrā of the Precious Genden Instruction Lineage

BY THE FOURTH PAṆCHEN LAMA,
LOSANG CHÖKYI GYALTSEN

[**General Promise to Compose**[157]]
Namo Mahāmudrāya!
Pervading nature of all mahāmudrā is
insep'rable, ineffable, mind's vajra expanse—
pervasive realized master who shows nakedly:
at peerless lama's feet I bow respectfully.

The Genden Great Seal Lineage condenses and imparts well the
sea's quintessence of personal advice on sūtra tantra both.
I will compose instruction on the Mahāmudrā heritage
of Dharmavajra father—great accomplished yogi—and his son.

[**Actual Instruction**]
Preparatory, actual,
concluding—from those three parts here:

[**Preliminaries**]
As teaching's port of entry, first,
and Mahāyāna's pillar chief,
not just by mouth, not just by words,
go fervently for refuge and
give rise to the awak'ning mind.

To see mind's nature furthermore
rests on amassing merit first, and cleansing obscurations, so

157. The guidelines in brackets are based on the divisions the Paṇchen Lama himself adds in the autocommentary.

at least a hundred thousand of the
mantra—hundred-syllables—
prostrations, many hundreds of, do with *Confessing Downfalls*
first.

Insep'rable from buddhas of
three times, to your root lama make
sincere requests, again, again.

[Actual Practice]
The actu'l practice of great seal
is many ways asserted, but
split into sūtra, mantra: two.

[Mantra-System Mahāmudrā, in Brief]
The latter is clear-light great bliss
from piercing skillfully the points
of vajra body and so forth:
great seal of Saraha and of
Nāgārj'na, Nāro, Maitrī too.
In *Essence* and in *Siddhis* taught,
it's highest tantra's quintessence.

[Sūtra-System Mahāmudrā]
The first's long, mid-, short's teaching direct:
to meditate on emptiness.
Nāgārjuna, best noble, said,
"No liberation path but this."

In line with his intention, here
on mahāmudrā I'll explain.
Like lineage lama's speech, I'll tell
the way to introduce the mind.

[Explanation for Mastering the Divisions of All the Excellent Traditions of Holy Beings]
Connate communion, amulet box,
same taste, four letters, five-endowed,

the pacifier, object to cut,
and dzokchen, middle view, so forth—
applied to it, names many, but
experi'nced yogis, masters of
both scripture, reason analyze:
the certain meaning falls to one thought.

[The Sequence of Mahāmudrā Meditation]

Thus has this systems two: upon
the view, seeking to meditate;
on meditation, seeking for
the view. Here is the latter one.

[The Six Preparatory Practices]

On a seat good to concentrate,
sit with the posture sevenfold.
Dispel stale air across nine rounds.
Divide well clear and murky minds.
With a pure, wholesome mind, first go
for refuge and produce the mind.
Apply deep guru yoga's path.
Intense requests, do hundreds, more—
then melt the lama into you.

[Actualizing Mental Settling on the Conventional Nature of the Mind]

Without a fabrication's trace
of hopes, fears, so on, enter free
of slightest flux, absorption in
ethereal appearance space.

It's not stopping attention like
in swoon or sleep; place the spy of
remembrance undistractedly.
Alertness prime for stirrings of mind.

With focus tight, look nakedly
at nature of the knowing and clear.

Whatever thoughts discursive rise,
catch sight of them for what they are.

[An Alternative Approach]
Or like a duelist, cut off
straightway whatever thoughts arise.

[What to Do When Conceptual Thoughts Calm Down]
When having cut, mind rests, relax.
Let go; lose recollection not.

[Machik Lapdrön:] "With focus tight, relax, let go:
that is the space to set the mind."
Such has been said, and furthermore,
[Brahmin Saraha:] "When mind in tangle bound lets go,
without a doubt it frees itself."
As said, let go, but do not drift.

Whatever thought comes, when you spot
its nature, then it vanishes—
vacuity dawns. Likewise too
when stilled, you check, void unobscured,
a vivid wakefulness you see:
"abiding, moving mixed," it's called.

[An Alternative Approach]
Whatever thought comes, don't block. Know
its movement. In its nature set,
like the example of a bird
that flies, imprisoned on a boat:
[Brahmin Saraha:] "As from a ship a raven flies,
swings round each side, alights again."
By practicing in just that way...

[*These examples are not part of root text; they are in the autocommentary*:
1. Place it like a cloud-free sun,
2. like great garuḍa soars in sky.

3. Place it like the great ocean's depth,
4. like a small boy looks at a shrine,
5. like flying bird's trace in the sky.
6. Place it like a cashmere spread.]

[The Result of Practicing in That Way]

Absorption, nature unobscured
by anything, is lucid, clear.
Not made of any form at all,
vacuity like the sky, and
it's vivid since all things can dawn.

[Refuting the View That This Is the Final Nature of the Mind]

[Past Tibetans:] "Indeed this mind's reality
with insight is directly seen.
But 'it's this' you can't hold or say.
What dawns, don't hold, but place in ease.
This is bestowed instruction for
to hold in your palm buddhahood":
these days so say with one mind most
of meditators in snow land.
But "this great method's skillful means
to settle mind, beginners for,
and point out mind's concealer truth":
so does Chökyi Gyaltsen say.

[Promise to Explain the Means of Introducing the Final Nature of the Mind]

And now, the way to introduce
the final nature of the mind.
I shall set forth the spoken advice
of my root lama who dispels
the murk confusing my mind and
is wisdom of all buddhas that
displays a guise as saffron-clad.

[Explaining the Final Nature by Indicating How the Object of Refutation Appears and How It Is Apprehended]

Not moving from absorption's space
like in a clear pond minnows dart,
with subtle mind incisively
inspect the meditator's make.

[Explaining That the Person Cannot Exist as He Appears, Because He Cannot Exist in Any of These Ways]

Nāgārj'na, Ārya, savior, said,
"A being is not earth, water not,
not fire, not wind, not space, and is
not consciousness, nor all of them.
Apart from these what being is there?

[How to Meditate on the Selflessness of Persons and Phenomena]

"Since a being's a collection of
six elements—authentic not.
Just so, each element is too
collected—thus authentic not."
If you have searched and as he said,
absorption, who absorbs, and such,
not one mere atom do you find,
sustain then space-like equipoise,
one-pointed, undistractedly.

[Meditating on the Final Nature of the Mind, as a Means of Going Deeper into the Very Subtle Mind]

Or from the space of equipoise,
all things appear, spread, unobscured
vacuity, not made as form.
A nonstop stream of knowing clear,
the mind engaging ceaselessly.

Determined object, held as seems—
relying not. Said Śāntidev':
"What's called 'continu'm,' 'gathering'

is false like mālās, armies, and such."
With scripture and such reasoning,
absorb one-pointed in the space
of nonestablished as appears.

[Advice from the Holy Spiritual Friend]
In short, from the blessed mouth of my friend
in virtue, Sangyé Yeshé, who
knows all phenom'na as they are:

"When you know fully what appears is what is grasped by concept-thought,
the ult'mate Dharma sphere appears, relying not on anything.
On entering awareness into space of that appearance then
to station single-pointedly, into absorption *e ma ho*!"

Thus he said, likewise Dampa said,
"Into the space of emptiness, whirl the spear of knowingness.
To the view there is no block, no difficulty, Dingriwa."
And so on—the intent's the same.

[Concluding Prayer]
To end, whatever wholesomeness comes
from meditating on the great seal,
with three times' virtue's ocean, too,
for full awak'ning, dedicate.

[(1) How to Practice in Postmeditation and (2) What to Do When Reentering Absorption]
Whatever, meditating thus,
appears as objects to six types,
inspect in close how it appears.
The naked mode will clearly dawn.
[Mitra Yogin] "The view's main point: discern what appears."

In short, whatever things appear—
your mind and such—don't grasp as that.

Instead determine its mode of
being, and always that sustain.

So knowing, join as essence one
all things of both saṃsāra and peace.

And in that vein, said Āryadev':
"Whoever's viewer of one thing,
is said to be a viewer of all.
Whatever's emptiness of one,
that is the emptiness of all."

[Answer to the Question "Do Conventional Imputed Phenomena Appear in the Face of Absorption on Final Reality?"]

Like that, in proper equipoise on
reality, there are no extremes—
no fabrications of saṃsāra
and peace, existence, non-, and such.

[Answer to the Doubt "In That Case, Are Karma and Its Results Totally Nonexistent?"]

Yet when you surface and you check:
mere name, just an imputed thing,
dependent relativity.
Acts, actors both indubitably
themselves dawn like mirages, dreams,
moons on a lake, illusions too.

[The Measure of Having Mastered the Practice]

Appearance shrouds not emptiness;
the empty stops appearance not.
Then manifests the exc'llent path—
dependent, empty: synonyms.

[Dedicating the Merit of Composing]

The speaker, learned renunciant,
is Losang Chökyi Gyaltsen called.
This virtue by may all beings soon

victor'ous be through this path that
lacks any second door to peace.

I have compiled this manner of introduction to mahāmudrā at the repeated requests of Nechupa[158] Gendün Gyaltsen and Káchupa[159] Sherab Sengé of Hamthong, both of whom have seen the eight mundane concerns of this life to be the drama of madmen, stayed in the manner of sages in isolated valleys, and taken this path as an essential practice.

Furthermore, many of my disciples, wishing to put into practice the definitive mahāmudrā, have also requested me to compose this.

Especially, the lord master of accomplishment, the all-knowing great Gyalwa Ensapa himself, having given instructions in the style of the Kadam tradition of lamrim in the form of a song of experience instructing himself and others on the stages, from the manner of relying on a virtuous friend up until calm abiding and special insight, said at the end:

Not well known now in this snow land,
and not the path explained above—
the great seal's ultimate advice,
I can't commit to letters now.

What was not committed to writing at that time, on account of seeing a drawback in doing so, was intended for a later time. It says in the *White Lotus [Sūtra] of the Genuine Dharma*[160]:

158. Tib. *gnas bcu pa*, "scholar of the ten disciplines." This most likely refers to someone who has mastered the five major sciences—grammar, logic, artistry, medicine, and the inner science (Buddhism)—and the five minor sciences—poetry, metrics, synonymy, drama (or rhetoric), and astrology.

159. Tib. *dka' bcu pa*, "scholar of the ten difficult subjects." This is a title similar to *geshé* that signifies one has mastered (1) Middle Way philosophy (Skt. *madhyamaka*; Tib. *dbu ma*), (2) perfection of wisdom literature (Skt. *prajñāpāramitā*; Tib. *shes rab kyi pha rol tu phyin pa*), (3) Vinaya (Tib. *'dul ba*), (4) Vasubandhu's *Treasury of Higher Knowledge* (Skt. *Abhidharmakośa*; Tib. *Chos mngon pa'i mdzod*), (5) Nāgārjuna's *Root Wisdom of the Middle Way* (Skt. *Mūlamadhyamakakārikā*; Tib. *Dbu ma rtsa ba shes rab*), (6) Candrakīrti's *Supplement to the Middle Way* (Skt. *Madhyamakāvatāra*; Tib. *Dbu ma la 'jug pa*), (7) Āryadeva's *Four Hundred Stanzas* (Skt. *Catuḥśaṭakavṛtti*; Tib. *Bzhi brgya pa'i 'grel pa*), (8) Maitreya's *Sublime Continuum* (Skt. *Mahāyānottaratantraśāstra*; Tib. *Theg pa chen po rgyud bla ma*), (9) higher knowledge (Skt. *abhidharma*; Tib. *chos mngon*), and (10) the *Guhyasamāja Tantra* (Skt. *Guhyasamājatantra*; Tib. *Gsang 'dus rtsa rgyud*).

160. Skt. *Saddharmapuṇḍarīkasūtra*; Tib. *Pad dkar dam chos kyi mdo*, 30a. This text, entitled *Sūtra of the Genuine Doctrine of the (White) Lotus*, is often known simply as the *Lotus Sūtra*.

> To realize buddha wisdom best,
> this method—some apply on their own.
> But to such ones, don't ever say,
> "You will become a buddha." Why?
> A savior takes heed of the time.[161]

In order to actualize Ensapa's assertion, which is similar to that from this sūtra, I, the renunciant Losang Chökyi Gyaltsen, who holds the lineage of personal instruction in sūtra and tantra, and who has become part of this lineage without damaging the pledges and without degenerating the stream of blessings of practice, which takes this path into direct experience stemming from the unequaled teacher, King of the Śākyas, and reaching down to my own root lama, Sangyé Yeshé Shab, who knows and sees all, have compiled this at Genden Nampar Gyalwai Ling Monastery [Ganden Monastery].

161. The meaning of this verse is that practitioners can only become buddhas through personal effort, not merely through the Buddha's blessings. For that reason, although it is certain that these practitioners will become buddhas, still the Buddha does not directly tell them so, because on hearing that they may become complacent. The verse is used as an example to illustrate that even though a teaching may be profound, depending on the circumstance, a teacher may choose to withhold it. Thanks to Gen Namgyal Chöphel for suggesting this reading. The grammar seems to imply that the method itself is "spontaneously devised," rather than that practitioners "apply the method on their own," but his reading makes sense of an otherwise-obscure passage so I have kept it.

NINE

The Preliminary Teaching

Taking the Essence of the Precious Human Rebirth by Means of Contemplating Impermanence

[99] This time around, we have attained a precious human body with the leisures and endowments,[162] which is difficult to obtain. We have met with the precious teachings of the Buddha, which are difficult to meet. We have encountered a Mahāyāna guru, who is difficult to encounter. At this time, when we have also from our own side a slight recognition of the points to be adopted and those to be abandoned, it is important that we make an effort to actualize a pure practice of Dharma.

Today those of us of who have gathered here for a Dharma purpose will listen to the Dharma in order to put it into practice. For that to come about, first it is important to put effort into remembering death and impermanence in the context of understanding the difficulty in obtaining the leisures and endowments. There is no certainty regarding young and old people: younger ones may die first, with the elder ones following after. There is also no certainty regarding sickness and health: [100] the sick patient may live on while his caretaker dies. Nor is there certainty regarding the coming together or not of conducive conditions: somebody might amass conducive conditions for life, but suddenly a condition for death arises, and he dies, while beggars without conducive conditions may live long lives. However you think about it, it is important to understand that the time of death is uncertain and to try to generate a mind that reflects, "I too am not beyond such a nature, and thus the time of my death is uncertain."

Merely generating such a mind will not benefit you. Even if you generate it, if you die without having practiced Dharma, you will not have fulfilled the purpose of obtaining the excellent basis with leisures and endowments. You must strive to generate a mind that thinks, "Now I will not waste this opportunity." Based on your reflection on the uncertainty of the time of

162. See note 106.

death, you think, "If I do not actualize a pure Dharma practice right now, there is nothing that can be done." If you were to die, what is the action that would benefit you after death? It is only having practiced pure Dharma. Youth and possessions will not benefit you, nor will friends, relatives, retinue, or servants. [101] You will even have to leave behind the physical aggregates with which you were born. Like pulling a wisp of hair from the middle of a lump of butter, your consciousness alone will travel the precipitous path of the bardo leading to the next life. What is it that follows you at that time? The imprints of your white and black actions will follow after you.

When we speak of "reflecting on death and impermanence," the generation of a fearful mind that comes from thinking, "Won't I be separated from my wealth and enjoyments, friends, relatives, retinue, servants, and even my body?" will not in and of itself benefit you, because that is how ordinary people make themselves fearful by thinking of death.

Well then, if here we need to remember death and impermanence, what kind of reflection is meant when we say, "Reflecting on impermanence and death, one must generate fear of death"? We need to generate a mind that fears death in the context of thinking something like, "If I die without actualizing the Dharma, I won't be all right at all." If we die without having actualized the Dharma, we will have to take birth somewhere. As for where we will be born, there are only two possibilities: unhappy migrations and happy migrations.[163] In our mental continua, there many tens of thousands—hundreds of thousands—of karmic imprints of our negative actions accumulated since beginningless time that are only causes for being born in Avīci, the greatest in suffering among the hell realms.

[102] If we die now without actualizing pure Dharma, the result of the karma with which we have the strongest habituation will ripen first, so through the force of the karma to be born in Avīci, with which we are habituated and which we accumulated first, we will be born in the Avīci Hell. On that basis, we must generate fear at the prospect of dying without having actualized the Dharma.

If you are born in hell, there will be no opportunity to generate even the intention to practice Dharma. Generally if somebody dies without actualizing Dharma, there is no possibility but to be born in an unfortunate

163. Respectively, Skt. *durgati*; Tib. *ngan 'gro*, and Skt. *sugati*; Tib. *bde 'gro*. Often these two terms are translated as "lower realms" and "upper realms." The first refers to birth as a hell being, hungry ghost, or animal, and the latter to birth as a human, demigod, or god.

migration. If you are born in the unfortunate migrations, there is limitless suffering of hot and cold, boiling and roasting in the hells, limitless suffering of hunger and thirst in the hungry ghost realms, and limitless suffering of stupidity, ignorance, and being used for labor and so forth in the animal realms. If such suffering were to befall you, you would be completely unable to bear it.

If on that basis we are able to arouse a mind of fear and dread toward the suffering of the unfortunate migrations, then as I explained before, we have in our mental continua many negative karmas that are causes for birth in the unfortunate migrations [so we must recognize that in order to avoid that suffering, we must purify these karmas]. If we properly confess these actions in the context of fulfilling the four opponent powers [see below], we may be able to purify them such that we will not have to experience a ripened result. However, it is extremely rare for us to perform a perfectly qualified confession. For that reason, if we die now, there is no possibility except to be born in the unfortunate migrations.

How to Go for Refuge by Contemplating Suffering

[103] Well then, what method can we employ to save ourselves from that? First we need to search for a source of refuge. If we take the Three Precious Jewels as our source of refuge, they fulfill all the criteria for being a suitable refuge. Mainly it is the Buddha Jewel who fulfills all of the qualifications for suitability: he himself is free of all fears, he is skilled in the method of freeing others from all fears, and with great compassion he engages equally for all without partiality, enacting their welfare whether or not they have benefited him. For what reason does the Buddha fulfill all of these? Originally, when he generated the holy mind of bodhicitta, he generated that mind for the welfare of all sentient beings. In the middle, while he was accumulating merit, he accumulated merit for the purpose of accomplishing the aims of all sentient beings. Finally, when he manifested complete and perfect buddhahood, he did so for the purpose of all sentient beings. Thus he fulfills all the qualifications for being a suitable refuge.

Also, his establishing himself as the Buddha Jewel was done in dependence on the cause of having practiced the holy Dharma. Likewise the Ārya Saṅgha who practice the Dharma themselves arose by practicing the Dharma.

If you entrust yourself, not with a two-pronged approach, [104] but by completely turning your mind toward refuge in the Three Precious Jewels, it is impossible that they will not provide refuge for you, because we have already established that the Buddha completely fulfills all the causes of being a refuge for us.

Well, if the Buddha possesses such qualities as these, why is it that right now we are left behind in this morass of suffering? Because from our side we have not completely directed our minds toward entrusting ourselves for refuge, we are left behind at present. Now we recollect the suffering of the unfortunate migrations and generate a mind of fear and dread toward that. Because we understand that the Three Precious Jewels have the power to provide refuge from that, we place our hopes in them from the depths of our hearts, thinking, "Precious Jewels of Refuge, I beseech you: please provide refuge from suffering." That is called "going for refuge." If we train in going for refuge in such a way and from the bottom of our hearts entrust ourselves to the Precious Jewels, for the time being we will be able to accomplish not being born in the unfortunate migrations.

For example, in a worldly context, if a person commits a crime and is about to face execution as a punishment, and he places his hopes in a powerful person who is able to save him, that powerful person may be able to provide refuge for him just this one time. But if he later commits many wicked deeds again and again, it will be very difficult to save him. Therefore the powerful person advises him, "If you wish to be completely free of punishment, from now on you will have to take responsibility for your own behavior. Now, just once, [105] I will enact a means to save you." If he puts this advice into practice, he will save his own life. Likewise if we go for refuge to the Three Jewels and practice as the Buddha instructed, we will be free from the suffering of the unfortunate migrations and enter onto the path to liberation.

The Actual Means of Practice

Well then, what is it that the Buddha advised us to practice? It is the practice of karmic cause and effect, engaging and abstaining—guarding yourself in accordance with karmic cause and effect, accumulating white karma and abandoning black karma. And as for white and black karmic cause and effect, because we have been strongly habituated to afflictions since beginningless time, whatever nonvirtuous, sinful, black action we accumulate, we do so fulfilling completely the three stages of preparation, the actual action, and the conclusion.[164] It becomes a karma whose ripened result is certain to be experienced.[165] When we exert ourselves in white virtuous actions, even though we have a good motivation, either the preparation, the actual action, the concluding dedication prayer or some other factor does not come about exactly right. In some cases, although we do the actual action well, we don't have a good motivation, or in other cases, even with a good motivation and action, when we dedicate it we dedicate for the purpose of this life alone, and so forth. [106] Whatever virtuous action we do, there is a danger that it will become very weak. For that reason, by means of fulfilling the four opponent powers, we must practice confession and restraint in regard to the imprints of nonvirtuous, sinful actions in our continuum.

Generating the mind of refuge and bodhicitta is (1) the power of the basis. Generating fierce regret toward the negativity you created in the past, as though it were poison that had penetrated into the depths of your system, is (2) the power of repudiation. As an antidote for the negative actions, one recites mantras and *dhāraṇīs*, chants the names of buddhas, erects statues, makes offerings, reads scriptures, and so forth. In short, whatever roots of virtue one creates for the purpose of purifying the negativity becomes an antidote, and so it is (3) the power of relying on an antidote. Without a mind of restraint that thinks, "From now on, I will not do this action," one will be unable to purify the negativity, so one definitely needs a mind of restraint [and this is the fourth power, (4) the power of not repeating the fault].

Having generated such a mind of restraint, now you must examine your own continuum; even regarding the faults and downfalls that you are very close to committing, you can think, "At the very least, I must restrain myself for one day or two days." After one or two days have passed, again think, "For another one or two days, I will restrain myself." If you gradually rely on the mind of restraint in that way, through the power of mental habituation

164. "Conclusion" in this context means that one completes the action and has a sense of accomplishment in doing so, rather than immediate regret. "Preparation" means that one correctly ascertains the nature of the action and the object on which one is acting, and has a clear motivation to carry through with it. Sometimes these two aspects of the stage of preparation are separated, making four stages in total.

165. Skt. *niyatakarma*; Tib. *rnam smin myong bar nges pa*. The point here is that a very heavy action will definitely bring a specific result *if* one does not apply any countermeasures. Although overcoming such powerful negative imprints requires significant force, it is possible to mitigate the effects of these actions if one earnestly applies the four opponent powers described below.

you will eventually be able to abandon the actions completely. [107] If you rely on the mind of restraint that thinks, "From now on, I won't do it," and perform confession by fulfilling the four powers, then it is said that you will even be able to purify karma that is definite to be experienced.[166] Therefore if by believing that statement, you practice confession properly, definitely you will purify your negativity.

When practicing confession, you shouldn't entertain doubts, wondering, "Although I did confession, I don't know if I purified the negativity or not." If you do confession, definitely you will purify negativity. While the Buddha said that if you create negativity, you definitely must experience a large collection of ripened results, he also said that if you practice confession, you can purify the negativity. Because the Buddha's explanation that negativity can be purified is an incontrovertible one,[167] it is important to have the conviction, "I practiced confession by fulfilling the four opponent powers, so my negativity has been purified."

If you go for refuge, guard against karmic cause and result, and perform confession fulfilling the four opponent powers, then not only will you not be born in the unfortunate migrations in the future, but also it is definite that you will achieve a distinctive physical basis of high status [that is, birth in happy migrations].

Merely achieving such a physical basis of high status once or twice is not sufficient. Until we are free of this saṃsāra, since we haven't abandoned afflictions, we will continue to accumulate negative karma under their power. [108] Because there is no certainty whatsoever—through the power of that karma, we will again have to be born in the unfortunate migrations,

166. See previous note.

167. Skt. *avisaṃvādaka*; Tib. *bslu ba med pa*. The concept of an "incontrovertible statement" has a specific meaning in Buddhist hermeneutics. Some of the Buddha's teachings can be personally verified through direct experience, or through the power of reasoning in the case of things we cannot at present experience directly, such as the existence of past and future lives. However, the content of certain teachings is beyond even the scope of reasoning: the Buddha might explain that a certain person's current actions will lead to specific results in a future life. While we can apply reasoning to karmic cause and effect in a general sense, we cannot know the details of particular effects without clairvoyance. In these cases, we can only generate conviction in the veracity of the teaching in an indirect manner. The more we come to trust the Buddha as a valid teacher and enlightened being by examining the teachings that are accessible to reason, the more confidence we will have in the authenticity of his wisdom. In this particular case, the Buddha has taught that sincere confession will mitigate the effects of past nonvirtue, and we can gain confidence in the truth of this teaching by gaining confidence more generally in the Buddha as an authentic teacher.

and so forth—we must employ a method to be free of saṃsāra. Saṃsāra is in the nature of suffering. Whatever contaminated happiness we might experience, it is only the suffering of change, so it is definitely not a sublime happiness.[168]

How to Practice the Three Higher Trainings, the Means of Achieving Liberation

What method should we employ to be free from this saṃsāra, which is in the nature of suffering? Even if the Buddha were to visit us directly, he would not describe anything superior to the practice of the three higher trainings. For that reason, we definitely must put into practice the unsurpassed method that he has taught. Among the three higher trainings to be practiced, the primary one is the higher training in wisdom, which cuts the root of saṃsāra. Furthermore, the root of all the various minds of attachment and hatred in our continua is delusion, the ignorance that conceives a self. That itself is the root that binds sentient beings in saṃsāra.

Other than meditation on the wisdom that realizes selflessness—wisdom whose mode of apprehension stands in direct contradiction to that ignorance—nothing else at all is able to cut the root of saṃsāra. Therefore, we definitely must generate the wisdom of realizing selflessness and meditate on it. [109] In order for that higher training in the wisdom of realizing selflessness to become an antidote for the apprehension of a self, it needs a firm meditative stabilization as a basis. Without a firm meditative stabilization, wisdom alone cannot abandon the apprehension of a self, so as a cause for that abandonment we need the higher training in concentration. In order to generate the higher training in concentration in our continua, we must guard pure ethical discipline as a cause for that. Because we have adopted many vows—pratimokṣa, bodhisattva, and tantric—mainly it is important to guard these. If one has gone forth as a monastic, one must guard the pratimokṣa trainings of novices, fully ordained monks, and so

168. "Contaminated happiness" (Skt. **sāsravasukha*; Tib. *zag bcas kyi bde ba*) refers to everyday happiness—happiness that is the result of virtuous deeds performed under the sway of the conception of true existence. Such happiness is the suffering of change because (a) it is unstable, eventually changing into suffering, and (b) by grasping at it as stable, one creates the causes for future suffering. "Sublime happiness" (Skt. **praṇītasukha*; Tib. *gya nom pa'i bde ba*) is the happiness of liberation, the permanent cessation of suffering.

forth, whereas if one is a householder, one guards the vows of an upāsaka[169] and so forth in accordance with the level of one's mind.

Even if one is unable to guard these vows, one can take the eight-branched vows of near abiding,[170] which are one-day vows, and guard these. In that way, something that we are able to practice right now with immediate, visible benefits is guarding the higher training in ethical discipline. One must guard whatever he or she is personally able to do. On top of that it is excellent if one is able to generate the higher trainings in concentration and wisdom. Even if you can't generate them, develop a mind wishing to do so and make a prayer, thinking, "May I generate these trainings." If you practice the three higher trainings, then on that basis you yourself will be able to achieve the state of liberation. [110] But is it sufficient merely to achieve the state of liberation for oneself? No, that alone is not sufficient.

What is the reason that it is not sufficient? Since all sentient beings have only been supremely kind to me, if I were to put aside the welfare of all these kind beings and work merely for my own liberation, it would resemble the following example: If I were together with all of my family—parents, siblings, and so forth—in a place with great terrors like thieves and predatory animals, but did not give the slightest thought to work to free them from these fears and escaped alone, others would consider me the worst scoundrel and completely shameless. Likewise, while all sentient beings are undergoing the sufferings of saṃsāra and the unfortunate migrations, if I were to disregard them and work for only my own liberation, it would be like that. Therefore, it is not sufficient simply to liberate oneself; one must enact the welfare of other sentient beings.

Since your rebirths have no beginning, each sentient being has been your mother countless times. When they acted as your mother, they kindly nurtured you, just as your mother of this life nurtures you now. You must contemplate their kindness in that way.

169. Tib. *dge bsnyen*, a lay follower of the Buddha.

170. These are eight vows that one maintains for a twenty-four-hour period, abstaining from (1) killing, (2) stealing, (3) sexual activity, (4) lying, (5) taking intoxicants, (6) reclining or sitting on large or high beds and seats, (7) eating food at wrong times (after noon), and (8) wearing perfumes, garlands, or ornaments, and singing or dancing. Many practitioners will be familiar with these vows in the context of the eight Mahāyāna precepts. While the eight Mahāyāna precepts are taken within the context of a bodhicitta motivation, these eight vows of near abiding are included within the individual liberation vows.

Generating Bodhicitta by Means of the Seven-Point Cause and Effect Instructions

Whatever collection of good qualities we possess comes about on the basis of sentient beings. [111] Our food, clothing, and reputation all must depend on sentient beings, and even our achieving the state of buddhahood depends on sentient beings. For that reason, when it comes to our achieving buddhahood, it is as though sentient beings and the buddhas are equal in their kindness to us. How is that? Achieving this human body with leisures and endowments depends on sentient beings. In past lives, in relation to sentient beings we guarded morality, practiced patience, and so forth, and based on that we have achieved the body, possessions, and health that we have now. In order for this bodily basis to arise, we needed to depend on sentient beings. Likewise, to have possessions and enjoyments, we must have practiced generosity, and for that we needed to depend on sentient beings. To achieve high status again in the future, as a cause for that we must again guard morality that abandons harming others together with the basis.[171] Even to achieve the states of liberation and omniscience, we must rely on sentient beings, so sentient beings are extremely kind. For that reason, in order to generate the mind wishing that all beings might attain the state of buddhahood, we must first remember the kindness of sentient beings and generate the mind wishing to repay that kindness.

[112] If we remember their kindness, the mind wishing to repay that kindness will arise. "Repaying kindness" and "returning kindness" have the same meaning. Even if we consider this lifetime, when somebody who has benefited us in the past meets with hardship, we think, "Before, he benefited me, and so he is very kind. Now, it is inappropriate if I don't return that kindness somehow." In the same way, now we consider, "I have attained high status. I have met with the teachings of the Buddha. I have encountered a virtuous friend teaching the path to liberation. From my side, I have generated, just a bit, the thought to abandon negativity and accomplish virtue. Many other sentient beings, obscured by ignorance, are undergoing unwanted suffering. Although they wish for happiness, they don't know how to create

171. The phrase "harming others together with the basis" refers to the ten nonvirtuous actions. The first seven nonvirtues of body and speech are "harming others," while the latter three, the nonvirtues of mind that lead to nonvirtues of body and speech, are the "basis." For the ten nonvirtues, see note 103.

its causes. Although they don't want suffering, they instinctively create its causes." From the space of considering their suffering, generate the mind wishing to repay their kindness, thinking, "Now, I must do something for their well-being."

Somebody who merely gives food and clothing to other sentient beings who are deprived of food, clothing, and the like is called, in ordinary parlance, "chief of those who repays kindness." We can't possibly care for all beings by means of food and clothing, and even if we could, it might only serve to bring them additional suffering. It would have no benefit in terms of stable happiness. Why? For example, if they get something, then based on that thing they might generate all kinds of desire and hatred. [113] By the power of that they will have to undergo suffering.

Well then, what should we do? We must create the causes to free them from all suffering and endow them with the sublime happiness of liberation and uncontaminated bliss. For that, we need to generate compassion that thinks, "How wonderful it would be if all sentient beings were free from the suffering of saṃsāra and the unfortunate migrations," and love that thinks, "How wonderful it would be if they had all happiness." By our meditating again and again on love that wishes for them to have happiness and compassion that wishes they were free of suffering, compassion grows increasingly powerful. When the mind arises that thinks, "I myself alone will endow them with happiness and free them from suffering," the altruistic intention is born. Spurred on by that altruistic intention, now we must do something to endow them with happiness and free them from suffering.

You may ask, "Do I currently possess the power to do such a thing?" If you yourself are not currently free of saṃsāra, how could you possibly free others from it? For example, for a person sinking in the mud to get out of the mud, he definitely needs somebody who is standing on dry land. [114] If two people sinking together in the mud pull each other, they will only sink deeper; there is no way for them to pull each other up. Likewise, if an uncontrived thought arises that considers, "In order that I may extricate all these sentient beings from the mud of saṃsāra and the unfortunate migrations, I shall swiftly attain the state of a buddha," we call that thought *bodhicitta*.

With regard to the limitless benefits of generating the mind that wishes, "For the welfare of all sentient beings, I shall achieve buddhahood," [Śāntideva explains] the following in his *Engaging in the Bodhisattva Deeds*: If it is explained in scripture that there is limitless benefit even in generating the mere thought "I must dispel the headaches of all beings!" what need is there to speak of the limitless benefit that would accrue if the thought "I shall endow all sentient beings, reaching the end of space, with all happiness, and free them from all suffering!" were to arise?[172]

Well then, if that thought has such endless benefit, is that mere thought able to bring us to the state of buddhahood? It alone is not sufficient: one must put effort into a method for achieving the state of buddhahood. [115] Therefore, generate an excellent motivation, thinking, "For the welfare of all sentient beings, I must achieve the precious state of buddhahood by whatever means I can. For that purpose, I will listen to the holy Dharma." Also think, "From my side, however long I must bear hardships for the welfare of sentient beings, for just that long, sentient beings will continue to undergo suffering, so there is no way I can remain indifferent to them. For that reason, for the welfare of sentient beings I must achieve that state of buddhahood *swiftly*. For that, today, in this place, I will receive the explanation on the Ganden oral tradition[173] of mahāmudrā, and by practicing that I will swiftly attain the state of buddhahood." You must listen with that thought in mind.

As I mentioned yesterday, generally there is both the sūtra system of mahāmudrā and the mantra system of mahāmudrā. Here I will explain based on the tradition of unsurpassed yoga tantra, so in order to receive this teaching, it is best if you have received an unsurpassed yoga tantra empowerment. Since this is an uncommon instruction of the Ganden Oral Instruction Lineage that traces back to Jé Rinpoché, if you have time you must recite 108 *miktsemas* every day in the context of the Ganden Lha Gyama practice.[174] If not, you must at least recite it a mere twenty-one times. As I explained before, generally please listen with a bodhicitta motivation, [116] and specifically please listen supported by a special kind of bodhicitta that thinks, "In one short life of this degenerate age, I will swiftly, swiftly achieve

172. Śāntideva, *Engaging in the Bodhisattva Deeds*, 1.21–22 (paraphrase).

173. "Ganden" (Tib. *dga' ldan*) is another term used to refer to the followers of Tsongkhapa, who are based at Ganden Monastery, which Tsongkhapa himself founded.

174. Ganden Lha Gyama (Tib. Dga' ldan lha brgya ma; literally "Hundred Deities of the Land of Joy") is a ten-verse praise to Tsongkhapa. It was originally written down by Dulnakpa Palden Sangpo (Tib. 'Dul nag pa dpal ldan bzang po, 1402–73) but is said to have been taught by Tsongkhapa himself. Geluk practitioners usually recite it daily, along with recitations of the associated mantra, Miktsema. For Rinpoché's own commentary on this text, see Chöden Rinpoché 2013.

that state of a perfectly completed buddha. For that purpose, I will listen to the holy Dharma."

The Meaning of the Name of the Text and the Expression of Homage

The Dharma text that we will listen to is called *Highway of the Conquerors: The Root Text of Mahāmudrā of the Precious Genden Instruction Lineage.* Generally speaking there is another Tibetan Dharma lineage called Instruction Lineage Mahāmudrā,[175] but this one is called "Precious Genden Instruction Lineage Mahāmudrā." Of the root text and its commentary, this is the root text composed by Losang Chökyi Gyaltsen, the Fourth Paṇchen Lama. The conqueror in the phrase "highway of the conquerors" is called so on account of having conquered the four māras.[176] The text explains how to achieve the state of a buddha by means of a skillful path that, like a broad and spacious highway, is free of wrong paths and faults of inferiority, so it is called by that name. When holy beings engage in a great activity, traditionally they begin by going for refuge to a special object, the Three Jewels. Likewise here, [117] in order that we may know that he is himself a worthy person, the author pays homage not to somebody like our teacher Śākyamuni Buddha, but to mahāmudrā itself.[177]

175. The Tibetan word Kagyü (*bka' brgyud*) simply means "(oral) instruction lineage." In the context of the Genden Mahāmudrā that Rinpoché is teaching, Rinpoché indicates that the word has no connotation beyond that. However, Rinpoché here is distinguishing this lineage from the Mahāmudrā taught in Kagyü school of Tibetan Buddhism, where the word "Kagyü" has the more specific connotation of a particular school. See also page 157. For an in-depth exploration of the connotation of "Kagyü" in the title of the Paṇchen Lama's text, see Jackson 2001.

176. The four māras (Skt. *caturmārāḥ/catvāro mārāḥ*; Tib. *bdud bzhi*) or four demons are four obstacles that a practitioner must overcome to achieve buddhahood. They are (1) the māra of afflictions (Skt. *kleśamāra*; Tib. *nyon mongs gi bdud*); (2) the māra of the aggregates (Skt. *skandhamāra*; Tib. *phung po'i bdud*), meaning the contaminated aggregates of body and mind that arise from karma and afflictions; (3) the māra of the lord of death (Skt. *mṛtyumāra*; Tib. *'chi bdag gi bdud*), meaning death under the power of karma and afflictions; and (4) the māra of the son of gods (Skt. *devaputramāra*; Tib. *lha'i bu'i bdud*). In a literal sense, this māra is the *deva* Garap Wangchuk (Tib. Dga' rab dbang phyug, also called 'Dod lha; Skt. Kāmadeva), a Cupid-like figure who inspires desire and other afflictions in Dharma practitioners. In a more general sense, this māra is the tendency to be distracted from Dharma practice by pursuing sense pleasures or rebirth as a god.

177. In the Buddhist tradition, an author begins a text with an expression of homage. Doing

And so, "Namo Mahāmudrāya." "Mahāmudrā" is the great seal.[178] "Namo" means "I prostrate," so "Namo Mahāmudrāya" is "I prostrate to the great seal." Here "mahāmudrā" is both mahāmudrā at the time of the path and the resultant mahāmudrā achieved by meditating on that path. The author says "I prostrate" to them both.

> **Pervading nature of all mahāmudrā is**
> **insep'rable, ineffable, mind's vajra expanse—**
> **pervasive realized master who shows nakedly:**
> **at peerless lama's feet I bow respectfully.**

Through this passage, Paṇchen Losang Chökyi Gyaltsen pays homage to his root lama who taught him this instruction. "Pervading nature of all mahāmudrā": With regard to emptiness, which is the mahāmudrā of the sūtra system,[179] that which pervades all phenomena in the sense of being the nature or final mode of abiding of all phenomena is called "mahāmudrā." "Insep'rable, ineffable, mind's vajra dance"[180]: [118] That object—emptiness—and great bliss [that is, the mind realizing that object] are "inseparable" like water poured into water.[181]

As it is said, "not said, thought, spoken . . ."[182] Because verbal expression

so indicates that the author is a worthy being (Skt. *satpuruṣa*; Tib. *skyes bu dam pa*) who is not merely composing the text for selfish purposes.

178. The Sanskrit term *mahāmudrā*, or Tibetan *chagya chenpo* (*phyag rgya chen po*), literally means "great seal." *Mahā* or *chenpo* means "great," and *mudrā* or *chagya* means "seal."

179. In the sūtra system, the term "mahāmudrā" specifically refers to the object of meditation, emptiness. See introduction.

180. In explaining the meaning of the verse, Rinpoché substitutes the term "dance" (Tib. *gar*) for "expanse" (Tib. *dbyings*).

181. By referencing the great bliss that is "inseparable" from the object of realization, this line is indicating the mantra system of mahāmudrā. See introduction.

182. Rinpoché is referring to a scriptural verse, which the Tibetan tradition considers to have been spoken by Śāriputra, the Buddha's chief disciple:

> *smra bsam brjod med shes rab pha rol phyin*
> *ma skyes mi 'gag nam mkha'i ngo bo nyid*
> *so sor rang rig ye shes spyod yul ba*
> *dus gsum rgyal ba'i yum la phyag 'tshal lo*
>
> Not said, thought, spoken, wisdom beyond,
> unborn, unceasing, nature of space,

is unable to imitate the way an ārya's meditative equipoise directly perceives the final mode of abiding, it is called "ineffable."

"Mind's vajra" is the primordial connate[183] wisdom, which engages clear light emptiness as one taste with it. The Paṇchen Lama calls his root lama, Sangyé Yeshé,[184] who "nakedly"—without obscuration—"shows" such connate wisdom, the "pervasive master," meaning he is inseparable from the sixth victor, the great master Vajradhara.[185] Also, his master has practiced as the text has instructed and reached the elevated "realized" state. The Paṇchen Lama pays homage saying, "At the kind lama's lotus feet I bow respectfully."

Promise to Compose

> **The Genden Great Seal Lineage condenses and imparts well the**
> **sea's quintessence of personal advice on sūtra tantra both.**
> **I will compose instruction on the Mahāmudrā heritage**
> **of Dharmavajra father—great accomplished yogi—and his son.**

This passage makes a promise to compose. The teachings of the great Tsongkhapa are like the condensed essence of all sūtra and tantra, [119] and

---

self-apprehending wisdom's scope,
to three times' victors' mother, praise!

183. I have chosen the word "connate" to translate the Tibetan *lhan cig skyes pa*, which literally means "born together." Traditionally most translators have used the term "innate" or "simultaneously born." In recent years some have started using this term, which is a more precise translation—the late Latin *con-* (together) + *nasci* (be born). The point is that while our mind is habituated to ignorance, coexistent with that ignorance has always been a potential for wisdom and bliss.

184. Sangyé Yeshé (Tib. Sangs rgyas ye shes, 1525–91) was the primary teacher of Paṇchen Losang Chökyi Gyaltsen. He underwent his monastic training at Tashi Lhunpo Monastery in Shigatsé and became a close student of Gyalwa Ensapa. When Losang Chökyi Gyaltsen was recognized as Ensapa's reincarnation, Sangyé Yeshé ordained the young boy and became his primary teacher in turn. Sangyé Yeshé also served twice as abbot of Riwo Gepel Monastery.

185. Vajradhara is called the "sixth victor" because he pervades all five of the buddha families. He is the sixth in addition to the five buddhas who are the lords of these five families. The five buddha families are Vajra, Ratna, Padma, Buddha, and Karma. The five lords of these families are Akṣobhya, Ratnasambhava, Amitābha, Vairocana, and Amoghasiddhi. Many modern texts refer to these five as the "five dhyāni buddhas," but this phrase, introduced into the English language by Brian Hodgson in the nineteenth century, has no corresponding term in Sanksrit or Tibetan.

the quintessence of those teachings coming from Jé the Great [Tsongkhapa] is clear in the requesting prayer to the mahāmudrā lineage that carried that quintessence.[186] From Jé Rinpoché, this lineage passed on to Tokden Jampal Gyatso,[187] followed by Baso Chökyi Gyaltsen[188] and then Drupchok Dharmavajra.[189] Thus the author states, "I will offer a teaching on becoming a buddha in one life according to this oral tradition." The name of the author of this treatise is Paṇchen Losang Chökyi Gyaltsen.

This sort of instruction on mahāmudrā was extant at the time of Jé Tsongkhapa and sons [Khedrup Jé and Gyaltsap Jé], but nobody put together the lineage of instruction in the form of a text until the time of Paṇchen Losang Chökyi Gyaltsen. Also, before Paṇchen Losang Chökyi Gyaltsen, there was the great Gyalwa Ensapa,[190] who reached the state of union [that is, enlightenment] in that very life. As the Paṇchen Lama clarifies in the colophon of his text, in one corner of his speech is an indication that the Gendenpa hold an instruction on mahāmudrā that is dissimilar

186. For this prayer, see the beginning of part 2.

187. Tokden Jampal Gyatso (Tib. Rtogs ldan 'jam dpal rgya mtsho, 1356–1428), a native of Tsongkha, was a close disciple of Tsongkhapa, from whom he received the Ganden Mahāmudrā transmission. He accompanied Tsongkhapa during the retreat at Olkha, after which time he set out on his own to practice in hermitages and caves in the Lhasa area. His primary disciples were Baso Chökyi Gyaltsen and Chenga Lodrö Gyaltsen.

188. Baso Chökyi Gyaltsen (1402–73), brother of Khedrup Gelek Pelsang, was an early holder of the Ganden mahāmudrā lineage of the Geluk tradition. He served as the sixth Ganden Tripa, from 1463–73. He was the disciple of Jampal Gyatso and the teacher of Chökyi Dorjé. He is considered to be the first incarnation of the Tatsak Jedrung line.

189. Drupchok Dharmavajra (Dharmavajra = "Chökyi Dorjé"; Tib. Chos kyi rdo rje, b. 1457) was an early holder of the Ganden mahāmudrā lineage of the Geluk tradition, which he received from Baso Chökyi Gyaltsen (Tib. Ba so chos kyi rgyal mtshan). He trained at both Ganden and Drepung before moving to Ensa Monastery in Tsang. His chief disciple was Ensapa Losang Döndrup (the "son" referred to in the root text). As for why the Paṇchen Lama singles out Dharmavajra as an object of praise here (rather than the earlier masters), His Holiness the Dalai Lama explains,

> This is because Dharmavajra was a very highly realized master who not only attained a single-pointed state of unity, but also received a clear vision of Tsongkhapa and composed *The Guru-Yoga of the Foremost Three-Part Composite Being*. (Gyatso and Berzin 1997, 109).

190. Gyalwa Ensapa Losang Döndrup (1505–56) was an early lineage holder of the Ganden oral lineage. After training with prominent lamas of his day, he spent an extended period of time in isolated retreat, living in the manner of an Indian siddha. He was a disciple of Gendün Gyatso, posthumously known as the Second Dalai Lama. Ensapa was himself posthumously recognized as the Third Paṇchen Lama. The phrase "and son" in the root text indicates Ensapa, who was a close student of Chökyi Dorjé.

from other schools; however, he explains that this is not the time to discuss that.[191]

As for the great Gyalwa Ensapa, being untainted by the stain of the eight worldly concerns,[192] he made the eight concerns of equal taste, [120] and manifesting crazy behavior externally, achieved the state of buddhahood in that very life. Because he showed the aspect of being crazy to ordinary appearance, there are those who call him "Crazy Ensa." He had already reached the state of union, so when he passed away his body shrank and was about to disappear into the sky as a rainbow. Because his disciples made requests, a body form the size of a mere cubit[193] remained.

As for Baso Chökyi Gyaltsen, he was a disciple of Jé Tsongkhapa, the all-knowing Khedrup [Gelek Palsang], and Tokden Jampal Gyatso. He became a holder of the treasure of Oral Lineage instruction. His disciples were the three Dorjé brothers—one named Drupchen Chökyi Dorjé,[194] who achieved the state of union in that very life, as well as Palden Dorjé[195] and the Khampa Rinchen Dorjé.[196] Gyalwa Ensapa listened to this instruc-

191. Gen Namgyal Chöphel explains the meaning of this passage. The Paṇchen Lama intends to indicate that there is something unique about the Geluk lineage of mahāmudrā, but because it is something hidden, he does not say so directly. Rather he subtly hints at this point through certain obscure phrases in the colophon (see root text). Also in the dedication verses to the autocommentary, he writes, "*unmixed* great seal, clear beautiful form . . . ," another insinuation that something is unique about this lineage.

192. The eight worldly concerns are gain and loss, renown and disrepute, praise and slander, and pleasure and pain. They are called "worldly" because attachment to the positive ones and aversion to the negative ones is the normal motivation of worldly people, but a motivation that Dharma practitioners seek to transcend. To "make them of equal taste" means not to approach them with attachment and aversion.

193. Tib. *khru gang tsam*. Jim Valby's Tibetan-English dictionary explains this length to be about fifteen inches, from elbow to fisted middle finger.

194. For Drupchen Chökyi Dorjé (also called Drupchok Dharmavajra), see note 187.

195. According to one account, Palden Dorjé of Tölung (Tib. Dpal ldan rdo rje, born in the fifteenth century) lived in Drip in a divine mansion of massive rocks that looked like piled-up vajras, while other accounts state that he lived in Gephel, a hermitage above Drepung. He both studied with and taught the Second Dalai Lama, Gyalwa Gendün Gyatso (Tib. Rgyal ba dge 'dun rgya mtsho, 1476–1542).

196. Khampa Yeshé Rinchen Dorjé (aka Dorjé Palwa, Tib. Khams pa ye shes rin chen rdo rje) lived in a solitary place in upper Jokpo in Phenyul. From Willis, *Enlightened Beings*, 46:

> Not much is known about his origins or whereabouts prior to his meeting with the others of the three Dorjés or regarding his stay at Gepel [Ri bo dge 'phel, a mountain behind Drepung Monastery], during which time he received the detailed practice instructions of the Oral Tradition from Paṇchen Chökyi

tion from the one called Drupchen Chökyi Dorjé from among the three Dorjé brothers.

As for Drupchen Chökyi Dorjé, he achieved the vajra rainbow body, and it is said that even now he abides in Tibet and that a few fortunate beings see him. When Ensapa was receiving this Dharma from Drupchen Chökyi Dorjé, [121] Drupchen Chökyi Dorjé condensed into a coarse bodily form. Since he had already achieved the state of rainbow body, he did not manifest an appearance to common trainees, but Gyalwa Ensapa met him in his meditation cave and listened to teachings from him.

Drupchen Chökyi Dorjé's lama, Baso Chökyi Gyaltsen, was the younger brother of the all-knowing Khedrup [Gelek Palsang]. He listened to personal instructions from Jé Tsongkhapa, the all-knowing Khedrup, and others, becoming a master of the Oral Lineage teachings.

Baso Chökyi Gyaltsen's primary lama was Tokden Jampal Gyatso. Tokden Jampal Gyatso listened to Dharma teachings directly from Jé Rinpoché. Before Jé the Great saw Mañjuśrī directly, Tokden Jampal Gyatso directly saw the noble lord Mañjuśrī. Initially, he was among the "eightfold pure retinue" when Jé the Great was about to enter into retreat. Later when Jé Rinpoché founded Ganden Monastery and was in the process of manifesting holy activities equaling the sky, Tokden remained single-pointedly in retreat for attainment and, undergoing worthy hardship, actualized the essence of accomplishment. [122] His main lama was Jé Tsongkhapa. In many sūtras and tantras there are passages indicating that the great Jé Tsongkhapa was an emanation of the noble lord Mañjuśrī.

Even from the point of view of his showing an ordinary aspect, Tsongkhapa did as he described in "Destiny Fulfilled":

> First, I sought much learning vast.
> Next, all texts dawned as advice.
> Last, I practiced day and night.
> I dedicate that teachings spread.[197]

Gyelpo. It is not known whether he had formerly lived amid ordinary people or in extraordinary dwelling places among *ḍākas.* (Willis 1995)

The three aformentioned masters are called brothers not because they were relatives but because they all had the name Dorjé and because they are all said to have achieved the vajra rainbow body (*dorjé* is Tibetan for "vajra").

197. "Destiny Fulfilled: An Expression of Realization" (Tib. *Rtogs brjod mdun legs ma*) is a poem Tsongkhapa composed describing his personal experience of gaining certainty in the

Initially, he extensively studied and contemplated all the sūtras and tantras. Furthermore, as for that vast learning, he was not content with mere superficial understanding but put it into personal practice. On the basis of having practiced, he manifested realizations. Having manifested realizations, he composed many treatises on the Buddha's supreme speech of sūtra and tantra, leaving them for the benefit of future trainees.

With regard to the compositions of Jé the Great, it is said that he never wrote something until he had attained stable ascertainment of the meaning of the scripture describing it. After a stable ascertainment had arisen in his holy mind, he would teach on it.

In order to demonstrate the noble source of the Dharma that I will teach, I have offered a brief description of the greatness of the composer of the treatise.

[123] As a Preparation, the Manner of Fervently Going for Refuge and Generating Bodhicitta

Preparatory, actual,
concluding—from those three parts here:

As teaching's port of entry, first,
and Mahāyāna's pillar chief,
not just by mouth, not just by words,
go fervently for refuge and
give rise to the awak'ning mind.

A meditator on this system of mahāmudrā must initially perform the preparatory practices of accumulating merit and purifying obscurations. Since going for refuge to the Three Jewels is what distinguishes a Buddhist from a non-Buddhist and is the port of entry for the Buddhist teachings, to begin one goes for refuge. And since bodhicitta is like the central pillar of the Mahāyāna path, one generates Mahāyāna bodhicitta. Thus it says, "go fervently for refuge and give rise to the awak'ning mind."

---

teachings of sūtra and tantra. This poem consists of three stages, corresponding to the three stages of hearing, contemplation, and meditation. This verse (verse 4) summarizes those three stages. Geshé Dorji Damdul has translated this poem as "Noble Pursuit: Revealing One's Personal Realizations," in Tibet House 2015, 194–205.

Although there are many different ways of going for refuge depending on the motivation, here it is the Mahāyāna manner of going for refuge. Since this text is explained in the context of the practice of mantra,[198] one definitely needs stability in the three causes of Mahāyāna refuge. Fear and faith alone are not sufficient; one needs fear, faith, *and* great compassion. The mind that (1) fears and dreads the suffering of the unfortunate migrations as described above and (2) goes for refuge on the basis of believing that the Three Jewels have the power to save one from that suffering goes for refuge in common with the being of lower capacity. [124] Having generated a mind of fright based on seeing not only the unfortunate migrations but all of saṃsāra in general as in the nature of suffering, and going for refuge by seeking a source of refuge that saves one from that suffering, is refuge in common with the being of middling capacity. If one not only has fear and dread toward the suffering of saṃsāra for oneself but generates a mind of fear and dread for the suffering of saṃsāra and the unfortunate migrations for both oneself and all other sentient beings, then goes for refuge on the basis of generating great compassion that thinks, "How wonderful it would be if all these beings were free of suffering," this is called "the refuge of the being of great capacity."[199] "Fervently" indicates that one must not merely move one's mouth or speak the words but definitely must mix their meaning with one's mind.

To see mind's nature furthermore
rests on amassing merit first, and cleansing obscurations, so
at least a hundred thousand of the mantra—
hundred-syllables—

198. The terms "practice of mantra" and "practice of tantra," as well as "mantric path" and "tantric path," are used interchangeably throughout this book, in accordance with the Geluk convention. I have translated them in accordance with Rinpoché's usage in Tibetan.

199. A being of lower capacity is one who goes for refuge with the thought to avoid rebirth in a lower realm and practices accordingly. A being of middling capacity sees not only the lower realms but all of saṃsāra as undesirable and goes for refuge with the intention to be free of saṃsāra. A being of great capacity goes for refuge not only for the purpose of personal liberation but with the intention to achieve full buddhahood and lead all beings to that state. Atīśa coined this manner of classifying spiritual practitioners in his text *Lamp for the Path to Enlightenment* (Skt. *Bodhipathapradīpa*; Tib. *Byang chub lam gyi sgron ma*), and Tsongkhapa adopted it in his lamrim literature.

prostrations, many hundreds of, do with *Confessing Downfalls*[200] first.

Since "mahāmudrā" is explained as the nature of the mind, being able to see that nature definitely depends on having accumulated merit and purified obscurations. Generally speaking, the primary obstacle-makers to whatever qualities we generate in our mind are negative actions and obscurations. Since we need an accumulation of merit as a conducive condition, any quality, whatever it may be, [125] depends on purifying negativity and obscurations—discordant conditions—and accumulating merit—the conducive condition. Since actualizing mahāmudrā also depends on having accumulated merit and purified obscurations, for the purpose of accumulating merit we must make prostrations, and for the purpose of purifying obscurations we must accumulate recitations of the hundred-syllable mantra of Vajrasattva[201] and so forth. Generally, as I mentioned above, any merit we accomplish will become an antidote for negativity. But as for "at least a hundred thousand of the hundred-syllable mantra": the hundred-syllable mantra is a requesting prayer to Vajrasattva. Since Vajrasattva arose in his holy form for the purpose of purifying negativity and obscurations, if you make requests to him, the purification of negativities has a great distinction that is dissimilar from other methods, so you must recite one hundred thousand of the hundred-syllable mantra.

Also with regard to the statement "at least a hundred thousand of the hundred-syllable mantra," in general, if you create negativity and do not confess it, each day it will increase exponentially. For example, if you create some negativity like killing and it remains without your being able to confess it, then the next day it will become like two negative actions of killing, the next day four, and so on. If you recite the hundred-syllable mantra twenty-one times a day without break, then beyond whatever negativity you already accumulated, you will at least be able to stop it from increasing.

200. Tib. *Ltung bshags*. This is a colloquial title for the *Sūtra of Three Heaps* (Skt. *Triskandhadharmasūtra*; Tib. *Phung po gsum gyi mdo*), a common prayer that practitioners recite while prostrating that includes the names of the thirty-five tathāgatas. For an explanation of this practice, see Geshé Jampa Gyatso 2016.

201. For explanations of this practice, see Lama Yeshe 2014, Khenpo Yeshe Phuntsok 2015, and Lama Zopa Rinpoché 2001.

[126] If you recite it one hundred thousand times, then you will thoroughly purify negativity. It says in *Ornament of the Essence*,[202]

> Recite a hundred thousand just,
> it absolutely purifies.

So it says even at the very least, you need to recite one hundred thousand.

Regarding the accumulation of merit, the text reads, "prostrations, many hundreds of, do . . . first," so you need to perform as many hundreds or hundreds of thousands of prostrations as you are able. By prostrating, you purify negativity accumulated with the body, and if you undergo hardship with your body there is a special forcefulness to the purification of negativity, so the Paṇchen Lama explicitly says, "However many hundreds of prostrations." Taking mantra recitation and prostrations as an illustration, he has described above the limb of confession within the seven-limbed prayer. On that basis, he implicitly indicates the limbs of prostration, offering, rejoicing, and so forth.[203]

> **Insep'rable from buddhas of**
> **three times, to your root lama make**
> **sincere requests, again, again.**

The root basis giving rise to all collections of good qualities without exception, in this and future lives, is making requests to one's lama. Gyalwa Götsangpa said,

> Train many in creation stage—
> tops lama meditation not.
> Though many count dhāraṇīs it
> surpasses not requesting prayers.[204]

202. Tib. *Snying po'i rgyan*. The full name of this text is *The Glorious Tantra That Is an Ornament of the Vajra Essence* (Skt. *Vajrahṛdayālaṃkāratantra*; Tib. *Dpal rdo rje'i snying po'i rgyan gyi rgyud*).

203. The seven-limbed prayer is a common means of accumulating merit and purifying negativity. The seven limbs are (1) prostration, (2) offering, (3) confession, (4) rejoicing, (5) requesting the buddhas/teachers to live long, (6) requesting them to teach the Dharma, and (7) dedicating the merit. For an explanation of this practice, see Pabongka 1991, 201–35.

204. Götsangpa Gönpo Dorjé (Rgod tshang pa mgon po rdo rje, 1189–1258) was an early

This passage explains that meditating on the lama is more beneficial than meditating on the deity and the generation stage, that it is more beneficial to make requests to the lama than to accumulate mantras of another deity, and that these will not deceive you in the long run. Thus, "make sincere requests, again, again."

We Need to Accumulate Merit and Purify Negativities in Order to Generate Realizations

If we put effort merely into cultivating an object of observation for the purpose of generating realizations, through that alone realizations will not arise. So that we might generate realizations, as explained above, we purify negativities and obscurations that are antagonistic conditions, accumulate merit as a supportive condition, cultivate an object of observation as our practice, and make requests to our lama, meditating on him as inseparable from the exalted deity. These and other practices we must combine and put into practice. This is extremely important.

Having examined for yourself whatever text you plan to put into practice, if you cultivate an object of observation as a practice, accumulate merit, purify negativity, and make requests to the lama inseparable from the exalted deity, then even though you may think, "At the moment, I am unable to generate any realizations," in the future you will be able to generate them with ease. The noble lord Mañjuśrī gave this advice to Jé Rinpoché, and Jé Rinpoché [128] himself also gave this advice. Likewise, here it is explained that one must meditate on guru yoga and make requests to the lama. Also, if when you meditate on guru yoga, you meditate on the lama as an ordinary person and make requests to him, there will be no significant benefit. If instead you consider the lama as inseparable from all the buddhas of the three times and make requests, on account of viewing him as inseparable from all the buddhas of the three times, there is in that respect a great blessing. If you make requests in this way, the blessing will come quickly, so you must consider the lama as inseparable from the exalted deity and make requests.

Usually when giving a commentary on mahāmudrā, there is a tradition

---

master of the Drukpa Kagyü school and is considered to have been the reincarnation of Milarepa. Rinpoché quotes part of a saying by him, of which these are the last two lines:

> Request nonstop; insep'rable
> experience is sure to come.

of combining commentaries on Lama Chöpa and mahāmudrā and teaching them together. The reason it is done that way is that one must practice having taken guru yoga as the lifeblood of the path.

Guru yoga has many forms, both extensive and condensed. Lama Chöpa, the six-session guru yoga, Ganden Lha Gyama, and so forth are all versions of guru yoga.[205] As for the meaning of "guru yoga," a ritual in which one meditates in order to be able to transform one's mind into that of a full-fledged guru is called "guru yoga." [129] "Able to transform into a full-fledged guru" means being able to transform into the *actual* guru.

Recall the benefits of correctly devoting to a spiritual friend and the drawbacks of not doing so. Then train in the root of the path—faith. Remember the lama's kindness and generate respect. In that manner, make requests to the lama. Viewing the lama as inseparable in nature from all buddhas, from the depths of your heart make requests to the lama and supreme deity. This was clarified above in the final verse of the mahāmudrā requesting prayer:

> Your holy form and, father, my form;
> Your holy speech and, father, my speech;
> Your holy mind and, father, my mind:
> Bless that insep'rably one in fact.

Thinking, "How wonderful it would be if my mind and the lama's holy mind were mixed," and making requests with intense longing in this way is also called "guru yoga." It is important to accumulate merit and purify obscurations in that way.

Having first accumulated merit, purified obscurations, and done guru yoga,

> **The actu'l practice of great seal**
> **is many ways asserted, but**
> **split into sūtra, mantra: two.**

> **The latter is clear-light great bliss**

205. The six-session guru yoga (Tib. *Thun drug bla ma'i rnal 'byor*) is a daily practice commitment for practitioners who have received an unsurpassed yoga tantra empowerment. For a commentary on this practice, see Tharchin 1999.

For Lama Chöpa (Tib. *Bla ma mchod pa*), see note 56, and also see Tenzin Gyatso 1988 and Kachen Yeshe Gyaltsen 2014. For Ganden Lha Gyama, see note 174.

from piercing skillfully the points
of vajra body and so forth: [206]
[130] **great seal of Saraha and of**
Nāgārj'na, Nāro, Maitrī too.[207]
In *Essence* and in *Siddhis* taught,
it's highest tantra's quintessence.

Although in general former scholars had many points of view regarding that which is called "mahāmudrā," these systems can be condensed into mahāmudrā of the sūtra system and mahāmudrā of the mantra system. Of the two—sūtra and mantra mahāmudrā—this text belongs to the latter—mahāmudrā of the mantra system.

"Mantra" means secret mantra. Since that must be practiced in great

206. In his commentary on the Paṇchen Lama's autocommentary, His Holiness the Dalai Lama elucidates the meaning of "and so forth":

> It refers to the fact that there are other methods as well for manifesting clear light mind. Those who practice the Nyingma system of meditation, for example, do not rely on actions for penetrating vital points of the vajra-body. They follow, instead, a guideline instruction for manifesting clear light mind by relying solely on meditation on a nonconceptual state. Thus, making manifest simultaneously arising greatly blissful clear light mind of deep awareness, either by relying on methods for penetrating vital points of the vajra-body or, for those of especially sharp faculties, by not having to do so, is the tantra tradition [mantra system] of mahamudra as explained in the texts of Saraha, Nagarjuna, Naropa and Maitripa. (Gyatso and Berzin 1997, 220)

207. Tradition holds that the elusive Indian figure Saraha was the first to introduce mahāmudrā meditation. Roger Jackson explains: "Saraha, the 'arrow-maker' disciple of a female tantric practitioner (and also known as the Great Brahmin, or Rāhulabhadra the Younger), is perhaps the greatest single individual in the history of Indian tantric Buddhism, famed as its most eloquent poet; as the fountainhead for lineages of practice related to the Yoginī tantras and to meditation on the 'great seal' of reality, mahāmudrā; and as a guru to the immortal Nāgārjuna. Yet we cannot locate him with any precision at all in time or place" (Jackson 2004, 7). See also note 210.

Nāgārjuna was the most renowned Buddhist paṇḍit of ancient India, likely living sometime in the early part of the first millennium. He is credited with founding the Madhyamaka (Middle Way) school, and his texts on sūtra and tantra underlie a significant part of the curriculum in all Tibetan monastic education.

Nāropā (died circa 1040) was a famous scholar of Nālandā Monastery who left the monastery to follow the elusive guru Tilopa, undergo many hardships, and ultimately reach supreme accomplishment. Through his Tibetan student Marpa, his teachings were transmitted to Tibet and became the basis for the Kagyü lineage.

Maitrīpa (also known as Maitrīpāda; circa 1007–85) lived in a hermitage in northeast India and was a student of Nāropā and a teacher to both Atiśa and Marpa.

secrecy, in this text it is only explained in a condensed way.[208] Also, in Lama Chöpa, except for condensed passages such as

> Bless in this life to actualize
> merged path: clear light, illusory form,[209]

secret mantra is not spoken of extensively. Since mantra must be practiced in great secrecy, in these texts it is only discussed briefly. The subject to be discussed includes both sūtra and mantra, but there is a difference in the number of words used to describe each one [that is, many more words are used for sūtra]. When there is no other particular need, it is the tradition of grammarians first to describe that which requires fewer letters. When the actual content of the subjects to be discussed also has both a condensed and an extensive subject, [131] it is moreover the custom to describe the condensed one first and the extensive one afterward. So here as well, since there is no more than a brief bit to say about mantra, he explains that first.

208. Because this text includes a brief description of mantra-system mahāmudrā, it is technically classed as mantra, even though the bulk of the text expounds sūtra-system mahāmudrā.

209. *Lama Chöpa*, v. 111cd.

TEN

The Mantra System of Mahāmudrā

Explanation of Mahāmudrā of the Mantra System

Again,

> **The latter is clear-light great bliss**
> **from piercing skillfully the points**
> **of vajra body and so forth . . .**

What sort of thing is this "mahāmudrā of the mantra system"? The practitioner pierces the vital points of the channels, winds, and drops in her own body and practices according to the manner of meditation explained in the texts. By practicing in that way, she condenses all the winds into the indestructible drop. All the external signs appear as in the stages of death, and the clear light shines forth. That clear light, moreover, is not just manifested purposely. Rather, it becomes the nature of a mind realizing emptiness called "the mixing of the mother emptiness and the son clear light." Such a clear light is called "path mahāmudrā." When the practitioner has condensed all the winds into the indestructible drop, that primordial, connate clear light, which has become the nature of a mind realizing emptiness, is the supreme essence of subjects explained in the ocean-like class of unsurpassed tantra and is the "great bliss" that is praised again and again in mantra teachings.

[132] The Kagyü school has a mahāmudrā that was well known in old times, before Jé the Great came. It is a mahāmudrā passed down from Nāropā and Maitrīpa. In actuality the primordial, connate clear light great bliss that has become the nature of a mind realizing emptiness is the final thought of Nāropā and Maitrīpa and is called "mahāmudrā."

"In *Essence* and in *Siddhis* taught": there are many texts, such as the *Seven Treatises of Accomplishment* [*Siddhis*] and so forth.[210] The intention of all

210. In his autocommentary, the Paṇchen Lama identifies the *Seven Treatises of Accomplishment* (Tib. *Grub pa sde bdun*) as follows:

of these is called "the primordial, connate clear light." To meditate on this, one needs to meditate on the completion stage and apply a method that condenses all the winds into the indestructible drop. To condense the winds in this way, one follows the instructions on the three channels and six channel wheels as explained in texts on Guhyasamāja, Heruka Cakrasaṃvara, Vajrabhairava, and so forth. At the outset of meditation, one meditates observing the navel, meditates on the heart, or meditates observing the tip of the secret region, and so forth: many modes of meditation have been explained. Again, if one meditates on mahāmudrā combining it with Lama

---

1. *Secret Accomplishment* (Skt. *Guhyasiddhi*; Tib. *Gsang ba grub pa*) by Protector Mahāsukha (Tib. Mgon po Bde ba chen po). The Paṇchen Lama says Mahāsukha is also called the Lake-Born Vajra (Skt. Saroruhavajra; Tib. Mtsho skyes rdo rje). He further explains that this text mainly explains the intention of the *Guhyasamāja Root Tantra* (Skt. *Guhyasamājatantra*; Tib. *Gsang 'dus rtsa rgyud*) and serves as the model text for the remaining six *Treatises* and *The Three Essence Cycles* (below).
2. *Accomplishment of Wisdom and Means* (Skt. *Prajñopāyaviniścayasiddhi*; Tib. *Thabs shes grub pa*) by Mahāsukha's student Anaṅgavajra (Tib. Yan lag med pa'i rdo rje).
3. *Accomplishment of Primordial Wisdom* (Skt. *Jñānasiddhi*; Tib. *Ye shes grub pa*) by Anaṅgavajra's student Indrabhūti.
4. *Nondual Accomplishment* (Skt. *Advayasiddhi*; Tib. *Gnyis med grub pa*) by Indrabhūti's consort Lakṣmīṃkarā.
5. *Connate Accomplishment* (Skt. *Sahajāsiddhi*; Tib. *Lhan cig skyes grub*) by Ḍombī Heruka.
6. *Accomplishment of Great Secret Suchness* (Skt. *Mahāguhyatattvasiddhi*; Tib. *Gsang ba chen po'i de kho na nyid grub pa*) by Dārika.
7. *Accomplishment of Suchness That Pervades All Things* (Skt. *Vyaktabhavānugatatattvasiddhi*; Tib. *Dngos po gsal ba'i rjes su 'gro ba'i de kho na nyid grub pa*) by Yoginīcintā ([Sahajā]yoginī Cintā, Tib. [Lhan cig skyes pa'i] rnal sbyor ma ci to), mid eighth century CE.

In his commentary on the Paṇchen Lama's text, Keutsang Losang Jamyang Mönlam (Tib. Ke'u tshang blo bzang 'jam dbyangs smon lam) identifies *Essence* as *The Three Essence Cycles*, which he equates with Saraha's three *dohās* (Rinpoché refers to these on page 206): the *Dohākośanāmacaryāgīti* (Tib. *Do ha mdzod ces bya ba spyod pa'i glu*), more commonly known simply as the "King's Dohā" (Tib. *Rgyal po'i do ha*), the *Dohākośopadeśagīti* (Tib. *Mi zad pa'i gter mdzod man ngag gi glu zhes bya ba*), less formally known as "Queen's Dohā" (Tib. *Gtsun mo'i do ha*), and the "Treasury of Dohā Songs"(Skt. *Dohākośagīti*; Tib. *Do ha mdzod kyi glu*), also known as the "Common Dohā" (Tib. *Dmangs kyi do ha*). Keutsang emphasizes that these texts are singled out because they give an especially lucid explanation, but that in a general sense mahāmudrā should be understood as the quintessence of all completion stage texts. The Paṇchen Lama mentions as an aside that some scholars, such as Butön, consider only the *Common Dohā* to be the work of Saraha, while the other two are instances of others borrowing his name. For a translation of the *King's Dohā*, see Khenchen Thrangu Rinpoché 2006. For translations of the *Common Dohā*, see Jackson 2004 and Schaeffer 2005. Guenther 1993 contains translations of all three dohās.

Chöpa, since Lama Chöpa is said to be mainly related with Guhyasamāja, one follows the stages of the path of Guhyasamāja.[211] In the Guhyasamāja system, the first stage is the isolation of body, followed by the isolations of speech and mind, which combine to form the second stage of observing the mind.[212] [133] Then comes illusory body, clear light, and unification; there are said to be these five stages of the completion stage. The ultimate object of accomplishment is actualizing the state of unification, which unifies clear light and illusory body. In order to actualize such a state of unification, one must first actualize individually the two parts that are to be unified—clear light and illusory body. "Illusory body" and "clear light" refer to the illusory body of the third stage and the meaning clear light of the fourth stage. In order to arise as the illusory body, one first needs to be able to condense all the winds into the indestructible drop, so one must cause to appear the example clear light which is the mental isolation of the second stage. In order for the example clear light of mental isolation to appear, one must make all the winds enter, abide, and dissolve into the heart. And for that, first of all, as a method for causing the winds to enter, one must loosen the knots in the channels. To loosen these, one must meditate on the vajra recitation that is isolation of speech.

Initially, for the purpose of causing the winds to enter into the central channel, one meditates placing one's focus on either the navel or the secret place. Applying such a method to cause the winds to dissolve in the cen-

211. For explanations of the Guhyasamāja practice, see Yangchen Gawai Lodoe 1995. For explanations of Heruka Cakrasaṃvara, see Ngülchu Dharmabhadra and the First Paṇchen Lama, Losang Chökyi Gyaltsen 2010, Kyabje Trijang Rinpoché Losang Yeshe 2013, and Lama Zopa Rinpoché 2000. For explanations of Vajrabhairava, see Ngülchu Dharmabhadra and the Fifth Ling Rinpoché, Losang Lungtog Tenzin Trinley 2012, Phabongkha 2000, Lama Zopa Rinpoché 2000, and Tri Gyaltsen Senge 1995. For general explanations of the practice of withdrawing the winds, see Ngülchu Dharmabhadra and the First Paṇchen Lama 2014.

212. Because the completion stage literally comprises six stages—isolations of body, speech, and mind, illusory body, clear light, and unification—different scholars have condensed the stages into five in different ways. One tradition, which stems from Candakīrti's commentary *The Clear Lamp* (Skt. *Pradīpodyotana*; Tib. *Sgron ma gsal bar byed pa*), is to group the first two isolations together with the isolation of mind as the "stage of observing the mind" and add the generation stage as the first stage. Another tradition, based on Nāgārjuna's *Five Stages* (Skt. *Pañcakrama*; Tib. *Rim pa lnga pa*) and Nāgabodhi's *Graded Presentation* (Skt. *Samājasādhanavyavastholi*; Tib. *Rnam gzhags rim pa*), groups the isolations of body and speech into the first stage and counts the isolation of mind alone as the second. Rinpoché here appears to be following a slightly modified presentation. The difference lies merely in the classification; the meaning of the stages is the same in all cases.

tral channel is called "isolation of body." In order to meditate on such a bodily isolation, first one must ripen one's continuum by meditating on the generation stage. [134] Regarding the generation and completion stages, during the completion stage one gains the ability to arise in actuality as the holy body of a deity, the basis to be actualized. During the generation stage, although one is not actually able to arise as the holy body of a deity, by means of aspirational mental engagement, one must *imagine* arising as the holy body.

Explanation of Taking the Three Bodies into the Path

The three bodies, in the context of taking the three bodies into the path, include the three bodies that are the bases, the three bodies that are the paths, and the three bodies that are the results. Ordinary (1) death, (2) intermediate state, and (3) taking rebirth are the bases; although they are not actually the three bodies, they are given the name "three bodies"—that is, three bodies that are the bases. In the context of the completion stage, (1) meditation on the clear light, (2) meditation on the illusory body, and (3) the illusory body again entering into the old aggregates are also not actually the three bodies but are called the three bodies that are the paths. On the basis of having purified the three bodies that are the bases to be purified by means of the three bodies that are the paths that purify them, one achieves the *actual* three bodies, which are the results of purifying: (1) the wisdom truth body, (2) the complete enjoyment body, and (3) the emanation body.[213]

Although the actual purifiers of the three bodies that are the bases arise

213. These are the three bodies or three embodiments of the Buddha. The term *body* is used loosely here; the point is that the Buddha appears in three different ways to different beings, depending on the stage of their development. To other buddhas, the Buddha appears as the wisdom truth body—omniscient consciousness. Nonbuddhas can conceive of this state but not perceive it directly. To advanced practitioners (bodhisattvas who have directly cognized emptiness), the Buddha appears in a resplendent, subtle form called the complete enjoyment body. Because ordinary beings cannot perceive this subtle body either, the Buddha also appears as the emanation body in accord with beings' karma. To beings with pure karma, the Buddha appears as a supreme emanation body, like the body of Śākyamuni Buddha, adorned with the major marks and signs and teaching the Dharma in its entirety. To beings with less pure karma, the Buddha appears as either an incarnate emanation body, such as a wise teacher who does not reveal he is a buddha, or as an artisan emanation body, which could be anything from a random person who appears briefly to give helpful advice at the right time to an inanimate object like a bridge, depending on the karma of the trainee. In this context

during the completion stage, to ripen the roots of virtue for these one must meditate on taking the three bodies into the path in the context of the generation stage. With regard to purifying the three bodies that are the bases, although the wisdom that realizes selflessness, by having a discordant aspect with the apprehension of a self, purifies that apprehension by means of directly contradicting its mode of apprehension, this manner of purifying the three basis bodies is not like that. Rather, it purifies by means of having a concordant aspect to that apprehension of a self.[214] [135]

When an ordinary person dies, the elements of the body gradually withdraw, and the mind becomes subtler and subtler. Finally, the primordial mind manifests, so for death that is the basis, one must meditate on taking death into the path as the wisdom truth body, with an aspect similar to that of ordinary death.[215]

Taking Death into the Path as the Wisdom Truth Body

Moreover, with regard to this meditation taking death into the path as the wisdom truth body, when meditating on the self-generation, first one must meditate on emptiness, and while meditating on emptiness, one must

---

of the generation stage, one is taking rebirth into the path as a *supreme* emanation body. For an insightful discussion of the bodies of the Buddha, see Makransky 1997.

214. The meaning of the wisdom that realizes selflessness having a "discordant aspect" with the apprehension of self is that these two minds observe the same object but apprehend it in contradictory ways. The apprehension of self observes the person and apprehends this person to be inherently existent. The wisdom that realizes selflessness observes that same person and recognizes its *lack* of inherent existence.

In the context of the generation stage, one is seeking to overcome the habitual adherence to ordinary appearances. One does not directly *contradict* the apprehension of self but rather *substitutes* a different conception. One replaces the conception that observes one's present body and mind, thinking, "This is me," with a conception that observes the holy body of the deity and thinks, "This is me." Although the deity is also not inherently existent, the deity is said to be closer to one's true nature than one's present body and mind. Combined with the wisdom of emptiness, this meditation helps one to overcome the habitual grasping at oneself as a limited saṃsāric being who exists in a findable way.

A question that remains is whether the conception of oneself as a deity is a wrong consciousness, even though it is effective for overcoming habitual grasping. Different teachers approach this question in different ways. Such a discussion is beyond the scope of the present work.

215. In other words, one replaces the conception "I am an ordinary person dying" with "I am dissolving my consciousness into the wisdom truth body."

meditate on this taking death into the path as the wisdom truth body. One recites the mantra *oṃ svabhāvaśuddhāḥ sarvadharmāḥ svabhāvaśuddho 'ham* and meditates on emptiness. At that time, the entire environment and the beings therein gradually condense and dissolve into oneself. One oneself also dissolves into the seed syllable of whatever deity one is meditating upon. For example, if it is Guhyasamāja, one dissolves into the *hūṃ* syllable [the seed syllable of Guhyasamāja]. The *zhabkyu* [the *u* letter] of the *hūṃ* dissolves into the *ha*. The *ha* dissolves into its head [top portion]. Imagine that the head dissolves into the crescent moon, the crescent moon into the drop, the drop into the *nāda*, and the nāda becomes emptiness, which is not observed.[216] These stages of dissolution are similar to the gradual dissolution of the coarse bodily winds at the time of death. When an ordinary person dies, the power of the earth element among the elements of the body decreases, and when the power of the water element becomes manifest, it is called "earth dissolving into water." [136] When earth dissolves into water, the dying person perceives an appearance like a mirage and feels as though he is sinking down into the earth. Take also the manner of water dissolving into fire to be the power of the water element decreasing and the power of fire becoming manifest.

At this point, there is an appearance like the diffusion of smoke inside a house. What are the external bodily signs at that time? The mouth becomes dry, the throat becomes dry, and so forth. Also, fire dissolving into wind: when the power of the fire element decreases and the power of the wind element becomes manifest, fire dissolves into wind. One's own inner appearance is like the appearance of fireflies. It is like, for example, fireflies at nighttime, when an appearance like sparks darting and flitting about arises. Wind dissolving into consciousness is the power of the wind element decreasing and the power of consciousness becoming manifest. One's own inner appearance is like a sputtering butter lamp that is about to go out. It appears as though the wind does not stir it, and it blazes brightly. At this juncture, one becomes unable to move one's body. After that, the white appearance,

216. Gen Namgyal Chöphel suggests that "not observed" in this context could have three levels of meaning:

1. Emptiness is the *nonobservation* of—that is, the negation of—inherent existence.
2. Emptiness is *not observed*—that is, not comprehended—by consciousnesses holding to extremes (of inherent existence or complete nothingness).
3. The nāda is *not observed*—that is, no longer exists—because it has dissolved into emptiness.

Meditation/Visualization of the Eight Stages of Dissolution at Death

Stage 1

The whole universe, including the Vajrabhairavas and their mandalas, melts into light and dissolve into Yamantaka.

Earth element dissolves into water element.

Stage 2

The outer Vajrabhairava dissolves into the syllable HUM at the heart level.

Water element dissolves into fire element.

Stage 3

The lower part (shabkyu) of the syllable HUM dissolves into the HAM part of the HUM.

Fire element dissolves into consciousness.

Stage 4

The HA part (including the crescent, drop, and nada) of the syllable HUM dissolves into the head of the HA.

Wind element dissolves into consciousness.

Stage 5

The head of the HA dissolves into the crescent (and drop and nada).

Inner sign: Clear White Appearance.

Stage 6

The cresent dissolves into the drop (and nada).

Inner sign: Radiant Red Increase.

Stage 7

The drop dissolves into the nada.

Inner sign: Black Near-Attainment.

Stage 8

The nada dissolves into emptiness.

Clear Light.

This image displays an example using Vajrabhairava; other deities would use different forms and syllables.

red increase, and black near-attainment will arise. First, as appearances dissolve, there is a vacuous white appearance like a spotless autumn sky pervaded by moonlight. [137] Next is the red increase: that white appearance vanishes and a blank redness dawns, like a spotless autumn sky pervaded by sunlight. After that is the black near-attainment: a vacuous blackness arises, like at dusk when a thick gloom descends. The near-attainment has two stages; during the former stage, that black appearance shows itself, and during the latter stage, one loses one's memory and there is no appearance at all. During this latter stage of the near-attainment, the clear light that is the basis appears. This is the clear light that arises at the time of death for an ordinary person. That clear light is said to be free of the three polluting faults. Above we discussed how the previous stages appear as though (1) pervaded by moonlight, (2) pervaded by sunlight, (3) pervaded by the thick gloom of dusk, and so forth. Here, without any of those faults, except for a vacuity that is like the self-radiance of the sky at dawn, there is no quality of color and so forth. Moreover, saying, "The mind is the root of all, saṃsāra and nirvāṇa," refers to this clear light.[217]

Practicing mantra, one employs a method to make that clear light manifest. By meditating on the basis clear light, also called the "mother clear light," [138] if one is able to mix it with the "son clear light,"[218] one can turn it into a path and achieve liberation and the state of all-knowing. As such, it is said to be the root of attaining nirvāṇa. If one does not support this clear light with skillful means and instead slips into ordinariness, through the force of that one is born into saṃsāra, so it is also the root of saṃsāra.

In that way, if you want to meditate on emptiness, you meditate on emptiness before deity yoga. During that meditation, the entire world and the beings therein gradually condense and dissolve into your body. When things are dissolving in this way, it appears to your imagination that earth has dis-

217. An astute student once questioned Rinpoché on the meaning of the clear light being "the basis of saṃsāra and nirvāṇa": does this mean that it is the *substantial cause* of these two states?

Rinpoché replied that the clear light is the basis in the sense that by not recognizing it, one wanders in saṃsāra, while by apprehending it for what it is and using it to meditate on emptiness, one achieves nirvāṇa. It is not that the clear light is literally the substantial cause of saṃsāra and nirvāṇa.

218. The mother clear light is the clear light mind that manifests naturally at the time of death. The son clear light is the clear light one manifests in order to meditate on emptiness. To mix the two means that having practiced during one's lifetime, then at the time of death one uses the naturally manifesting clear light to meditate on emptiness.

solved into water. As a sign of earth dissolving into water, you think, "The mirage-like sign has appeared," and then you should think, "The appearance of smoke is about to arise."

If you are meditating on a *hūṃ* syllable at your heart, then imagine that your body gradually dissolves from the top and bottom into the *hūṃ* at your heart. During that, you should think, "The appearance of smoke, the sign of water dissolving into fire, has arisen. The appearance of the mirage has already gone. Next, the appearance of fireflies is about to arise."

After that, imagine the *zhab-kyu* of the *hūṃ* dissolves into the *ha*. During that dissolution, think, "The appearance of fireflies, the sign of fire dissolving into wind, has arisen. The appearance of smoke has already gone. At the end of this, the appearance of a sputtering butter lamp is about to arise." [139]

The *ha* dissolves into its head. As it dissolves, imagine, "The appearance of a sputtering butter lamp has arisen. The appearance of fireflies appearance has already passed. Now the appearance of a sputtering butter lamp is here, and afterward the white appearance is about to arise."

Usually *hūṃ* does not have a crescent moon on top of it, but here imagine that it does. Above that is a drop or a circle, and above that is a nāda with three twists. When the head of the *ha* dissolves into the crescent moon, imagine that the white appearance arises. Think, "The appearance of a sputtering butter lamp has gone. Next the red increase is about to appear." As I explained above, the white appearance is like a vacuity pervaded by moonlight that appears at the basis—that is, for ordinary people when they die. When you are meditating, imagine that vacuity to be also the vacuity empty of inherent existence. At that time you must remember emptiness. You don't think it's the emptiness that is complete nothingness but rather the emptiness that is empty of true existence. Imagine, "After this, the red increase will appear."

After that, the crescent moon dissolves into the drop. As the crescent moon dissolves into the drop, imagine that the red increase is appearing. [140] That is a red vacuity, and also it is the vacuity of inherent existence. Imagine, "Next, the black near-attainment will appear."

The drop dissolves into the nāda. As the drop dissolves into the nāda, think, "The black near-attainment is arising. The red increase has already gone. After this, the clear light will appear." Also think, "When the clear light appears, I will not fall into ordinariness. I will recognize it and will be able to transform it into the nature of a mind that realizes emptiness."

And when the clear light does appear, you should think, "This is the actual wisdom truth body." That wisdom truth body possesses four special qualities: (1) the appearance factor of that mind is a vacuity, (2) the ascertainment factor is the ascertainment of lack of inherent existence, and (3) the mind has become the nature of clear light great bliss, so (4) its experienced object is said to be bliss. You meditate by applying the pride that thinks, "This is the actual wisdom truth body, and it is who I really am." That is called "meditation taking death into the path as the wisdom truth body." During the generation stage you must meditate on taking death into the path as the wisdom truth body. By meditating on that, you ripen roots of virtue to have the actual clear light appear during the completion stage. Through the force of meditating and having pierced the vital points of the vajra body during the completion stage, all appearances appear as before, so the basis and the path are said to have a concordant aspect. [141] Meditating on emptiness before the self-generation is meditating on taking death into the path as the wisdom truth body, and of the two collections of merit and wisdom that you must accumulate to become Buddha, it becomes an accumulation of the collection of wisdom.

As for the need for purifying one's aggregates into emptiness of inherent existence: afterward when one places one's mind in the pride of the deity, it is easier to stop adherence to ordinary appearances and appear purified as a deity. Having purified into emptiness, imagine that the clear light appears, and place your mind in the pride of thinking, "This is the actual wisdom truth body." For most ordinary people, when they die they abide in the clear light for about three days. At the end of that, the previous order of dissolution reverses, and the appearances come in reverse order without getting mixed up: the black near-attainment appears, then the red increase, then the white appearance. In your imagination, you think, "I have achieved the actual wisdom truth body."

Explanation of Taking the Bardo into the Path as the Complete Enjoyment Body

As for arising as the complete enjoyment body: in a corner of your mind, impel yourself, thinking, "If I remain for a long time in the space of the wisdom truth body, there will not be vast benefit for sentient beings, because that wisdom truth body is only the object of experience of other buddhas; others cannot directly meet it. Therefore, I will arise as the form body, which achieves the welfare of others by appearing to all sentient beings.[219] [142] At the time of the basis, if ordinary people arise from the clear light, they encounter the black near-attainment. Simultaneous with that, they must actualize the bardo. In the imagination of the yogi, having recognized taking death into the path as the wisdom truth body, one placed the mind in pride of thinking, "This is the actual wisdom truth body." After that, while in equipoise on the clear light, wind stirs and the near-attainment appears. At the same time, as a substitute for the bardo that appears for ordinary people at the basis, imagine that one directly arises as the very subtle body—the complete enjoyment body. Think, "This is the actual complete enjoyment body." If when meditating on taking the three bodies into the path, the deity one is meditating on is, for instance, Guhyasamāja, then one generates oneself as the primal protector.[220] If it is Vajrabhairava, one generates as the causal vajra holder, the youthful Mañjuśrī. If Vajrayoginī, one meditates on the syllable *bam*, if Cakrasaṃvara, a nāda, and so forth. These are "taking the bardo into the path as the complete enjoyment body." When meditating on the *bam* syllable, meditate that it is in nature the complete enjoyment body and in aspect the syllable *bam*. One must place one's mind in the pride of thinking, "This is the actual complete enjoyment body. It is who I really am." That is called "taking the bardo into the path as the complete enjoyment body," and it is like a substitute for the establishment of the bardo that arises for ordinary people. At the basis, for ordinary people, that bardo being [143] takes birth in a womb, and completely transforms into a physical body, so that is what is to be purified. The purifier of that has a similar aspect to it: during the generation stage, simultaneous with achieving the near-attainment, one manifests in the aspect of a very subtle body, the complete enjoyment body, and thinks it is the actual complete enjoyment body.

219. The form body (Skt. *rūpakāya*; Tib. *gzugs sku*) includes both the complete enjoyment body and the emanation body.

220. In the context of the visualization of Guhyasamāja, one first generates oneself in the form of the primal protector (Tib. *dang po'i mgon po*), who is Guhyasamāja appearing in a white-colored, peaceful form. Some schools take the meaning of "primal" to imply that a sentient being is, in essence, a buddha and has been so since beginningless time. Geshé Ngawang Thokmé points out that for the Geluk school, such an interpretation is unacceptable, and so an alternate way to understand "primal" is that when one becomes a buddha, one initially arises as the complete enjoyment body, so this is the primal, or first, buddha.

Taking Rebirth into the Path as the Emanation Body

The complete enjoyment body, moreover, can only be perceived by those who have achieved the Mahāyāna ārya stage, so it is unable to achieve vast benefit for sentient beings. For that reason, one impels oneself with the thought "I will arise in a body that all trainees, both advanced and beginner, can perceive." Out of that thought arises the complete supported deities and supporting maṇḍala. One places one's mind in the pride of thinking, "This is the actual resultant time emanation body." This is called "taking birth into the path as the emanation body." If you habituate yourself well in this way, then at the time of death such signs of having meditated will appear. As you pass through the stages of dissolution at the time of death, you will be able to think, "Now it is that stage. I will recognize the subsequent stages as they arise." Also, if you think, "I will not allow that clear light to slip into ordinariness; I will be able to transform it into the path," then even if you are unable to transform it directly, there will be great benefit. If you meditate extensively on these stages of dissolution, then when earth dissolves into water, you imagine that the earth element, form aggregate, eye sense power (a form that is included in your continuum),[221] [144] and the basis-time mirror-like wisdom all dissolve. Having meditated in this way, then gradually the twenty-five stages of gross dissolution[222] will arise. If you can gain an understanding of these stages of dissolution, it is said that you will not be born in the unfortunate migrations.

This mahāmudrā has both sūtra-system and mantra-system mahāmudrā. Of these, the mantra system of mahāmudrā, beyond a few brief verses, is not explained extensively in the mahāmudrā root text that I am explaining. As for the mahāmudrā exalted wisdom in the mantra context: (1) the exalted wisdom of connate great bliss that arises from the winds having entered,

221. Buddhist philosophy recognizes five sense powers in the continuum of a person. These are different than the gross sense powers, such as the eyes and ears. Rather, they are a subtle kind of form that is intertwined with the mind, and at the time of death these sense powers dissolve into the subtle mind, are carried with it, and remanifest in the bardo state.

222. The "twenty-five stages of dissolution" actually refers to the eight stages of dissolution at the time of death, during which twenty-five gross objects gradually dissolve: the five aggregates, the five basic wisdoms, the four constituents, the six sense sources, and the five objects of these senses. For a clear explanation of this process, see Lati Rinbochay and Hopkins 1979, especially the table on pages 33–34 of that book.

abided, and dissolved into the central channel and which is the example clear light that realizes emptiness by means of a meaning-generality,[223] as well as (2) the meaning clear light that directly realizes emptiness, is called "mahāmudrā" in this context of mantra-system mahāmudrā.[224] In order to generate in your continuum the exalted wisdom of connate great bliss that arises from piercing the vital points of the vajra body and causing the winds to enter, abide, and dissolve into the central channel, first, as a method for causing the winds to enter the central channel, you must take the isolation of body and isolation of speech as preliminaries. And as a means of priming yourself to generate such a realization, in order to ripen roots of virtue [145] you must meditate on taking the three bodies into the path during the generation stage.

Explanation of the Five Stages

The five stages are (1) isolation of body; (2) isolation of speech and isolation of mind, which together are called "the stage of observing the mind"; (3) illusory body; (4) meaning clear light; and (5) unification.[225] On the basis of practicing these, ultimately one will be able to achieve the unification of no more learning. In order to generate the connate bliss on the basis of the winds entering, abiding, and dissolving in the central channel, you must understand the properties of the vajra body.

Explanation of the Three Channels and Four Channel Wheels

Many coarse and subtle attributes of the vajra body are described, but here the most important ones are the three channels and four channel wheels. In your body, in the center of the left and right sides, and on the back side if you divide by front and back, is the central channel, blue on the outside and red on the inside, about the thickness of a wheat straw. On the right and left sides

223. A meaning-generality (Skt. *arthasāmānya*; Tib. *don spyi*) is a generic image that appears to thought consciousness through the force of bringing an object to mind. Unlike a directly appearing object, it lacks specific qualities, because it is only as detailed as the thinker can imagine it. See also the introduction.

224. For an explanation of the difference between the example and meaning clear lights, see introduction.

225. See note 212.

of this are two secondary channels, the red *roma* on the right and the white *kyangma* on the left. At the channel wheel at the navel, there is a knot where the right channel twists around behind both the central channel and the left channel, and the left channel also twists around behind. [146] Also at the level of the heart, the right channel wraps around thrice, and the left channel wraps around thrice—that is, the right channel twists once, then the left one, then again the right, the left, and finally again the right and then the left channel twists around. This is counted as three knots. At the channel wheel at the throat, there is said to be one knot—one twist for each, the right and left channels. At the channel wheel at the crown, the right and left channels each wrap around, but when you combine the two, it is counted as one knot.

Although I don't need to explain in detail the manner in which the secondary channels branch out, at the heart where there are eight secondary channels, the root of these eight secondary channels penetrates into the central channel in four places, from which four secondary channels branch out. Each of these again branches into two, so there are said to be eight secondary channels at the heart. At the crown, there are thirty-two secondary channels, and at the throat, sixteen. The secondary channels at the crown are as though facing downward, and those at the throat are as though facing upward, signifying the unification of method and wisdom. The sixty-four secondary channels at the navel face upward, and the eight at the heart face downward, again signifying method and wisdom. The uppermost tip of the central channel is called the *min tsam*.[226] It is at the place where peaceful deities have a tuft of hair and where wrathful deities have a wisdom eye. [147] The bottommost tip reaches the tip of the sexual organ. The uppermost tips of the right and left channels penetrate into the nostrils.

When meditating, before you visualize the channels you must meditate on the hollow interior. Initially you meditate on yourself in the aspect of a particular deity. Having purified the inside of the deity's body into emptiness, it is good if you can imagine light rays filling that emptiness and from that space visualize the channels. Since the right and left channels continuously abide as though constricting the central channel, wind flows through the right and left channels but is unable to flow in the central channel. The wind that flows through the right and left channels is the wind of karma for an ordinary person and is the cause of birth in saṃsāra, so we need to be able to gather that wind inside the central channel.

226. Skt. *bhrūmadhya*; Tib. *smin mtshams*. This is the spot between the eyebrows.

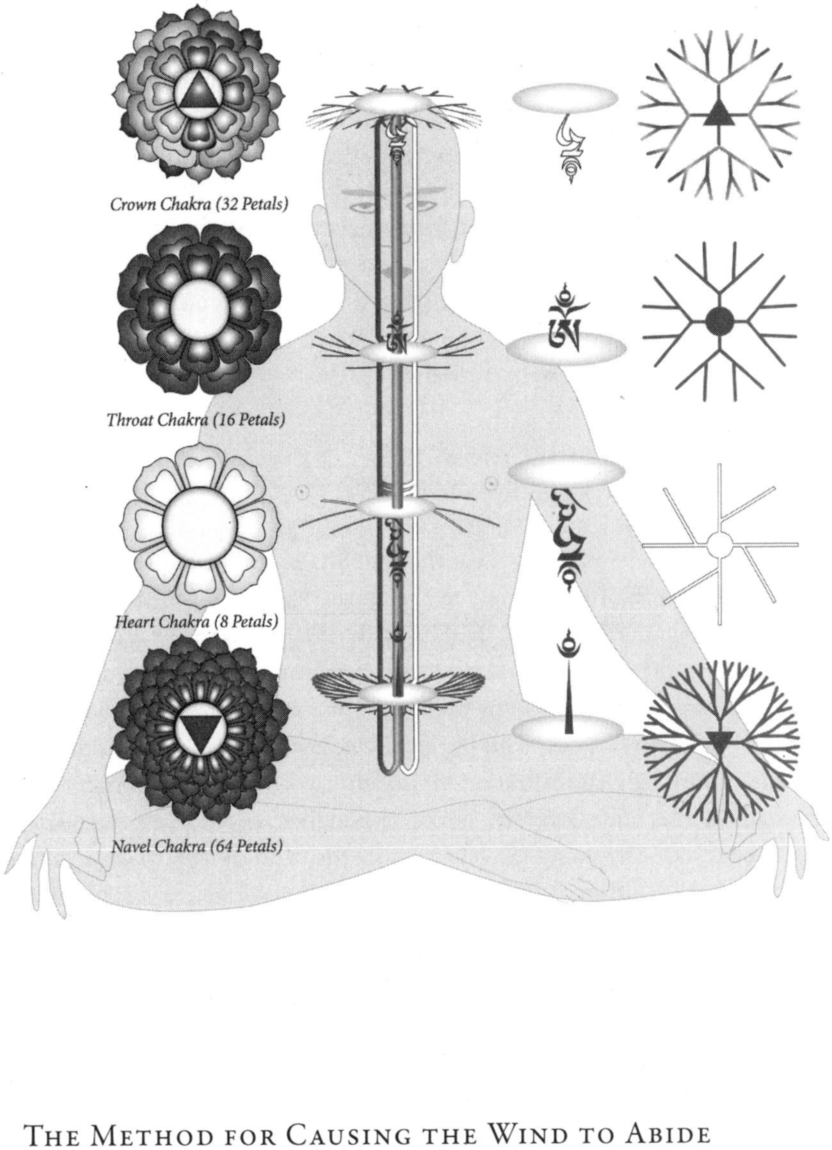

The Method for Causing the Wind to Abide in the Central Channel

Although we mainly need to cause the winds to enter, abide, and dissolve in the indestructible drop at the center of the mantra wheel at the heart, if right away we meditate observing the heart, there is a danger that we will be unable to gather the winds and that "heart wind"—that is, a disorder of the heart energy—will arise.[227] For that reason, initially we should meditate observing another vital point of the body. If our ultimate goal is to make effort at a method for generating realizations of the completion stage, first we need a stable realization of the generation stage. Take as an illustration first meditating on isolation of body. [148] Before that, we have to recite the hundred-syllable mantra in conjunction with the meditation recitation of Vajrasattva. We then meditate on guru yoga, visualize the channels of the body, and purify them.

Request to the lama, making the request "Please bless me to generate an unmistaken realization of the completion stage." If your guru yoga practice is Lama Chöpa, request with this verse:

> Requested thence, my lama supreme:
> to bless, with joy alight on my crown.[228]

If it is the six-session guru yoga, then meditate up until "alights on my crown, *samāja*."[229] Then request to the lama, "Please bless me to generate in my continuum the realization of isolation of body." Initially visualize the channels, and then request that the channels may appear clearly and that blockages in the channels and winds may not arise. After that, if you meditate on isolation of body from the space of clear appearance of yourself as the deity, it is said that realizations of isolation of body will arise. After that, the lama abides on your crown, or the lama abides at your heart, according to some texts. Wherever you visualize him, the main thing is to make your mind inseparable from the lama yidam and then generate the visualization of your mind entering into either a drop, a *hūṃ* syllable, or something like that. [149] Initially cause the *hūṃ* syllable to descend either to the channel wheel at the navel or to the tip of the jewel [sexual organ] at the secret place. If you meditate in that way, then the winds will gather wherever you place your visualization. Since the wind and mind exist together and travel together, then wherever you place your mind, the wind will gather there.

227. Tib. *snying rlung*. This condition can be severe, leading to physical and psychological problems. Some practitioners have destabilized their minds, resulting in hallucinations and psychosis. Needless to say, readers are prudent to take Rinpoché's warnings seriously and proceed carefully under the guidance of a qualified teacher.

228. *Lama Chöpa*, v. 115.

229. *Six-Session Guru Yoga*, v. B-1. The Sanskrit term *samāja* literally means "union," "meeting," or "assembly," but in this context it implies "to become inseparable."

If you place your observation as explained above, it will be easy to gather the winds. Imagine that rays of light emanate from your heart or from the syllable there and purify the faults of the whole world and its beings. All worlds, in the form of celestial palaces, and all beings, in the form of gods and goddesses, melt into light. All worlds melt into light and dissolve into the beings, and those beings also dissolve into your body. You also melt into light from top and bottom, and then imagine dissolving into the drop. If you do so, the winds will condense inside. If the winds merely enter into the central channel but are unable to abide there, it won't be of benefit, so you must cause them to abide. By meditating again and again on the winds inside the central channel, you will cause them to abide there.

The Sign of the Winds Abiding in the Central Channel

What kinds of signs arise when the winds abide in the central channel? The wind of the nostrils stops moving—that is, air ceases to flow through the nostrils. When doing concentration meditation, even when subtle laxity accrues, the wind of the nostrils ceases to flow. When wind ceases to flow through the nostrils *and* the abdomen is not moving, [150] that is a sign that the wind is abiding in the central channel. After that, one must dissolve the winds in the central channel, so as for the sign of that: as I explained above in the context of taking death into the path as the wisdom truth body, there are the signs of earth dissolving into water and so forth. The signs like a mirage, like smoke, like fireflies, like a sputtering butter lamp, the white appearance, red increase, and black near-attainment arise successively. When you meditate in this way, although the wind enters, abides, and dissolves in the central channel at channel wheels other than the heart, the signs of it dissolving exactly like at the stages of death do not arise. However, a simulacrum of that arises, so at that time you make effort to recognize the signs. First the white appearance arises, followed by the red increase, black near-attainment, and finally the clear light.

Before meditating on the completion stage, you must apply yourself to gain an understanding of emptiness, because when the clear light appears, that clear light appears as an utter vacuity called "arising like the experience," which is like the direct realization of emptiness. Rather than just using that vacuity for no purpose, you should be able to meditate by combining it with the emptiness that is empty of inherent existence. When you meditate like that, you can meditate on the tip of the secret organ or at the navel. By meditating in that way, the winds will gather there. [151] Through the power of that gathering, the *tummo* fire will ignite at the navel. The tummo will generate heat, which will melt the bodhicitta at the crown. The bodhicitta will descend from the crown to the throat, giving rise to the wisdom of joy. By descending to the heart, the supreme wisdom of joy will arise, when it reaches the navel, special joy will arise, and when it reaches the tip of the secret place, connate joy will arise. The bodhicitta gradually descends, and if one is equally familiar with both the wind and with joy, the four joys and four empties will arise.[230] When the connate joy arises, everything will appear as empty clear light. Thus, that appearance, from the point of view of empty appearing, is the appearance of everything as empty clear light, and from the point of view of experiencing bliss, is connate bliss. It is called "the primordial clear light of connate great bliss," or, in the context of mantra, it is what we call "mahāmudrā."

Explanation of the Nine Rounds of Mixing

By first meditating on that primordial connate clear light, when you combine it with the view, it becomes the nature of a mind that realizes emptiness by means of a meaning-generality. That is called the "example clear light." In order for the example clear light to arise, you need to pierce the vital points at the heart. When you place your observation on the secret place and so forth and the clear lights appears, [152] although you are unable to cause the example clear light of the final stage of isolation of mind to appear, a simulacrum of that will appear. When that simulacrum becomes manifest, you mix it with the wisdom truth body. That is called (1) "mixing the clear light with the wisdom truth body": you place your mind in the pride of having actually attained the wisdom truth body and realize emptiness with the connate bliss. When you arise from the equipoise, along with the reverse process of the near-attainment appearing, from your perspective you arise as the complete enjoyment body. That is called (2) "mixing with the complete enjoyment body." Then you generate the conviction in your mind that you are arising as the emanation body and that you are again entering into your

230. For explanations of tummo, bodhicitta, the four joys, and the four empties, see Ngülchu Dharmabhadra and the First Paṇchen Lama 2014, and also the glossary in this present book.

old aggregates. That is called (3) "mixing with the emanation body." When you are not sleeping, you meditate on these three rounds of mixing during the waking state.

When you get a good and stable meditation on that, then even while sleeping, things will appear as before [the clear light and so on], and so you can (4) mix deep sleep with the wisdom truth body. When sleep gets lighter and you are dreaming, you arise in a subtle dream body and (5) mix the dream state with the complete enjoyment body. When you awake, you (6) mix waking with the emanation body. These are the three rounds of mixing during sleep.

If you get a good meditation on those three, then at the time of death, the winds will condense through the force of karma. As the winds condense, then when all the appearances arise similar to those when you meditated before, [153] you will recognize them. Along with all the stages of dissolution appearing just as at the stages of death, you combined them with the stages of emptiness. When the actual clear light of death appears through the power of karma, you mix it with the clear light of the path that you meditated on before in the waking state and generate it in the nature of a mind realizing emptiness. That is called (7) "mixing death with the wisdom truth body." If you get a good mixing of death with the wisdom truth body, then just as the bardo is established, without even a slight volition the bardo will arise as the complete enjoyment body. That is called (8) "mixing the bardo with the complete enjoyment body." That subtle body itself that has arisen in the nature of the complete enjoyment body will then transform into a gross body that is able to appear to common trainees. That is called (9) "mixing birth with the emanation body." The nine rounds of mixing are thus: three rounds of mixing during the waking state, three rounds during sleep, and three at the time of death. If you get a good practice of those, then on that basis you will be able to actualize buddhahood.

In order to gather the winds in the central channel, first you must apply yourself to being able to cause them to enter the central channel by piercing the vital points at a different place from the heart [either the navel or the secret region]. In order for them to enter at the heart, you need to release the channel knots at the heart. And to release those, you need to meditate on the vajra recitation of the isolation of speech.

[154] The Manner of Meditating on the Vajra Recitation that Releases the Channel Knots

What we call the "vajra recitation" is a recitation of the vajras of the three syllables [*oṃ āḥ hūṃ*]. At the center of the channel wheel of the heart, at the indestructible drop, is a *hūṃ*, a drop, or a seed, and so on—one meditates on whatever is appropriate to meditate on, based on the context. At that time, when the wind is going out, the tone of the wind is the sound of a *hūṃ*. It is not like listening to a *hūṃ* sound coming from somewhere else. Rather, the sound of one's own breath when one exhales is the sound of *hūṃ*, and when one inhales inward, the sound of the breath takes on the tone of an *oṃ* sound. Imagine that when it again goes out from that drop, it goes out from the heart in the manner of a *hūṃ* sound, and when it comes back, it comes as the tone of *oṃ*. Since ordinary beings like us don't have anything except wind going out and coming back in, we need to observe that especially and actualize an abiding [in one place, rather than flowing in and out]. When abiding, imagine that it abides in the tone of *ah*. By observing like that again and again at the crown, navel, or secret place, we will clear out the blockages in the central channel. That is called "speech isolation vajra recitation." It is a part of the isolation of speech; that is, it is included in the isolation of speech.

After you have purified the central channel in that way, you place your observation at the heart, and, in a relaxed manner, gradually condense the winds inward. [155] When you have condensed them, then as I explained before, the four empties will arise, and if you condense the winds along with those four, the wisdom of the four joys will arise. The wisdom which is the fourth joy—connate joy—will arise as one nature with but a different isolate from the clear light that is the emptiness of everything.[231] At that time, one realizes emptiness by means of a meaning-generality. If you have generated the final stage isolation of mind that arises from causing the winds to enter,

231. "One nature but different isolate" means that two things do not appear separately to direct perception and therefore are substantially one entity, but they can be conceptually separated by thought consciousness. For example, one man may be both his mother's son and his wife's husband. When one looks at him, one only sees one person, but conceptually one can consider him through two distinct frameworks. Likewise the subtlest wind and mind are substantially one entity, but we can conceive of them, or talk about them, from two different perspectives.

abide, and dissolve in the heart, just as at the stages of death, then it pervades [that is, is definite] that you will achieve buddhahood in this life.

The Benefits of the Illusory Body and an Introduction to Unification

When one arises from such an equipoise on clear light, then as I explained previously, along with the reverse process appearance of the near-attainment, one arises as the impure illusory holy body. Since the very subtle wind and mind are of one nature but different isolates, it is an illusory holy body that arises on the basis of wind as a substantial cause and mind as a cooperative condition. It appears as though without nature, like a rainbow in the sky. It appears with all limbs complete—in the aspects of the complete supporting and supported maṇḍala, as when one meditated on the yidam deity. In the end, one will be able to arise directly as the holy body of whatever deity one meditated upon. Until that time, one meditates in the manner of faith of conviction. [156] After that, one arises as the illusory holy body. Although according to the sūtra system, one must accumulate the collections of merit and wisdom for three countless great eons before becoming a buddha, if one achieves the illusory body according to the mantra system, then it becomes a substitute for the collections of three countless great eons. To put it another way, achieving the illusory body is similar to having accumulated the collections of three countless great eons, so we say, "By relying on mantra, the path is swifter." The swift path of mantra is like that.

You might want to know "What does one do to accomplish such an illusory body, and what kind of thing is this 'illusory body'?" Even by just gaining a good understanding that "first one causes the winds to enter, abide, and dissolve in the central channel. When, from that, one actualizes a holy body that is actualized merely from wind and mind, that is called 'illusory body,'" it is said that one thereby achieves benefits similar to having completed the generation stage. The practitioner of illusory body also arises from the illusory body and again enters into the old aggregates, and goes about the activities of the postmeditation period. Having gone about those activities, again and again he enters into equipoise on the clear light. By doing that, when the fourth stage—the meaning clear light—arises, he directly realizes emptiness. In the space of that realization, there is absolutely no dualistic appearance of conventional appearances and so forth; [157] in emptiness everything becomes one taste, like water poured into water.[232] This clear light that directly realizes emptiness is called "fourth stage, the meaning clear light." When one enters into equipoise on the meaning clear light, not only does one abandon grasping at the self of persons, but also the impure illusory holy body one had before dissolves by itself, along with its similar continuum. When one arises from that meaning clear light, one arises as the pure illusory holy body—a pure illusory holy body which is different from the impure illusory holy body. The meaning clear light acts as the direct antidote to the afflictive obscurations.[233] If one then arises as an illusory holy body, because one has abandoned or purified afflictive obscurations, that illusory holy body is called the "pure illusory holy body." From that time on, it does not change; one has gained the deathless vajra holy body, so the continuum of that holy body cannot be severed. When such a practitioner of the pure illusory body arises as that pure illusory holy body, although she has arisen from the clear light, when she again enters into equipoise on the clear light, she achieves the main unification, called "realizational union."

When one achieves the learner's unification, which is the fifth stage, one has not yet abandoned all the knowledge obscurations; they are left over. In order to abandon the knowledge obscurations, that practitioner of unification meditates on the rest of the paths, and by accumulating the collections of merit and wisdom [158] gains the ability to abandon all knowledge obscurations without exception. The exalted wisdom into which one enters in equipoise after attaining that ability is called the "meaning clear light of the end of learning." That is the end of the learner's path and is also the

232. The analogy of water poured into water can have three distinct meanings in this context: (1) Within the direct perception of emptiness, there is no appearance of conventional objects, only emptiness. (2) The object—emptiness—and the mind realizing it are experienced as nondual, without any filter of a meaning-generality between them. (3) Within the realization of emptiness, all conventional objects are understood to be of one taste in emptiness.

233. The obscurations that one must abandon to achieve buddhahood are twofold: the afflictive obscurations and the knowledge obscurations. The afflictive obscurations include afflictive mental states like anger and attachment, and also the apprehension of true existence that lies at their root. The knowledge obscurations are the imprints left over by these afflictions. One who has abandoned the afflictive obscurations no longer experiences confusion or pain but is still obscured from full omniscience until abandoning the knowledge obscurations. This abandoning of the afflictive obscurations at the moment of directly perceiving emptiness is a unique feature of the tantric path. According to the sūtra path, one does not abandon these until reaching the eighth bodhisattva ground, many lifetimes after the initial direct perception of emptiness.

direct antidote to the knowledge obscurations. If one achieves the path of release that is freed from knowledge obscurations and is induced by that direct antidote, one has achieved the exalted wisdom that knows all aspects as well as the state of a buddha. At that time, according the sūtra system one achieves the complete enjoyment body endowed with the five certainties,[234] and according to the mantra system, the state endowed with the seven-branched union.[235]

On the basis of ascertaining those stages, one must meditate on mantra-system mahāmudrā and understand the manner of traversing the paths. Since in the commentaries there are no more than brief explanations of this mahāmudrā for mantra, I have explained it extensively. All the other points are clear in the two commentaries that have come from Tibet,[236] so there is no need to explain extensively beyond just that.

234. These are the five certainties that characterize the complete enjoyment body:

1. Certainty of abode: It abides only in Akaniṣṭha (Tib. *'Og min*), a pure realm situated in the fourth level of the form realm.
2. Certainty of holy body: It is adorned with the thirty-two major marks and eighty minor signs.
3. Certainty of retinue: The surrounding retinue of disciples is comprised entirely of ārya bodhisattvas.
4. Certainty of Dharma: It only teaches Mahāyāna Dharma.
5. Certainty of time: It will continue to exist until all beings have been liberated from saṃsāra.

However, in the context of tantric practice, one achieves this body in the desire realm, and so it does not have the certainty of abode.

235. The seven branches of union are

1. complete enjoyment body: having all the major and minor marks of a Buddha,
2. embracing: union of father and mother deities,
3. great bliss: manifesting a subtle bliss consciousness,
4. lack of inherent existence: a bliss consciousness realizing emptiness in a nondual manner,
5. completely filled with compassion: always having great compassion for sentient beings,
6. uninterrupted continuity: not abiding in cyclic existence, and
7. noncessation: abiding until cyclic existence is emptied.

The Tibetan term *kha sbyor* (translated as "union") literally means "to kiss" ("to join mouths"), though in this context it is a metaphor for the state of union.

236. The two commentaries to which Rinpoché refers here are Paṇchen Losang Chökyi Gyaltsen's autocommentary (to the text explained here), entitled *The Lamp That Further Clarifies*, and Ngülchu Dharmabhadra's notes to that text, entitled *Dispelling All Illusions*. See note 288.

ELEVEN

Introducing Sūtra-System Mahāmudrā

IN THAT CASE, what exactly is this mahāmudrā of the sūtra system? The text continues:

> **The first's long, mid-, short's teaching[237] direct**
> **to meditate on emptiness.**
> **Nāgārjuna, best noble, said,**
> **"No liberation path but this."[238]**
>
> **In line with his intention, here**
> **on mahāmudrā I'll explain.**
> **Like lineage lama's speech, I'll tell**
> [159] **the way to introduce the mind.**

Usually we speak of two subject matters of the extensive, middling, and condensed mothers[239]: the explicit teaching—the stages of meditation on emptiness—and the hidden meaning—the stages of realization. Of these two, the manner of meditating on emptiness is the manner of meditation

237. "Long, mid-, short's teaching" refers to the extensive, middling, and condensed perfection of wisdom sūtras, the primary texts that most Tibetan schools rely upon for their exposition of the Buddha's final thought on emptiness. Although there is some disagreement as to which actual sūtras are the extensive, middling, and condensed, most Geluk scholars posit the *Perfection of Wisdom in One Hundred Thousand Verses* as the extensive, *Perfection of Wisdom in Twenty-Five Thousand Verses* as the middling, and *Perfection of Wisdom in Eight Thousand Verses* as the condensed. For an English translation of the *Perfection of Wisdom in Eighteen Thousand Verses*, see Conze 1975.

238. In his liturgical poem "Praise to the One Gone Beyond the World" (Skt. *Lokātītastava*; Tib. *'Jig rten las 'das par bstod pa*), Nāgārjuna wrote,

> "Without realizing signlessness,
> no liberation comes," you [Buddha] said.

239. The perfection of wisdom sutras are often called "mothers" because meditating on their central topic, emptiness, gives birth to realization.

of sūtra-system mahāmudrā. Without meditating on the mind that realizes emptiness, it is impossible to attain liberation. The protector Nāgārjuna said, "In order to attain liberation, one must generate the mind that realizes emptiness." As for the need to take the protector Nāgārjuna as a valid authority when explaining the meaning of emptiness: the Blessed One himself prophesied, "The protector Nāgārjuna will clarify the freedom from the two extremes of permanence and annihilation."[240] Paṇchen Losang Chökyi Gyaltsen says that here he will explain the manner of meditating on emptiness in accordance with the intention of the supreme Ārya Nāgārjuna. That is, he will first explain the meditation on the mahāmudrā commentary and then the introduction to the nature of the mind and so forth in accordance with the personal instruction of his lama Khedrup Sangyé Yeshé. As for the view of the object—emptiness—there is nothing extra in the context of mantra over and above what the protector Nāgārjuna explained in his commentaries on the thought of the extensive, middling, and condensed mothers. [160] In terms of delineating the object—emptiness—since there is nothing extra in mantra that is not in sūtra, then in terms of the object (emptiness) there is no difference. However, in terms of the *object-possessor*, we come upon a difference. In the sūtra system, the mind that realizes emptiness is a gross consciousness realizing emptiness; there is no talk in sūtra of a very subtle wind and mind or a primordial mind. As I explained before in the context of mantra, there is a difference in terms of what object-possessor is combined with realizing emptiness. Having gathered all the winds in the central channel, one stops the gross winds and manifests the subtle, primor-

240. This prophecy is found in the *Descent in Laṅkā Sūtra* (Skt. *Laṅkāvatārasūtra*; Tib. *'Phags pa lang kar gshegs pa'i theg pa chen po'i mdo*), 165b5–6. Many of Nāgārjuna's texts have been translated into English, along with commentaries. Nāgārjuna's central philosophical works, called by Tibetans the sixfold collection of reasoning, include (1) *Root Wisdom of the Middle Way* (Skt. *Mūlamadhyamakakārikā*; Tib. *Dbu ma'i rtsa ba shes rab*; there are many translations of this text in English—for example, see Jay L. Garfield 1995), (2) *Finely Woven* (Skt. *Vaidalyasūtra*; Tib. *Zhib mo rnam thag*; for an English translation with commentary, see Westerhoff 2018), (3) *Seventy Stanzas on Emptiness* (Skt. *Śūnyatāsaptatī*; Tib. *Stong nyid bdun cu pa*; for an English translation with commentary, see Komito 1987), (4) *Dispeller of Disputes* (Skt. *Vigrahavyāvartanī*; Tib. *Rtsod zlog*; for an English translation with commentary, see Westerhoff 2010), (5) *Sixty Stanzas on Reasoning* (Skt. *Yuktiṣaṣṭikā*; Tib. *Rigs pa drug cu pa*; for an English translation with commentary, see Loizzo 2007), and (6) *Precious Garland* (Skt. *Ratnāvalī*; Tib. *Rin chen phreng ba*). There are many translations of this last text in English. For example, see Hopkins 1998. These and other works of Nāgārjuna can also be found in Lindtner 2011.

dial mind. By observing emptiness with that mind, one realizes emptiness with the connate bliss, and so forth.

The protector Nāgārjuna explained the thought of the extensive, middling, and condensed perfection of wisdom sūtras, just as the Blessed One prophesied that he would explain the meaning of profound emptiness. There have been many followers of the protector Nāgārjuna, and they have had a variety of takes on his thought. However, among those followers, mainly one should follow after the glorious Candrakīrti.[241] The glorious Jowo Atiśa explained that while the glorious Candrakīrti was in fact a great bodhisattva who had attained the grounds, he intentionally took birth as a man in order to spread the view that the protector Nāgārjuna explained. Therefore, Atiśa said, we should follow after the glorious Candra's explanation of the thought of the protector Nāgārjuna.

[161] What should we do in order to realize emptiness? The protector Nāgārjuna was prophesied to explain the thought of the Victor, and if we follow after his disciple the glorious Candra we will gain an unmistaken realization of emptiness. If we follow after any system other than that, we will be unable to realize emptiness. Why must we call emptiness "mahāmudrā"? The Blessed One himself said in the *King of Concentrations Sūtra*, "All dharmas' nature is the seal [*mudrā*]." That is, all phenomena are as though sealed by emptiness, and since any phenomenon whatsoever is by nature empty, that emptiness seals it (*rgyas btab pa*). Or, to use the nonhonorific, it stamps it (*dam phrug btab pa*). All phenomena are empty of inherent existence, and since nothing has passed beyond that seal, we call emptiness a "seal" (Skt. *mudrā*; Tib. *phyag rgya*). Why do we need to call it "great" (Skt. *mahā*; Tib. *chen po*)? Because if you realize it you attain the liberation that is liberation from saṃsāra and you are freed of all adversity, we call it "great."

241. Candrakīrti (circa 600–650) composed four main texts on emptiness: (1) *Clear Words* (Skt. *Prasannapadā*; Tib. [*Dbu ma rtsa ba'i 'grel pa*] *tshig gsal ba*), a word commentary on Nāgārjuna's *Root Wisdom of the Middle Way* (for an English translation from the Sanskrit, see Sprung 1979), (2) *Supplement to the Middle Way* (Skt. *Madhyamakāvatāra*; Tib. *Dbu ma la 'jug pa*), a meaning commentary on that same text, along with its *Autocommentary* (for English translations of the root text, see Candrakīrti, translation by Ven. Fedor Stracke, and also Huntington 1989), (3) *Commentary on [Āryadeva's] Four Hundred Stanzas* (Skt. *Catuḥśaṭakavṛtti*; Tib. *Bzhi brgya pa'i 'grel pa*; for a partial translation, see Tillemans 1990, and also Lang 2003), and (4) *Commentary on Sixty Stanzas on Reasoning* (Skt. *Yuktiṣaṣṭikāvṛtti*; Tib. *Rigs pa drug cu pa'i 'grel pa*; for an English translation, see Loizzo 2007).

[162] The Way in Which All Mahāmudrās Are the Same in Being a Means of Attaining Unification

Connate communion, amulet box,
same taste, four letters, five-endowed,
the pacifier, object to cut,
and dzokchen, middle view, so forth—
applied to it, names many, but . . .

Great holy beings of old had many diverse ways of asserting that mahāmudrā. Some called it "connate communion," others "amulet box," "endowed with the five," "six rounds of equal taste," and "the four letters." Still others called it "the pacifier," "the object to be cut," "the great perfection" [dzokchen], "the view of the middle," and so forth.[242] The different Dharma lineages each had diverse ways of naming it. However, as for the actual meaning,

242. In his commentary on the Paṇchen Lama's text, Keutsang Losang Jamyang Mönlam explains the meaning of these various terms:

> In the system of Jé Gampopa [founder of the Dakpo Kagyü school], it is called "connate communion," because one unifies with the truth body of the mind, which is not adventitiously fabricated, but is connate since beginningless time [this is the system used today by the Karma Kagyü tradition]. In the system of Khyungpo [Khedrup Khyungpo Naljor, founder of the Shangpa Kagyü school], it is called "amulet box," because appearance and emptiness cannot be separated into upper and lower parts [an amulet box has two equal opposing sides that snap shut]. The main [inheritor of this system] is said to be the Shangpa [Kagyü] system of meditation on the clear light within the six yogas of Niguma. The "five-endowed" is the system of the Dakpo [Kagyü, and especially, according to the autocommentary, developed by Jikten Gönpo, founder of the Drigung subsect of the Dakpo Kagyü], who practice with the following five: (1) [generating] the awakening mind as the preliminary, (2) generating one's body as a deity, (3) [arousing] a mind of devotion [to the lama], (4) [being] without discursive thought [this stage being actual mahāmudrā], and (5) dedicating at the end. [Tsongkhapa himself received this five-endowed lineage from the Drigung abbot Chen Nga Chökyi Gyalpo.] The "six rounds of equal taste" is the system of Chöjé Gyaré [Tib. Chos rje rgya ras ye shes rdo rje, founder of the Drukpa Kagyü school, who discovered these teachings as a *terma* treasure hidden by Réchungpa Dorjé Drak]. This system takes into the path (1) conceptual thought, (2) afflictions, (3) sickness, (4) gods and demons, (5) suffering, and (6) death. [Maitrīpa's tradition of] the "four [Sanskrit] letters," *a-ma-na-si* [from Skt. *amanasikāra*; literally "not (*a*) fabricating/proliferating (*kāra*) with respect to/in the mind (*manasi*)" or "not in/toward the mind"], which are the [Sanskrit] equivalent of the Tibetan "not engaging the mind" [Tib. *yid la mi byed pa*], describes a way of sequentially

experi'nced yogis, masters of
both scripture, reason analyze:
the certain meaning falls to one thought.

He is saying that all the different ways of naming mahāmudrā in accordance with the individual assertions of holy lamas of old—the holy great beings of the Kagyü tradition stemming from Marpa, Milarepa, and [Nyammé] Dakpo [Lhajé, also known as Gampopa],[243] and also the Nyingma tradition of the old translation, and so forth—all of these, in short, are the same in being a means of attaining the state of mahāmudrā unification.

[163] Each of these teachers explained his thought in accordance with the level of mind of the intended trainees present when he spoke. At that particular time, speaking in that way became a pure Dharma in accordance with the level of mind of the trainees. Since that way of speaking did not go beyond the level of mind of trainees of inferior intellect, it is difficult to put it into practice.[244] However, it is said that "it is possible that teachers who

---

> (1) cutting down to the root basis of the mind, (2) teaching the manner for placing the mind, (3) cutting off deviations of mind, and (4) taking the mind into the path. [Pha]dampa Sangyé's holy Dharma is the "pacifier" of suffering. [In] Machik [Lapdrön]'s profound Dharma it is "the object to be cut." In the system of the Ācārya Padma[sambhava] it is the "great perfection": the three instructions of the *Garland of Views*, *Garland of Words*, and *Garland of Assembly*. In the Ri-wo Gendenpa [Geluk] system it is called "Instructions on the View of the Middle."

From Keutsang Jamyang Mönlam, *The Excellent, Always Virtuous Path to Liberation: Notes on the Genden Oral Lineage of Mahāmudrā*, 146–47. His Holiness the Dalai Lama adds that the term "and so forth" in the root text is meant to include traditions of the Sakya lineage (Gyatso and Berzin 1997, 262).

For a clear explanation of these systems, see First Paṇchen Lama 1981, Gyatso and Berzin 1997, 263ff, and Jackson 2019, 497–500.

243. Marpa Chökyi Lodrö, or Marpa Lotsawa (1012?–1097), was a great Tibetan lay practitioner who traveled to India to study with Nāropā and other masters, bringing back the lineages that would become the basis for the Kagyü tradition. See Heruka 1982.

Milarepa (1040–1123) was a student of Marpa. Having meditated for years in solitude, he is renowned in Tibet as an outstanding example of a yogi who achieved enlightenment in a single lifetime. See Lhalungpa 1979.

Dakpo refers to Nyammé Dakpo Lhajé (Tib. Mnyam med dwags po lha rje), often better known as Gampopa Sonam Rinchen (Tib. Sgam po pa bsod nams rin chen, 1079–1153). Gampopa was a doctor who ordained as a monk when his wife and child both died. He later became one of Milarepa's chief disciples and helped to codify the lineage of teachings into the Kagyü order. See Stewart 1995.

244. The point here is that certain ways of expressing emptiness were beneficial for particular students at particular times, but their meaning may not be easily accessible to modern

have not studied the textual systems a great deal may not know the way of applying terminology." That is, something that is unmistaken as to the meaning but doesn't have good terminology may be a case of somebody's not having studied the textual systems a great deal, not of their failing to understand.

The manner of counting the five and six in "endowed with five" and "six rounds of equal taste" in this text, and the way of calculating the eight great instructions[245] and so forth, are clear in the commentaries, so there is no need to give a long explanation.

> **Thus has this systems two: upon**
> **the view, seeking to meditate;**
> **on meditation, seeking for**
> **the view. Here is the latter one.**

What sort of stages of meditation does one require for this mahāmudrā? There are two systems: searching for meditation within the view of emptiness and searching for the view within meditation. There are two kinds of people: (1) those who first gain certainty about the view, realize the view, and from within the view, actualize calm abiding, and (2) those who first actualize calm abiding, [164] and having actualized calm abiding, gain certainty about the view. Of those two, the explanation in this context is

---

readers. For that reason, the Geluk school especially considers it of great importance to study the clear and extensive explanations of Nāgārjuna, Candrakīrti, and others and not to expect to gain a full understanding of emptiness by reading only some pith instructions. Only in certain exceptional cases can one gain understanding in that latter way.

245. Tib. *Khri chen brgyad* (or *'Khrid chen brgyad*). In the autocommentary (p. 72), the Paṇchen Lama identifies these eight texts as the following:

1. *Instructions on the Lama, the Three Exalted Bodies* (Tib. *Bla ma sku gsum gyi 'khrid*).
2. *Instructions on Love and Compassion* (Tib. *Byams snying rje' 'khrid*).
3. *Instructions on the Dependent Relativity of Cause and Effect* (Tib. *Rgyu 'bras rten 'brel gyi 'khrid*).
4. *Instructions on the Nectar Drops Endowed with Five* (Tib. *Lnga ldan bdud rtsi thigs pa'i 'khrid*).
5. *Instructions on Connate Communion* (Tib. *Lhan cig skyes sbyor gyi 'khrid*).
6. *Instructions on the Six Yogas of Nāropā* (Tib. *Na ro'i chos drug gi 'khrid*).
7. *Instructions on Impartiality for the Eight Dharmas* (Tib. *Chos brgyad mgo snyoms kyi 'khrid*).
8. *Instructions on Secret Conduct Reverse Order Meditation* (Tib. *Gsang spyod ldog bsgom gyi 'khrid*).

These eight texts are part of the six rounds of equal taste lineage of Chöjé Gyaré.

an explanation of the means of first actualizing calm abiding [taking as an object the mind's conventional nature of clarity] and then after that gaining certainty about the view.

The Manner of Meditating on Calm Abiding

So if one first meditates on calm abiding, then the manner of meditating on calm abiding has two sections: (1) preparation and (2) the actual session. The preparation includes relying on the collection of causes for calm abiding. In the context of meditating on the lamrim, before the actual meditation, one must first perform the six preparatory practices.[246] Likewise here as well, one must first perform the six preparatory practices.

> **On a seat good to concentrate,**
> **sit with the posture sevenfold.**
> **Dispel stale air across nine rounds.**
> **Divide well clear and murky minds.**
> **With a pure, wholesome mind, first go**
> **for refuge and produce the mind.**
> **Apply deep guru yoga's path.**
> **Intense requests, do hundreds, more—**
> **then melt the lama into you.**

He is saying that you need to do like that when meditating on calm abiding. Initially to actualize calm abiding, one needs to rely on the collection of causes for calm abiding. The great Jowo Atiśa explained that without relying on the collection of causes for calm abiding, then even somebody who meditates for many eons will be unable to actualize calm abiding. [165] Also, as an abode of meditation, one needs one that fulfills all the characteristics. Maitreya explains in the *Ornament for the Mahāyāna Sūtras*:

> The place where wise ones practice is
> found well, a pleasant dwelling, and
> a pleasant land, with pleasant friends,
> with easy yoga's assets complete.[247]

246. See note 55.

247. See note 37.

Since one must abide actualizing the Dharma, then at that time one needs to find food, clothing, and so forth in a good way. That is, one must depend on a good way of finding them that is not mixed with obtaining food by evil deeds. "A pleasant dwelling" means that previous holy beings have practiced meditation there and blessed the abode. "Pleasant land" means a pleasant environment that will not give rise to illness and so forth. Since there are cases of Dharma practitioners being afflicted with illness due to not tolerating the environment, it should not be like that. A pleasant companion is somebody whose view and behavior accords with one's own. It should be a person who, among Dharma and worldly activities, mainly engages in Dharma activities, and somebody whom you can look up to as a good example.

On top of that, "with easy yoga's assets complete": a yogi who has already ascertained in his own mind all the requisite points of practice possesses the requisites conducive to yoga. If somebody is practicing calm abiding, he should know well the way of sustaining the object of calm abiding, the way of dispelling faults of laxity, excitement, and so forth if they should arise, and so on. It shouldn't be that one has already arrived at the retreat house but still doesn't understand something and needs to go and question others. [166] A secluded, tranquil abode without noises from people in the daytime and water, dogs, and so forth in the nighttime is said to be a place conducive to calm abiding.

As for possessing ethical discipline, being pure in the ethical discipline to which one has committed is the most important factor. Generally it is said that ethical discipline is the basis for generating all good qualities. Especially for somebody meditating on calm abiding, pure ethical discipline is the most important factor. Having few wants and contentment: if somebody lacks the qualities of having few wants and contentment, then she will be distracted to various activities and won't get around to meditating on calm abiding. If one is practicing for actual calm abiding, then it is said, "Thoroughly abandon the bustle of many activities"—one shouldn't engage in many activities. Even though the activities may involve engaging in virtue, other than recitations that one absolutely must do on a daily basis, one shouldn't engage in many activities. Mainly one should meditate on calm abiding.

One should thoroughly abandon excessive thoughts about objects of desire and so forth. This is aspiring for things like name, fame, food, clothing, and dwellings out of attachment. For example, a being of the desire realm is attached to earthly pleasures, [167] while a being in the higher realms is attached to meditative stabilization.[248] Since such desire can arise, one should thoroughly abandon such discursive thoughts.

Especially, one also needs to possess the oral instructions of a holy lama who is skilled in the manner of actualizing calm abiding. There are many people who say, "I practiced for calm abiding and got to the fourth or fifth mental settling. But I wasn't able to achieve actual calm abiding." Well then, what is the reason that they didn't achieve it? Although one definitely must assemble the collection of causes as branches of calm abiding, they didn't assemble them. Somebody who does assemble the collection of causes will not take more than six months to achieve actual calm abiding.

A place that fulfills all the characteristics is called "a platform for easy concentration" [translated above as "a seat good to concentrate"]. For example, if the seat where one stays is slightly higher in the back and lower in the front, one's body will become straight, and it will be easy to breathe in and out. A seat such as this is [also] called "a platform for easy concentration." With regard to having a body with the seven aspects of Vairocana's posture, no matter what virtuous activity one engages in on an ongoing basis, it is said that if one practices with one's body in the sevenfold posture of Vairocana, then it is the nature of things that realizations will arise easily. So, sit in the sevenfold posture of Vairocana.[249]

[168] "Dispel stale air over nine rounds": Dispelling stale air is for the purpose of clearly visualizing and purifying the channels, so dispel stale air in nine rounds. As for the nine rounds, three times, inhale through the right nostril and exhale through the left. Then three times, inhale through the left and exhale through the right. Finally, three times, inhale through both nostrils and exhale through both—nine rounds. When exhaling through both, imagine the winds entering into the central channel.

Take a good look at your mind, examining whether afflictions are manifest or whether a virtuous mind is manifest. If afflictions are manifest in your mind, it is said that you should separate clear and murky awareness and count the breath coming and going. The reason is that you cannot immediately transform a mind under the power of afflictions into virtue. So for the purpose of transforming it into the nature of a neutral mind, you observe the coming and going of the breath, thinking, "The breath went out; it came

248. See note 89.

249. See page 77.

back in." Put your observation on that. By putting your observation on that, it is as though you will gradually forget the nonvirtuous thought that was in your mind. If you are able to transform the mind into a neutral state by observing only the coming and going of the breath, [169] thereafter you can observe a virtuous object.

"With a pure, wholesome mind": to generate only calm abiding, one doesn't need the support of bodhicitta. Non-Buddhists also have fully characterized calm abiding. In this context, since the explanation is in relation to mahāmudrā, "With a pure, wholesome mind" is saying that one's practice must be supported by bodhicitta. "Pure" means purified of the intention for one's own purpose. Think that you are taking upon yourself the purpose of others and that in order to place all other limitless sentient beings in the state of a buddha, you are meditating on mahāmudrā and meditating on calm abiding. If you do that, everything you meditate on will be supported by bodhicitta, so it is said to be especially superior.

As I explained before with regard to refuge and bodhicitta, refuge distinguishes one's practice from the wrong paths of forders,[250] and bodhicitta distinguishes it from the lower paths of hearers and solitary realizers. So you definitely need to meditate on those two. In that context, meditate on guru yoga, and make fervent requests to the lama. Saying "apply guru yoga," [170] as it says in this text, is saying to do a separate practice of guru yoga, like Lama Chöpa.

When practicing guru yoga, initially you need to perform the six preparatory practices. The first is cleaning the place, then setting up representations of the holy body, speech, and mind, then setting up and beautifully arranging offerings without deceit,[251] and so on. The fourth preparatory practice—visualizing the merit field, performing the seven-limb prayer along with a maṇḍala offering, making requests, and so forth—is included in the Lama Chöpa itself. For that reason, it says that the six preparatory practices must go first. Meditate on guru yoga in that way, and make requests to the lama. Since the occasion is meditating on calm abiding, make the request "Please bless me to generate easily the realization of calm abiding." Imagine that nectar descends, and purify yourself. Imagine that obstacles to calm abiding

250. See note 24.

251. "Offerings without deceit" means that one offers the best one can, without trying to deceive the objects of refuge. Alternatively, it can imply offerings that are obtained through right livelihood.

like laxity, excitement, and so forth are pacified and you have been blessed to achieve actual calm abiding. After that, it is also all right if you meditate on the lama.[252] When giving a commentary on the Oral Lineage, there is a tradition of doing so by "explaining by means of the three explanations."[253] We don't count what I said yesterday [in the general introduction], [171] and what I said today has become the first explanation, so we still have two more explanations to go.

The Second Explanation of Mantra-System Mahāmudrā

As for mantra-system mahāmudrā: the connate great bliss that arises from causing the winds to enter, abide, and dissolve in the central channel and that realizes emptiness is called "mantra-system mahāmudrā." This is a realization of the completion stage, and to generate a realization of the completion stage, one must first meditate on the generation stage. The main practice of the generation stage is taking the three bodies into the path. To meditate on that, first perform the first three of the six preparatory practices: cleaning the place, arranging representations of the holy body, speech, and mind, and setting up and beautifully arranging offerings without deceit. After that, go for refuge and generate bodhicitta, definitely combining it with tantra.[254] In order to purify discordant conditions, negativities, and obscurations, perform the meditation recitation of Vajrasattva. So that the blessing may enter you, meditate on guru yoga and so forth. All of these must be done first. If you are in the middle of meditating on another sādhana, it is sufficient to meditate on taking the three bodies into the path in the context of that. Otherwise, if you are doing, for instance, Lama Chöpa, then first go for refuge and generate bodhicitta. After that, it is all right to meditate on taking the three bodies into the path in the context of the verse "From within great bliss . . ." [172] Alternatively, you can recite Lama Chöpa and

252. One can meditate on the lama by remembering his qualities, making requests, and so forth.

253. Generally one first gives a brief explanation, followed by an extensive one, and finally recaps with a summary and prayer of dedication. Rinpoché varies that pattern slightly here by starting with the long explanation.

254. To "combine bodhicitta with tantra" means that, in addition to generating the mind to achieve enlightenment, one generates the special motivation to utilize the tantric path and achieve enlightenment in this very life.

withdraw the merit field, and request, "Precious Lama, please dissolve into my crown, and grant me blessings to generate realizations of the generation stage." After that, the lama dissolves into you, causing the environment and its being to condense, and you meditate on taking death into the path as the wisdom truth body. After that, you should meditate on taking the complete enjoyment body into the path and then taking the emanation body into the path.

If you are meditating based on the six-session guru yoga, then meditate on taking death into the path as the wisdom truth body during the verse ". . . again gladly turns one taste with me."[255] The lama becomes of equal taste with you, and that causes the whole environment and its beings to dissolve into you. Imagine that you also gradually dissolve into emptiness, and meditate on taking death into the path as the wisdom truth body. From the space of emptiness, meditate on taking the bardo into the path as the complete enjoyment body. It is sufficient to meditate on the subtle holy body—the complete enjoyment body—as in the aspect of light, and it is also permissible to meditate on it in the form of a mantra or seed syllable. In any case, meditate on a holy body that is established merely from wind and mind. During the verse "I, with pride of Vajrasattva . . . ," meditate on taking rebirth into the path as the emanation body. That is how to meditate on taking the three bodies into the path.

Mainly, you need to meditate on the clear light, mahāmudrā. [173] For that, first meditate on your body with a hollow interior. Next, visualize the three channels along with the four channel wheels. After that is purifying the channels: a drop moves up and down inside the channels, drawing all the winds[256] and purifying the channels. Meditate on taking the three bodies into the path. If you first meditate by placing your observation on the heart, there is a danger of creating a disturbance, so initially meditate by taking either the secret place or the center of the channel wheel at the navel as the objective support. On that basis, you generate the wisdom of great bliss of the four empties, which arises from having caused the winds to enter, abide, and dissolve in the central channel.

During that time, if you are a practitioner of the nine rounds of mixing, you practice isolation of body, and after isolation of body the vajra recitation

255. *Six-Session Guru Yoga*, v. B-2.

256. Gen Namgyal Chöphel suggests that we use the image of a needle pulling a thread to visualize "drawing the winds."

of isolation of speech. I already explained about the vajra recitation, which is one part of the isolation of speech. During that, when you exhale out, you imagine that the breath goes out in the tone of *hūṃ*, and when you inhale in, you imagine it comes back in the tone of *oṃ*. When it abides, the tone is *ha*. For example, if you puff air onto chinaware, you make the sound *hang*; imagine it abides like that. At that time, do not imagine that the breath goes out. [174] If you do, since you need to condense the winds inside in order to generate realizations of the completion stage, it will harm your condensing it in that way, so don't imagine the wind going out.

Well then, what should you do? Inhale, hold briefly, and then release the breath out. By meditating on the vajra recitation, the channel knots in the central channel will start to loosen. Once they have loosened, you should meditate by placing your observation on the heart. When you place your observation on the heart and gradually condense the winds, they will enter, abide, and dissolve in the central channel from both above and below. That is, they will enter, abide, and dissolve in the central channel at the heart. However, it has not yet become the final stage of the example clear light. The final stage of the example clear light is the winds entering, abiding, and dissolving into the indestructible drop at the heart just as at the stages of death. If the stages of dissolution occur like at the time of death, the example clear light of the isolation of mind will appear. You don't just leave that clear light purposelessly but generate it in the nature of a mind realizing emptiness in the manner of a meaning-generality. Generating it in that way is called "the example clear light that is the final stage of the isolation of mind."

When you arise from absorption on such a clear light, [175] you arise in the illusory holy body. That illusory holy body, moreover, is not just a single deity; it arises in the aspect of the complete supporting and supported maṇḍala. That illusory holy body arises on the basis of (1) the wind, which is the mount for that clear light, as the substantial cause, and (2) the clear light mind itself acting as the cooperative condition. It is not a flesh and blood body of matter but an unobstructed illusory holy body established from mere wind and mind. If we take a flower as an example, the seed acts as the substantial cause, and water and fertilizer act as cooperative conditions. Likewise here, the wind that is the mount of the clear light acts as the substantial cause, and that clear light mind acts as the cooperative condition. On that basis, it is not a flesh and blood body of matter, but rather it arises as an unobstructed, rainbow-like holy body established from mere wind and mind. This is the illusory body of the third stage. If that practitioner keeps entering into absorption on the clear light again and again, that connate bliss will generate in the nature of a direct realization of emptiness. That is called the "meaning clear light of the fourth stage." From that, one arises as the pure illusory holy body. That practitioner will then accumulate whatever collections she needs to accumulate to abandon the obscurations to knowledge. Having completed the collections, she again enters into absorption on the clear light. [176] When she actualizes the direct antidote to the obscurations to knowledge, it is called "the clear light at the end of learning." At the second moment of that, she achieves the path of release, and thereby achieves the stage of the victor Vajradhara, possessing the seven-branched union. That is the second explanation.

The Third Explanation of Mantra-System Mahāmudrā

First go for refuge, generate bodhicitta, confess negativities, and meditate on guru yoga as preliminaries. After that, imagine the stages of dissolution—earth dissolving into water and so forth—and think that thereby the clear light of death appears. Place your pride in that as the wisdom truth body. Next, arise as the complete enjoyment body, which is established from mere wind and mind and is like a substitute for the bardo. Meditate on taking the bardo into the path as the complete enjoyment body, thinking, "This is the actual complete enjoyment body." Again, imagine reentering into your old aggregates, and as you do so think, "Birth is arising as the emanation body." Mantra-system mahāmudrā requires the connate bliss that realizes emptiness. To get to that, first one must meditate on the isolation of body as a method for causing the winds to enter into the central channel. One meditates on the isolation of speech in order to release the channel knots at the heart. One meditates on the isolation of mind in order to cause the winds to enter, abide, and dissolve into the indestructible drop at the heart. [177] After the example clear light that is the final stage of isolation of mind appears, then upon arising from absorption one actualizes the illusory body. That practitioner of the impure illusory body enters into absorption on the clear light again and again, and then the meaning clear light that is the direct antidote to afflictive obscurations appears. Upon arising from the meaning clear light, one actualizes the pure illusory holy body. The holy body of unification, which is a unity of holy body and mind that the practitioner of the pure illusory body achieves by again entering into absorption on the clear light, is called "learner's unification." That practitioner of unification must accumulate the collections in order to abandon the obscurations to knowledge, so he accumulates them. When he attains the power to abandon the obscurations to knowledge and then actualizes the direct antidote to them, that stage is called "meaning clear light at the end of learning." At the next moment when he attains the path of release, that is called "attaining the state of Vajradhara." This completes the third explanation.

Those who give commentaries need to sustain the object of observation as they give the commentary. Whether it is extensive or condensed, if one keeps it all in mind and then maintains awareness of that, then when one explains the Dharma in order three times, one maintains the object of observation three times, and so that fulfills the role of three sessions. If in one's room one then performs one session maintaining the object of observation, it becomes the yoga of four sessions. [178] As the lama is explaining the commentary, he should try to be able to meditate in accordance with what he explains. If he meditates in that way, it fulfills the role of three sessions. Out of the preliminary, actual session, and postsession, as a preliminary, one goes for refuge, generates bodhicitta, and confesses negativities.

TWELVE

The Actual Practice of Sūtra Mahāmudrā

The actu'l great seal fits into
divisions: sūtra, mantra two.[257]

THE MANTRA SYSTEM of mahāmudrā involves piercing the vital points of the vajra body and then entering into absorption on emptiness with the primordial, connate clear light mind. Both the example clear light that realizes emptiness by means of a meaning-generality and the meaning clear light that directly realizes emptiness are called "mantra-system mahāmudrā." I already explained how, in order to manifest that clear light, one must first meditate on isolation of speech, isolation of body, and so forth.

As for the sūtra system of mahāmudrā, the protector Nāgārjuna faultlessly explained the intended meaning of the perfection of wisdom sūtras. The profound emptiness that is settled upon by following after Nāgārjuna and according with his explanations is called "sūtra-system mahāmudrā." With regard to the reason for calling emptiness "mahāmudrā," [179] because emptiness exists on all phenomena as though profound emptiness were sealed upon them, it is a seal [*mūdra*]. On the basis of that emptiness, the paths of the three vehicles increase endlessly,[258] and one must practice by taking that as an object of observation. On account of its great import, we call it the "great seal" [*mahāmudrā*]. Furthermore, there are two approaches to that: first settling upon the view, and from within the view, seeking out meditation, or first actualizing calm abiding, and then within meditation, seeking out the view. Here, I am explaining from the point of view of first actualizing calm abiding and then actualizing special insight.

257. This stanza is not in the root text but is paraphrasing a stanza from page 153.

258. The "three vehicles" are those of hearers (Skt. *śrāvaka*; Tib. *nyan thos*), solitary realizers (Skt. *pratyekabuddha*; Tib. *rang sangs rgyas*), and bodhisattvas. To say that they "increase endlessly" on the basis of emptiness means that by meditating on emptiness, one advances on the path and increases one's positive qualities.

The manner of meditating on calm abiding has two sections: (1) preparatory practices and (2) the actual session. The preparatory practices are relying on the collection of causes for calm abiding that I explained above. A place where you actualize calm abiding should fulfill the requisite characteristics. The place where one practices should at a minimum accommodate the four bodily activities: If you stand up, you shouldn't have to bow your head. If you lie down, you should be able to fold and extend your legs without obstruction. If you move about, you should be able to take three steps in every direction. If you sit, it shouldn't interfere with your assuming the cross-legged position. You also need to have few wants and contentment, must abandon the bustle of many activities, need pure ethical discipline, and must thoroughly abandon excessive thoughts about objects of desire and so forth. Among those, [180] the main one you need is pure ethical discipline. Sit with your body in the sevenfold vajra posture of Vairocana. Dispel stale air in nine rounds. Separate clear and murky minds, and if you notice that a nonvirtuous thought has arisen, count your breath as a way of moving away from the nonvirtuous mind. If on that basis your mind becomes of a neutral nature, then train in bodhicitta. Endowed with bodhicitta, earnestly go for refuge and generate bodhicitta.[259]

Meditate on guru yoga, and imagine that the lama sits on your crown. At this juncture, you should recite the requesting prayer to the mahāmudrā lineage lamas.[260] If you are in the process of reciting Lama Chöpa, then you recite the mahāmudrā requesting prayer just before the verse "Source of good qualities . . ."[261] If your practice is the six-session guru yoga, then you recite it at the end of the maṇḍala offering.[262] When reciting the mahāmudrā requesting prayer, imagine that the lamas abide in a vertical column and that above the highest one sits Vajradhara. The victor Vajradhara is in the normal aspect of Vajradhara, and then from Mañjuśrī [181] up until your supremely kind root lama, you should imagine that all the lamas are in nature that particular lama but in the aspect of Mañjuśrī. Request to the lamas sequentially, starting with the top one. As you request sequentially, Vajradhara dissolves

259. It would seem redundant to say "endowed with bodhicitta . . . generate bodhicitta." But the point is that with the *mental* motivation of bodhicitta, one then *verbally* recites the prayers of refuge and bodhicitta.

260. For this prayer, see the beginning of part 2.

261. *Lama Chöpa*, v. 43.

262. *Six-Session Guru Yoga*, v. A-11.

into Mañjuśrī, and then Mañjuśrī dissolves into Jé Rinpoché, who is in the aspect of Mañjuśrī. Jé Rinpoché dissolves into Tokden Jampal Gyatso. They successively dissolve into each other, as explained in the instructions on the manner of meditation, and finally dissolve into your kind root lama. Since your root lama is in the nature of combining all the lamas, make fervent requests to him. Finally, imagine that he also dissolves into you.

When you have meditated on guru yoga in this way, you make these fervent requests to the lama: "Please bless me to generate, in general, all the realizations of the grounds and paths," and because here calm abiding is what you are intending to actualize, "Especially bless me to generate in my continuum the particular realization of calm abiding." Imagine that nectar descends and purifies you. Thinking, "I have now purified all the obstacles to actualizing calm abiding and have been blessed to generate a special realization of calm abiding," make requests hundreds of times. When the lama dissolves into you, [182] then you should have faith in and reverence for the lama by recollecting his qualities. Recollecting his qualities, you have faith, and recollecting his kindness, reverence. It should be to the point that through fervent faith and reverence, tears fall from your eyes, and the hairs of your body stand on end. Imagine that the lama is on the verge of dissolving into you out of great affection.

By your thinking and requesting in this way, the lama dissolves into you. By his dissolving into you, the Paṇchen Lama says that you should imagine abiding in "a space of ethereal appearance"[263]—that is, abide in a state of no other conceptions save being filled with bliss.

> **Without a fabrication's trace**
> **of hopes, fears, so on, enter free**
> **of slightest flux, absorption in**
> **ethereal appearance space.**

Through the objective support—your lama, dissolving into you—you place your mind in equanimity, without any other discursive thoughts and without the slightest fluctuation, in the space of ethereal appearance described

263. Tib. *snang ba ban bun*. This term literally implies a state of evanescent appearance, like fog that billows and vanishes. When applied to a mental state, it usually implies confusion or lack of clarity. However, in this context, Gen Namgyal Chöphel suggests it means a combination of relaxation and freedom from hope and fear.

above. Don't allow discursive thoughts of hope and worry to arise for even an instant—hopes of "In the future, I hope I will gain such renown and so forth" and worries thinking "May such harmful conditions and tragedies not befall me."

> [183] **It's not stopping attention like in swoon or sleep; place the spy of remembrance undistractedly.**

As for the object of observation in this context: observe your clear and knowing mind, free of any trace of discursive thought. Your concentration must combine the two branches of (1) intensity of clarity and (2) single-pointed abiding [the factor of stability]; it is not simply a lack of any mental engagement at all, like thoughtless, heedless fainting and sleep. If you are to practice by observing the mind, you need to practice by relying again and again on an undistracted recollection of that mind, which is your objective support.[264] When actualizing meditative stabilization, recollection is the most important factor. Since you need to actualize it by means of a recollection that does not forget the objective support and that continuously sustains it, the text says "place the spy of . . . remembrance."

When placing the mind in absorption on meditative stabilization, the two greatest hindrances obstructing stabilization are laxity born of mental sinking and excitement that scatters to other objects under the power of desire. For that reason, the text explains [see the root text on page 204], "Before laxity and excitement actually arise, you *prime* a mind which is a sentry—'introspection that checks whether laxity and excitement are arising.'" So you need to make a kind of preparation. [184] Generally speaking, any virtuous mind needs to have both a factor of mental stability and a factor of individual analysis. There is a manner of speaking: "From the factor of stability, it approximates calm abiding, and from the factor of individual analysis, it approximates special insight." Having in mind these simulacra of

264. In the first half of this book, Rinpoché presented a manner of actualizing calm abiding by observing a visualized object. Here he presents an alternative method of taking the mind itself as the object. Practitioners should bear in mind that many experienced teachers warn that while this latter method can in some cases be more expedient, the danger it presents is that it is much more difficult to recognize subtle dullness. With a visualized image, a meditator can check if the image is appearing vividly, but with the mind itself as an object, it is easy to think one is abiding in genuine concentration when in fact the mind is slightly dull.

calm abiding and special insight, the Buddha said [in the *Sūtra Unraveling the Thought*], "Generally speaking, all good qualities of the three vehicles are the result of calm abiding and special insight."[265]

The Nature of Calm Abiding and How to Actualize It

As for fully qualified calm abiding, if you don't assemble the collection of causes, you will be unable to actualize it. Generally speaking, since the meditative stabilization of calm abiding arises in both Buddhists and non-Buddhists, it is an object of practice common to both of them. Thus, in terms of its nature, we cannot posit it as a path.[266] What do we need to do in order to actualize a fully qualified calm abiding? We need to actualize it on the basis of the method of the nine mental settlings. The great texts speak of (1) initially relying on the eight applications that are antidotes abandoning the five faults, based on seeing the benefits of calm abiding, and of (2) the manner of actualizing it by means of the six powers and four mental engagements.[267] If our practice accords with the explanations in the great texts, then we will get a fully qualified calm abiding. If we are practicing in that way, occasionally a thought of not wishing to actualize meditative stabilization will arise. [185] That thought arises through the power of laziness, so to counter it we need to generate faith that sees the good qualities of meditative stabilization. Since without achieving calm abiding we will be unable to generate clairvoyance, an uncontrived determination to be free of cyclic existence, bodhicitta, and so forth, then in order to generate realizations

265. Tsongkhapa cites this quote from the "Chapter Requested by Maitreya" of the *Sūtra Unravelling the Thought* (Skt. *Saṃdhinirmocanasūtra*; Tib. *Mdo sde'i dgongs 'grel*) at the beginning of his exposition on calm abiding in *The Great Treatise on the Stages of the Path to Enlightenment*. He goes on to explain that the quote should not be taken literally; it is not that somebody cannot generate any qualities without calm abiding and special insight, but that one needs at least a *simulacrum* of these. That is, one needs the ability to focus and analyze. For an English translation of this sūtra, see Powers 1995a.

266. The definition of a "path [consciousness]" is "a clear realizer supported by an uncontrived determination to be free of cyclic existence." According to Buddhist philosophy, non-Buddhist practitioners cannot possibly generate such a mind, because they do not recognize all-pervasive compounding suffering and thereby do not fully recognize cyclic existence for what it is. One can generate calm abiding without having such an uncontrived determination, so calm abiding is not necessarily a path.

267. See introduction and part 1 of this book.

of the higher paths, we definitely need to attain calm abiding. So with the thought "If I don't achieve calm abiding, there is no way to achieve the path," generate faith that sees the benefits of calm abiding. That faith induces an aspiration that strives to produce calm abiding. On that basis, one generates enthusiasm. On the basis of generating enthusiasm, one achieves the pliancy in which the body and mind can be utilized for virtue however one wishes. These four—faith, aspiration, enthusiasm, and pliancy—are the antidotes to laziness.

Calm abiding needs first to observe a particular objective support and then not to forget it. If one forgets the objective support, it is the fault of forgetting the instructions, so as an antidote to that, one generates stable recollection and introspection. If while one is absorbed single-pointedly on the object of observation, laxity or excitement arise, that is a fault. If when laxity and excitement arise one does not make recourse to applying an antidote, it is the fault of not applying the antidote. Later, even though one is already free of laxity and excitement, if one still makes recourse to an antidote, [186] it will harm the factor of stability, so one must abide without applying an antidote. The antidotes of the first fault, laziness, are the four—(1–4) faith and so forth. The antidote of forgetting the instructions is (5) recollection. (6) Introspection is the sentry who checks whether or not laxity and excitement are arising. When laxity and excitement arise, one (7) applies the antidote to pacify them. When one is free of laxity and excitement, one (8) does not apply the antidote. These eight are called "the eight applications that are antidotes for abandoning."[268]

For the purpose of abandoning the five faults, one relies on the eight applications that are antidotes, and on that basis achieves the nine means of settling the mind: (1) First one places the mind on an object of observation and abides there. (2) Next, one abides for a little longer duration. (3) Next, when the mind is distracted, one is immediately able to draw it back. (4) Then, by not losing the objective support, one is not distracted. (5) Next one pacifies both gross laxity and excitement.[269] (6) Then one pacifies subtle laxity and excitement. (7) Then laxity and excitement do not arise at

268. As described in the introduction and part 1 of this book, the last two antidotes, applying the antidote and not applying the antidote, are technically called "intention" and "equanimity," because these are the primary mental factors that carry out the intended task.

269. Gross excitement was already pacified by stage four, but here one pacifies gross laxity, and thus *both* are pacified.

all. (8) Next, at the beginning of the session, by relying ever so slightly on recollection and introspection, one is able to complete the session successfully without distraction. (9) Then without any need for effort, spontaneous achievement arises. These are called "the nine means of settling the mind."

[187] In terms of the object of observation for calm abiding, some non-Buddhists even actualize calm abiding observing sticks, stones, and so forth, so there is no certainty in terms of the objective support. Generally speaking, if a person practices by observing something that is compatible with her disposition and inclination and with which she has familiarity, it will be easier to actualize calm abiding. A story goes that in old times there was a cattle herdsman who, when practicing for meditative stabilization, practiced using various other objects but could not actualize it. Later when he practiced by observing a bullhorn, he was able to achieve it. Based on that, we can see that if one practices calm abiding by taking as an objective support something with which one has strong familiarity, it will be easier to actualize it. If Buddhists observe horns and so forth and practice calm abiding, beyond merely actualizing calm abiding there is no great purpose. If one observes the holy body of the Buddha and actualizes it, then since the objective support is the holy body of the Buddha, if one actualizes a good calm abiding, afterward there will be a significant difference in ease when one meditates on a deity. Since one is observing the holy body of the Buddha, one will accumulate vast merit, so most Buddhist practitioners of calm abiding practice observing the holy body of the Buddha as the objective support. In this context, previous lamas of this lineage of mahāmudrā instruction have said, "When meditating on mahāmudrā, practice by observing the mind." [188] If a person practices observing the mind by observing the interrupted intervals of the five sense consciousnesses, which sometimes arise and sometimes don't, she will not actualize calm abiding. Instead, one practices by observing a mental consciousness. Specifically, it is the primordial mind which comes uninterruptedly from the last life—not the subtle primordial mind, but a coarse sort of primordial mind.[270]

270. The "subtle primordial mind" is the clear light mind that one utilizes in the mantra system of mahāmudrā. In this sūtra-system context, one does not observe that mind but still observes a subtler level of mind than the one we typically experience in daily life. So calling this mind "coarse" is only in comparison with the subtlest clear light mind. From the point of view of sūtra, the mind one observes here is still subtle, and it is subtle compared to the normal thinking mind. Regarding this distinction, which he traces to the master Gyalrong Tsultrim Nyima's commentary to this text, His Holiness the Dalai Lama explains,

Thus, by making fervent requests to the lama, the lama dissolves into you. From his dissolving, all discursive thoughts and grasping at appearances cease, and the text states that one should observe and enter absorption on the mind abiding in the state of ethereal appearance. As to this mind, moreover, "Don't try to forget thoughts of hope and fear that were there before": by not calling to mind discursive thoughts of things you have already done, you don't actually try to forget them.[271] By not engaging in hope and worry, thinking, "What if this happened in the future?" this mind does not anticipate the future. Even regarding the present, it does not fall under the power of desire and attachment but is clear and knowing. It is the clear, knowing mind when one is not clearly apprehending any object at all.

Alertness prime for stirrings of mind.

With focus tight, look nakedly
at nature of the knowing and clear.

The mind [in its untrained state] abides as though it is without anything to obstruct it. Whatever object you observe, [189] the mind does not even stay on it a little, and you are unable to find an objective support. If you are able to recognize such an objective support as this clear and knowing mind, you have found an objective support. Alternatively, if you meditate by observing something like the holy body of a deity, it will be like the mind has something to obstruct it, and you have thereby found an objective support. If you practice by observing the holy body of a deity, and especially if you practice by observing the holy body of the teacher Śākyamuni, at first all the features of mouth, hands, and so forth may not clearly appear. But it is said that if you initially can have your mind abide on a yellow shaft of light, then you should actualize a factor of stability on that basis. If you get your mind to abide on the clear and knowing mind, then you shouldn't immediately try to make that appearance clearer and so forth [because in so doing you may lose stability]. Rather, from within that state, you should use recollection to

"According to his presentation, the unique feature of mahamudra is its use of a decisive understanding of the devoid nature of coarse primordial mind as a special, uncommon aid for manifesting subtle primordial mind" (Gyatso and Berzin 1997, 227).

271. The point here is that while one should not get caught up in past thought patterns, one also shouldn't make an intentional effort to forget them. Simply by not engaging with them, they will settle of their own accord.

be able to hold the mind there, with recollection *focus tightly*, and observe while staying single-pointedly.

At that time, if discursive thoughts that are improper mental engagement arise,[272] then from their arising one will be unable to see the nature of the mind, to which any object at all is suitable to appear. The nature of the mind is like the vacuity of empty space, without anything obscuring it at all. But as for being unable to see it, it is due to those discursive thoughts obscuring it. [190] Since you need to recognize and put to rest whatever discursive thoughts arise, first of all you need to do something to recognize the discursive thoughts. Above the text read, "Alertness prime for stirrings of mind." It is saying to place observation single-pointedly on the basic space or the mere generality of the mind. You must apply stable recollection and not forget the object of observation that you have previously ascertained.

As for the manner of sustaining concentration, in short, it is only referring to the manner of sustaining it by using recollection not to forget the object of observation. It is said that if you get a stable recollection, then it's as though introspection also will naturally arise.

> **Whatever thoughts discursive rise,**
> **catch sight of them for what they are.**

Whatever discursive thoughts should arise, you should use introspection to recognize them, and then put them to rest by applying the antidote.

> **Or like a duelist, cut off**
> **straightway whatever thoughts arise.**

In old times, powerful people would have both archers and sword-wielders. Of these two, the sword-wielder is called a "duelist." No matter how many arrows the archer fired, the sword-wielder would spin his sword and chop away all the arrows, such that they would not strike his body. [191] Paṇchen Losang Chökyi Gyaltsen uses this as an example. In a similar way, when you are absorbed on the clear and knowing mind, you should not simultaneously

272. "Improper mental engagement" (Tib. *tshul min yid byed*; Skt. *ayoniṣomanasikāra*) means deluded, destructive thought patterns that give rise to afflictions. Thoughts like "This object is so wonderful" and "This person is so beautiful" give rise to attachment, thoughts like "He did this terrible thing to me!" give rise to anger, and so on.

stir up discursive thought but should stop it. He says that if you pacify discursive thoughts that arise, then you should look at the nature of the clear and knowing mind, and with recollection not forget it.

> **When having cut, mind rests, relax.**
> **Let go; lose recollection not.**

If you have finished putting to rest other discursive thoughts, then for the time being place the mind on that nature of clarity, and apply an intense recollection not to forget it. At this point, you loosen the exertion of arousing an antidote, and immediately you relax. Although the mind is internally focused and the body is relaxed, still the mind must apprehend the object with a tight mode of apprehension. Furthermore, the mind is not excessively tight; you are relaxed, and without losing recollection, although you relaxingly *let go*, do not actually let go of the mode of apprehension.

Machik Lapdrön[273] and the great brahmin Saraha[274] explain:

> **[Machik Lapdrön:] "With focus tight, relax, let go:**
> **that is the space to set the mind."**
> **Such has been said, and furthermore,**
> **[Brahmin Saraha:] "When mind in tangle bound lets go,**
> **without a doubt it frees itself."**
> **As said, let go, but do not drift.**

Generally if the mode of apprehension is too tight, [192] it will harm the factor of stability, while if you relax and let go too much, it will harm the factor of clarity. So Machik says, "With focus tight, relax, let go," and [Saraha's] dohā[275] says, "When mind . . . lets go, without a doubt it frees itself." Based on these explanations that one needs to let go, earlier Tibetans would say, "When practicing for meditative stabilization, you need to relax your mind."

273. Machik Lapdrön (Tib. Ma cig lab sdron, 1055–1149) was a Tibetan female practitioner best known for her teachings on chöd (Tib. *gcod*) and shiché (Tib. *zhi byed*) (see note 242). For a biography of Machik Lapdrön and a history of chöd, see Edou 1996.

274. For Saraha, see note 207.

275. Saraha composed three sets of spiritual songs or dohā. See note 210. This verse is drawn from his *Common Dohā*. See Jackson 2004, 78, v. 42h.

The Need for a Spacious Mind Where the Mode of Apprehension Is Not Lost

If your mind is too relaxed inwardly, laxity will arise. On the basis of subtle laxity arising, the factor of stability will become slightly stable. But because laxity would arise if the mind's mode of apprehension was too relaxed, holy beings of old did not say, "You need a relaxed mode of apprehension." The Kadampa lamas would say that when you meditate, "Take a long view; don't squeeze yourself."[276] All these sayings have the same meaning. Well then, what are they saying? "Tangle" is saying that you should get rid of the claustrophobic mind and not think, "I need to accomplish it right now!" Rather, you need to take a long view, thinking, "If I practice slowly and steadily, I will accomplish it."

[193] This skillful means is the most important thing at all times. For example, even when you are practicing for calm abiding, you should not tighten your body and mind with fierce exertion, thinking, "If I achieved calm abiding right now, how wonderful that would be!" Rather, "take a long view" is saying that on the basis of a mind that remembers the past and thinks about what will occur in the future, you need to think, "If I relax, slowly, slowly, I will be able to generate calm abiding."[277] Moreover, whenever we engage in any virtuous activity, while doing it, it is especially important to think like that. There are some people who have the hope "In a short time, I will swiftly generate realizations in my continuum," and then for a few days they apply strong effort to think about death and impermanence, karmic cause and effect, renunciation, bodhicitta, and so forth. When merely doing that doesn't generate realizations, they say, "It's not happening," and give up. If you don't act like that, and instead practice slowly, slowly, by taking a long view, you will reach accomplishment.

276. Tib. *mig rgyang sring / khong srang lhod*; literally "extend the length of your vision and relax inside." I am borrowing this liberal but effective translation from Lama Zopa Rinpoché 2010.

277. Remembering the past in this context means that one keeps in mind the wisdom gained from past experience and doesn't get obsessively caught up in a superficial assessment of what is happening in the present moment. Thinking about the future means setting realistic long-term goals and not being overly concerned about having happiness and avoiding suffering right now.

For example, Longdöl Lama Rinpoché[278] said, "For eleven or twelve years, I sustained meditation. However, on top of the mind with which I began, no addition of positive mental qualities arose at all. Later, by making effort in conjunction with accumulation and purification, realizations arose in my continuum." [194] Likewise, Khedrup Norsang Gyatso[279] was somebody who attained the state of buddhahood in this very life. He also said, "I meditated for fourteen years, achieved other's benefit, and so forth." We too should not contemplate for just a few days and then give up, thinking, "Now, I won't accomplish anything." Furthermore, in previous times there was one lama who stayed in *nyungné* retreat his entire life, completing over twenty-thousand nyungnés.[280] One of his expert disciples asked him, "If somebody performs so many nyungnés, realizations must arise, so what realizations have you had?" He replied, "Although you are renowned as an expert, you don't know how to apply reasoning. I don't have any hope of swiftly generating realizations right away. From now until I die, I will stay in nyungné. I hope that in the future life, I will again stay in nyungné, and that

278. Longdöl Ngawang Losang (Tib. Klong rdol ngag dbang blo bzang, 1719–94) was born in Kham. He was known for creating an encyclopedia of technical terms from all the disciplines of traditional Tibetan scholarship. He received monastic ordination from Phurbuchok Ngawang Jampa. He was known as Longdöl Lama because of his long meditations at Nyetang Longdöl cave. A publication of his collected works, in two volumes, is forthcoming from Lhopa Khangtsen at Sera Jé. Longdöl Lama was a member of Lhopa Khangtsen, Rinpoché's house group at Sera, where he is remembered each year with a special pūjā on the third day of the fourth Tibetan month.

279. Khedrup Norsang Gyatso (Tib. Mkhas grub nor bzang rgya mtsho, 1423–1513) was an early master of the Geluk tradition and a teacher of the Second Dalai Lama, Gyalwa Gendün Gyatso. He composed a famous text on Kālacakra in addition to his texts on mahāmudrā. For the Kālacakra text, see Khedrup Norsang Gyatso 2004. His short mahāmudrā commentary "Bright Lamp of Mahāmudrā" (*Bka' dge dgongs pa gcig bsgrub kyi phyag rgya chen po'i gsal ba'i sgron ma*) is available in English in Jackson 2019.

280. Nyungné (Tib. *myung gnas*; literally "abiding in the fast") is a two-day intensive retreat that includes strict fasting, prostrations, and extensive prayers to Avalokiteśvara, the buddha of compassion. Twenty-thousand nyungnés would take forty thousand days, or over 109 years. I have to speculate that perhaps Rinpoché meant this meditator had stayed in nyungné retreat for twenty thousand *days*, meaning he had completed ten thousand nyungnés. Many English language materials detail this practice, such as FPMT 2005, Lama Zopa Rinpoche 2017, and Wangchen Rinpoche 2009.

slowly, slowly, with the Ārya Avalokiteśvara looking after me, realizations will come. Beyond that, I don't hold out hope that I will quickly have such realizations." We definitely should think over these great life stories. The meaning of the saying "Within internal focus, stay relaxed" has something substantial to it.[281]

> [195] **Whatever thought comes, when you spot**
> **its nature, then it vanishes—**
> **vacuity dawns. Likewise too**
> **when stilled, you check, void unobscured,**
> **a vivid wakefulness you see:**
> **"abiding, moving mixed," it's called.**[282]
>
> **Whatever thought comes, don't block. Know**
> **its movement. In its nature set,**
> **like the example of a bird**
> **that flies, imprisoned on a boat.**

If discursive thoughts arise, then if you examine and analyze, "From what cause did this arise? What sort of nature does it have?" then sometimes it will be like the thoughts vanish by themselves. So, it says you should do like that. Moreover, it is saying that when discursive thoughts arise, you should not immediately stop them; by examining their nature, some will stop by themselves. For example,

281. Geshé Ngawang Thokmé explains that internal "focus" (Tib. *grim*) or "tightness" in this context means that one does not lose the object of apprehension; in the context of having an intensity of the factor of clarity, one relaxes, rather than relaxing in an uncontrolled way. He gives the example of a Dharma practitioner who relaxes in social contexts without actually losing his mindfulness and certainty of purpose, rather than relaxing in the sense of letting go of all conscientiousness.

282. In the autocommentary (p. 83), the Paṇchen Lama clarifies the meaning of this obscure passage:

> (1) At that time, when you have overpowered conceptual thoughts, whatever conceptual thought arises, when you look at its nature, a vacuity will dawn into which the conceptual thoughts have vanished. (2) Likewise, when your mind abides without fluctuation, if you analyze it, it is an unobscured vacuity, a vivid wakefulness. Seeing *the former and latter states [of fluctuation and stillness] as without any difference* is known to great meditators as "still and moving are mixed," and they call it by that name. (italics mine)

> **"As from a ship a raven flies,**
> **swings round each side, alights again."[283]**
> **By practicing in just that way . . .**

The text explains an example for the way discursive thoughts are pacified by examining their nature. If from a ship in the middle of the ocean you send out a bird, then because there is nowhere to land in the ocean, after some time it will arrive back at the ship. Likewise by examining the nature of discursive thoughts, sometimes discursive thoughts will stop by themselves. At that time, you should place your mind in equipoise on the clear and knowing nature, as before.

[196] When you examine the nature of discursive thoughts, then discursive thoughts calm down. The mind becomes clear, unobscured by anything, like a vacuity. A "vivid wakefulness" appears, where any object is suitable to appear. When discursive thoughts calm down, such a thing appears. Likewise, when the mind is abiding without fluctuation, if you look to see how that mind is, what you get is a vacuity—a clear appearance of vivid wakefulness where there is no distinction of past and future. When discursive thoughts arise, when you look at their nature, afterward that vacuity appears, and when the mind abides without fluctuation, by looking to see how that mind is, you get a vacuity—a mind of clearly appearing vivid wakefulness, with no distinction of past and future. In that context, great meditators use the term "mixing abiding and movement." Observing that mind, apply single-pointed placement. At that time, you need a tight mode of apprehension endowed with intensity of the factor of clarity. However, if the mode of apprehension is *too* tight, then the mind needs to focus forcefully, and there is a danger that the mind will be unable to stay on the object of observation and will scatter to other objects. Since such a danger is there, you should relax your mind a bit. But again if you relax too much, the mind will sink and laxity will come.

Laxity has many kinds, both gross and subtle. When somebody has intensity of the clarity factor but the force of the focus relaxes slightly, [197] it is a sign that laxity has arrived, and one has lost that intensity. As for that, you need to know from your own experience that when the tightness is too

283. This is another quote from Saraha's *Common Dohā* (Jackson 2004, 93, v. 70). Interestingly, in that context this example is used to illustrate yogis who focus too narrowly on emptiness meditation.

much, excitement arises and you need to relax slightly. Also when relaxation is too much, laxity arises and you need to tighten a bit, and so forth. You should know tight and relaxed modes of apprehension by analyzing your own experience.

Explanation of How to Place the Mind

The text[284] speaks of six ways of placing the mind. When placing your mind on an object, what are you supposed to do? If you practice by means of the six ways of placing the mind, it becomes like following the king of instructions. What are these?

1. **Place it like a cloud-free sun . . .**

A sun free of clouds is clear, and likewise when you observe the nature of the mind, which is clear and knowing, it is free of the clouds of discursive thought, laxity, and excitement, and is clear and lucid like the sun.

2. **like great garuḍa soars in sky.**

When the "great garuḍa," the king of birds, moves through the sky, he does not have to flap his wings or exert much effort but can soar great distances through his own force, unlike small birds who have to flap their wings while flying. Likewise, if the mind is too tight, excitement arises, and through excessive relaxation, laxity arises. So without excessive tightness or relaxation, [198] you should practice the internal focus explained above (page 208): not outside the bounds of recollection and introspection, endowed with intensity of the factor of clarity, it sustains through its own force.

3. **Place it like the great ocean's depth . . .**

Although huge waves are there on the surface of the great ocean, they cannot disturb it from its depths. Likewise when the mind is placed in equanimity, even though subtle discursive thoughts arise, they cannot incite

284. These six examples are not in the root text, but the Paṇchen Lama includes them in his autocommentary, on page 87.

gross conceptual thought. So you should do like that, so gross thoughts cannot disturb you.

> **4. like a small boy looks at a shrine . . .**

When a small child looks at the paintings in a temple, he doesn't inspect all the subtle details of the painting. Rather, he will look without being distracted from the gross picture. Likewise when placing the mind on the object of observation, don't inspect whatever objects appear to the five senses. Instead, you should place your observation upon the mere clarity and knowing of the mind.

> **5. like flying bird's trace in the sky.**

When a bird flies in the sky, we can't point to something and say, "These are the traces of flight." Likewise whatever feelings arise—pleasure, suffering, or equanimity—an ordinary person will continuously react with attachment, hatred, and dullness. Whenever she experiences pleasure, she will become attached. When experiencing suffering, she will get angry. [199] When experiencing neither pleasure nor suffering, dull ignorance will arise. However, in this context when you are training in meditative stabilization, then whatever feelings arise—pleasure, suffering, or equanimity—do not allow yourself to be under the control of attachment and hatred. The text says you need to place your mind single-pointedly on the object of observation.

> **6. Place it like a cashmere spread . . .**

That is, it should be like the smooth surface of a spread of cloth. After you cut up fleece and lay it out evenly, it is smooth and relaxed. Likewise with the mind placed in equanimity, it is free of the roughness of laxity and excitement and manifest afflictions of the three poisons. Since laxity and excitement are the greatest fault, it is explained that you should not allow laxity, excitement, and other discursive thoughts to arise.

What kind of result comes from meditating in this way?

> **Absorption, nature unobscured**
> **by anything, is lucid, clear.**
> **Not made of any form at all,**

vacuity like the sky, and
it's vivid since all things can dawn.

By meditating on the basis of the nine means of settling the mind, you reach the ninth mental settling. Observing the mind that is in the nature of equipoise, you see that "mind" is not established as form, [200] so it is lucid and clear. It is a vacuity, like the sky. [In the autocommentary] the Paṇchen Lama says of the mind that if it meets an object, then like an image appearing in a mirror, it is a vivid wakefulness wherein that object can appear. When it abides without meeting an object, it is capable of giving rise to an experience wherein it is difficult to identify what it is and what it is not. When you achieve that ninth mental settling, the mind is free of the faults of laxity and excitement. You are able to stay in that equipoise for a long time. A clear experience arises such that you are able to count all the particles in a wall, from the subtlest up.[285] However, it is said that if it is not supported by the bliss of pliancy, then it is not actual calm abiding. As for the bliss of pliancy: if your mind and body become serviceable for whatever virtuous activity you like, you have achieved pliancy of body and mind. On that basis, bodily bliss arises. Bodily bliss causes mental bliss to arise. When that mental bliss is free of the faults of excessive fluctuation and supports concentration, it has become a fully characterized calm abiding.

Explanation of the Conventional Nature of the Mind

What is the nature of this calm abiding that takes the mind as an object?

[Past Tibetans:] "Indeed this mind's reality
with insight is directly seen.
But 'it's this' you can't hold or say.
What dawns, don't hold, but place in ease.
This is bestowed instruction for
to hold in your palm buddhahood":[286]

285. See note 97.

286. Some translators have translated this line as "holding the spark of buddhahood" or even "holding *until* buddhahood." However, Gen Namgyal Chöphel interprets *sbar bcangs* as "holding in the palm of your hand." *Sbar* does not mean "spark" here but is instead short

these days so say with one mind most
of meditators in snow land.
But "this great method's skillful means
to settle mind, beginners for,
and point out mind's concealer truth":
so does Chökyi Gyaltsen say.

As was said before, the nature of such a mind is lucid and clear. It is a vacuity, similar to the sky, and is a clear, vivid wakefulness. By seeing that conventional nature of the mind, these days many great meditators, when introduced to this nature of the mind, say, "I have seen the final reality of the mind." They say that all the explanations that teach such a nature are instructions bestowed for holding buddhahood in the palm of your hand—that is, instructions for taking buddhahood into your hand for personal practice.

According to his own perception, Paṇchen Losang Chökyi Gyaltsen says that this recognition of the conventional nature of the mind is not a mind realizing emptiness, and he thereby posits that the nature of the mind includes both a conventional nature [translated as "concealer" nature above] and an ultimate nature. He calls the emptiness of the mind, which is the emptiness of inherent existence, the "ultimate nature of the mind" and calls the mind's unique mode of existence its "conventional nature." [202] What appears to the absorption explained above, which is placed in equanimity on the mind, is the conventional nature of the mind, not the ultimate nature. So he is saying that merely on the basis of that, one cannot achieve the state of a buddha. There is no need for me to offer further explanation.[287]

---

for *sbar mo*. *Sbar mo* usually means claws or talons but can also refer to a human hand or palm. This interpretation also agrees with Rinpoché's commentary.

Likewise other translators have not included the first stanza as part of the quotation, but again Gen Namgyal Chöphel thinks the entire first six lines, and not only the fifth and sixth, are all quoting a prevalent view of previous scholars. "Reality" in the first line translates the Tibetan *chos nyid* (Skt. *dharmatā*), a term that usually refers to the final nature of something. Thus to take this conventional nature of mind as its final nature is part of the wrong view being presented.

287. Rinpoché is making an important point here. According to the Geluk interpretation, recognizing the vivid wakeful nature of the mind does not constitute a recognition of emptiness. This wakefulness is merely the conventional nature of the mind. Even so, recognizing this conventional nature is a significant feat. In this context, after recognizing that conventional nature, one takes that wakefulness itself as the *basis* (Tib. *stong gzhi*) for meditation on emptiness. See introduction.

Just because you are able to sustain an object of observation, you should in no way think, "I have achieved calm abiding!" In the context of what I explained yesterday about taking the three bodies into the path, you had to *imagine* "I have generated realizations" and meditate holding that pride. [But here, you certainly must *not* do that.] In this present context, you must not forget this manner of actualizing calm abiding that takes mind as its object of observation. Thinking, "I need such an unmistaken means of actualizing it," then if later you get an opportunity to actualize real calm abiding, you should actualize it in that way.

The mahāmudrā commentary that Paṇchen Losang Chökyi Gyaltsen composed himself is called *The Lamp That Further Clarifies*, and there are also notes on that by Ngülchu Dharmabhadra called *Dispelling All Illusions*. It is good if you can take a look at these two. Of the two commentaries that have already been translated into Chinese, one is the commentary by Paṇchen Losang Chökyi Gyaltsen, and the other is the notes composed by Ngülchu Dharmabhadra.[288]

Ngülchu Dharmabhadra is somebody who stayed in retreat practicing for fifty-two years.[289] [203] Given that meditators have the greatest familiarity with how to meditate, and because he composed these notes himself, you should definitely have a look at them.

Of the three—preparation, actual explanation, and concluding activities—the actual explanation has two parts: mantra-system mahāmudrā and sūtra-system mahāmudrā. I have already explained the mantra-system mahāmudrā. In the context of explaining sūtra-system mahāmudrā, the student must first actualize calm abiding and afterward the teacher must

288. Rinpoché mentions the texts having been translated into Chinese because in this context he was speaking to a Chinese-language audience. For English speakers, Roger Jackson's *Mind Seeing Mind: Mahāmudrā and the Geluk Tradition of Tibetan Buddhism* includes a translation of the Paṇchen Lama's autocommentary and a summary of Ngülchu Dharmabhadra's text. Additionally, His Holiness the Dalai Lama's commentary on *The Lamp That Further Clarifies* is included in Gyatso and Berzin 1997. For the Tibetan texts, see Losang Chökyi Gyaltsen, the Fourth Paṇchen Lama, *The Lamp That Further Clarifies: An Extensive Commentary on the Root Text of Mahāmudrā, the Precious Teaching Tradition of the Genden Oral Lineage*, and Ngülchu Dharmabhadra, *Dispelling All Illusions: Notes Taken During Profound Instructions on the Root Text of Mahāmudrā, Highway of the Conquerors* in the bibliography.

289. Ngülchu Dharmabhadra (Tib. Dngul chu Dharma Bha dra, 1772–1851) was one of the greatest Geluk scholars of the nineteenth century, studying at Tashi Lhunpo and spending most of his life in retreat at Ngülchu Hermitage.

explain emptiness. We have already covered the means of actualizing calm abiding.

Mind is a vacuity that is not established as a physical form. It is a clarity free of obscurations. It is a vivid wakefulness to which any object at all is suitable to appear. One is introduced to such a mind and, taking that mind as an object of observation, actualizes calm abiding. One does so with an unmistaken mode of maintaining recollection, which makes recourse to recollection by means of possessing an irreversible factor of stability and an intense clarity. The object of observation of calm abiding is the mind called "vacuity," "clarity," and "vivid wakefulness"—that is, the conventional nature of the mind.

THIRTEEN

Meditation on Emptiness

FROM HERE, the text explains the introduction to the ultimate nature of the mind—the mind's final reality:

> **And now, the way to introduce**
> **the final nature of the mind.**
> **I shall set forth the spoken advice**
> [204] **of my root lama who dispels**
> **the murk confusing my mind and**
> **is wisdom of all buddhas [Sangyé Yeshé][290] that**
> **displays a guise as saffron-clad.**

Here is a stanza that is a promise to compose. Although Paṇchen Losang Chökyi Gyaltsen already inserted a promise to compose at the beginning of the main body of the text [page 144], he was making a promise to compose in the context of the introduction to the conventional nature of the mind. The present one is a promise to compose because he is going to introduce us to the final reality, the ultimate nature of the mind.

Paṇchen Losang Chökyi Gyaltsen's lama was called Khedrup Sangyé Yeshé. Since one must view one's lama as the buddha, he says, "The exalted wisdom of all the buddhas, condensed into one, takes on the aspect of a saffron-robed [monk]." Because all the good qualities in Paṇchen's holy mind arose in dependence on his lama, he says, "Here I will set forth the oral instructions of my root lama, who dispels all the darkness of unknowing."

Here, the manner of introducing has two divisions: (1) the general explanation and (2) a teaching which condenses the essence. There are also sayings in

290. The Paṇchen Lama is here playing on the name of his teacher, Sangyé Yeshé (Tib. *Sangs rgyas ye shes*). This name literally means "Buddha Wisdom," and so in referring to him the Paṇchen Lama says he is in actuality "all the wisdom of all the buddhas" (Tib. *sangs rgyas rnams kyi ye shes kun*).

sūtra such as "If you subdue your mind, you are a buddha; you won't need to search for the buddha elsewhere" and "Because the mind itself is the buddha, do not search for the buddha elsewhere!" Because these sayings can be a basis for misunderstanding, the Paṇchen Lama explains [in the autocommentary] that he elucidated these divisions in terms of the two means of introduction to the nature of the mind. [205] The meaning of "Because the mind itself is the buddha, do not search for the buddha elsewhere!" according to the sūtra system is that the final reality of the mind is the basis for accomplishing buddhahood and is called "buddha lineage."[291] Having in mind that when this lineage is freed from obscurations, it becomes the nature of buddha, the sūtra says, "The mind itself is the buddha. You should not look for the 'buddha' somewhere else." So it is saying, "The basis for accomplishing buddhahood is there in your continuum. There is no need to search for it somewhere else."

According to the mantra tradition, it is as I explained above. If through

291. Skt. *buddhagotra*; Tib. *sangs rgyas kyi rigs*. This concept of a naturally abiding potential in the mind is often construed as "buddha nature," although that term does not literally correspond to any term in Sanskrit or Tibetan and can also be somewhat misleading. To say "buddha nature" implies that sentient beings are in actual nature buddhas, or that at the deepest level there is already a fully enlightened buddha waiting to manifest. Some schools of Tibetan Buddhism, notably the Jonang school of Dölpopa Sherap Gyaltsen and later followers of his view, do in fact take this position, but Tsongkhapa vehemently opposes it, and all Geluk scholars have followed suit. The basis for this teaching on buddha lineage is primarily the *Sūtra of the Essence of the Tathāgathas* (Skt. *Tathāgatagarbhasūtra*; Tib. *De bzhin gshegs pa'i snying po'i mdo*) and Maitreya's commentary to it entitled *Sublime Continuum* (Skt. *Mahāyānottaratantraśāstra*; Tib. *Theg pa chen po rgyud bla ma*). The reader might note a discrepancy in primary meaning of the Sanskrit "womb," or "that issued from the womb" (*garbha*), and the Tibetan rendition thereof as "essence" (*snying po*). As Prof. Zimmermann notes, this stems from a divergent approach to the simile of deluded sentient beings, who have the potential to reach enlightenment, as being like "withered lotuses with beautiful tathāgatas sitting in the center of their calyxes (*padmagarbha*)." See Zimmerman 2002, 12–13 and 40.

In any case, in the Geluk context, this buddha lineage is understood to be the emptiness of the mind rather than a functioning thing like an obscured aspect of the mind. The term *lineage* is used to emphasize that while beings may belong to different castes by birth—priestly caste, warrior caste, peasant caste, etc.—all of them are equal in that their minds are suitable to transform into a buddha, and thereby they possess the buddha lineage. In his text *Golden Garland of Eloquence*, Tsongkhapa breaks the Sanskrit *gotra* ("lineage") into two parts: *guṇa* ("qualities") and *uttāraṇa*, a term he takes to mean "to liberate." He explains this etymology to imply that because the mind is empty of inherent nature, there is the potential to transform it into a buddha, and furthermore that by meditating on this very emptiness, one can "liberate" those qualities. Thus it is the "lineage"—the "source of qualities." For English-language explanations of this important concept, see Tsongkhapa 2008, 1:367ff; also, Ārya Maitreya et al. 2000, Brunnhölzl 2014, and Gyatso and Chodron 2018.

skillful means you recognize the primordial connate clear light, then on the basis of that you will achieve the state of a buddha very quickly. If that clear light of death is lost in ordinariness, it becomes the cause of saṃsāra, so the mind is said to be "the root of both saṃsāra and nirvāṇa." According to mantra, the saying "If you realize the mind, you are a buddha" means that if you recognize the primordial connate clear light and are able to mix the mother and son clear lights, then you will actualize the higher and higher paths and become a buddha. So that is the meaning of "If you realize the mind, [206] you are a buddha" in accordance with the thought of all the sūtras and tantras.

If you recognize the final reality of the mind, that is "having cut the root basis of the mind within the actual meaning."[292] There are many ways of interpreting that statement. Some interpret it to mean, "A mind with aspects does not judge later about past events. A future mind does not anticipate things before they occur. The present mind is uncontrived naturalness." That is, one should abide without allowing any conceptual thought to arise at all. There are also those who say, "'Vacuity, clarity, suitability for any object at all to appear, vivid wakefulness.' If initially you place your mind in that way, you will see the naked nature of the mind, and that is introduction to the mind. You are introduced to the mind, and having been introduced to the mind, the realization spoken of in the statement 'If you subdue the mind, you are a buddha' will arise. If you are introduced to the mind, then through that you do not need to do any other work of adopting virtue and discarding negativity." Some people have said these kinds of things, but they are mistaken. Also, it is mistaken to say, "Based on seeing the final reality of the mind, one need not have regard for the results of karma."

Why is it mistaken? If a person has the realization of emptiness, then emptiness and dependent arising will become mutually supportive. [207] Furthermore, taking "empty" as a reason should increase one's faith in dependent arising, and taking "dependently arisen" as a reason should sharpen one's ascertainment of emptiness. If you realize emptiness, it should *increase* your regard for the results of karma.

For example, Jetsün Milarepa achieved buddhahood in this very life. He said, "From the ultimate point of view, there is no buddha, and also

292. Geshé Ngawang Thokmé explains that "actual meaning" refers to the final nature of the mind. "Cutting the root basis" means realizing the final nature of the mind and thereby cutting the root basis for cycling in saṃsāra. The mind can be both the root basis for cycling in saṃsāra and the root basis for liberation, depending on whether one adheres to true existence or refutes it.

no sentient being." He was not saying that in general there is no buddha, but that from the standpoint of true establishment there is no buddha and so forth. He explained that the Buddha himself said, "From the conventional point of view, all of these exist." On account of his saying, "From the ultimate standpoint, it does not exist," there were some people who denigrated him, saying, "Milarepa is a nihilist." When they said, "He is a nihilist," Jetsün replied, "If you want to know whether or not I am a nihilist, look at my behavior." His meaning was "I am not a nihilist."

Well then, what is the point? It is said that some people may be householders, but their level of regard for the results of karma, and their manner of guarding ethical discipline, is superior to those gone forth as monastics. In short, if by realizing the view one need not have regard for the results of karma, then Jetsün Milarepa would not need to have regard for the results of karma. As for Milarepa, the chief of all the accomplished ones of the Tibetan snow land, [208] although he realized the view, he held the results of karma in high regard. So those ways of speaking I talked about before are mistaken.

So, as for our own system of how to practice mahāmudrā and our own system of the manner of introduction to the final reality of the mind: when you first realize emptiness, it is profoundly meaningful, and it is difficult to realize. With regard to that, from the perspective of appearances to common trainees, at first the Blessed One stayed for forty-nine days without teaching the Dharma. After that time he exclaimed,

> This profound, peaceful, unembellished, clear light, uncompounded is
> a nectar-like phenomenon, uncovered such a thing have I!
> Whomever to I teach, to understand they will unable be.
> So I will not communicate. The forest in, I will abide.[293]

By saying, "Although I have uncovered a profound phenomenon, no matter to whom I teach it, they will be unable to understand. So for the time being, I won't teach this thing to others and will stay here," he indicated that it is difficult to realize. If you don't realize it, you cannot be liberated from saṃsāra, so without realizing it there is no method. Furthermore, the

293. This is a quote from the *Extensive Sport Sūtra* (Skt. *Lalitavistarasūtra*; Tib. *Rgya cher rol pa'i mdo*), chapter 24.

Buddha said that every Dharma he taught was for the purpose of liberating trainees from saṃsāra, so he indicated that in order to free yourself from saṃsāra, you definitely need to realize emptiness. As for the excellent teachings of the Buddha, some of them directly teach emptiness and cause trainees to enter into realizing emptiness. [209] There are others that do not directly teach emptiness but that indirectly cause trainees to enter into the path of realizing selflessness. Śāntideva said in *Engaging in the Bodhisattva Deeds*,

> Regarding all these branch concerns,
> for wisdom's purpose taught the sage.[294]

He is saying that the Buddha's teaching the other five of the six perfections—giving, guarding ethics, practicing patience, generating enthusiasm, absorption into meditative stabilization, and so forth—was only for the purpose of generating the sixth perfection, the mind realizing emptiness.

Jowo Jé Atiśa said,

> Of eighty-thousand heaps and four
> of Dharma, all that has been taught,
> flows down to this reality.[295]

He is saying that the teacher Buddha's explaining the 84,000 heaps of Dharma all comes down to the purpose of realizing emptiness, which is like the place where they all descend. Ācārya Kamalaśīla[296] explained in a similar way in his *Stages of Meditation*.[297] The intention of all of the great Indian scholars comes down to one. As for the most profound view, it is the view of the Consequence school,[298] which is that all phenomena are empty

294. Śāntideva, *Engaging in the Bodhisattva Deeds*, 9.1.

295. Atīśa (var. Atiśa), *Introduction to the Two Truths* (*Satyadvayāvatara, Bden gnyis la 'jug pa*), v. 15. See Sherburne 2000, 357.

296. Kamalaśīla (740–95) was an Indian scholar from Nālandā who accompanied Śāntarakṣita to help bring Buddhist teachings and monasticism to Tibet.

297. Skt. *Bhāvanākrama*; Tib. *Sgom rim*. For an English translation of the *Stages of Meditation*, see Sharma 1997. For a commentary, see Tenzin Gyatso 2001.

298. Tibetan doxography groups Indian scholastic Buddhism into four broad categories: the Great Exposition school (Skt. Vaibhāṣika; Tib. Bye brag smra ba), the Sūtra-Following school (Skt. Sautrāntika; Tib. Mdo sde pa), the Mind Only school (Skt. Cittamātra; Tib.

of being established by way of their own character. "In order to be liberated from saṃsāra, [210] you must realize emptiness" is saying that you need to realize emptiness as it is explained in this school. By teaching that directly, the Buddha caused trainees to enter into realizing emptiness. There are some cases where he did not directly say "empty of being established by way of their own character" but rather explained in accordance with the various ways of accepting selflessness of the four schools of tenets.[299] In the end, he explained these as only methods [stepping stones] for realizing selflessness as it is accepted by the Middle Way Consequence school. He explained two selflessnesses: the selflessness of persons and the selflessness of phenomena. In the Middle Way Consequence system, the selflessness of persons has a different basis of negation [the person], but as for the object of negation, it is no different than the object of negation of the selflessness of phenomena.[300] There are four proponents of tenets: Middle Way, Mind Only, Followers of Sūtra, and Great Exposition school.

Among these four, some are superior to others, and the supreme one is Middle Way. Below that is Mind Only, below that, Followers of Sūtra, and

---

Sems tsam pa), and the Middle Way school (Skt. Madhyamaka; Tib. Dbu ma pa). This latter school is further subdivided into the Autonomy school (Skt. Svātantrika; Tib. Rang rgyud pa) following Bhā(va)viveka (sixth century), and the Consequence school (Skt. Prasaṅgika; Tib. Thal 'gyur ba) following Buddhapālita (sixth century) and Candrakīrti. For a clear explanation of these schools of tenets, see Tsering 2008. For an in-depth presentation, see Hopkins 2003.

299. See previous note.

300. In the Mind Only and Middle Way Autonomy schools, the selflessness of persons and the selflessness of phenomena are differentiated in terms of what is being negated. For example, in the Middle Way Autonomy school, on a single basis—a person—there are two levels of selflessness. The person's emptiness of being substantial in the sense of being self-sufficient is the selflessness of persons, and the person's emptiness of true existence is the selflessness of phenomena, a subtler emptiness. For example, a man in a dream may appear to be one's enemy. On closer examination, one realizes he is a friend. That is like the selflessness of persons. On a deeper level, one realizes that he is not a man at all but simply a dream object. That subtler level of negation is like the selflessness of phenomena.

According to the Consequence school, the two selflessnesses are *not* two levels of negation on a single base, but rather the same negation on different bases. A person being empty of true existence is the selflessness of persons, and an object other than a person being empty of true existence is the selflessness of phenomena. Using the same example, in this case, recognizing the dream man to be not a real man corresponds to realizing the selflessness of persons, and recognizing the dream landscape to be not a real landscape corresponds to realizing the selflessness of phenomena. These two kinds of selflessness are no different in their level of subtlety; only the basis is different.

finally Great Exposition school. The Middle Way school is further subdivided into the Autonomy and Consequence schools. All schools from the Autonomists down accept the selflessness of persons to be no more than the person's emptiness of being a substantial self in the sense of being self-sufficient. Beyond that, they are unable to negate that the person is inherently established.[301] [211] The Great Exposition school and the Followers of Sūtra do not accept anything subtler than that—they do not accept a selflessness of phenomena. The Mind Only school does assert a selflessness of phenomena, but beyond the emptiness of duality, which is empty of a substantial separation of form and the valid cognition apprehending form, they do not assert an emptiness of true establishment.[302] They accept that emptiness of duality as being truly established.

The Middle Way Autonomy school accepts that while there is no true

301. If a person were substantial in the sense of being self-sufficient, he would have to be able to appear to the mind without relying on the mind ascertaining something else. For example, the color blue can appear to the eye consciousness without relying on something that is not blue, but a forest can only appear to the eye consciousness by relying on things that are not a forest—trees, squirrels, moss, etc. Thus blue is substantial in this sense, and the forest is not. Likewise a person cannot appear to the mind without relying on things that are not the person—the five aggregates of body, feelings, discrimination, compounding factors, and consciousness. For the lower schools, recognizing the way that we habitually grasp at the person as existing in a substantial way that can appear on its own, and recognizing that grasping as mistaken, constitutes recognizing the selflessness of persons.

The Consequence school considers this recognition as only a stepping stone to a deeper realization. According to them, one can negate the person as being substantial in the sense of being self-sufficient but still subtly cling to the idea that the person is substantial in the sense of there being something *among* the bases of designation that *is* the person. For example, one might conceive that the aggregates themselves *are* a person, or that some combination of them is, or that a particular one of them is, especially the mental consciousness (and indeed, all the lower schools do in fact posit one or another of these things as *being* the person). Taking the above example, one might suspect that the combination of the trees, moss, and animals constitute a forest. In that case many logical fallacies would ensue, such as (a) if one tree were removed, it would no longer be "the forest" and (b) in order to see the forest, one would have to see every single individual tree. The Consequence school asserts that none of the individual aggregates nor any combination thereof can be the person, and one must negate any trace of grasping at inherent existence in order to realize selflessness. For a more detailed explanation, see Jinpa 2002.

302. The Mind Only school asserts that, for example, the color blue is not substantially different from the eye consciousness perceiving blue, and that realizing this lack of substantial difference constitutes realizing emptiness. However, according to them, both blue and the eye consciousness are truly existent, because if they were not truly existent they could not perform functions outside of our imagination.

establishment, there is establishment by way of one's own character. They accept that if there were no establishment by way of one's own character, or establishment from one's own side, and if a cause did not from its own side have the power to generate a result, then results would not arise from causes. Moreover, on the basis of a particular cause, we could not say "achieved liberation" or "achieved the state of all-knowing." If things were not established by way of their own character, then the cause would not from its own side have the power to generate a result. In that case, all the sayings such as "From the side of the cause, the result arose" and "On the basis of that cause, she achieved the state of liberation" beyond mere mental presumption would become meaningless. Because it is unfeasible for there to be no cause and effect in reality, there is establishment by way of one's own character. In the end, as the reason for why this is so, they posit, "Because causes arise from results." However, they do say that true establishment is completely nonexistent.[303]

As for the Mind Only school, as the reason for why all compounded phenomena are truly established, [212] they posit that causes give rise to effects.

The Middle Way Consequentialists say, "There is no establishment by way of one's own character. If there *were* establishment by way of one's own character, then it would be unfeasible for causes to give rise to results. *Because* causes give rise to results, they must not be established by way of their own character." Thus, the Consequentialists go deeper into reasoning and, taking what the lower schools posit as the reason for establishment by way of one's own character, posit it as the reason there is *not* establishment by way of one's own character.

The various ways of accepting selflessness of the higher and lower tenets only become methods for realizing emptiness, either directly or indirectly. First, in order to reverse the imprint of the view adhering to a self-sufficient, substantial self, a view that comes from habituation with the view of

303. The Autonomy school asserts that things are not truly existent because they depend on other things—their parts and their causes. However, things do possess a level of intrinsic or findable existence. For example, a chariot is composed of parts that are not a chariot, but *the collection of the parts* is a chariot. If the collection of parts were not the chariot, then we would have to say there is no chariot at all and therefore would be unable to talk about cause and effect.

According to the Consequence school, the collection of parts is not the chariot. When you search and analyze, you cannot find a chariot, but conventionally we can still speak of a chariot existing and functioning.

forders,[304] the Buddha initially taught the mere emptiness of a substantial self in the sense of being self-sufficient. For those whose minds have become superior through habituation to that selflessness, he gradually taught emptiness of duality, emptiness of true existence, and emptiness of establishment by way of one's own character. So each earlier tenet becomes a method for realizing the view of the latter one, and in this way it is said, "Directly or indirectly, all of it comes down to emptiness." In short, all Dharma explained by the sage was only spoken as a method of realizing selflessness. Why did he need to teach in that way? Without realizing selflessness, one cannot be liberated from saṃsāra, [213] and through seeing selflessness, one will be liberated from saṃsāra. With those points in mind, he taught as he did.

We Need to Realize Selflessness

Why do we need to realize selflessness in order to be liberated from saṃsāra? Merely through calm abiding, we will be unable to escape from saṃsāra. Even people who are able to stay in absorption on calm abiding for many eons are unable, through that, to abandon saṃsāra. Furthermore, the story goes that when our teacher Buddha came to this world, there was a forder named Udraka Rāmaputra.[305] Udraka Rāmaputra entered into absorption on calm abiding and thought, "Now my mind has achieved liberation." So he stayed in absorption. While he remained in absorption for a long time, this forder let his matted locks flow freely. A rat began chewing on his locks, causing him to arise from absorption. Seeing the rat chewing on his locks, he became angry. Through the force of his anger, his calm abiding degenerated. Because his calm abiding degenerated, he generated the wrong view, thinking, "Alas, there is no liberation after all!" and was thereby born in hell.

Merely by actualizing calm abiding, one cannot achieve liberation. However, we ought to actualize calm abiding and, using calm abiding as a basis, generate the wisdom that realizes selflessness. Using that wisdom as the direct antidote to the apprehension of a self, we can then achieve liberation. For that reason, in order to attain liberation, we do in fact need calm abiding.

304. See note 24.

305. See note 25.

[214] What kind of thing is this concentration which causes the attainment of liberation? From the *King of Concentrations Sūtra*,[306]

> As selfless, if you check all things
> then meditate as you have checked,
> that's cause to gain nirvāṇa's fruit.
> Through other causes, peace won't come.

It is saying that on the basis of the wisdom realizing selflessness, one achieves liberation; no other cause will bring about liberation. As for that selflessness, according to the teaching of Hashang,[307] "Be it a wicked thought or a wholesome thought, you should not allow any thoughts to arise at all. Rather, you should abide without engaging your mind with anything whatsoever. If you do like that, you will achieve liberation." This is incorrect. "As selfless, if you check all things . . ." is saying that in order to achieve liberation, you need to realize selflessness. In order to realize that, you need to analyze with the wisdom of individual examination. If at the end of analysis you see the meaning of emptiness, you need to meditate on that and achieve liberation. Apart from that, no other cause at all will give rise to liberation. So it is clearly saying that you need to meditate on the basis of having analyzed with

306. Skt. *Samādhirājasūtra*; Tib. *Ting nge 'dzin rgyal po'i mdo*. For a commentary on this sūtra, see Thrangu Rinpoché 1994. A complete translation is available at http://read.84000.co/translation/toh127.html.

307. Hashang Mahāyāna (Mohoyen [和尚摩訶衍] or Héshang Móhēyǎn) was a Chinese teacher who visited Tibet in the eighth century and gathered a following there. According to the tradition and sparse, but largely factual—though idealized, and most likely instrumentalized—historical documentation (especially the oft-quoted, early-ninth-century *dBa' bzhed*), the king Trisong Detsen arranged a debate at Samyé Monastery between Hashang and Kamalaśīla, an Indian scholar. According to the generally accepted narrative, Hashang lost the debate, and the king proceeded to banish him.

Although Tsongkhapa's presentation of Hashang's teachings is likely somewhat of a caricature, it does highlight a common wrong view that has gained prevalence in various locations over Buddhism's varied history. According to this teaching, conceptions of right and wrong are obstacles to comprehending emptiness, and therefore a practitioner should do away with all concepts of right and wrong and abide in a nonconceptual state. For an account of the Samyé debate, see Bretfeld 2004, Houston 1980, and especially Pasang and Diemberger 2000. See also Powers 1995, 130–33. For indigenous Tibetan accounts of the debate, refer to Buton's *Chos 'byung* and the *Bsam gtan mig sgron* by Gnubs chen Sangs rgyas ye she. For Chinese historical attestation, refer to Dunhuang Manuscript Pc 4646 (頓悟大乘正理決). We gratefully acknowledge the expert input of Ben Manbun Luk (University of Hong Kong) on the historical veracity of the Samyé debate.

the wisdom of individual examination. Although there are many different views, mainly if you take into practice the view that is most concordant with your individual mind, there is the greatest advantage and least danger. For example, if you have a strong inclination for the Mind Only view, [215] for the time being you should meditate on the Mind Only view. For the purpose of realizing the final view, if you make effort, accumulate merit, purify negativities, and repeatedly make prayers to realize the unerring view, then one day when you meet with the right conditions, you will come to realize the Middle Way view. If instead you right away take on the Consequentialist view, saying, "All phenomena lack establishment by way of their own character," then there is a danger you will start to think, "No phenomenon exists at all. Karmic cause and effect is also nonexistent," and you will fall into the extreme of nihilism. When we talk about the Consequentialist view, saying, "No establishment by way of its own characteristics . . . ," then fear does not even arise in our minds. Legend has it that in earlier times, when our teacher Buddha lived, if he explained emptiness to somebody who was not a suitable vessel for teaching emptiness, then their mind would not tolerate it. They would vomit blood and die on the spot.[308]

For that reason, in the advice to bodhisattvas, it says that you should not teach emptiness to the untrained. In this context, we should explain the view in accordance with the Consequentialist assertion. According to that school, selflessness has both the selflessness of persons and the selflessness of phenomena, and these two do not have any difference in terms of coarseness and subtlety. However, by virtue of the basis of negation being different, [216] the selflessness of persons is easier to realize, so I will explain that first.[309] Selflessness of persons is said to be the nonestablishment by

308. The point here is that if one truly understands the import of the teachings on emptiness, initially one will experience fear. The fact that fear does not arise in our minds when we hear about emptiness is a sign that we do not really comprehend the import of the teaching. Rinpoché has said elsewhere:

> At the end of examining, by way of many reasons, the mode of apprehension of the mind that holds to true establishment, when a vacuity that is the absence of true establishment appears, you have realized emptiness. When that mind realizing emptiness arises, a person of sharp faculties will have a joyous feeling, as though they have discovered a stable support. A person of lesser faculties will have an experience as though they have lost their most cherished jewel. (Chöden Rinpoché 2018, 105).

309. Jé Tsongkhapa clearly states in his *Middle-Length Lamrim* (Tsongkhapa 2012, 253) that while the objects of negation of selflessness of persons and selflessness of phenomena are not

way of one's own character on the basis of a person. In order to realize the basis, a person, you need to realize the "I" that is posited on the basis of any one of the five aggregates that are the basis of the self. Using dependent relativity—which is dependence on labeling—as a reason proving it, you are going to establish selflessness. Therefore, since (1) if you realize the person, you have to realize a gross imputed existent,[310] (2) if something were truly established, it would have to be established as self-sustaining without relying on anything at all, and (3) if you realize the person, you need to realize its dependence on the aggregates, which are the basis of the self, it is said to be easier to realize the selflessness of persons by virtue of the basis [the person].

Explanation of the Manner of Identifying the Object of Negation

Without recognizing the object of negation, you will be unable to establish the subtle emptiness that is the negation of that. So in order to come to certainty about the selflessness of persons, you first need to identify the self that is the object of negation. Having identified that, you must refute away that self that is the object of negation and establish selflessness, so the self that is established from the side of the object is called the "self that is the object of negation." When identifying the object of negation, you must identify an object of negation of an appropriate magnitude. If you do not, and instead

---

distinguished by their level of subtlety, still by virtue of the basis (person or phenomena) it is easier to realize selflessness on the basis of the person.

One common way to understand this distinction is that the person's being an imputed existent is more obvious. Most people would agree that the collection of the aggregates cannot be said to constitute the person—obviously my hand is not "me," nor is my belief system, nor are the two of these together. We can understand that what we call "me" is in some way a conceptual designation based on a variety of different physical and mental factors, even though it takes time for this understanding to deepen and affect our habitual thinking and behavior. It is more difficult to understand how the collection of the arms, legs, head, and torso do not constitute a "body," because all of these parts are physical forms.

Another way to understand this distinction is that the selflessness of persons is easier to realize because it is easier to recognize the way our mind habitually grasps at the inherent existence of a person. It is easier to recognize that because our grasping is so strong.

310. If you realize a person, you realize a being that is posited on the basis of the five aggregates. This is "gross imputation," as opposed to the subtler kind of imputation—imputation on the basis of a conceptual consciousness labeling it. The point is that, in realizing a person, you necessarily realize gross imputation, so it naturally becomes easier to realize subtle imputation (see previous note).

you negate too much, it is improper because you will negate all existents and fall into the extreme of nihilism. Alternatively, if your object of negation is too narrow—if you mentally fabricate an object of negation, [217] then call the negation of that "selflessness"—then beyond merely negating something you yourself have created, you will not negate the actual object of negation. So you definitely need to identify the object of negation. The apprehension of a self, the apprehension of "I," or the apprehension that thinks "I"—this mind can have three different modes of apprehending its object[311]: (1) the mind that apprehends that very "I," which is qualified by being established from its own side, as though it existed in a sturdy, autonomous way without depending on anything else; (2) the mind that apprehends an "I" that is qualified by being not truly established and not existing apart from mere imputation over there by names and concepts; and (3) the mode of apprehension that apprehends by merely thinking "I" without qualification as either truly established or not truly established.

The third mode of apprehension that thinks "I" without qualification as either true or false is the mode of apprehending the "I" that exists in mere name. The "I" that accords with that mode of apprehension does exist. For example, it is the "I" in the context of "I eat," "I wear clothes," "I practice Dharma," or "I achieve liberation." The "I," in accordance with the first mode of apprehension, which apprehends the "I" qualified as truly established, is not established and so we must negate it. The second mode of apprehending—within the qualification of not being truly established—is only the way somebody would apprehend it after they have gained an understanding of selflessness. A person who has not gained such an understanding would not have such a mode of apprehension.[312]

The mind that apprehends the self as truly established is called "apprehension of the self of persons," [218] and it is the root of saṃsāra. It exists when somebody is bound by the apprehension of a self of phenomena that apprehends the aggregates to be truly established. These two—apprehension of self of persons and apprehension of self of phenomena—are equal in being

311. The point here is *not* that (1) the apprehension of a self, (2) the apprehension of "I," and (3) the apprehension that thinks "I" are three different things with three different objects of apprehension. These are three different ways of referring to the same mind. The point is rather that this apprehension of a self can apprehend that self in three different ways, as Rinpoché goes on to explain.

312. An ordinary person would have both the first and the third apprehensions, but not the second one.

the root of saṃsāra.[313] In order to apprehend the person as true, one first needs to apprehend the aggregates as true. The reason is that in order for the person to appear as an object of mind, first the aggregates need to appear as an object of mind, and then an "I" which is imputed on the basis of those aggregates appears. Before the person even appears to the mind, as soon as the aggregates appear as an object of mind, through the force of strong prior habituation to the apprehension of true existence, one apprehends the aggregates as true. So before one apprehends the person as true, one apprehends the aggregates as true.[314]

What is the mode of existence of all phenomena? Whatever phenomenon there is, it exists merely by being imputed over there by names and posited over there by the force of concepts; the phenomenon does not have even a mere atom of existence from its own side.[315] The principles of actions and agents for all phenomena are logically sound, so in general they do exist. If they were established not as merely posited by the force of names and

313. Being the "root of saṃsāra" means that these two misapprehensions give rise to all other afflictions and that both of them can act as the ignorance that is the first of the twelve links of dependent origination.

314. "Apprehending the aggregates as true" in this context does not mean one necessarily has the thought "These aggregates are truly established," but rather that one merely assents to the way they habitually appear without questioning that appearance. Because they appear to untrained consciousness as being truly existent, then merely assenting to that appearance constitutes apprehending them as truly existent.

Geshé Ngawang Sangyé gives an example to illustrate this stepwise process. When you meet a person for the first time, you initially see their physical body and hear the sound of their voice, and you unconsciously assent to the way these aggregates appear—as inherently existent. Then when somebody tells you, "This is Michael," you start forming a concept of a truly existent person.

315. The term "posited over there by names and concepts" (Tib. *ming dang rtog pa'i dbang gis phar bzhag pa tsam*) negates existence from its own side. According to the Autonomy school, things are *both* posited by thought *and* existent from their own side; both factors must be present for something to exist. They are "posited by thought" but not "posited *over there* by thought." For the Consequence school, things are posited by thought without existing from their own side, so they are posited "over there." For the Consequence school, there is no problem of things not being able to exist before somebody thinks about them, because in this school, causes can be dependent upon their effects. Why? Because (1) something being called a "cause" is only in relation to an "effect," and (2) things only exist in mere name, so if the name of X is dependent on Y, then X is also dependent on Y. An illustrative example would be this: Dr. Donald Johanson discovered the bones of a human ancestor and called them "Lucy." Dr. Johanson did not apply this name until the present day, but still it is conventionally correct to say "Lucy lived over three million years ago." Lucy depends upon Dr. Johanson for her existence.

concepts, that establishment would become an object of negation, so their mode of existence does not go beyond existence that is posited by the force of names and concepts. For that reason, the opposite of that—existence that is not posited by the force of names and concepts—is the object of negation.

Well then, what is "posited by the force of names and concepts"? [219] When it is coiled, a variegated rope is similar to a snake. If you look when dawn has not yet broken, because its color and way of being coiled is like a snake's, through the force of concepts the thought will arise, "It's a snake!" On that basis, fear arises, so the manner of being posited by the force of thought is like that. When the thought arises, "It's a snake!" does the snake exist upon the rope? Other than fear arising on account of thought positing a snake, there is no snake established whatsoever within the rope. It is not as though there is a snake established from the side of the rope, and then fear arises. One's own concepts impute it as a snake, and through the force of that, fear arises.

In the same way, all phenomena, beyond mere imputation by thought, have no establishment whatsoever from their own side. Positing such an example is merely positing an example of imputation by thought; it is not saying that just as the snake does not exist in the rope, all phenomena do not exist.[316]

The apprehension of a self of persons apprehends the "I" of the thought "I" as an existent that is not imputed by names and concepts. It apprehends it as though it were concretely here from the side of the basis of imputation and not posited over there by the force of names and concepts. So we must identify that mode of apprehension. In order to negate the self, which is the object of negation, and establish selflessness, [220] initially it is important to do the work of identifying the manner in which that object of negation appears to your mind. Furthermore, the mere explanation in the text and the lama's merely saying it will not help. You need to think about it and be able to identify it based on your own experience. What method should you apply to identify it through your own experience? When you experience a strong feeling of joy or when strong fear arises, and somebody says, "You!" then the "I" of the thoughts "Ooh, I am attractive!" and "I am *so* likeable!"

316. The point is, the snake in the rope is both posited by thought *and* is nonexistent. A chariot, on the other hand, is also posited by thought but is not nonexistent. Things posited by thought can be either nonexistent or existent, but initially it is easier to understand the way thought posits nonexistent things, so these are used as examples.

arises. Something that is concrete—not imputed by names and concepts—appears as an object of mind. At that moment, you need to have an astute awareness and be able to identify it. If you identify that object of negation, then it will be easier to establish the negation that negates it, so you must identify the object of negation.

Generally to realize selflessness you do not need calm abiding, but you do need a slight mental factor of stability. If you get a factor of stability in your mind, then by analyzing with the wisdom of individual analysis, you will be able to realize selflessness. What I spoke of before—"seeking meditation within the view" [on page 186]—will come about. Here, the Paṇchen Lama is explaining according to the system of seeking the view within meditation: first one actualizes calm abiding. Having actualized a stable calm abiding, then within that calm abiding, [221] one must engage in analysis.

> **Not moving from absorption's space**
> **like in a clear pond minnows dart,**
> **with subtle mind incisively**
> **inspect the meditator's make.**

Seeking meditation within the view is from the point of view of not having actualized a stable calm abiding. [In the context of this stanza,] from the point of view of *having* actualized a stable calm abiding, set your mind in equipoise on the conventional nature of the mind. From within that absorption and without moving from that absorption, examine the nature of a being: What sort of thing is this, a "person"? What sort of thing is this, a "self of persons"? For example, in clear water, although underneath minnows or small fish dart to and fro, the surface of the water does not oscillate. Likewise, the Paṇchen Lama is saying that when you engage in subtle analysis without moving your mind from absorption, the ability to analyze without moving from absorption comes about. In terms of searching for the "I" within that absorption, initially within that absorption, as I explained above, you incite a feeling of joy or distress. When a strong feeling of joy or distress arises, with a corner of your mind you check to see what sort of mode of apprehension it has. Like the sentry of introspection that I explained above [on page 200], [222] this is a corner of the mind that is like a sentry. When a strong feeling of joy or distress arises, the mind thinking "I" does not arise for more than a brief instant, so that mind standing watch has to be able to recognize it quickly. Because it soon gets mixed with our usual [nonerroneous] mode of apprehension of "I" and thereafter does not arise clearly, you should examine it as quickly as possible.

As I explained before about needing to rely on the collection of causes to achieve calm abiding, likewise to generate special insight, one needs to rely on the collection of causes for special insight. Rely on a holy being, and listen to his instructions. You yourself must also study texts that explain emptiness. For the purpose of realizing emptiness, meditate on your kind root lama himself in the aspect of the exalted supreme deity, the noble lord Mañjuśrī, and make requests. The noble lord Mañjuśrī is the deity of wisdom. Among his many aspects, you should meditate on his usual one—orange Mañjuśrī—and make requests. Go for refuge and generate bodhicitta, confess negativities, and so forth. If you meditate on guru yoga, you also meditate on the lama in the aspect of the noble lord Mañjuśrī. As a preliminary, perform the seven-limbed prayer, one hundred prostrations, and so forth. Make a request: "Please allow me to be able to realize the unmistaken view." [223] By doing that, streams of [white] nectar flow down from the noble lord's holy body. Imagine that they purify all the ignorance of apprehending a self, sickness, spirit harm, negativities, and obscurations in your continuum. Again, yellow nectar flows down. By filling your entire body, imagine that you are blessed to generate the wisdom that realizes the view.

Meditate on guru yoga. After that, contemplate the fault of not realizing selflessness—that you will not be liberated from saṃsāra—and the benefit of realizing it—that you will be liberated. The four proponents of tenets each have different ways of accepting selflessness. From within the three modes of apprehending the "I" [explained on page 229], the mode of apprehension that apprehends an "I" that is neither qualified as true nor false is the mode of apprehension of the nominally existent "I." The "I" in accordance with that apprehension does exist. In accordance with the mode of apprehension that apprehends an "I" qualified as truly established, the "I" does not exist. When based on your own experience you identify the "I" in accordance with that latter mode of apprehension, it will appear as though it is something existing sturdily from its own side, not something posited over there by the force of names and concepts. When you identify the "I" that exists sturdily from its own side, not posited by the force of names and concepts, and then analyze whether or not that mode of establishment exists, you see that that mode of establishment is completely nonexistent. Initially, [224] it is difficult for the view of selflessness to appear to your mind. For that reason, the Blessed One said, "To whomever I may teach this profound emptiness, they will be unable to understand. So for the time being, I will not teach." Nevertheless, you should not become depressed, thinking, "I can't understand these things." Make requests to the deity and the lama. Think it over yourself. If you do like that, it is said that because compounded things do not stay the same, one day understanding will arise.

Although you may not have generated the actual mind realizing the view at this point, you can think, "'Selflessness' seems to be like that," and make progress toward that mind. If you think, "All phenomena are not established by way of their own character. They are merely posited by the force of names and concepts," then although familiarity may not arise in your mind, you must make a determination to move your mind in that direction.

As for searching for the view within meditation, without moving or arising from that absorption, with that subtle mind you analyze. If the end result of analysis is to induce pliancy, you have achieved special insight.[317] In order to search for the view within the space of calm abiding meditation, first "with subtle mind incisively inspect the meditator's make." You must enter absorption on the generality of the mind, and then with a subtle mind examine what precisely is the determined object of the apprehension that apprehends an inherently existent being or "I." [225] When you haven't identified that object of negation, but still you prematurely analyze whether the object of negation exists on any part of the body, then if, although examining, you fail to locate it on any part of the body, you may have the thought "A self, or 'I,' that exists in name and is the basis for karmic results is completely nonexistent." In that case you have fallen into the extreme of nihilism, so first "incisively inspect the meditator's make." That is, examine what is the object of negation and what is the mode of apprehension of the mind apprehending it. If you thereby ascertain the mode of apprehension of that apprehender, *then* you should analyze whether or not such an "I" exists among the bases of designation.

Furthermore,

Nāgārj'na, Ārya, savior, said . . .

Because he provides refuge for all those who are without refuge, he is called "savior." From his *Precious Garland*,[318]

317. If analysis does not disturb but actually enhances concentration and bliss, one has achieved special insight. See introduction.

318. Nāgārjuna, *Precious Garland*, 1.80–81. For English, see Hopkins 1998.

> **"A being is not earth, water not,**
> **not fire, not wind, not space, and is**
> **not consciousness . . ."**

If there were such a being who was established from his own side, then if you searched for him on each of the six elements,[319] you would have to locate such a being. A "being" is designated on the basis of the aggregation of the six elements. So when you observe the being's body, which is an aggregation of the six elements, and search for the being among these six elements, the earth element is not the being. Nor is the water, nor is the fire, nor is the wind, nor is the space, nor is the consciousness element the being. [226] Since you search in each part but do not locate him, you have established that all parts of the six elements are not "I." If you wonder, "Well then, each individual part is not the being, but isn't the collection of the parts 'I'?" Nāgārjuna continues,

> **"nor all of them."**

He is saying that even the collection is not "I."[320] He then adds,

> **"Apart from these what being is there?"**

The aggregates and six elements that are the bases of designation are not each individually the person, and the aggregation of the six elements is also not the person. Therefore, upon the bases of designation you do not find an "I" that is established by way of its own character. Well in that case, other than that is there an "I," established from its own side, to be found? In this case also there is no such thing to be found at all.

319. Skt. *ṣaḍdhātu*; Tib. *khams drug*. The six elements are the six listed in the root text above. Like the five aggregates, this list is a way of expressing the constituents of a person.

320. See also note 301. Several reasons can be used to establish that the collection of parts is not the person. For example, if the collection of body parts were the person, then merely by seeing a person's face, I could not say, "I see the person," because the person would be the collection of all the parts and not merely the face. Likewise, when my hand is in pain, I could not say, "I am in pain," because the entire collection of parts, which would be me, is not in pain. Alternatively, if my hand were amputated, we would have to say that I ceased to exist, because the entire collection of parts would no longer exist. These reasons take on even more force when we consider that the mind and mental factors—and not merely the parts of the body—are included in the collection of parts.

Having analyzed in that way, you conclude that an "I" that is established by way of its own character does not exist anywhere. It does not exist on the aggregates, which are the bases of designation, and it also does not exist on anything else apart from the aggregates. Keeping this conclusion in mind, use your mind to analyze repeatedly whether or not that object of negation exists.

Well then, generally does the being not exist? While a being who is established by way of his own character does not exist, there is a being who is merely posited by conventions. Again, Nāgārjuna says,

> **"Since a being's a collection of**
> **six elements—authentic not."**

A being is posited as a being or person merely by designation over there on the basis of the aggregation of the six elements. So he is not authentic [227] or established from his own side. "Authentic" has the same meaning as "established from its own side" or "inherently established," so such a thing is nonexistent.

That *Precious Garland* explains that the person is not inherently established and goes on to delineate the lack of inherent existence of the aggregates. Taking "not authentic" as an example, just as the being is not inherently established,

> **"Just so, each element is too . . ."**

Even each of the six elements is established on the basis of the aggregation of its many parts, so it is not inherently established. Taking the earth element of a being's body as an example, that element is also established out of the aggregation of its many parts. Since it is established by aggregation, like the aggregates there is no inherently existent earth element to be found. Nāgārjuna concludes,

> **"collected—thus authentic not."**

The Paṇchen Lama continues,

> **If you have searched and as he said . . .**

If you search in the way it was explained in *Precious Garland*, there is no person existing on the collection, nor is there any existing on each individual constituent. So there is no authentically established person at all.

Explanation of the Manner of Realizing Emptiness

absorption, who absorbs, and such . . .

If you divide up the three—the action of entering absorption, the actor who enters into absorption, [228] and the objects of absorption (emptiness and so on)—then even if you search for them, there is nothing to be found.

not one mere atom do you find . . .

Having identified the object of negation, if you analyze each part and discover that nothing is found, you have realized emptiness.

sustain then space-like equipoise,
one-pointed, undistractedly.

At that point, since you have realized emptiness, enter into absorption on that. Just as we posit the mere negation of obstructive contact as space, we enter into the mere negation of the object of negation, so it is called "space-like."

The preceding verses have delineated how the "I" lacks inherent existence and how the aggregates of that "I" lack inherent existence.

Or from the space of equipoise,
all things appear, spread, unobscured
vacuity, not made as form.
A nonstop stream of knowing clear,
the mind engaging ceaselessly.

Determined object, held as seems—
relying not.

Earlier we discussed how within the space of single-pointed equipoise on calm abiding, you analyze with a subtle awareness. Checking what kind of thing is this mind, you identify that mind is not established from its own side and is thereby a clear vacuity. It has no obscuration at all, and various objects appear and scatter. It does not cease—each moment sequentially follows the next, [229] so it is without cessation. It is clear and knowing. Such is the mind, which you recognize. Having identified the mind, you might ask, "How does this mind apprehend the object, inherent existence?" It appears as nonreliant—a self-powered thing that does not rely on anything. The apprehension of true existence, which apprehends the object as truly being established in the way that it appears, apprehends it like that. If that apprehension of true existence apprehends it in that way, what must you do to negate its determined object?[321]

> **. . . said Śāntidev':**
> **"What's called 'continu'm,' 'gathering'**
> **is false like mālās, armies, and such."[322]**
> **With scripture and such reasoning . . .**

What we call "time" and "mind" are designated on the conjoining of an earlier and later continuity. Beyond that, they are not established from their own side. With a collection as well, on the basis of many parts, if they aggregate we designate it a "collection." Beyond that, there is no collection established from its own side. As an example of that, Śāntideva posits a rosary [*mālā*] and an army. With a rosary, we do not call each individual bead a rosary. We can only say "rosary" for a collection of a series of many beads. So the mere designation over there of "rosary" on the abiding of a series of many beads on a string is a rosary. Beyond that, if we search among the bases of

321. In the context of a conceptual consciousness like the apprehension of true existence, "to apprehend" is synonymous with "to determine," and "apprehended object" is synonymous with "determined object." So the point here is that (a) the object (the mind, in this case) appears (to *both* direct perception and thought consciousness) to be nonreliant, or inherently existent, (b) *thought* consciousness apprehends/determines it to exist in the way it appears, as nonreliant, and (c) nonreliance, the apprehended/determined object of that thought consciousness, is incorrect.

322. These two lines are a quote from Śāntideva's *Engaging in the Bodhisattva Deeds* (*Bodhisattvacaryāvatāra*), 8.101ab.

designation, [230] there is nothing to be found. Likewise if we say, "An army is coming!"—if one soldier is coming, we don't say, "An army is coming!" We say, "A soldier is coming." As for an army, if many soldiers congregate we designate an "army." Just as each individual soldier is not an army, likewise the continuity or the continuum of mind is a mere designation on a collection without establishment from its own side.

> **absorb one-pointed in the space**
> **of nonestablished as appears.**

Granted that the continuity or continuum of mind exists as a collection of many earlier and later moments, well then, on what do we designate "continuity of mind"? Do we designate it on the first moment or on the second moment? If you analyze, you do not find anything, because that continuity, other than mere designation over there on a collection, is nonexistent.

If we look at the way it appears to our mind, when the aggregates and so forth appear, they appear as not depending on anything, as though they were established from their own side. If they existed in accordance with the way they appear, there would need to be something findable on each individual part, but no such findable thing exists. If you realize this nonestablishment in accordance with the manner of appearance, you have realized emptiness. As I explained above, analyze by means of identifying the object of negation. If you analyze in this way but do not find it, [231] you realize emptiness, so then enter single-pointed absorption on that very nonfindability, within the space of the union of calm abiding and special insight.

> **In short, from the blessed mouth of my friend**
> **in virtue, Sangyé Yeshé, who**
> **knows all phenom'na as they are . . .**

The one called Sangyé Yeshé is in accordance with actuality. He is like the exalted wisdom (*yeshé*) of all the buddhas (*sangyé*) condensed into one. So the Paṇchen Lama is giving a meaning to his name.

> **"When you know fully what appears is what is grasped by**
> **concept-thought,**
> **the ult'mate Dharma sphere appears, relying not on anything.**

On entering awareness into space of that appearance then
to station single-pointedly, into absorption *e ma ho*!"[323]

At present, no matter what appears to you, it is merely posited over there by conceptual thought. There is not even a mere atom existing from the object's own side. If you thoroughly understand—that is, see—that it is merely posited over there by conceptual thought, then without depending on another reason, you will be able to cause the emptiness that is empty of inherent existence, or the ultimate final reality, to appear as an object to your mind. Once you enter *into* awareness within the space of such an emptiness, he says, "To station single-pointedly, into absorption *e ma ho*!" If you enter absorption into the space of such an emptiness, then since the object of your realization is the emptiness of all phenomena, [232] he says, "*E ma ho*! It is a great wonder!"

Thus he said, likewise Dampa said,
"Into the space of emptiness, whirl the spear of knowingness.
To the view there is no block, no difficulty, Dingriwa."[324]
And so on—the intent's the same.

323. This verse of Sangyé Yeshé is found in his collected works, Item *ca* 67 (vol. 1, 135–276). A literal translation of the final two lines of this verse would seem to be

To situate awareness into the space of that appearance
And enter single-pointedly, into absorption *e ma ho*!"

However, in his commentary, Rinpoché adds the suffix *ra* to the term *rig pa* ("awareness"), clarifying that the meaning is not that one places awareness but enters *into* awareness. My translation reflects Rinpoché's reading, and Rinpoché's reading likewise reflects the Paṇchen Lama's own explanation in the autocommentary (p. 115). There he explains that "in the space of that appearance" actually means that the appearance of emptiness as an object of mind and the object-possessor mind realizing it merge as one, and you enter into absorption on that. So "entering into the space of that appearance" and "entering awareness" are both correct. The Paṇchen Lama also clarifies that "grasped by concept-thought" means *posited* by thought, and "ultimate Dharma sphere appears" means that mind *engages*—that is, realizes—the ultimate nature of reality. Because realizing the conventional level, in which things are posited by thought, leads directly to realizing the ultimate level of emptiness, he says this is the meaning of Candrakīrti's statement (*Supplement to the Middle Way*, 6:80)

Convent'nal truth's a method and
the ult'mate truth, from method comes.

324. This is a quote from Phadampa Sangyé's (Tib. Pha dam pa Sangs rgyas) text *One Hundred Verses of Advice for the People of Dingri* (Tib. *Ding ri brgya rtsa ma*), v. 52. Phadampa Sangyé was an Indian master who traveled and taught in Tibet and China in the eleventh

Because he stayed at Dingri, when he gave a kind of advice to himself Phadampa Sangyé would say, "Dingriwa, Dingriwa" [one from Dingri]. When you analyze in that way, the appearance of establishment without depending on anything at all shows itself. You then analyze whether or not things are established in the way the mind apprehends them, when it apprehends them to be established as they appear. At the end of analysis, you think, "They are not established in that way," and such a vacuity appears. "Into the space of emptiness, whirl the spear of awareness." If you "whirl" or launch a spear, just as it falls onto its target, place your mind on this. If you do like that, then "to the view there is no block, no difficulty, Dingriwa": he is talking about the manner of meditating on emptiness, saying, "You have realized the actual view."

In our system, regarding mahāmudrā, having settled upon the final reality of the mind, meditation on that is called "mahāmudrā meditation." Many earlier practitioners, upon discovering the conventional nature of the mind—utter vacuity, clarity, and vivid wakefulness—would say, "This is instruction bestowed for holding buddhahood in the palm of your hand." However, in Paṇchen Rinpoché's holy opinion, [233] "This is the conventional introduction to the mind"—it is a mere introduction and is not the actual mahāmudrā that is the final reality of the mind. The actual mahāmudrā is the conclusive view of the final reality of the mind when you have settled upon that final reality of the mind.

In Conclusion, Dedicating the Virtue to Complete Enlightenment

> **To end, whatever wholesomeness comes**
> **from meditating on the great seal,**
> **with three times' virtue's ocean, too,**
> **for full awak'ning, dedicate.**

---

and twelfth centuries. In his early life he was known as Kamalaśīla, though not the same person as the author of *Stages of Meditation*.

Some Tibetan historians, starting with the Mongolian Changkya Rölpai Dorjé, have even identified him as the Indian master Bodhidharma, who brought Ch'an Buddhism to China (see Hopkins 1983, 536–37, and Hopkins 1987, 18). For a translation of this text with commentary, see Khenchen Thrangu 2015. For a biography of Phadampa Sangyé, see Molk 2008.

"To end": of the three parts of the initial outline—the preparation, actual explanation, and conclusion or afterword—what are the concluding activities? He makes a dedication, saying, "Whatever wholesomeness, or virtues, have arisen from meditating on mahāmudrā—and not only that virtue alone, but the ocean-like collection of virtues accumulated by myself and all other sentient beings over the three times—I combine into one. May it become a cause for the great unsurpassed enlightenment!"

If you meditate on how all phenomena are merely posited over there by thought, and there is not even mere slight establishment from the side of the object,

> **Whatever, meditating thus,**
> **appears as objects to six types,**
> **inspect in close how it appears.**
> **The naked mode will clearly dawn.**
> [234] **"The view's main point: discern what appears."**[325]

By meditating in that way, then whatever appears as an object of the six classes of consciousness,[326] you should closely examine its mode of appearance. That is, check, "What sort of mode of appearance is there?" As for the mode of appearance, whatever the phenomenon may be, when it appears as an object to the mind, it appears as though the object was established from its own side. Actually it is merely posited over there by thought, without even a mere slight establishment from its own side. So if you closely examine or analyze such a mode of appearance, then it will clearly appear to your mind that the mode of existence is mere imputation over there by mind, without even mere slight establishment from its own side. No matter what appears to the mind, that appearance is merely imputed over there by mind

325. The autocommentary (p. 118) explains that "the mode" refers to "the mode of dependent arising, free of any essence of self-power, which will nakedly, clearly dawn. On that basis, one's ascertainment of final reality will grow stronger." Because this stanza relates to practice in the postmeditation session, it describes the means of viewing the objects of the senses-objects which appear as inherently existent—to be illusion-like dependent arisings. "The view's main point: discern what appears" is a source quote from the Indian master Mitra Yogin, restating the same instruction. Mitra (twelfth to thirteenth centuries) was one of the last great Indian tantric adepts, who transmitted the Mitra Gyatsa (Mi tra brgya rtsa) cycle of initiations to Tibet. He was a student of Lalitavajra, who was in turn a student of Tilopa.

326. These are the five sense consciousnesses and the mental consciousness.

and does not exist in the way it appears to exist, from its own side. So he says, "The view's main point: discern what appears."

The essence of all that is stated succinctly:

In short, whatever things appear—
your mind and such—don't grasp as that.
Instead determine its mode of
being, and always that sustain.

In short, whenever any object—your mind and so forth— appears, although it appears as though established from its own side and not merely imputed over there, the appearing object is not established as it appears. If you hold to it as established as it appears, [235] that holding becomes the apprehension of true existence, so do not apprehend it in that way. Given that it does not exist as it appears, if you examine how exactly it does exist, you ascertain that apart from imputation over there, the object lacks even mere slight existence as it appears from its own side. Having generated ascertainment of such a mode of existence, always sustain it.

In short, as for the mode of appearance, whatever phenomenon it may be, it appears as though established here from its own side and not as merely posited over there. Do not hold it as it appears, but hold to it as it actually exists. What mode of existence does it have? It does not exist as it appears—that is, the object exists without even the slightest establishment from its own side.

So knowing, join as essence one
all things of both saṃsāra and peace.

If you understand the emptiness of one phenomenon, then by applying that same reasoning elsewhere you will come to understand the emptiness of all phenomena. Having gained certainty of the final reality of the person, the aggregates, and, among the aggregates, the mind, if you then move on to the nature of all phenomena included in saṃsāra and nirvāṇa, their unmistaken mode of existence will appear. Whatever phenomenon it is, it is the same in being free of inherent establishment. "Saṃsāra and peace": all phenomena included in saṃsāra are empty of inherent establishment, [236] and all phenomena of nirvāṇa are also empty of inherent establishment. Since they are all the same, connect all phenomena as of one nature.

And in that vein, said Āryadev':
"Whoever's viewer of one thing,
is said to be a viewer of all."

The viewer who views the emptiness of inherent existence of one thing, like the aggregates, when moving on to other phenomena will realize their emptiness of inherent establishment. So he says "viewer of one thing."

"Whatever's emptiness of one,
that is the emptiness of all."[327]

If you understand emptiness on one phenomenon, that mode of emptiness is said to be the same mode of emptiness that is on all phenomena. With that in mind he says that the *mode* of emptiness is the same. He is not saying that the very emptiness of a pot is the emptiness of a pillar.

Like that, in proper equipoise on
reality, there are no extremes—
no fabrications of saṃsāra
and peace, existence, non-, and such.

Having analyzed in that way, then from the perspective of the equipoise that is single-pointedly absorbed on the final reality—that is, for the ascertainment factor that ascertains the final reality—there is no conventional phenomenon at all. Except for a vacuity, there is no existent or nonexistent, no proliferation of saṃsāra and nirvāṇa. [237] Although the exalted wisdom realizing all aspects—which is absorbed single-pointedly on the final reality—sees all phenomena, from the perspective of its factor of seeing the final reality there is said to be no conventional phenomenon at all.[328]

From the perspective of [a sentient being's] equipoise that realizes the lack of inherent existence of the self, there is not even a nominally exis-

327. Āryadeva, *Four Hundred Stanzas* (Skt. *Catuḥśataka*), v. 191. For an English version of this text along with commentary, see Āryadeva et al. 1994.

328. "The exalted wisdom realizing all aspects" is the Buddha's omniscient mind. The Buddha's omniscient consciousness simultaneously cognizes both emptiness and all conventional phenomena. However, from the *point of view* of its cognizing emptiness, nothing else appears except emptiness, meaning that nothing else appears to be the final reality.

tent "I." If from that perspective there is no "I," does it realize the "I" as nonexistent? Although the "I" does not exist from the perspective of that equipoise, it does not *realize* the "I" as nonexistent.[329] When one arises from the equipoise and examines things, the "I" appears as something established from its own side and not merely posited over there. Since there is no "I" that is established in accordance with such an appearance, well then, is the "I" completely nonexistent? Although there is no inherently established "I," we must posit a nominally existent "I." How should we posit such a nominally existent "I"? It is not suitable to say "mere name" means nothing exists except for names. Rather, because nothing exists except what is imputed over there by names, we say "mere name." Apart from such mere imputed existence, which is merely imputed over there by thought, nothing exists. On that basis, the action, agent, and object of a cause generating a result, the action, agent, and object of fire burning kindling, and so forth—all actions, agents, and objects are feasible on the basis of mere imputation over there. [238] Furthermore, if you directly realize the feasibility of the dependent relativity of all actions and agents, without any room to raise objections, they will appear as though in a dream, a mirage, a moon in the water, and an illusion. In a dream, although a horse appears, in actuality there is no establishment as a horse. Likewise, although inherent establishment appears, there is no inherent establishment. In the same way, a water mirage appears as water, and a moon in the water appears as a moon and so forth, but none of them exists in that way. Although not established in that way, there is no room to deny that the appearance arises. In the same way, all phenomena included in saṃsāra and nirvāṇa are the same in being empty—not inherently established. Nevertheless, nobody can deny that saṃsāra and nirvāṇa, actions and agents, like dreams and illusions, merely appear and arise as mere imputations.[330]

329. The distinction being made here is between not finding the "I" and finding the "I" to be nonexistent. When wisdom analyzing the ultimate searches for an "I" that exists from its own side, it does not find it and is left with emptiness. However, that does not mean that this wisdom finds the "I" to be nonexistent. It still exists conventionally.

330. Things appear *as* mere imputations *after* one has realized emptiness. Before that time, they *are* mere imputations, but they don't appear that way—they appear to be truly existent. Rinpoché here is describing the experience of somebody who has realized emptiness and who is viewing things during postmeditation. This person has recognized that things are not inherently established, but he cannot deny that they still appear.

Yet when you surface and you check:
mere name, just an imputed thing,
dependent relativity.
Acts, actors both indubitably
themselves dawn like mirages, dreams,
moons on a lake, illusions too.

Appearance shrouds not emptiness;
the empty stops appearance not.
Then manifests the exc'llent path—
dependent, empty: synonyms.

If you unerringly realize emptiness, then if an appearance of a conventional subject arises, it does not obscure emptiness but rather becomes a support for emptiness. If an appearance of emptiness arises, [239] that emptiness does not negate the principles of actions and agents existing conventionally. At that time, the path where emptiness and dependent arising are of one meaning directly manifests.

As long as you haven't realized emptiness, you will not know how to distinguish the conventional "I" from the inherently established "I." So when you posit the conventional "I" as existing, the inherently established "I" must exist. And when you negate the inherently established "I," it is like you are negating the conventional "I." Emptiness and appearance do not become mutually supportive but negate each other in turns. If you realize emptiness just as it is, then by the reason of appearance existing, you establish it as empty. By the reason of it being empty, you establish appearance as existing. Because they do not negate each other but instead mutually support each other, emptiness and dependent arising are called of "one meaning."

The speaker, learned renunciant,
is Losang Chökyi Gyaltsen called.
This virtue by may all beings soon
victor'ous be through this path that
lacks any second door to peace.

Because he possesses vast learning, he is called "learned." Because he has applied himself to actualizing the meaning of what he has learned, he calls himself "the renunciant Losang Chökyi Gyaltsen." On the basis of that virtue, may all beings practice this path, which is free of two doors to peace, [240] and swiftly become victors. The state of nirvāṇa—peace—does not have two doors to traverse to get there. There is only one door. What is that one? It is the mind that realizes emptiness. "On the basis of the path realizing emptiness, which is free of two doors to peace, may all beings swiftly attain victory over the four māras."[331] Thus he makes a prayer.

This manner of introduction to mahāmudrā was spoken
by the Bhikṣu Losang Chökyi Gyaltsen.

May virtue increase.

331. For the four māras, see note 176.

FOURTEEN

Questions and Answers

If you fall into the unfortunate migrations, when do you fall?
Above I explained that after the clear light, when the near-attainment is established, the bardo is established. After the bardo, one is born into the unfortunate migrations.

Do we call the mind of clear light possessing four distinguishing features[332] "unification"?
It is only a mere aspirational one; it is not actual. To achieve the actual unification, after the clear light directly appears, one arises directly as the illusory body. The unification which unifies those two only arises in the context of the completion stage. The one we are talking about here is a generation stage mind, which is a mental contemplation of belief.

[The following questions are drawn from Chöden Rinpoché 2018, 108–9]
I've received some teachings regarding emptiness. When I recite the ritual of self-generation, I say, "from the space of emptiness . . ." What is that "space"? What relation does it have to emptiness?
When you say, "everything becomes emptiness," it's not like everything becomes just nothing at all. You are imagining that it is the emptiness of inherent establishment. "Empty" must be understood as the object. When you say, "from the space of emptiness," from the space of *the mind that realizes that object*—emptiness—not moving from its observation of emptiness, you need to activate a corner of your mind [to generate the deity]. That is called "from the space of emptiness."

332. As Rinpoché described on page 166, the "four distinguishing factors" of the clear light (that realizes emptiness) are this: (1) the appearance factor of that mind is a vacuity, (2) the ascertainment factor is the ascertainment of lack of inherent existence, and (3) the mind has become the nature of clear-light great bliss, so (4) its experienced object is bliss.

One only manifests the actual clear light during the completion stage, but in this context, one is *imagining* the clear light with these four factors, so it is a generation stage practice.

Is it possible to take the mind itself as the object of observation, for example when practicing mahāmudrā? Is it difficult to do that? Please give some explanation about that.

There are diverse ways of thinking about that. Taking us Geluks as an example, if we actualize calm abiding observing the mind, it is good if we hold the object of observation in conjunction with mahāmudrā. Mahāmudrā includes both the mind's conventional nature and its ultimate nature. As the mind's ultimate nature we posit the mind's emptiness of true existence, and as its conventional nature we posit the mere clear and knowing aspect. If you practice in that way, then the object of absorption is the mind, the absorber is also mind, and introspection acting as a sentry must also be something the mind does.

Translator's Acknowledgments

IT IS ONLY DUE to the unparalleled monastic education I have received at Sera Jé that I have been able to translate this book. For that reason, I must express tremendous gratitude to Chöden Rinpoché for insisting to a zealous but callow college graduate that study within the monastic community was the most expedient path to spiritual development and the best preparation for long-term meditation. After fifteen years, I am only starting to comprehend the vastness of Rinpoché's vision. Although Rinpoché was unfortunately not present in body to field questions during the process of translation, still when I had doubts about difficult points, and especially when considering how to write the introduction, I would focus my mind during the prayer sessions with hundreds of Rinpoché's students at Lhopa Khangtsen and ask, "What does Rinpoché want me to say?" Though I cannot promise I always interpreted the answer correctly, I do hope that Rinpoché's blessing is present in this work.

Many others, too numerous to mention, have contributed as well. I will specify a few. Lama Zopa Rinpoché had the discerning insight, during our first meeting, to foresee that Chöden Rinpoché would become my primary teacher. Within the monastery, Geshé Ngawang Sangyé, a realized master in an ordinary guise, has been a constant source of knowledge and inspiration. Geshé Ngawang Thokmé, Geshé Ngawang Rabga, and Gen Losang Gyatso, all students of Chöden Rinpoché and members of Lhopa Khangtsen, have also offered expert guidance through the traditional texts. Geshé Thupten Chimé, who is sincerely devoted to Rinpoché, has acted as my *kasha gen* (advisor) since my first day at Sera. Gen Namgyal Chöphel, a senior member of the Khangtsen who edited Rinpoché's book in Tibetan, generously offered his time to help me through some of the more ambiguous parts of the translation. Gen Chöphel was originally a student of Rinpoché's brother Gen Thupten Yarphel, who also insisted that the young Chöphel travel to India to study at Sera. He will be completing the highest degree of *lharampa geshé* shortly after the publication of this book. I wish him the best in his future pursuits, both in personal practice and in teaching the Dharma.

The most important factor of my education at Sera has been my classmates in debate. Our group, which originally numbered well over two hundred, is still one hundred strong, with a good number of truly exceptional debaters who continuously expose and challenge my incomplete understanding.

Next, I must acknowledge the Western monks of Sera IMI House, whose support has been invaluable in allowing me to thrive in this challenging environment. Especially I would like to thank Geshé Tenzin Namdak and Gen Jampa Kaldan for initiating this community and acting as my mentors during my early years as a monk.

Gen Sherab Dhargyé was my Tibetan teacher during my initial months of study in Dharamsala. I can still recall many details of his articulate lessons, which gave me a firm foundation in the language. I hope he will be pleased to see this work.

Thank you also to Geshé Gyalten, Rinpoché's longtime student and attendant, for offering me the opportunity to translate Rinpoché's works. I hope I have lived up to the task.

Regarding the English side of the translation, I am exceptionally fortunate to have had the opportunity to work with the team at Wisdom Publications on this text. Their professionalism and care have refined and streamlined my initial translation. Thanks especially to Daniel Aitken and Tim McNeill (under whom I worked many years ago) for their initial enthusiasm about this project. Laura Cunningham has done a superb job as editor, always providing prompt and detailed responses to my queries. I hope to continue working with them again in the future.

Voula Zarpani, translator of several of Rinpoché's previous works, offered valuable advice on the overall process of translation and publication, as well as details of some difficult phrases. Roger Jackson, who was simultaneously working on his own translation of mahāmudrā texts, offered some helpful exchanges regarding obscure points. Art Engle helped to clarify some obscure references in the lineage prayer.

Ven. Gyalten Jigdrel, a student of Rinpoché and a PhD candidate at the University of Hamburg, read through an early version of the manuscript, added in the Sanskrit diacritics, and helped to research some obscure points. Anita Dudhane was the first to read the preface and introduction and offered valuable feedback on these. Tim Brown was the first to read through the body of the text and offered many constructive comments. Ven. Losang Dönyö assisted with the formatting.

I owe a debt of gratitude to all of my superb English teachers at Milton Academy and Tufts University for never being satisfied with what I thought was good composition, and always insisting there was room for improvement.

Suffice it to say, any errors in the translation are my own.

Lastly, I would like to thank my parents, Debb Colony and Bill Roiter, who not only acquiesced to their only son pursuing a monastic career in faraway country but have continuously offered their unconditional support through this long process. May the results of their boundless generosity and patience ripen in the future as a path to enlightenment.

Paṇchen Losang Chökyi Gyaltsen

Biography of Paṇchen Losang Chökyi Gyaltsen

This biography of the Fourth Paṇchen Lama was composed by Alexander Gardner, director and chief editor of the Treasury of Lives. Gardner completed his PhD in Buddhist studies at the University of Michigan in 2007.

Published October 2009. Reprinted and adapted with permission.[333]

LOSANG CHÖKYI GYALTSEN (blo bzang chos kyi rgyal mtshan) was born in a village called Drukgya (brug brgya) in the Lhan valley, in Tsang, in either 1567 or 1570. His father, Kunga Ozer (kun dga' 'od zer), was a nephew of Wensa Sangyé Yeshé (dben sa sangs rgyas ye shes, 1525–1590/1591), and a member of the illustrious Ba (sba) clan. His mother's name was Tsogyal (mtsho rgyal). They gave him the name Chögyal Palden Sangpo (chos rgyal dpal ldan bzang po). The boy was recognized by Langmikpa Chökyi Gyaltsen (glang mig pa chos kyi rgyal mtshan) as the reincarnation of Ensapa Losang Döndrub (dben sa pa blo bzang don sgrub, 1505–1566) and given the name Chökyi Gyaltsen.

As a youth Chökyi Gyaltsen studied with Sangyé Yeshé, then the abbot of Tashi Lhünpo (bkra shis lhun po) and Ensapa monasteries (dben sa pa). For the first years of his life he was tutored in the autumn by Sangyé Yeshé in Drukgya, receiving from him many blessings and empowerments. There he also received teachings and initiations from his brother and grandfather. At the age of thirteen Chökyi Gyaltsen left Drukgya for Wensa Monastery to further his instruction with Sangyé Yeshé. He took novice vows with his master, received the name Losang Chökyi Gyaltsen, and began instruction in *The Stages of the Path* (*lam rim*). Chökyi Gyaltsen remained at Wensa for the next five years.

In his eighteenth year Chökyi Gyaltsen went to Tashi Lhünpo, where he entered the Thösam Ling college (thos bsam gling grwa tshang), studying

333. Alexander Gardner, "The Fourth Paṇchen Lama, Losang Chökyi Gyaltsen," Treasury of Lives, accessed April 28, 2018, http://treasuryoflives.org/biographies/view/Losang-Chökyi-Gyaltsen/9839. For a more extensive biography, see Willis 1995.

with Paljor Gyatso (dpal 'byor rgya mtsho, d.u.). He spent the next three summers at Wensa, however, receiving further teachings and transmissions from Sangyé Yeshé, including the Ganden Mahāmudrā of Tsongkhapa. In 1591 he received the news that Sangyé Yeshé was ill with smallpox, and he quickly returned to visit with him one last time, shortly before Sangyé Yeshé passed away. Following a successful examination in *Pramāṇavārttika* (Dharmakīrti's *Commentary on Valid Cognition*) at Tashi Lhünpo, Chökyi Gyaltsen returned to Wensa to oversee the funeral.

Chökyi Gyaltsen received full monastic ordination that same year, 1591, with Paṇchen Damchö Yarphel (paN chen dam chos yar 'phel, d.u.), Peljor Gyatso, and Paṇchen Lhawang Lodrö (paN chen lha dbang blo gros, d.u.) officiating. He then traveled to Lhasa, making offerings at the Jokang, and proceeded to Ganden, where he continued his education with Namkai Tsenchen (nam mkha'i mtshan can, d.u.), with whom he studied Kālacakra, and Gendün Gyaltsen (dge' 'dun rgyal mtshan, 1532–1605/1607), the Twenty-eighth throne holder of Ganden, who taught him the collected works of the Second Dalai Lama. Chökyi Gyaltsen in turn taught Gendün Gyaltsen the Ganden mahāmudrā, making him his successor in the oral lineage of that tradition. Damchö Pelbar (dam chos dpal 'bar, 1523/1546–1599), the twenty-sixth throne holder of Ganden, also taught him chö (*gcod*).

Having returned to Wensa, which he enlarged with new temples and statues, Chökyi Gyaltsen gave public teachings on lamrim and other topics, but soon felt the urge to enter retreat. He closed himself off from the public for six or seven months, reading scripture between sessions of meditation. It was during this short retreat that he had a vision of Tsongkhapa, and in his sleep received a number of important transmissions from him. He shifted his retreat to his home village, living for a time like a "cotton-clad one" (*ras pa*) in the tradition of the Kagyu ascetics, before returning to Wensa.

In 1601, his fame now widespread, Losang Chökyi Gyaltsen was asked to assume the abbacy of Tashi Lhünpo. The thirty-one-year-old was already abbot of Wensa and, beginning in 1598, abbot of Gangchen Chöphel (gangs can chos 'phel), having been requested to assume that post by Lhüntse Depa (lhun rtse sde pa, d.u.). That same year he initiated a Great Prayer Festival, or Mönlam Chenmo (*smon lam chen mo*), at Tashi Lhünpo, installing a number of new statues in the temples. Eight years later, in 1609, he established a tantric college at the monastery, the Tashi Lhünpo Gyüpa Dratsang (bkra shis lhun po rgyud pa grwa tshang).

Soon after Losang Chökyi Gyaltsen assumed abbacy of Tashi Lhünpo,

Yönten Gyatso (yon tan rgya mtsho, 1589–1616), the Fourth Dalai Lama, visited there, arriving in Tibet from Mongolia for the first time. It would seem that Chökyi Gyaltsen played a role in the Tibetan acceptance of the Mongolian boy as the legitimate incarnation of Sönam Gyatso (bsod nams rgya mtsho, 1543–1588). The Fourth Dalai Lama requested Chökyi Gyaltsen to accompany him to Drepung, where he taught for some time. Afterward he traveled to various Kadampa and Gelukpa monasteries in the region, including Reting (rwa sgreng) and various sites connected to Tsongkhapa's activities in Lhoka.

In 1612 Chökyi Gyaltsen visited Bhutan on invitation from the Lhapa hierarchs of Nyö (gnyos). This clan, Drukpa Kagyu followers who were strong in both Tsang and Bhutan, were rivals to Zhapbdrung Ngawang Namgyal (zhabs drung ngag dbang rnam rgyal, 1594–1651). Their loss of influence in Bhutan, and the close relations with Chökyi Gyaltsen, led to the Lhapa conversion to the Geluk tradition late in the century. They were but one clan-based religious tradition that Chökyi Gyaltsen brought under the Geluk tradition. Chökyi Gyaltsen was again involved in Bhutanese-Tibetan affairs, negotiating a truce to conflicts between the two in the mid-1650s. Among hostages freed by Bhutan was a son of the house of Nenying (gnas rnying), another clan-based religious tradition whose merger with the Geluk was accomplished by Chökyi Gyaltsen.

Chökyi Gyaltsen continued to go back and forth between Shigatsé and Lhasa, teaching at Tashi Lhünpo, Drepung, Sera, Ganden, and other Geluk monasteries. In 1617 the Fourth Dalai Lama passed away, and Chökyi Gyaltsen assumed the abbacy of both Drepung and Sera. These were not the last monasteries where he served as abbot; in 1626 he was made abbot of Ganden's Jangtsé college, and in 1642 of Zhalu (zha lu).

In 1618 the ruling family of most of Tibet, the Phakmodrupa (phag mo dru pa), was overthrown by the ruling family of Tsang, based in Shigatsé. Supporters of the Kagyu tradition, the new rulers repressed Gelukpa institutions and religious practice, including the large Geluk monasteries of the Lhasa region, although they tolerated the presence of Tashi Lhünpo and Chökyi Gyaltsen. Curing him of a disease the king believed to have been inflicted by the Fourth Dalai Lama, Chökyi Gyaltsen was able to secure permission from the king of Tsang to confirm the reincarnation of the Fourth Dalai Lama in the person of a boy he named Losang Gyatso (blo bzang rgya mtsho, 1617–1682), who later became the Fifth Dalai Lama, although he was forbidden to install him in Lhasa.

Over the next decade relations between Lhasa and Shigatsé continued to deteriorate, and Chökyi Gyaltsen was forced to mediate time and again. He was also forced to confront Mongol invasions, first in 1621 when Mongolian troops, brought in after secret negotiations with Geluk hierarchs, laid siege to Tsang authority in Lhasa and drove Tsang forces to Chakpori (lcags po ri), a small rocky hill in Lhasa. Only after Chökyi Gyaltsen's intervention were the forces allowed to retreat to Shigatsé. With Tsang forces out of Lhasa, in 1622 Chökyi Gyaltsen was able to enthrone the Fifth Dalai Lama at Drepung.

Following the defeat of the Tsang king and the ascent of the Fifth Dalai Lama as king of Tibet in 1641, the fortunes of Chökyi Gyaltsen grew greater still. Chökyi Gyaltsen was given the title of Paṇchen Lama. Two separate systems of enumeration exist; according to the system of Tashi Lhünpo, three previous lamas, identified as Chökyi Gyaltsen's previous incarnations, are identified as the First through Third Paṇchen Lamas: Khedrup Gelek Pelsang (mkhas grub dge legs dpal bzang, 1385–1438), Sonam Chökyi Langpo (bsod nams phyogs kyi glang po, 1439–1505), and Ensapa Losang Dondrub. For this reason, Chökyi Gyaltsen is either listed as the First or the Fourth Paṇchen Lama (this book lists him as the Fourth, following common standard).

Chökyi Gyaltsen continued to teach for the next two decades, passing away in 1662.

APPENDIX 2

Biography of His Eminence Chöden Rinpoché

This short biography of Chöden Rinpoché is adapted with permission from my "Obituary for Chöden Rinpoché," Mandala Magazine, *January–June 2016, and supplemented with material from "The Life of a Hidden Meditator,"* Mandala Magazine, *July–August 2000, from the Ananda Dharma Center website, and from my own recollections and stories others have shared.*

CHÖDEN RINPOCHÉ (Chos ldan Rin po che), Losang Gyalten Jikdrel Wangchuk (Blo bzang rgyal bstan 'jigs bral dbang phyug), was born in Rongpo, Kham, Eastern Tibet, in 1930, on the fifteenth of the fourth Tibetan month (Saka Dawa), the anniversary of the Buddha's birth, enlightenment, and pārinirvāṇa. The young boy showed signs of previous Dharma imprints, such as displaying his hands in the mudrā of teaching and pretending to give Dharma teachings or administer medicine to other children.

Reting Rinpoché, the regent of Tibet, officially recognized this boy as the reincarnation of Losang Chöden, a locally renowned yogi and abbot of Rongpo Monastery, and as the third incarnation of the Chöden lineage. His monastic education began at age three, from which time he showed remarkable aptitude in memorizing and studying Buddhist texts. At age six, he met Phabongkha Rinpoché, whom he took as his main teacher and from whom he took ordination as a novice monk. He recounts,

> I really admired everything that Rinpoché did: the way he walked, the way he dressed, everything. I felt, "if only I could be like him," because I had such admiration for him.[334]

Phabongkha Rinpoché also initiated the young boy into the unsurpassed yoga tantra practice of Vajrabhairava. From then until he passed away, Chöden Rinpoché performed the long sādhana of this deity daily without break, and he first completed the approximation retreat at age ten.

At age fifteen, Rinpoché traveled with his brother Thupten Yarphel to

334. "The Life of a Hidden Meditator," 63.

Sera Jé Monastery in Lhasa (Thupten Yarphel also went on to become a great scholar-practitioner, composing many commentaries on sūtra and tantra, before passing away in Tibet in 1997). The two brothers joined Lhopa Khangtsen, the house group at Sera corresponding to their region of Tibet.

Rinpoché excelled in his studies, memorizing thousands of pages of philosophical texts, including the entire text *Golden Garland of Eloquence* by Tsongkhapa, a sprawling twelve-hundred-page commentary on the perfection of wisdom sūtras. He consistently topped his class in debate and periodically attended teachings on lamrim and tantra by contemporary luminaries like Pari Rinpoché, Trijang Rinpoché, and Ling Rinpoché.

Although as a reincarnate lama he could have received sponsorship and special treatment, Rinpoché maintained the appearance of an ordinary monk during his years at Sera, forgoing the yellow *donka* (vest) traditionally worn by tulkus and living in extremely basic conditions with the other monks.

By the age of twenty-eight, Rinpoché had completed all the requisite studies to qualify for the highest degree of lharam geshé. Trijang Rinpoché and others advised him to complete his studies and enter retreat, but his primary teacher at Sera, the abbot Geshé Losang Wangchuk, instructed him to continue studying *vinaya* (monastic discipline) at Sera. During these years Rinpoché also studied auxiliary subjects like Sanskrit, poetry, and astrology with a private tutor in Lhasa.

That same year, just before the Tibetan uprising of March 10, 1959, Rinpoché was one of two Sera Jé scholars chosen to debate publicly His Holiness the Dalai Lama during the latter's geshé examinations. He chose to debate the subject of the two truths according to the Middle Way Consequence interpretation. Rinpoché later recounted how impressed he had been with His Holiness' sharpness of mind, and His Holiness likewise praised Rinpoché's skill in debate.

After the uprising, life for monks in Lhasa entered a dark period, and for several years Rinpoché struggled to maintain his freedom to study and practice, even spending a month in prison at one point. Finally, in the early 1960s he left Lhasa to enter retreat in the mountains, mastering the practice of *chü-len*, or "taking the essence,"[335] but the ravages of the Cultural Revolution created obstacles even for solitary practice, so in 1965 Rinpoché arranged to

335. This practice involves complete abstention from solid food. A practitioner instead relies on "essence pills," small pills composed mainly of ground dried flowers.

stay in a small, unlit dugout beneath the house of a relative in Lhasa. Rinpoché did not leave this room for nineteen years, all the while performing various retreats, reciting the rituals from memory. He recounted:

> You don't need external things to do Dharma practice. It's all in your heart, your mind. As for the realizations: you do not experience the realizations of the three principle aspects of the path, but you do have a little renunciation, and because of that you are able to stay like that . . . The main thing I wanted to do was to practice Dharma sincerely, no matter what external factors were arising. This was my main motivation, to be completely against the eight worldly concerns. The future life is more important than this life—this life is just like a dream. So if you went and did as the Chinese said, you would get a good house and car, you could enjoy so many things, but this would have caused you to fall to the lower realms, where you would experience sufferings for so many eons. Future lives are much more important than this life. In order to work for the future lives, I stayed inside to practice . . . The future is very long, many eons. This life is so short, it's just fiction, just a dream. Your mind continues infinitely, and when you die in the next life, again it doesn't vanish, and again you continue to the next life, and the next—many lives you have to go through. So all of these are determined by the present actions. You have no choice. So the present action is very important. This life is so short, perhaps only one hundred years—very small compared to the future lives.[336]

His previous practice of chü-len allowed Rinpoché to continue with minimal sustenance, and even after retreat he continued to take only meager amounts of food. And despite his humble account, his disciples (and anyone else who had the fortune to meet him) all recognized that Rinpoché had attained profound realization during his time in retreat.

In 1985, during a period of a slight lenience in Chinese policy, Rinpoché was able to leave Tibet and travel to India. His Holiness the Dalai Lama encouraged Rinpoché to teach, and after a brief stint in Nepal, Rinpoché returned to Lhopa Khangtsen at the newly reestablished Sera Jé Monastery

336. "The Life of a Hidden Meditator," 68–69.

in South India. There he acted as a *petri gen* (dpe khrid rgan)—philosophical debate instructor—for the younger generation of monks. Rinpoché maintained an utterly humble aspect and when not teaching would spend all his time sitting in his room, studying or meditating in dim lighting.

Rinpoché held the monastic life in high esteem, encouraging the young monks to always attend the daily pūjās and debate, and to live simple lives, adhering to the regulations of the monastery. Geshé Ngawang Sherap, who was a young boy in Lhopa Khangtsen at the time, recalls how Rinpoché would come to everyone's door before dawn to make sure they were up and had gone to the pūjā. Occasionally, Rinpoché would compose short, practical texts at the request of students, but primarily he would focus on study and retreat, commenting, "Many people have asked me to compose books, but I don't like to do that. The main purpose of learning poetry, grammar, and astrology is to understand Dharma properly and to put it into practice. I didn't learn it to compose books. When people ask me I say we have so many books—we have enough books. What's lacking is practicing the instructions in the books."[337] He eschewed any kind of position in the monastic hierarchy, preferring to remain a quiet yogi and teacher for devoted students. Nevertheless, his reputation as an immense scholar, meticulous vinaya holder, and supreme master of meditation spread, and his public teachings usually attracted the majority of the monastic population.

Geshé Gyalten, who for many years served as Rinpoché's close attendant, recalls one occasion where Rinpoché intimated that he may have had some recollection of a past life as Sthavira Aṅgaja (Tib. Gnas brtan yan lag 'byung), who is counted as one of the "sixteen arhats," sixteen disciples of the Buddha who appeared as arhats but were in actuality bodhisattvas who had pledged to preserve the teachings from life to life. As a young boy, Rinpoché had apparently been able to recite the common Tibetan prayer to the sixteen arhats (*gnas bcu*) by memory after reading it only once.

In 1998, at the requests of His Holiness the Dalai Lama and Lama Zopa Rinpoché, Chöden Rinpoché began traveling to the West and East Asia to teach foreign students. For the next fifteen years, he spent most of the year touring, returning to Sera at the end of each year to give extensive public teachings to thousands of monks. Even during his years of almost constant travel, Rinpoché never wasted a single opportunity for practice. During car or plane rides, he would make maṇḍala offerings and recite his prayer com-

337. "The Life of a Hidden Meditator," 68–69.

mitments. During teachings, when he paused for the translator, he would quietly recite mantras and meditate.

Rinpoché finally began to slow down in 2014, when a Taiwanese doctor diagnosed him with terminal-stage stomach cancer. Surprising the doctor, Rinpoché made a temporary recovery and was able to give important teachings on the Mañjuśrī Dharmacakra at Sera in December.

Rinpoché spent most of 2015 resting in Taiwan. In August, His Holiness the Dalai Lama, observing ominous signs, urged Rinpoché to return to India. On August 29, His Holiness met Rinpoché in Delhi, praising him as a faithful disciple who had come to the end of a successful life. His Holiness also assured Rinpoché that they would meet again in future lifetimes, continuing to work together for the benefit of sentient beings.[338]

On August 31, Rinpoché returned to his *labrang* (house) at Sera. Coming out of the car in a wheelchair, Rinpoché sat on his front porch as an assembly of monks came to offer *khataks*. Many of the monks were crying, but Rinpoché, smiling broadly, maintained his usual appearance of utmost peace and detachment. As though he had planned it ahead of time, Rinpoché then commenced the work of preparing to transition to his next life. A group of students, led by Sera Mé Gen Thupten Rinchen, over five days performed the self-empowerments of Rinpoché's five main deities: Vajrabhairava, Guhyasamāja, Heruka Cakrasaṃvara, Vajrayoginī, and Cittamaṇi Tārā. Lying in bed in the next room, Rinpoché listened through a radio. His attendant noted that despite being unable to move his body, Rinpoché perfectly recited all of the rituals from memory and performed the appropriate hand mudrās. Geshé Yama Sönam, a longtime student of Rinpoché's, commented that although he had seen many accomplished meditators die in peace, "None of them were like Rinpoché. Their minds were at peace, but when they had to move around, the flash of distress on their face would belie their physical discomfort. Rinpoché was not like that at all. He never showed the slightest sign of mental or physical strain."

After completing the rituals, Rinpoché took some fruit juice and yogurt (pure white foods) and then stopped taking any more food or medicine. For several days, he meditated and made strong prayers in front of the statues on his altar, especially Avalokiteśvara. Shortly before passing away, Rinpoché

338. See the transcript of this conversation, available at https://fpmt.org/wp-content/uploads/2015/09/11/his-eminence-choden-rinpoche-passes-away/Meeting-of-HHDL-and-Choden-Rinpoche-29-8-15-PDF.pdf.

sat up on his throne and successively displayed three mudrās of teaching and meditation. He then lay down in the lion's posture—on the right side, the posture the Buddha adopted at death. Calmly he said, "The most important thing is to remember the kindness of the Buddha and abide in that kindness." Then he recited a verse from Ārya Nāgārjuna's *Five Stages*:

> Whatever thing a yogi sees,
> he views it as illusion-like.
> Who sees like a reflection in
> a mirror, dream, illusion, or
> a bubble, a trick of the eye:
> that one is foremost, so is said.

As he finished speaking, Rinpoché entered a state of profound meditation, progressively actualizing the three empties and the clear light. Shapdrung Rinpoché, who was present, described "an atmosphere of extreme peace." After Chöden Rinpoché stopped breathing, he remained in meditation for three days, as his disciples again performed the self-empowerments, in reverse order. Rinpoché had said he would not remain long in meditation so as to reincarnate and return quickly. Outside his house, every evening thousands of monks would gather on the lawn to recite great Indian and Tibetan philosophical texts, with a substantial group always staying until dawn.

Jangtsé Chöjé Losang Tenzin Rinpoché[339] and monks from Gyütö tantric college presided over Rinpoché's cremation on September 15, in the courtyard of Lhopa Khangtsen. Four days later, Gen Thupten Rinchen guided the process of opening the cremation stūpa. Under the hearth, dust had condensed in the form of a small vajra. Rinpoché's students enthroned his relics in his house as an auspicious sign for his swift return.

Karma Gönpo Tsering was born on May 21, 2016, again corresponding to the fifteenth of the fourth Tibetan month. In 2017, His Holiness the Dalai Lama indicated that Chöden Rinpoché had been reborn, and late that year, he advised a search party of monks from Lhopa Khangtsen to look for a young boy in a Tibetan settlement in Odisha, a state in eastern India. Espe-

339. The former Jangtsé Chöjé Rinpoché has subsequently ascended to the rank of Ganden Tripa, supreme head of the Geluk lineage.

cially impressed by Tsering, the party brought him to His Holiness in Bodh Gaya in January 2018. His Holiness confirmed that this was the true reincarnation of Chöden Rinpoché and renamed the young boy Tenzin Gyalten Rinpoché.

Gyalten Sangpo, a former American monk who served as Chöden Rinpoché's attendant for several years, shared many remarkable stories of his time with this exceptional yogi and teacher. The following one is especially illustrative of the quiet power that Rinpoché exuded:

> One night at Rinpoché's house at Sera, everyone was gone but him and me. The guests had gone after the completion of H.H. Dalai Lama's lamrim teachings, and Geshé Gyalten was away in America. Our guests at the labrang had departed. To conserve energy, electricity went off for about an hour every night at different parts of the monastery, so the lights were out at the house around 7 PM. I was in my room. I got the notion to go to the kitchen. I got there, but didn't understand why I even went—I didn't want anything. I walked back to my room and stopped at the bottom of the stairs, feeling an urge to just wait there. A few moments later, I heard some movement upstairs. I thought it strange as it was only myself and Rinpoché in the house, so who could be there? Rinpoché was in his room practicing in retreat before leaving for Australia and New Zealand to teach. I thought maybe someone else was up there. Next thing, I see Rinpoché coming down the stairs. I was concerned for Him walking down the stairs when I saw his foot hit the first stair down, but when he turned the corner and I saw Him in full view—he lit up the room. He was translucent and just luminous radiating light. Just glowing and resplendent. It was astonishing. Like many things I experienced living with Him, I think he wanted me to see this.

Glossary

absorption. *See* equipoise.

access concentration (*a.k.a. preparatory stage [of concentration]*) (Skt. *sāmantaka*; Tib. *nyer bsdogs*). A preparatory state to any of the four dhyānas or four formless absorptions. When one first achieves calm abiding, one achieves the access concentration of the first dhyāna. Although this access concentration is included within the level of the first dhyāna, it is not an actual first dhyāna because the meditator still has afflictions included within the desire realm during postmeditation. If the meditator makes effort and suppresses these afflictions through concentration such that they do not arise even in postmeditation, the access concentration becomes an actual first dhyāna.

actual dhyāna absorption (Tib. *bsam gtan gyi dngos gzhi'i snyoms 'jug*). Often known in the West by its Pāḷi name *jhāna*, this is a subtle level of concentration that is accessed via an access concentration and that has passed beyond the ground below it. For example, the first actual dhyāna has passed beyond the desire realm, the second actual dhyāna has passed beyond the first, and so forth. Practitioners can utilize these dhyānas to meditate on the path, but tantric practitioners forgo their intentional cultivation.

actual formless absorption (Tib. *gzugs med kyi dngos gzhi'i snyoms 'jugs*). These are four further refined levels of meditation beyond the four dhyānas. They differ not in terms of the accompanying mental factors but in terms of their respective objects of observation: (1) infinite space, (2) infinite consciousness, (3) nothingness, and (4) neither [gross] discrimination nor non-[subtle] discrimination.

afflictions (Skt. *kleśa*; Tib. *nyon mongs*). Mental factors that, by their very nature, disturb mental peace. Examples include desire-attachment, anger, and the apprehension of true existence. The latter one disturbs the mind because it naturally gives rise to desire and other strong afflictions.

afflictive obscurations (Skt. *kleśāvaraṇa*; Tib. *nyon sgrib*). Along with knowledge obscurations, one of the two classes of obscurations. Afflictive obscurations include afflictions themselves, along with their concomitant main minds and mental factors, and their seeds. This class of obscuration mainly obstructs liberation, and when one abandons these, one attains liberation.

arhat (Skt. *arhan*; Tib. *dgra bcom pa*). A person who has abandoned afflictive obscurations and attained liberation. A Hīnayāna arhat has abandoned afflictive obscurations but not knowledge obscurations. A Mahāyāna arhat has abandoned both and is a buddha. The Sanskrit *arhat* can mean "worthy of homage," although an alternative reading of *arihan* translates as "one who has subdued the enemy [of afflictions]." The Tibetan translation reflects this latter reading.

assumption of bad states (Skt. *dauṣṭhulya*; Tib. *gnas ngan len*). Uncouth behavior of body and speech and agitated mental states, which are the ripening of imprints of afflicted behavior in the past and which obstruct using the body and mind as one wishes for virtuous practice. These behaviors are not necessarily motivated by afflictions. For example, somebody might walk in an unsettled manner or speak in vulgar language. When one achieves calm abiding, one gains deep inner composure, and these behaviors and mental states diminish significantly, though they do not completely disappear. In other contexts, this same term can refer to rebirth in unfortunate realms.

bardo (Skt. *antarābhava*; Tib. *bar do*). Literally "in-between"; the state of existence between death and rebirth, when a being is driven by karma to search for a new body. This experience is often compared to a dream state.

being of great capacity (Skt. *mahāpuruṣa*; Tib. *skyes bu chen po*). A spiritual practitioner whose primary motivation is to attain full enlightenment for the benefit of others.

being of middling capacity (Skt. *madhyamapuruṣa*; Tib. *skyes bu 'bring*). A spiritual practitioner who mainly strives to be free of cyclic existence but not to achieve full enlightenment.

being of small capacity (Skt. *adhamapuruṣa*; Tib. *skyes bu chung ngu*). A spiritual practitioner who primarily strives to achieve a positive rebirth as a god or human.

black near-attainment (Tib. *nyer thob nag lam*). The appearance of pervasive darkness during the third of three subtle levels of mind that one experiences before the clear light dawns. This term also refers to the mind experiencing that appearance. During the process of death, one experiences this state just before the clear light, and when one arises and enters the bardo, one experiences this state first.

bliss of pliancy (Skt. *praśrabdhisukha*; Tib. *shin sbyangs kyi bde ba*). A sense of joy that arises as a result of the pliancy one achieves with calm abiding. This is not literally a pleasant sensation but rather a freedom from agitation.

bodhicitta (Skt. *bodhicitta*; Tib. *byang chub kyi sems*). Literally "the mind of awakening," this is the aspiration to achieve the state of buddhahood, motivated by wishing to free all sentient beings from suffering and place them in the state of buddhahood. This same term is used to refer to the white drop (*see* drops).

buddha (Skt. *buddha*; Tib. *sangs rgyas*). A person who has abandoned all afflictive and knowledge obscurations, thereby attaining an unobstructed consciousness that can perfectly see the temperaments and needs of each being and can emanate a form to guide them accordingly.

buddha lineage (Skt. *buddhagotra*; Tib. *sangs rgyas kyi rigs*). The emptiness of the mind is the naturally abiding "lineage" present in all sentient beings, and it allows for them to transform into the state of a buddha.

calm abiding (Skt. *śamatha*; Tib. *zhi gnas*). Achieved by means of the nine mental settlings, this is a concentration that is supported by the bliss of pliancy and is able to abide focused on a chosen object for as long as one wishes.

central channel (Skt. *avadhūtī*; Tib. *dbu ma*). One of the three main channels of the subtle body, it extends from the forebrow (center of the forehead) over the crown and down the spine, and terminates at the tip of the genitals. For ordinary people, knots obstruct wind from flowing in this channel, but advanced practitioners employ means to draw the winds into this channel to achieve pristine concentration.

channel knot (Tib. *rtsa mdud*). A blockage in the energy channels that obstructs the proper flow of wind energy in the central channel. The main channel knots occur above and below the channel wheels, where the left and right channels wrap around the central channel.

channels (Skt. *nāḍī*; Tib. *rtsa*). Subtle pathways of energy in the body through which flow wind energy and that also contain drops.

channel wheels (Skt. *cakra*; Tib. *rtsa 'khor*). Major energy centers in the body where the left and right channels wrap around the central channel. The five primary channel wheels are at the crown, throat, heart, navel, and secret region, where the right and left channels wrap around the central channel.

clairvoyance (Skt. *abhijñā*; Tib. *mngon shes*). A mental consciousness that directly perceives its object on the basis of an actual dhyāna, which acts as its empowering cause. The six main kinds of clairvoyance are (1) magical emanation, (2) divine ear, (3) divine eye, (4) knowing others' minds, (5) recollection of past lives, and (6) knowledge of the extinction of contaminants. In the context of tantric practice, it is also possible to achieve clairvoyance without an actual dhyāna, by instead manifesting subtle levels of mind.

clear light mind (Skt. *cittaprabhāsvara*; Tib. *sems kyi 'od gsal*). The subtlest level of mind, also known as the primordial mind and the very subtle mind. It resides within the indestructible drop at the heart, inextricable from the very subtle wind that acts as its mount. For ordinary people, it only manifests fully at the time of death. In tantric practice, a meditator intentionally manifests this mind to meditate on emptiness. One first gains such an ability during the isolation of mind, the third stage of the completion stage. At this point, the clear light mind realizes emptiness through a meaning-generality and is called "example clear light." During the fifth stage of the completion stage, one realizes emptiness directly, and this is called the "meaning clear light."

collection of merit (Skt. *puṇyasaṃbhāra*; Tib. *bsod nams kyi tshogs*). One of the two collections a practitioner accumulates in order to achieve enlightenment, this mainly becomes the cause for the Buddha's form body. One collects merit mainly through the practices of generosity, ethical discipline, and patience. In tantric practice, one accumulates merit through deity yoga. Unlike the wisdom collection, the merit collection is unstable and can wane on account of strong nonvirtue.

collection of wisdom (Skt. *jñānasaṃbhāra*; Tib. *ye shes kyi tshogs*). One of the two collections a practitioner accumulates in order to achieve enlightenment, this mainly becomes the cause for the wisdom truth body. The main cause for this collection is meditation on emptiness, though one also accumulates wisdom through meditation on impermanence, the four noble truths, and other topics, as well as through study and experience.

complete enjoyment body (Skt. *saṃbhogakāya*; Tib. *longs sku*). One of the three bodies of the Buddha, this is a subtle form body perceptible only to ārya bodhisattvas. It is characterized by the five certainties, although in the context of tantra, it need not have the certainty of abode—it does not need to abide only in the pure land of Akaniṣṭha but may be attained within the desire realm (see note 234).

completion stage (Skt. *sampannakrama*; Tib. *rdzogs rim*). The second stage of unsurpassed yoga tantra, this stage is mainly characterized by the practice of causing the winds to enter, abide, and dissolve in the central channel. It has six stages: (1) isolation of body, (2) isolation of speech, (3) isolation of mind, (4) illusory body, (5) clear light, and (6) unification. These six stages are often condensed into five, as explained in note 212.

concentration (Skt. *samādhi*; Tib. *ting nge 'dzin*). In general, the mental formation that is present when any mind is able to maintain an object for a duration, even a few seconds. A practitioner develops this natural ability, gradually extending the length of time he or she can keep an object in mind.

conventional nature of the mind (Tib. *sems kyi kun rdzob pa'i ngo bo*). The clear and knowing aspect of the mind, as distinguished from its ultimate nature, emptiness. For example, conventionally the nature of fire is heat, even though its ultimate nature is emptiness. Recognizing the conventional nature of the mind still represents a significant achievement, because a practitioner recognizes that the mind is not physical and is not inextricably bound up with thoughts and emotions. "Clear" is that which allows for a corresponding aspect to arise or appear unobstructedly, like a mirror. "Knowing" is an engaging with or pervading of an object in such a way as to render it something that is known, unobstructedly, in one way or another.

conventional phenomena/truth (Skt. *saṃvṛtisatya*; Tib. *kun rdzob bden pa*). Literally "truth for a concealer," this is truth as it appears to an everyday consciousness that is obscured from seeing the ultimate nature of things. On a day-to-day basis, we can distinguish fact from fiction, but even what we ordinarily consider factual is not true in an ultimate sense. The great Indian scholar Buddhapālita provides a helpful analogy: we can correctly distinguish a painting of the deity Śiva from one of Viṣṇu, but ultimately it is neither Śiva nor Viṣṇu; it is only a painting.

deity yoga (Skt. *devayoga*; Tib. *lha'i rnal 'byor*). Meditation that focuses on the holy body of an enlightened being within the space of absorption into—or at the very least awareness of—emptiness.

desire-attachment (Skt. *rāga*; Tib. *'dod chags*). Although this term is often translated as "desire," I have intentionally translated it as "desire-attachment" to distinguish it from a similar term, *'dun pa*, translated as "desire." Desire is an aspiration that can be either virtuous or nonvirtuous, depending on its object. But desire-attachment is the wish to possess or not to be separated from an object, based on having projected imagined qualities that exceed its nature. Desire-attachment is an afflictive mind and can never be virtuous. Often this term is abbreviated as simply "attachment" (Skt. *lobha*; Tib. *chags pa*).

desire realm (Skt. *kāmadhātu*; Tib. *'dod khams*). The realm that human beings inhabit and that arises mainly from desire for sense pleasures. This "realm" includes both the physical objects as well as the minds of its beings. Hell beings, hungry ghosts, animals, and desire realm gods also inhabit this realm. Unless a person achieves calm abiding and an actual dhyāna, they will definitely be reborn in this realm and never experience anything outside of it.

direct antidote (Tib. *dngos gnyen*). A mind that abandons a particular obscuration from the root by means of counteracting the wrong conception that underlies it. For example, the direct antidote to the wrong conception of true existence is a mind that (a) directly realizes emptiness and (b) is supported by such strong merit that once it arises, the wrong conception of true existence will never arise again. A bodhisattva following the sūtra path does not attain such a direct antidote until the eighth ground, but with the tantric path one achieves it at the path of seeing, with the meaning clear light.

drops (Skt. *bindu*; Tib. *thig le*). Essences or seeds of bliss that abide as various types of limpid residue within the channels. Like wind energy, these drops are a subtle kind of form, imperceptible to our ordinary senses but capable of inducing physical sensations, especially the bliss of orgasm. The main drops are red and white, coming from the mother and father, respectively. Part of the white drop is at the crown, part is at the heart, and the rest is spread throughout the body. Part of the red drop is at the navel, part at the heart, and the rest is spread throughout the body. The parts of the red and white drops at the heart together form the indestructible drop. Meditation on mother tantras, such as Heruka Cakrasaṃvara, place more emphasis on utilizing these drops, while meditation on father tantras like Guhyasamāja emphasize gaining control over the winds. Ultimately, both systems lead to the same goal of manifesting the mind of clear light.

eight applications (Skt. *aṣṭasaṃskāra*; Tib. *'du byed brgyad*). These are eight mental factors that a practitioner cultivates as antidotes to the five faults. The first four—faith, aspiration, effort, and pliancy—counteract the first fault, laziness. Recollection counteracts forgetting the advice. Introspection works to counteract laxity and excitement. Intention (to apply the antidote) counteracts not applying the antidote. Equanimity counteracts (unnecessarily) applying the antidote.

eight stages of dissolution (Tib. *thim rim brgyad*). At the time of death, as the coarse levels of mind become dormant and the subtler levels become manifest, a person has certain recognizable experiences and internal visions before the clear light of death finally appears. The first seven stages are the earth element dissolving into the water element, that into the fire element, that into the wind element, that into consciousness, and then that into the white appearance, red increase, and black near-attainment. The seven internal visions associated with these are a mirage, smoke, fireflies, a sputtering butter lamp, white appearance, red increase, and black near-attainment. At the end of all these, the eighth stage of clear light dawns.

emanation body (Skt. *nirmāṇakāya*; Tib. *sprul sku*). Of the three bodies of the Buddha, the one that appears to ordinary beings. Ordinary beings cannot perceive the complete enjoyment body, and so the Buddha emanates forms to teach them in accordance with their karma.

emptiness (Skt. *śūnyatā*; Tib. *stong pa nyid*). Emptiness is a nonaffirming negation, meaning it negates one thing without affirming something else. When the word "emptiness" is used generically, it means the emptiness of inherent existence (see below).

emptiness of duality (Skt. *dvayaśūnyatā*; Tib. *gnyis stong*). This is the emptiness posited by the Mind Only school. It is the emptiness of substantial difference between an object and the valid cognition apprehending it. The Consequence school rejects this emptiness, on the grounds that it affords too much ontological status to the mind at the expense of objects. According to this latter school, minds and their objects are equal in being empty of inherent existence, but both must exist conventionally because there cannot be an internal mind if there is no external object, just as there cannot be a right side without a left side. Furthermore, emptiness of duality implies that when you deeply analyze the nature of physical form, you find that it is in the nature of mind. For the Consequence School, when you deeply analyze form, you find that it has no findable nature at all.

emptiness of establishment by way of inherent existence (Skt. *svabhāvasiddhiśūnyatā*; Tib. *rang bzhin gyis grub pas stong nyid*). For the Consequence school, this is the subtlest form of emptiness. When an object is empty of inherent existence, the object does not exist from its own side, meaning that if one searches among the bases of designation, one does not find anything that *is* the object. For example, the individual parts of a chariot are not a chariot, the collection of the parts is not the chariot, and the arrangement of parts in a particular configuration also is not the chariot.

emptiness of establishment by way of one's own character (Skt. *svalakṣanasiddhiśūnyatā*; Tib. *rang gi mtshan nyid kyis grub pas stong nyid*). This is another way of expressing emptiness of inherent existence.

emptiness of a substantial self in the sense of being self-sufficient (Tib. *rang rkya thub pa'i rdzas yod kyi bdag gis stong nyid*). The nonexistence of a person who can appear to consciousness without depending on any of the aggregates appearing. According to the Consequence school, this emptiness exists and is a genuine object of meditation, but it is not the final or subtlest emptiness.

emptiness of true existence (Skt. **satyasiddhiśūnyatā*; Tib. *bden par grub pas stong nyid*). According to the Consequence school, this is synonymous with emptiness of inherent existence. The Autonomy school distinguishes the two—for that school, objects are empty of true existence but are *not* empty of inherent existence.

equipoise (Skt. *samāhita*; Tib. *mnyam gzhag*). Literally "to place in equilibrium," this word is also translated as "absorption." Generally it refers to a deep state of meditation in which coarse thoughts subside and a meditator maintains single-pointed focus on a chosen object. "Equilibrium" can refer to the body and mind being balanced or can denote that in such equipoise, only this mind is manifest, while all other mental states—thoughts and sense consciousnesses—have temporarily subsided.

exalted wisdom that knows all aspects (Skt. *sarvākārajñāna*; Tib. *rnam mkhyen*). This is the omniscient consciousness of a buddha. "Knows all aspects" describes the manner in which a buddha's mind simultaneously knows all objects. The buddha's mind does not literally need to go out to each object individually, but rather each object's "aspect" appears, like a reflection in a mirror.

excitement (Skt. *auddhatya*; Tib. *rgod pa*). This is a subtle form of desire-attachment that serves to scatter the mind and disrupt meditative concentration through attraction to pleasant objects. With gross excitement, the meditator loses the objective support altogether. With subtle excitement, the mind stays on the objective, but a corner of the mind is fantasizing about another object, like rushing water beneath still ice.

factor of clarity (Tib. *gsal cha*). Within meditative stabilization, the aspect of the objective support appearing clearly to the mind, free of gross laxity.

factor of stability (Tib. *gnas cha*). Within meditative stabilization, the aspect of the objective support appearing unwaveringly, free of gross excitement.

final reality (Skt. *dharmatā*; Tib. *chos nyid*). Literally "the thing itself," this is a synonym for emptiness.

five aggregates (Skt. *pañcaskandha*; Tib. *phung po lnga*). The factors that comprise a person: form, feeling, discrimination, compounding factors, and consciousness. Students often find this list arbitrary, but there is a specific purpose for the presentation. The first aggregate is the body and the latter four are mind, so essentially this is the body and the mind. Within mind, the final factor is the main mind, the mere aspect of clarity and knowing, while the first three are the mental factors, the specific qualities and functions of the mind. Again, feeling and discrimination are separated out, and "compounding factors" includes all other mental factors. Feeling and perception are separated because they are the main causes of circling in cyclic existence. Beings cycle primarily due to attachment to pleasant feelings and aversion to unpleasant ones. Furthermore, they act motivated by their (often mistaken) beliefs about which actions will cause pleasant feelings and minimize unpleasant ones, and beliefs are forms of discrimination. Based on feeling and discrimination, beings develop the volition to act, and so volition is the primary factor among the remaining ones. Thus the fourth aggregate takes the name "compounding factors," another way of expressing volition.

five faults (Skt. *pañcadoṣa*; Tib. *nyes pa lnga*). The five major obstacles to calm abiding. (1) Laziness is an obstacle before one begins practice. (2) Forgetting the instructions is an obstacle in the initial stages of practice. (3) Laxity and excitement become obstacles as one gains some degree of stability. (4) Not applying an antidote is an obstacle when laxity and excitement arise. (5) (Unnecessarily) applying an antidote is an obstacle when one is close to achieving calm abiding, and laxity and excitement no longer arise.

forder (Skt. *tīrthika*; Tib. *mu stegs pa*). A spiritual practitioner who is following a non-Buddhist path. This term indicates that such a person is making a sincere effort to "cross the stream" toward liberation.

four classes of tantra (Tib. *rgyud sde bzhi*). All tantric practices are included in one of these four classes: action tantra, performance tantra, yoga tantra, and unsurpassed yoga tantra. Each class involves progressively more refined and difficult forms of meditation. Mantra-system mahāmudrā belongs to the unsurpassed yoga tantra class.

four empties (Skt. *catuḥśūnya*; Tib. *stong pa bzhi*). Empty, very empty, great empty, and all empty, which are synonymous respectively with the four progressively subtler levels of mind associated with the four visions: the (1) white appearance, (2) red increase, (3) black near-attainment, and (4) clear light.

"Empty" in this context does not mean empty of inherent existence, but rather refers to the mind being empty of, or free from, progressively subtler levels of dualistic appearance. These four empties are empty of, respectively, (1) coarse conceptual thought, (2) the white appearance, (3) the red increase, and (4) the black near-attainment. Thus the clear light is free of all traces of conceptual or dualistic appearance regarding its object.

His Holiness the Dalai Lama points out that "emptiness" here is not the "self-emptiness" of the *Perfection of Wisdom Sūtras*, but instead relates to the "other-emptiness" espoused by Dölpopa Sherap Gyaltsen and his Jonang followers. "Self-emptiness" is emptiness of *being* something, like how a rope mistaken for a snake is empty of *being* a snake—that is, it is not a snake. Likewise, phenomena are empty of being inherently existent. "Other-emptiness," conversely, is emptiness of *possessing* something, like in the example "the temple is empty of monks." So in this context, the object—emptiness—remains the same, but the mind experiencing it grows progressively subtler as it is freed from subtler levels of dualistic appearance.

four joys (Skt. *catvāra ānandāḥ*/*caturānandāḥ*; Tib. *dga' ba bzhi*). Joy, supreme joy, extraordinary joy, and connate joy. By causing the white drop at the crown to descend into the central channel, a meditator experiences progressively more intense levels of physical bliss at the throat, heart, navel, and secret region. Using this bliss as the immediately preceding condition, he generates subtle levels of mind that meditate on emptiness. These minds meditating on emptiness are not actual joy or bliss, but based on their immediate cause—physical bliss—take the name "four joys." Usually these four joys are combined with the four empties, although some practitioners cultivate the joys first before manifesting the subtlest minds.

four māras (Skt. *caturmāra*; Tib. *bdud bzhi*). Four major obstacles to overcome in achieving enlightenment: (1) the māra of afflictions (Skt. *kleśamāra*; Tib. *nyon mongs kyi bdud*), (2) the māra of the aggregates (Skt. *skandhamāra*; Tib. *phung po'i bdud*), (3) the māra of the lord of death (Skt. *mṛtyupatimāra*; Tib. *'chi bdag gi bdud*), and (4) the māra of the son of the gods (Skt. *devaputramāra*; Tib. *lha'i bu'i bdud*). See note 176.

four mental applications (Skt. *caturmanaskāra*; Tib. *yid byed bzhi*). Four levels of meditation that successively become primary at different stages of cultivating calm abiding. During the first two mental settlings, one practices (1) focused engagement. From the third to the seventh, one practices (2) interrupted engagement. At the eighth, one practices (3) uninterrupted engagement. During the ninth and final mental settling, one practices (4) spontaneous achievement.

four opponent powers (Skt. *catuḥpratipakṣabala*; Tib. *gnyen po'i stobs bzhi*). Four states of mind one cultivates to counteract the effects of past negative deeds. They are the power of the basis, the power of repudiation, the power of relying on an antidote, and the power of not repeating the fault.

front generation (Skt. *sākṣādutpatti*; Tib. *mdun bskyed*). In tantric practice, the visualization of a deity in the space in front of oneself, which is distinguished from self-generation—visualizing oneself as a deity.

generation stage (Skt. *utpattikrama*; Tib. *bskyed rim*). The first stage of unsurpassed yoga tantra practice, this stage primarily involves creative imagination taking death, the bardo, and rebirth into the path without causing the winds to enter, abide, and dissolve in the central channel. This stage ripens the mindstream for the completion stage. During the gross generation stage, a practitioner visualizes deities at a normal size, while during the subtle generation stage, one visualizes the entire maṇḍala of deities in a space the size of a mustard seed.

happy migration (Skt. *sugati*; Tib. *bde 'gro*). Birth as a human or god.

hearer (Skt. *śrāvaka*; Tib. *nyan thos*). A Buddhist practitioner who has entered the path and whose primary concern is achieving self-liberation under the guidance of a teacher.

ignorance that apprehends a self (Tib. *bdag 'dzin ma rig pa*). A mental factor that observes a person or object, and apprehends that person or object to be inherently existent.

illusory body (Skt. *māyādeha*; Tib. *sgyu lus*). The fourth stage of the completion stage. Having actualized the clear light, a practitioner causes the very subtle wind to arise in the form of the deity he or she previously visualized during the generation stage. Before the direct perception of emptiness, this is the impure illusory body, and after that direct perception, it is the pure illusory body, whose substantial continuum will become the complete enjoyment body of a buddha.

improper mental engagement (Skt. *ayoniśomanaskāra/ayoniśomanasikāra*; Tib. *tshul min yid byed*). Habitual conceptual thought patterns that exaggerate the qualities of objects, giving rise to afflictions like desire-attachment, anger, and jealousy. Although these can take many forms—thoughts like "He harmed me!" and "She is so beautiful!"—the most important ones to recognize are (1) apprehending impermanent things to be permanent, (2) apprehending the causes of suffering to be the causes of happiness, (3) apprehending impure things (like the human body) to be pure, and (4) apprehending that which is selfless to possess an enduring, independent identity. These thoughts cycle constantly just below conscious awareness, so when one meditates they can seem to increase, but that is merely because one starts to notice them. Some modern scholars, aware of developments in psychology, suggest the translation "maladaptive cognitive appraisals." Such a term captures the general idea of what is happening here, though many of the traditional forms of improper mental engagement, such as the conception of true existence, may not be classified as "maladaptive" in modern psychological circles.

indestructible drop (Skt. *akṣarabindu*; Tib. *mi shigs pa'i thig le*). The combined parts of the white and red drops residing at the center of the heart, which houses the very subtle wind and mind. This drop is "indestructible" because it continues from birth until death. During the stage of mental isolation, a tantric practitioner intentionally causes this drop to split open. The term "indestructible drop" can also be used to refer to the completely indestructible drop, which is the very subtle wind associated with the primordial clear light mind. This latter indestructible drop continues from lifetime to lifetime.

intensity of the factor of clarity (Tib. *gsal cha'i ngar*). An appearance of the objective support that is not only clear but vivid and forceful. One achieves this intensity when subtle laxity subsides. Some translators render this term as "sharpness."

introspection (Skt. *samprajanya*; Tib. *shes bzhin*). A mental factor that maintains awareness of the contents of consciousness, especially whether or not afflictions are present.

isolation (Skt. *viveka*; Tib. *dben pa*). In everyday life, ordinary beings experience their minds and environment as "polluted"—as the reflection of imprints of afflictions and the conception of true existence. Completion stage tantric practice involves isolating or separating oneself from these appearances and conceptions so that one can instead experience oneself and one's surroundings as pure—seeing oneself as a deity, one's surroundings as the deity's palace and retinue, and all appearances as empty of true existence.

isolation of body (Skt. *kāyaviveka*; Tib. *lus dben*). The first stage of the completion stage. During this stage, a practitioner begins to cause the winds to enter, abide, and dissolve in the central channel at channel wheels other than the heart—usually the navel or secret region. In so doing, one isolates oneself from the ordinary appearance and conception of one's body, and begins to manifest a wisdom of bliss and emptiness.

isolation of mind (Skt. *cittaviveka*; Tib. *sems dben*). The third stage of the completion stage. During this stage, a practitioner causes the winds to enter, abide, and dissolve in the indestructible drop at the heart. In so doing, one "isolates" oneself from ordinary appearance and conceptions of one's mind. At the end of this stage, one achieves the example clear light.

isolation of speech (Skt. *vāgviveka*; Tib. *ngag dben*). The second stage of the completion stage. During this stage, using vajra recitation, a practitioner begins to cause the winds to enter, abide, and dissolve in the central channel at the heart, but not in the indestructible drop. In so doing, one "isolates" oneself from ordinary appearance and conceptions of one's speech.

knowledge obscurations (Skt. *jñeyāvaraṇa*; Tib. *shes sgrib*). Along with afflictive obscurations, one of the two classes of obscurations. These include the imprints of the afflictions as well as the appearance of true existence to thought and sense consciousnesses. When they are abandoned, the mind lacks any obstruction and achieves the omniscient consciousness of a buddha.

laxity (Skt. *laya*; Tib. *bying ba*). A mental factor which functions to make an object of meditation appear in a dull or loose manner. With gross dullness, the object appears but not clearly, and with subtle dullness, it appears clearly but not intensely.

left channel (Skt. *lalanā*; Tib. *rkyang ma*). One of the two main channels that wrap around the central channel and through which wind energy flows for ordinary beings.

lethargy (Skt. *styāna*; Tib. *rmugs pa*). A mental factor that causes sleepiness and apathy. Although related to laxity, unlike laxity, lethargy can be nonvirtuous and occurs in ordinary people, not only in meditators.

liberation (Skt. *mokṣa*; Tib. *thar pa*). Freedom from cyclic existence; it is synonymous with nirvāṇa.

mahāmudrā (Skt. *mahāmudrā*; Tib. *phyag rgya chen po*). The "great seal." Sūtra-system mahāmudrā is emptiness, the object of meditation. Mantra-system mahāmudrā is the connate great bliss wisdom that realizes emptiness.

manner of apprehension (Skt. *muṣṭibandha*; Tib. *'dzin stangs*). The way consciousness engages or holds an object. For example, with the thought "That man is tall," "man" is the object of observation, and "tall" is the manner of apprehension. In the case of meditative stabilization, the manner of apprehension includes not only the quality the mind apprehends but also the way it apprehends it—tightly or loosely.

meditative stabilization (Skt. *samādhi*; Tib. *ting nge 'dzin*). A degree of concentration that, through cultivation, has attained some factor of stability.

meaning clear light at the end of learning (Tib. *slob pa mtha' yi don gyi 'od gsal*). The connate great bliss wisdom that realizes emptiness at the last moment of the continuum of a sentient being. It acts as the direct antidote to the knowledge obscurations, so at the next moment a practitioner attains the state of a buddha.

meaning-generality (Skt. *arthasāmānya*; Tib. *don spyi*). A generic image that appears to thought consciousness through the force of bringing an object to mind. Unlike a directly appearing object, it lacks specific qualities, because it is only as detailed as the thinker can imagine it.

merely posited over there by thought/merely imputed over there by names (Tib. *rtog pas phar bzhag pa tsam/ming gis phar btsags pa tsam*). To be "posited by thought" and "imputed by names" means that something's coming into existence depends in some way on the thought that apprehends it and the term that designates it. "Over there" negates existence from its own side. According to the Autonomy school, things are *both* posited by thought *and* existent from their own side; both factors must be present for something to exist. They are posited by thought but not posited *over there* by thought. For the Consequence school, things are posited by thought without existing from their own side, so they are posited "over there." For the Consequence school, there is no problem of things not being able to exist before somebody thinks about them, because in this school, causes can be dependent upon their effects. Why? Because (1) something being called a "cause" is only in relation to an "effect," and (2) things only exist in mere name, so if the name of X is dependent on Y, then X is also dependent on Y. An illustrative example would be this: Dr. Donald Johanson discovered the bones of a human ancestor and called them "Lucy." Dr. Johanson did not apply this name until the present day, but still it is conventionally correct to say, "Lucy lived over three million years ago." Lucy depends upon Dr. Johanson for her existence.

Middle Way school (Skt. *madhyamaka*; Tib. *dbu ma pa*). A school of Buddhist philosophy initiated by the Indian master Nāgārjuna. Its defining feature is its rejection of the true existence of all phenomena. Bhāvaviveka's interpretation of Nāgārjuna gave rise to the Autonomy school (Svātantrika), and Candrakīrti's interpretation gave rise to the Consequence school (Prāsaṅgika).

mind of refuge (Skt. *śaraṇacitta*; Tib. *skyabs 'gro'i sems*). A firm mind of faith that entrusts oneself to the Three Jewels of refuge, based on (a) fear of the suffering of the lower realms and of cyclic existence in general and (b) confidence that the Three Jewels have the power to free one from that suffering. Mahāyāna refuge is also based on the third quality of compassion that wishes to free others from suffering.

Mind Only school (Skt. *cittamātra*; Tib. *sems tsam pa*). A school of Buddhist philosophy initiated by the Indian master Asaṅga. Its defining feature is the assertion that all phenomena are of one nature with consciousness. Some, but not all, Mind Only adherents assert the existence of the mind basis-of-all (Skt. *ālayavijñāna*; Tib. *kun gzhi'i rnam shes*).

mother emptiness/mother clear light (Skt. *mātrāprabhāsvara*; Tib. *ma'i 'od gsal*). The clear light mind that manifests naturally for ordinary beings at the time of death.

nine mental settlings (Skt. *navākārā cittasthitiḥ*; Tib. *sems gnas dgu*). Nine progressively more focused stages of meditation that lead to the actualization of calm abiding.

nine rounds of mixing (Tib. *bsre ba skor dgu*). Mixing death with the wisdom truth body, the bardo with the complete enjoyment body, and rebirth with the emanation body during the waking state, in sleep, and at the time of death. To "mix" death with the wisdom truth body actually means to *replace* ordinary death with the experience of the wisdom truth body, and so forth for the others.

nominally existent "I" (Tib. *tha snyad du yod pa'i nga*). The self that performs actions and that we can conceive of and talk about. This self exists conventionally—it is not incorrect to say, "I am meditating"—but when searched for under analysis, one cannot locate any specific thing that corresponds to the conception.

objective support (Skt. *viṣayālambana*; Tib. *dmigs rten*). The basis one uses as an object of meditation. It is called a "support" because focusing on it grounds the mind.

object of negation (Skt. *pratiṣedhya*; Tib. *dgag bya*). In the context of meditation on emptiness, this is inherent existence, the nonexistent superimposition one must recognize and negate in order to establish emptiness. The first step in meditating on emptiness is to recognize the way the mind projects this nonexistent quality.

path mahāmudrā (Tib. *lam gyi phyag rgya chen po*). In mantra-system mahāmudrā, the primordial clear light mind that realizes emptiness, in the continuum of a sentient being.

path of release (Skt. *vimuktimārga*; Tib. *rnam grol lam*). A path that (1) is induced by its immediate cause, an uninterrupted path acting as the direct antidote to a particular object of abandonment, and (2) has abandoned that object. For example, after the meaning clear light acts as the direct antidote to afflictive obscurations, the path of the next moment is the path of release, which has abandoned the afflictions.

pliancy (Skt. *praśrabdhi*; Tib. *shin sbyangs*). A factor of body or mind induced by meditative concentration whose function is to make the body and mind serviceable for virtuous practice by eliminating the assumption of bad states and other obstructions to serviceability. Physical pliancy is a pleasant lightness of body, free of agitated energies, and mental pliancy is a mental factor that keeps the mind fresh and focused.

perfection vehicle (Skt. *pāramitāyāna*; Tib. *phar phyin gyi theg pa*). Nontantric Mahāyāna practice, so called because the main focus is the practice of the six perfections of generosity, ethical discipline, patience, joyous effort, concentration, and wisdom.

primordial mind (Skt. *anādicitta*; Tib. *gnyug sems*). A synonym for the mind of clear light. It is "primordial" because it has existed continuously for beginningless lifetimes in cyclic existence and will continue on until buddhahood. A literal translation of this term might be "fundamental mind," although His Holiness the Dalai Lama also suggests "innermost mind."

recollection (Skt. *smṛti*; Tib. *dran pa*). Often translated as "mindfulness." A mental factor that observes an object with which one has familiarity, that has the aspect of nonforgetfulness, and whose function is to prevent distraction from that object. In the context of meditation, it is the factor that keeps the objective support in mind without slipping into forgetfulness or distraction.

red increase (Tib. *mched pa dmar lam pa*). The appearance that accompanies the second of the three subtle levels of mind that arise sequentially before the clear light, either through meditation or naturally at death. This term can also be used to refer to the mind experiencing that appearance.

right channel (Skt. *rasanā*; Tib. *ro ma*). One of the two main channels that wrap around the central channel and through which wind energy flows for ordinary beings.

sādhana (Skt. *sādhana*; Tib. *sgrub thabs*). A structured series of meditations related to a particular tantric deity.

samaya (Skt. *samaya*; Tib. *dam tshig*). Pledges that one takes at the time of receiving tantric initiation. These include both (1) vows to refrain from certain actions and (2) commitments to continually engage in particular practices and especially to maintain pure perception of one's teacher.

saṃsāra (Skt. *saṃsāra*; Tib. *'khor ba*). Cyclic existence—the body and mind in their ordinary, undeveloped state, which powerlessly cycle through the twelve links of dependent arising under the power of karma and afflictions.

Saṅgha (Skt. *saṅgha*; Tib. *dge 'dun*). The actual Saṅgha are ārya beings—those who have directly realized emptiness. The example Saṅgha is a gathering of at least four fully ordained monks.

scattering (Skt. *visaraṇa*; Tib. *'phro ba*). The mind wandering to unintended objects through the force of habit. Scattering induced by desire-attachment is excitement, though scattering can also be induced by anger or virtuous thoughts.

self-generation (Skt. *ātmotpatti*; Tib. *bdag skyed*). In tantric practice, the visualization of oneself in the form a particular deity, with or without a supporting maṇḍala.

selflessness (Skt. *nairātmya*; Tib. *bdag med*). According to the Consequence school, this is a synonym for emptiness. The "self" of selflessness does not refer to a person but to an independent essence, so both persons and other phenomena are empty of self.

sevenfold posture of Vairocana (Skt. *saptadharmavairocana*; Tib. *rnam snang gi chos bdun*). An ideal sitting posture for meditation: (1) the legs arranged in the vajra position, (2) the hands placed in the mudrā of equipoise, (3) the hips (or lower back) straight, (4) the teeth and lips even and the tip of the tongue lightly pressed against the roof of the mouth, (5) the head slightly bent forward, (6) the eyes cast toward the tip of the nose, and (7) the shoulders straight. Often known in the West by its name in Hindu yoga traditions, the "lotus posture" (*padmāsana*).

sixfold collection of causes (Tib. *rgyu tshogs drug*). Six important causes that allow for successful practice of calm abiding: (1) having a pleasant abode, (2) maintaining pure morality, (3) thoroughly abandoning the bustle of many activities, (4) having few wants, (5) having contentment, and (6) thoroughly abandoning discursive thoughts about desire and so forth.

six powers (Skt. **ṣaḍbala*; Tib. *stobs drug*). Six factors that become primary at successive stages of actualizing calm abiding. The power of hearing is primary at the first stage, the power of reflection at the second, the power of recollection at the third and fourth, the power of introspection at the fifth and sixth, the power of zeal at the seventh and eighth, and the power of thorough familiarization at the ninth.

six preparatory practices (Skt. *ṣaṭ prayogadharmāḥ*; Tib. *sbyor ba'i chos drug*). Six activities that help lay the ground for successful meditation. See note 55.

son clear light (Skt. **putraprabhāsvara*; Tib. *bu'i 'od gsal*). The clear light mind that a meditator intentionally induces in order to meditate on emptiness during the path.

special insight (Skt. *vipaśyanā*, literally "diligent viewing"; Tib. *lhag mthong*, literally "higher seeing"). Within the space of calm abiding, a mental factor of wisdom that not only does not disturb concentration but actually enhances bliss through the force of individual analysis.

stage of observing the mind/focusing on the mind (Skt. *cittālambanakrama*; Tib. *sems dmigs kyi rim pa*). The second of the five stages of the completion stage, which comprises the three isolations of body, speech, and mind. The tradition of grouping these three stages together into one stems from Candrakīrti's commentary *The Clear Lamp* (Skt. *Pradīpo-*

dyotana(nāmaṭīkā); Tib. *Sgron ma gsal bar byed pa*), wherein the generation stage comprises the first stage. Rinpoché gives a slightly different presentation, wherein the isolation of body is the first stage, and the isolations of speech and mind together comprise the second stage of observing the mind.

supporting and supported maṇḍala (Skt. *ādhārādheyamaṇḍala*; Tib. *rten dang brten pa'i dkyil 'khor*). The visualized deities (the supported) along with their abode, which supports them.

sūtra (Skt. *sūtra*; Tib. *mdo*). A discourse of the Buddha that does not involve tantric themes, or a system of practice based on that.

taking the three bodies into the path (Tib. *sku gsum lam 'khyer*). During the generation stage, imaginarily transforming ordinary death, the bardo, and rebirth into, respectively, the wisdom truth body, complete enjoyment body, and emanation body of a buddha. This practice creates the causes such that during the completion stage, a practitioner actualizes the clear light mind and manifests as an illusory body, eventually becoming an actual buddha.

tantra (Skt. *tantra*; Tib. *rgyud*). A discourse of the Buddha that involves, at the very least, the four purities: taking the pure body, abode, enjoyments, and enlightened activities of a resultant buddha into a causal path, or a system of practice based on such a teaching.

three classes of vows (Skt. *trisaṃvara*; Tib. *sdom pa gsum*). The vows of individual liberation, bodhisattva vows, and tantric vows.

three higher trainings (Skt. *triśikṣa*; Tib. *lhag pa'i bslab pa gsum*). The three fundamental Buddhist practices of ethical discipline, concentration, and wisdom. All other Buddhist practices either fit into one of these three practices or act as their branch or support.

Three Precious Jewels (Skt. *triratna*; Tib. *dkon mchog gsum*). The three objects of refuge for Buddhists: Buddha, Dharma, and Saṅgha.

thought of definite emergence (Skt. **niḥsaraṇacitta*; Tib. *nges 'byung gi bsam pa*). Often translated as "renunciation," this is the determination to be free of cyclic existence and is the distinguishing feature that demarcates a Buddhist path.

torma (Skt. *bali*; Tib. *gtor ma*). An offering of food, ideally arranged in a traditional shape with coloring, with many levels of symbolic significance, that a practitioner makes to meditational deities, protectors, or local spirits.

tummo (Skt. *caṇḍālī*; Tib. *gtum mo*). Literally "fierce lady." A method cultivated during the stages of isolation of body and speech for melting the white drop at the crown in order to experience the four joys. In the practice of Heruka Cakrasaṃvara, a practitioner intentionally cultivates this inner heat at the navel. In the Guhyasamāja system, one does not intentionally cultivate this heat, but a similar process naturally occurs as a practitioner begins to dissolve the winds during the isolation of body.

unfortunate migration (Skt. *apāyaḥ/durgati*; Tib. *ngan song*). States of rebirth where suffering predominates and precludes any intentional spiritual development. These include birth as a hell being, hungry ghost, or animal.

unification (Skt. *yuganaddha*; Tib. *zung 'jug*). The sixth and last stage of the completion stage. One achieves the unification of abandonment after arising from the meaning clear light and the unification of realization when again entering into meditation on emptiness after having already achieved the pure illusory body. These are both subsumed under the category of "learner's union." The union of no more learning is the stage of a buddha.

union of calm abiding and special insight (Skt. *śamathavipaśyanāyuganaddha*; Tib. *zhi lhag zung 'brel*). A synonym for special insight.

unsurpassed yoga tantra (Skt. *anuttarayogatantra*; Tib. *bla na med pa'i rnal 'byor gyi rgyud*). The fourth and most advanced class of tantric teachings and practices. This includes the generation and completion stages.

vajra recitation (Skt. *vajrajāpa*; Tib. *rdo rje bzlas pa*). Primarily a part of the isolation of speech stage, although practitioners also cultivate this practice to some extent during isolation of body and mind and there is a simulacrum of this practice during the generation stage. The purpose of this practice is to cause the winds to dissolve into the indestructible drop at the heart and to clear out obstructions in the central channel. One focuses on the winds in the sound of *oṃ āḥ hūṃ*, and by focusing the mind, the winds naturally gather where the mind is focused.

vital points of the vajra body (Skt. **vajramarman*; Tib. *rdo rje gnad*). Points to focus on within the central channel, either at the six major channel wheels or at the top and bottom tips of the channel. Through different means of absorbed concentration on these points, a practitioner pierces them—that is, gathers the wind energies there—in order to cause the winds to enter the central channel.

white appearance (Tib. *snang ba dkar lam pa*). The appearance like a clear autumn sky that occurs during the first of the three subtle levels of mind that precede the clear light. This term also refers to the mind experiencing that appearance.

winds (Skt. *vāyu*; Tib. *rlung*). Subtle energies that flow throughout the body and act as the mount for consciousness. Because of their intimate relationship with consciousness, a tantric practitioner manipulates them as a means of gaining control over the subtle mind. Note that the subtle wind has the following five subtypes:

1. The life-supporting wind / vital wind (Skt. *prāṇa*; *srog 'dzin*)
2. The downward-voiding wind (Skt. *apāna*; Tib. *thur du sel ba*)
3. The upward-moving wind (Skt. *udāna*; Tib. *gyen du rgyu ba*)
4. The equally-abiding wind (Skt. *samāna*; Tib. *me dang mnyam du gnas pa*)
5. The pervading wind (Skt. *vyāna*; Tib. *khyab byed*)

wisdom truth body (Skt. *jñānadharmakāya*; Tib. *ye shes chos sku*). Synonymous with the mind of a buddha, the exalted knower of all aspects, this is the aspect of a buddha that appears directly only to other buddhas.

Sanskrit additions were supplied by Ven. Gyalten Jigdrel, with substantial assistance from Prof. Harunaga Isaacson (University of Hamburg), who not only offered clear and plentiful advice on matters of Sanskrit terminology, but generously offered to proofread the entire English section of the final draft, bringing to light several points that needed mending. Likewise warmly appreciated are the efforts of Dr. Nirajan Kafle, University of Leiden, Netherlands, Prof. Michael Zimmermann, University of Hamburg, and equally Elisabeth Steinbückner, founding member of the Kringellocken Kloster (Germany), in clarifying Sanskrit terms. Prof. Halkias's help (University of Hong Kong) in assessing ambiguous aspects of bibliographical references for the primary literature is likewise gratefully appreciated. It goes without saying that Ven. Jigdrel takes full responsibility for any potential errors in the rendition of the Sanskrit, errors that doubtlessly remain despite the extensive help that has been gracefully offered by the aforementioned specialists.

Suggestions for Further Reading

Selections marked with an asterisk (*) are especially recommended.

On Calm Abiding

Lamrimpa, Gen. 1995. *How to Practice Shamatha Meditation*. Translated by B. Alan Wallace. Ithaca, NY: Snow Lion Publications.

*Lati Rinbochay and Denma Locho Rinbochay. 1997. *Meditative States in Tibetan Buddhism*. Translated and edited by Leah Zahler and Jeffrey Hopkins. Somerville, MA: Wisdom Publications.

*Lodrö, Geshe Gedün. 1998. *Calm Abiding and Special Insight*. Translated by Jeffrey Hopkins. Ithaca, NY: Snow Lion Publications.

Khenchen Thrangu. 1993. *The Practice of Tranquillity and Insight*. Ithaca, NY: Snow Lion Publications.

*Shankman, Richard. 2008. *The Experience of Samādhi: An In-Depth Exploration of Buddhist Meditation*. Boston: Shambhala Publications.

*Sopa, Geshe Lhundub, with James Blumenthal. 2016. *Steps on the Path to Enlightenment: A Commentary on Tsongkhapa's Lamrim Chenmo: Volume 4: Śamatha*. Somerville, MA: Wisdom Publications.

Wallace, B. Alan. 1998. *The Bridge of Quiescence*. Ithaca, NY: Open Court.

———. 2011. *Stilling the Mind: Shamatha Teachings from Dudjom Lingpa's Vajra Essence*. Somerville, MA: Wisdom Publications.

Zahler, Leah. *Study and Practice of Meditation*. 2009. Ithaca, NY: Snow Lion Publications.

On Geluk Mahāmudrā

Dhargay, Geshe Ngawang. 1981. Commentary on *The Great Seal of Voidness*. In First Panchen Lama. *The Great Seal of Voidness: The Root Text for the Gelug/Kagyu Tradition of Mahamudra*; *The Main Path All Buddhas Have Travelled*. Translated by Geshe Ngawang Dhargay, Sharpa Tulku, Khamlung Tulku, Alexander Berzin, and Jonathan Landaw. In *Four Essential Buddhist Texts*, H.H. the Fourteenth Dalai Lama et al., 53–81. Dharamsala, India: Library of Tibetan Works and Archives.

*Gyatso, Tenzin, the Fourteenth Dalai Lama, and Alexander Berzin. 1997. *The Geluk/Kagyü Tradition of Mahāmudrā*. Ithaca, NY: Snow Lion Publications.

Gyatso, Tenzin, the Fourteenth Dalai Lama, Khöntön Peljor Lhündrub, and José Ignacio Cabezón. 2011. *Meditation on the Nature of the Mind*. Somerville, MA: Wisdom Publications.

Jackson, Roger R. 2001. "The dGe ldan-bKa' brgyud Tradition of Mahāmudrā: *How Much gGe ldan? How Much bKa' brgyud?*" In *Changing Minds: Contributions to the Study of Buddhism and Tibet, in Honor of Jeffrey Hopkins*, edited by Guy Newland, 155–91. Ithaca, NY: Snow Lion Publications.

*———. 2019. *Mind Seeing Mind: Mahāmudrā and the Geluk Tradition of Tibetan Buddhism*. Somerville, MA: Wisdom Publications.

Panchen Losang Chökyi Gyaltsen. 2014. *A Debate between Self-Grasping and the Wisdom Realizing Selflessness, Arising out of an Identification of the Nature of the Basis, Path, and Resultant Mahamudra*. With commentary by Ven. Chöden Rinpoche, translated by Ven. Fedor Stracke. Available for free download at https://happymonkspublication.org/publications/a-debate-between-self-grasping-and-the-wisdom-realizing-selflessness-arising-out-of-an-identification-of-the-nature-of-basis-path-and-resultant-mahamudra/.

Willis, Janice. 1995. *Enlightened Beings: Life Stories from the Ganden Oral Tradition*. Somerville, MA: Wisdom Publications.

Yeshe, Lama. 2018. *Mahamudra*. Somerville, MA: Wisdom Publications.

Bibliography

Kangyur (Canonical Scriptures)

The Descent into Laṅkā Sūtra. Laṅkāvatārasūtra (= *Āryalaṅkāvatāramahāyānasūtra*). *'Phags pa lang kar gshegs pa'i theg pa chen po'i mdo.* Tōh 107, mdo sde *ca* (49), 56a1–191b7.

The Extensive Sport Sūtra. Lalitavistarasūtra (= *Āryalalitavistaranāmamahāyānasūtra*). *Mdo rgya cher rol pa.* Tōh 95, mdo sde *kha* (46), 1b1–216b7.

The Glorious Tantra Which Is an Ornament of the Vajra Essence. Vajramaṇḍalālaṃkāratantra (= *Śrīvajramaṇḍalālaṃkāranāmamahātantrarāja*). *Rdo rje'i snying po'i rgyan gyi rgyud.* Tōh 490, rgyud 'bum *tha* (86), 1b1–82a7.

King of Concentrations Sūtra. Samādhirājasūtra (= *Āryasarvadharmasvabhāvasamatāvipañcitasamādhirājanāmamahāyānasūtra*). *Mdo ting nge 'dzin gyi rgyal po.* Also known as *Candrapradīpasūtra* (Tib. *Zla ba sgron me'i mdo*). Tōh 127, mdo sde *da* (55), 1b1–170b7.

Ornament of the Essence. Vajrahṛdayālaṃkāratantra (= *Śrīvajrahṛdayālaṃkāratantranāma*). *Dpal rdo rje'i snying po'i rgyan gyi rgyud.* Tōh 451, rgyud 'bum *cha* (82), 36a1–58b3.

Sūtra of the Essence of the Tathāgatha(s). Tathāgatagarbhasūtra (= *Āryatathāgatagarbhanāmamahāyānasūtra*). *De bzhin gshegs pa'i snying po'i mdo.* Tōh 258, mdo sde *za* (66), 245b2–259b4.

Sūtra of Three Heaps. Trīskandhadharmasūtra (=*Āryatriskandhakanāmamahāyānasūtra*). *Phung po gsum gyi mdo* [aka *Ltung bshags* (*Confession of Downfalls*)]. Tōh. 284, mdo sde *ya* (68), 57a3–77a3.

Sūtra Unravelling the Thought. Saṃdhinirmocanasūtra (= *Āryasaṃdhinirmocananāmamahāyānasūtra*). *Dgongs pa nges 'grel.* Tōh 106, mdo sde *ca* (49), 1b1–55b7.

Three Continuities. Rgyun chags gsum pa. Handwritten manuscript accessible via TBRC Resource ID W1KG22482, https://www.tbrc.org, as of March 3, 2019.

———. 2009. In *Zhal 'don gces btus.* Rumtek, East Sikkim: Dhorphen Publications.

White Lotus of the Genuine Dharma Sūtra (= *"Lotus Sūtra"*). *Saddharmapuṇḍarīkasūtra. Dam chos padma dkar po'i mdo.* Tōh 113, mdo sde *ja* (51), 1b1–180b7.

Tengyur (Canonical Treatises)

Anaṅgavajra. *Accomplishment of Wisdom and Means. Prajñopāyaviniścayasiddhi. Thabs shes grub pa.* Tōh 2218, rgyud *wi* (51), 28b4–36b7.

Asaṅga. *Grounds of Yogic Practice* (= *Treatise on the Grounds of Yogic Practice*). *Yogācārabhūmiśāstra* (*Yogācārabhūmiśāstra** or *Bhūmivastu*). *Rnal 'byor spyod pa'i sa / Sa'i dngos gzhi.* Tōh 4035, sems tsam *tshi* (229), 1b1–283a7.

a. *Compendium of Ascertainments. Viniścayasaṃgrahaṇī* (= *Yogacaryābhūmiviniścayasaṃgrahaṇī*). *Gtan la dbab pa bsdu ba.* Tōh 4038, sems tsam *zhi* (232), 1b1–289a7.

b. *Compendium of Enumerations. Paryāyasaṃgrahaṇī* (= *Yogacaryābhūmau paryāyasaṃgrahaṇī*). *Rnam grangs bsdu ba.* Tōh 4041, sems tsam *'i* (234), 22b1–47b7.

c. *Compendium of Explanations. *Vivaraṇasaṃgrahaṇī/*Vyākhyā(na)saṃgrahaṇī* (= *Yogacaryābhūmau *Vivaraṇasaṃgrahaṇī*). *Rnam par bshad pa bsdu ba.* Tōh 4042, sems tsam *'i* (234), 47b7–68b7.

d. *Compendium of Grounds. Vastusaṃgrahaṇī* (= *Yogacaryābhūmau vastusaṃgrahaṇī*). *Sa gzhi bsdu ba.* Tōh 4039, sems tsam *zi* (233), 127a4–335a7.

Candragomin (Tsandra go min, seventh century). *Praise of Confession. Deśanāstava. Bshags pa'i bstod pa.* Tōh 1159, bstod tshogs *ka* (1), 204a5–206b5.

Candrakīrti. *Clear Lamp. Pradīpodyota* (= *Pradīpodyotananāmaṭīkā*). *Sgron ma gsal bar byed pa.* Tōh 1785, rgyud *ha* (29), 1b1–201b2.

———. *Clear Words. Prasannapadā* (= *Mūlamadhyamakavṛttiprasannapadānāma*). *Dbu ma rtsa ba'i 'grel ba tshig gsal ba.* Tōh 3860, dbu ma *'a* (204), 1b1–200a7.

———. *Commentary on [Āryadeva's] "Four Hundred Stanzas." Catuḥśaṭakaṭīkā* (= *Bodhisattvayogācāracatuḥśatakaṭīkā*). *Bzhi rgya pa'i rgya cher 'grel pa.* Tōh 3865, dbu ma *ya* (205), 30b6–239a7.

———. *Commentary on Sixty Stanzas on Reasoning. Yuktiṣaṣṭīkāvṛtti. Rigs pa drug cu pa'i 'grel pa.* Tōh 3864, dbu ma *ya* (205), 1b1–30b6.

———. *Entering the Middle Way. Madhyamakāvatāra* (= *Madhyamakāvatāranāma*). *Dbu ma la 'jug pa.* Tōh 3861, *dbu ma 'a* (204), 201b1–219a7.

Dārika (dA ri ka). *Accomplishment of Great Secret Suchness. Mahāguhyatattvasiddhi* (= *Śrī Uḍḍiyānavinirgataguhyamahāguhyatattvopadeśa*). *Gsang ba chen po'i de kho na nyid grub pa.* Tōh 2221, rgyud *wi* (51), 62a6–63a5.

Dharmakīrti (Chos kyi grags pa). *Commentary on Valid Cognition. Pramāṇavārttika* (= *Pramāṇavārttikakārikā*). *Tshad ma rnam 'grel.* Tōh 4210, *tshad ma ce* (276), 94b1–151a7.

Ḍombī Heruka. *Connate Accomplishment. Sahajasiddhi* (= *Śrīsahajasiddhināma*). *Lhan cig skyes grub.* Tōh 2223, rgyud *wi* (51), 68b5–70b5.

Indrabhūti (Indra bhU ti). *Accomplishment of (Primordial) Wisdom. Jñānasiddhi* (= *Jñānasiddhināmasādhanopāyikā*). *Ye shes grub pa.* Tōh 2219, rgyud *wi* (51) 36b7–60b6.

Kamalaśīla (Padma'i ngang tshul). *Stages of Meditation. Bhāvanākrama. Bsgom rim.* 3 sections. Tōh 3916–7, dbu ma *ki* (212), 22a1–68b7.

a. [Section 1]. Tōh 3915, dbu ma *ki* (212), 22a1–41b7.

b. [Section 2]. Tōh 3916, dbu ma *ki* (212), 42a1–55b5.
c. [Section 3]. Tōh 3917, dbu ma *ki* (212), 55b6–68b7.

Lakṣmīṃkārā. *Nondual Accomplishment, Advayasiddhi* (= *Advayasiddhisādhana-nāma. Gnyis med grub pa.* Tōh 2220, rgyud *wi* (51), 60b7–62a6.

Maitreya (Rje btsun byams mgon). *Differentiating the Middle from Extremes. Madhyāntavibhāga* (= *Madhyāntavibhāgakārikā*). *Dbus mtha' rnam 'byed.* Tōh 4021, sems tsam *phi* (225), 40b1–45a6.

———. *Distinguishing Dharma and Dharmatā. Dharmadharmatāvibhaṅga. Chos dang chos nyid rnam par 'byed pa.* Tōh 4022, sems tsam *phi* (225), 46b1–49a6.

———. *Ornament for Clear Realization. Abhisamayālaṃkāra* (= *Abhisamayā laṃkāranāmaprajñāpāramitopadeśaśāstrakārikā*). *Mngon rtogs rgyan.* Tōh 3786, *bstan'gyur, shes phyin,* ka (80), 1b1–13a7.

———. *Ornament for the Mahāyāna Sūtras. Mahāyānasūtrālaṃkāra* (= *Mahāyānasūtrālaṃkārakārikā*). *Theg pa chen po mdo sde'i rgyan.* Tōh 4020, sems tsam *phi* (225), 1b1–39a4.

———. *Sublime Continuum. Mahāyānottaratantraśāstra* (= *Mahāyānottara-tantraśāstraratnagotravibhāga*). *Theg pa chen po rgyud bla ma.* Tōh 4024, sems tsam *phi* (225), 54b1–73a7.

Nāgārjuna (Klu sgrub). *Dispelling Disputes. Vigrahavyāvartanī* (= *Vigrahavyāvar-tanīkārikānāma*). *Rtsod zlog.* Tōh 3828, mdo *tsa* (198), 27a1–29a7.

———. *Finely Woven. Vaidalyasūtra* (= *Vaidalyasūtranāma*). *Zhib mo rnam 'thag.* Tōh 3826, dbu ma *tsa* (198), 22b6–24a6.

———. *Precious Garland. Ratnāvalī* (= *Rājaparikathāratnāvalī*). *Rin chen phreng ba.* Tōh 4158, spring yig *ge* (274), 107a1–126a4.

———. *Root Wisdom of the Middle Way. Mūlamadhyamakakārikā* (= *Prajñā-nāmamūlamadhyamakakārikā*). *Dbu ma'i rtsa ba shes rab.* Tōh 3824, dbu ma *tsa* (198), 1b1–19a6.

———. *Seventy Stanzas on Emptiness. Śūnyatāsaptati* (= *Śūnyatāsaptatināma*). *Stong nyid bdun cu pa.* Tōh 3827, dbu ma *tsa* (198), 24a6–27a1.

———. *Sixty Stanzas on Reasoning. Yuktiṣaṣṭikā* (= *Yuktiṣaṣṭikākārikānāma*). *Rigs pa drug cu pa.* Tōh 3825, dbu ma *tsa* (198), 20b1–22b6.

[Sahajā]yoginī Cintā ([Lhan cig skyes pa'i] rnal sbyor ma ci to). *Accomplishment of Suchness That Pervades All Things. Vyaktabhavānugatatattvasiddhi. Dngos po gsal ba'i rjes su 'gro ba'i de kho na nyid grub pa.* Tōh 2222, *bstan 'gyur,* rgyud *wi* (51), 63a6–68b5.

Śāntideva (Rgyal sras zhi ba lha). *Engaging in the Bodhisattva Deeds. Bodhicaryā-vatāra (= Bodhisattvacaryāvatāra). Byang chub sems dpa'i spyod pa la 'jug pa.* Tōh 3871, dbu ma *la* (207), 1b1–40a7.

Saroruhavajra (Mtsho skyes rdo rje). *Secret Accomplishment. Guhyasiddhi* (= *Sakalatantrasaṃbhavasaṃcodanī śrīguhyasiddhināma*). *Gsang ba grub pa.* Tōh 2217, rgyud *wi* (51), 1b1–28b4.

Tibetan-Language Works

Atiśa Dīpaṃkaraśrījñāna (Dpal mar med mdzad ye shes). 2012. *Lamp for the Path to Enlightenment. Bodhipathapradīpa. Byang chub lam gyi sgron me.* In *Byang chub lam gyi rim pa'i khrid yig*, Vol. 1. Mundgod: Yongzin Lingtsang Labrang.

Chöden Rinpoché. 2018. *Thun drug bla ma'i rnal 'byor gyi 'grel pa dang / zhi lhag gi yams len gyi skor bcas.* Bylakuppe, Karnataka, India: 'jam dbyangs rol pa'i rtsom sgrig sde mtshan.

Gyaltsap Darma Rinchen (Rgyal tshab dar ma rin chen). 2006. *Clarifying the Path to Liberation. Tshad ma rnal 'grel gyi tshig le'ur byas pa'i rnam bshad thar lam phyin ci ma log par gsal bar byed pa.* Varanasi: wA Na dbus bod kyi ches mtho'i gtsug lag slob khang gi dge ldan spyi las khang. Dge ldan pod phreng ang 77, 78.

———. 2008. *Ornament of the Essence. Rnam bshad snying po'i rgyan.* Mundgod: Drepung Loseling Library Society.

Keutsang Jamyang Mönlam (Ke'u tshang blo bzang 'jam dbyangs smon lam). 1999. *The Excellent, Always Virtuous Path to Liberation: Notes on the Genden Oral Lineage of Mahamudra. Dge ldan snyan brgyud kyi bka' srol phyag rgya chen po'i zin bris rnam grol kun tu dge ba'i lam bzang.* In *Blo bzang dgongs rgyan mu tig phreng mdzes deb so bzhi pa*, 146–47. Mundgod: Drepung Loseling Educational Society.

Khedrup Sangyé Yeshé (Mkhas drub Sangs rgyas ye shes). 1973–76. *The Collected Works* (gsuṅ- 'bum) *of Mkhas-drub san-rgyas-ye-śes.* New Delhi: Don 'grub rdo rje.

Khetsun Sangpo. 1973. *Biographical Dictionary of Tibet and Tibetan Buddhism: Compiled by Khetsun Sangpo.* Vol. 5, *The Bka'-gdams-pa Tradition (Part One).* Dharamsala, India: Library of Tibetan Works and Archives.

———. 1975. *Biographical Dictionary of Tibet and Tibetan Buddhism: Compiled by Khetsun Sangpo.* Vol. 6, *The Bka'-gdams-pa Tradition (Part One)* [sic]. Dharamsala, India: Library of Tibetan Works and Archives.

Losang Chökyi Gyaltsen (Blo bzang chos kyi rgyal mtshan), the Fourth Paṇchen Lama. 2011a. *Highway of the Conquerors: The Root Text of Mahāmudrā of the Precious Genden Instruction Lineage. Dge lden bka' brgyud rin po che'i phyag chen rtsa ba rgyal ba'i gzhung lam zhes bya ba.* In *Phyag chen rtsa 'grel.* Hunsur, Karnataka, India: Gyudmed Tantric University.

———. 2011b. *The Lamp That Further Clarifies: An Extensive Commentary on the Root Text of Mahāmudrā, the Precious Teaching Tradition of the Genden Oral Lineage. Dge ldan bka' brgyud rin po che'i bka' srol phyag rgya chen po'i rtsa ba rgyas par bshad pa yang gsal sgron me.* In *Phyag chen rtsa 'grel.* Hunsur, Karnataka, India: Gyudmed Tantric University. (Referred to in text as "the autocommentary.")

———, et al. 2011c. *Requesting Prayer to the Mahamudra Lineage. Phyags chen brgyud pa'i gsol 'debs*. In *Phyag chen rtsa 'grel*. Hunsur, Karnataka, India: Gyudmed Tantric University.

———. 2012. *The Easy Path to All-Knowing. Byang chub lam rgyi rim pa'i dmar khrid thams cad mkhyen par bgrod pa'i bde lam*. In *Byang chub lam gyi rim pa'i khrid yig*. Vol. 3. Mundgod: Yongzin Lingtsang Labrang.

Losang Yeshé (Blo bzang ye shes), the Fifth Panchen Lama. 2012. *The Swift Path to All-Knowing. Byang chub lam gyi rim pa'i dmar khrid thams cad mkhyen par bgrod pa'i myur lam*. In *Byang chub lam gyi rim pa'i khrid yig*. Vol. 3. Mundgod: Yongzin Lingtsang Labrang.

Ngawang Losang Gyatso (Ngag dbang Blo bzang Rgya mtsho), the Fifth Dalai Lama. 2012. *Mañjuśrī's Oral Instruction. Byang chub lam gyi rim pa'i khrid yig 'jam dpal zhal lung*. In *Byang chub lam gyi rim pa'i khrid yig*. Vol. 3. Mundgod: Yongzin Lingtsang Labrang.

Ngülchu Dharmabhadra (Dngul chu Dharma Bha dra). *Dispelling All Illusions: Notes Taken During Profound Instructions on the Root Text of Mahāmudrā, Highway of the Conquerors. Phyag rgya chen po'i rtsa ba rgyal ba'i gzhung lam gyi steng nas zab 'khrid gnang skabs kyi zin bris 'phrul ba kun sel*. https://www.tbrc.org/#library_work_ViewByOutline-O4CZ251254CZ138939%7CW6493.

Phabongkha Dechen Nyingpo (Pha bong kha bde chen snying po). 1973. *Rigs brgya'i khyab bdag rdo rje sems dpa'i ngo bo rje pha bong kha pa'i gsan yig bsam 'phel nor bu'i do shal*. In *Collected Works of PHA-BON-KHA-PA BYAMS-PA-BTSAN-'DZIN-PHRIN-LAS-RGYA-MTSHO*. Vol. 1. New Delhi.

———. 2012. *Liberation in the Palm of Your Hand. Rnam grol lag bcangs su gtod pa'i man ngag zab mo tshang la ma nor ba mtshungs med chos kyi rgyal po'i thugs bcud byang chub lam gyi rim pa'i nyams khrid kyi zin bris gsung rab kun gyi bcud bsdus gdams ngag bdud rtsi'i snying po*. In *Byang chub lam gyi rim pa'i khrid yig*. Vol 5. Mundgod: Yongzin Lingtsang Labrang.

Phadampa Sangyé (Pha dam pa sangs rgyas). 2011. *One Hundred Verses of Advice for the People of Dingri. Ding ri brgya rtsa ma*. In Pha Dampa Sangs Rgyas's *One Hundred Spiritual Instructions to the Dingri People*. Edited and translated by Lozang Jamspal and David Kittay. New Delhi: Ladakh Ratnashridipika.

Thupten Samdrup (Thub bstan bsam grub). *Sgom sde tshig mdzod chen mo*. Taiwan: Corporate Body of the Buddha Educational Foundation.

Tsongkhapa Losang Drakpa (Tsong kha pa blo bzang grags pa). 2012a. "Destiny Fulfilled: An Expression of Realization." *Rtogs brjod mdun legs ma*. In *Byang chub lam gyi rim pa'i khrid yig*. Vol. 2. Mundgod: Yongzin Lingtsang Labrang.

———. 2012b. *The Great Treatise on the Stages of the Path to Enlightenment. Byang chub lam rim che ba*. In *Byang chub lam gyi rim pa'i khrid yig*. Vol. 1. Mundgod: Yongzin Lingtsang Labrang.

———. 2012c. *Middle-Length Stages of the Path. Byang chub lam rim 'bring po*. In *Byang chub lam gyi rim pa'i khrid yig*. Vol. 2. Mundgod: Yongzin Lingtsang Labrang.

———. 2012d. "Song of Experience." *Lam rim nyams mgur*. Also known as "Condensed Stages of the Path" (*Lam rim bsdus don*). In *Byang chub lam gyi rim pa'i khrid yig*. Vol. 2. Mundgod: Yongzin Lingtsang Labrang.

English Works

Ārya Asaṅga. 2016. *The Bodhisattva Path to Unsurpassed Enlightenment: A Complete Translation of the* Bodhisattvabhūmi. Translated by Artemus B. Engle. Boulder, CO: Snow Lion Publications.

Āryadeva et al. 1994. *Yogic Deeds of Bodhisattvas: Gyel-tsap on Āryadeva's Four Hundred*. Ithaca, NY: Snow Lion Publications.

Bretfeld, Sven. 2004. "The 'Great Debate' of bSam yas: Construction and Deconstruction of a Tibetan Buddhist Myth," *Asiatische Studien* 58, no. 1: 15–56.

Brunnhölzl, Karl. 2011. *Gone Beyond: The Prajñāparamitā Sūtras, The Ornament of Clear Realization, and Its Commentaries in the Tibetan Kagyü Tradition*. Ithaca, NY: Snow Lion Publications.

———. 2014. *When the Clouds Part: The Uttaratantra and Its Meditative Tradition as a Bridge Between Sūtra and Tantra*. Boston: Snow Lion Publications.

Buddhaghosa, Bhadantācariya. 1991. *The Path of Purification*. Translated by Bhikkhu Ñāṇamoli. Kandy, Sri Lanka: Buddhist Publication Society.

Chandrakirti, Venerable Master. n.d. *Introduction to the Middle Way* (aka *Supplement to the Middle Way*). Translated by Ven. Fedor Stracke. Available for free download at https://happymonkspublication.org/publications/introduction-to-the-middle-way/.

Chöden Rinpoché. 2012. *Stairway to the State of Union: A Collection of Teachings on Secret Mantra*. Translated by Ian Coghlan and Voula Zarpani. Churchill, Australia: Awakening Vajra Publications.

———. 2013. *Hundreds of Deities of Tuṣita*. Translated by Ian Coghlan and Voula Zarpani. Churchill, Australia: Awakening Vajra Publications.

Chos-'byor, Ngag-dbang. 2001. *Jorchö: The Six Preparatory Practices*. Dharamsala, India: Library of Tibetan Works and Archives.

Conze, Edward. 1975. *The Large Sūtra on Perfect Wisdom*. Delhi: Motilal Banarsidass.

Edou, Jérôme. 1996. *Machig Labrön and the Foundations of Chöd*. Ithaca, NY: Snow Lion Publications.

Foundation for the Preservation of the Mahayana Tradition. 2005. *Nyung Nä: The Means of Achievement of the Eleven-Face Great Compassionate One*. Portland, OR: FPMT.

———. 2006. *Essential Buddhist Prayers: An FPMT Prayer Book*. Vol. 1, *Basic Prayers and Practices*. Portland, OR: FPMT.

Garfield, Jay L. 1995. *The Fundamental Wisdom of the Middle Way*. New York: Oxford University Press.

Goleman, Daniel, and Richard J. Davidson. 2017. *Altered Traits: Science Reveals How Meditation Changes Your Mind, Brain, and Body*. New York: Avery.

Guenther, Herbert. 1993. *Ecstatic Spontaneity: Saraha's Three Cycles of Doha*. Berkeley, CA: Asian Humanities Press.

Gyatso, Geshe Jampa. 2016. *Purification in Tibetan Buddhism: The Practice of the Thirty-Five Confession Buddhas*. Somerville, MA: Wisdom Publications.

Gyatso, Khedrup Norsang. 2004. *Ornament of Stainless Light: An Exposition of Kālacakra Tantra*. Translated by Gavin Kilty. Somerville, MA: Wisdom Publications.

Gyatso, Lobsang, and Graham Woodhouse. 2011. *Tsongkhapa's Praise for Dependent Relativity*. Somerville, MA: Wisdom Publications.

Gyatso, Tenzin, the Fourteenth Dalai Lama. 1988. *The Union of Bliss & Emptiness: A Commentary on the Lama Choepa Guru Yoga Practice*. Ithaca, NY: Snow Lion Publications.

———. 2001. *Stages of Meditation*. Ithaca, NY: Snow Lion Publications.

———. 2002. *Illuminating the Path to Enlightenment*. Long Beach, CA: Thubten Dhargye Ling. (Available from Lama Yeshe Wisdom Archive.)

———, and Alexander Berzin. 1997. *The Geluk/Kagyü Tradition of Mahāmudrā*. Ithaca, NY: Snow Lion Publications.

———, and Thubten Chodron. 2018. *Saṃsāra, Nirvāṇa and Buddha Nature*. Somerville, MA: Wisdom Publications.

Heruka, Tsang Nyon. 1982. *The Life of Marpa the Translator: Seeing Accomplishes All*. Boston: Shambhala Publications.

Hopkins, Jeffrey. 1983. *Meditation on Emptiness*. London: Wisdom Publications.

———. 1987. *Emptiness Yoga*. Ithaca, NY: Snow Lion Publications.

———. 1998. *Buddhist Advice for Living & Liberation*. Ithaca, NY: Snow Lion Publications.

———. 2003. *Maps of the Profound: Jam-yang-shay-ba's Great Exposition of Buddhist and Non-Buddhist Views on the Nature of Reality*. Ithaca, NY: Snow Lion Publications.

Houston, G. W. 1980. *Sources for a History of the bSam yas Debate*. Sankt Augustin: VGH Wissenschaftsverlag.

Huntington, C. W., Jr., with Geshe Namgyal Wangchen. 1989. *The Emptiness of Emptiness: An Introduction to Early Indian Mādhyamika*. Honolulu: University of Hawaii Press.

Jackson, Roger R. 2001. "The dGe ldan-bKa' brgyud Tradition of Mahāmudrā: *How Much gGe ldan? How Much bKa' brgyud?*" In *Changing Minds: Contributions to the Study of Buddhism and Tibet, in Honor of Jeffrey Hopkins*, edited by Guy Newland, 155–91. Ithaca, NY: Snow Lion Publications.

———. 2004. *Tantric Treasures: Three Collections of Mystical Verse from Buddhist India*. Oxford: Oxford University Press.

———. 2019. *Mind Seeing Mind: Mahāmudrā and the Geluk Tradition of Tibetan Buddhism*. Somerville, MA: Wisdom Publications.

Jinpa, Thupten. 2002. *Self, Reality and Reason in Tibetan Philosophy: Tsongkhapa's Quest for the Middle Way*. London: RoutledgeCurzon.

———. 2008. *The Book of Kadam: The Core Texts*. Somerville, MA: Wisdom Publications.

Kachen Yeshe Gyaltsen. 2019. *Manjushri's Innermost Secret: A Profound Commentary of Oral Instructions on the Practice of Lama Chöpa*. Translated by David Gonsalez. Somerville, MA: Wisdom Publications.

Kimiaki, Tanaka. 2016. *Samājasādhanavyavastholi of Nāgabodhi/Nāgabuddhi: Introduction and Romanized Sanskrit and Tibetan Texts.* Tokyo: Watanabe Publishing.

Koch, Christof. 2013. "The Brain of the Buddha." *Scientific American Mind,* July/August, 28–31.

Komito, David Ross. 1987. *Nāgārjuna's "Seventy Stanzas": A Buddhist Psychology of Emptiness*. Ithaca, NY: Snow Lion Publications.

Kyabje Trijang Rinpoché Losang Yeshe. 2013. *The Ecstatic Dance of Chakrasamvara: Heruka Body Mandala Practice & Commentary*. Translated by David Gonsalez. Seattle: Dechen Ling Press.

Lang, Karen C. 2003. *Four Illusions: Candrakīrti's Advice to Travelers on the Bodhisattva Path*. Oxford: Oxford University Press.

Lati Rinbochay and Jeffrey Hopkins. 1979. *Death, Intermediate State and Rebirth in Tibetan Buddhism*. Ithaca, NY: Snow Lion Publications.

Lhalungpa, Lobsang P. 1979 *The Life of Milarepa*. New York: Penguin Compass.

"The Life of a Hidden Meditator." 2000. *Mandala Magazine*, July–August, 62–74.

Lindtner, Chr. 2011. *Nagarjuniana: Studies in the Writings and Philosophy of Nāgārjuna*. Delhi: Motilal Banarsidass.

Loizzo, Joseph. 2007. *Nāgārjuna's Reason Sixty*. New York: American Institute of Buddhist Studies at Columbia University.

Losang Chökyi Gyaltsen, the First Panchen Lama. 1981. *The Great Seal of Voidness: The Root Text for the Gelug/Kagyu Tradition of Mahamudra, the Main Path All Buddhas Have Travelled*. Translated by Geshe Ngawang Dhargay, Sharpa Tulku, Khamlung Tulku, Alexander Berzin, and Jonathan Landaw. In *Four Essential Buddhist Texts*, Tenzin Gyatso, the Fourteenth Dalai Lama, et al., 53–81. Dharamsala, India: Library of Tibetan Works and Archives.

——— and Gyudmed Khensur Lobsang Jampa. 2013. *The Easy Path*. Edited by Lorne Ladner. Somerville, MA: Wisdom Publications.

Maitreya et al. 2000. *Buddha Nature: The Mahayana Uttaratantra Shastra with Commentary*. Translated by Rosemarie Fuchs. Ithaca, NY: Snow Lion Publications.

———. 2004. *Maitreya's Distinguishing Phenomena and Pure Being, with Commentary by Mipham*. Translated by Jim Scott. Ithaca, NY: Snow Lion Publications.

———. 2006. *Middle Beyond Extremes: Maitreya's Madhyāntavibhāga*. Translated by the Dharmachakra Translation Committee, with commentaries by Khenpo Shenga and Ju Mipham. Ithaca, NY: Snow Lion Publications.

———. 2014. *Ornament of the Great Vehicle Sūtras: Maitreya's Mahāyānasūtrālaṃkāra*. Translated by the Dharmachakra Translation Committee, with commentaries by Khenpo Shenga and Ju Mipham. Boston: Snow Lion Publications.

Makransky, John. 1997. *Buddhahood Embodied*. Albany, NY: State University of New York.

Molk, David, with Lama Tsering Wangdu Rinpoche. 2008. *Lion of Siddhas: The Life and Teachings of Padampa Sangye*. Ithaca, NY: Snow Lion Publications.

Ngülchu Dharmabhadra and Losang Chökyi Gyaltsen, the First Paṇchen Lama. 2010. *Source of Supreme Bliss: Heruka Chakrasamvara Five Deity Practice & Commentary*. Translated by David Gonsalez. Ithaca, NY: Snow Lion Publications.

———. 2014. *Blazing Inner Fire of Bliss & Emptiness: An Experiential Commentary on the Practice of the Six Yogas of Naropa*. Translated by David Gonsalez. Seattle: Dechen Ling Press.

——— and Losang Lungtog Tenzin Trinley, the Fifth Ling Rinpoché. 2012. *The Roar of Thunder: Yamantaka Practice & Commentary*. Translated by David Gonsalez. Ithaca, NY: Snow Lion Publications.

Pabongka Rinpoche. 1990–2001. *Liberation in Our Hands, Parts One to Three*. Translated by Sermey Khensur Lobsang Tharchin with Artemus B. Engle. Howell, NJ: Mahayana Sutra and Tantra Press.

———. 1991. *Liberation in the Palm of Your Hand*. Boston: Wisdom Publications.

———. 2000. *Meditation on Vajrabhairava*. Translated by Sharpa Tulku and Richard Guard. Dharamsala, India: Library of Tibetan Works and Archives.

Pasang, Wangdu, and Hildegard Diemberger. 2000. *dBa' bshed: The Royal Narrative Concerning the Bringing of the Buddha's Doctrine to Tibet (Translation and Facsimile Edition of the Tibetan Text)*. Vienna: Verlag der Österreichischen Akademie der Wissenschaften.

Perdue, Daniel. 1992. *Debate in Tibetan Buddhism*. Ithaca, NY: Snow Lion Publications.

Phuntsok Khenpo Yeshe. 2015. *Vajrasattva Meditation: An Illustrated Guide*. Somerville, MA: Wisdom Publications.

Powers, John. 1995a. *Introduction to Tibetan Buddhism*. Ithaca, NY: Snow Lion Publications.

———. 1995b. *Wisdom of the Buddha: The Saṁdhinirmocana Mahāyāna Sūtra*. Berkeley, CA: Dharma Publishing.

Śāntideva. 1997. *A Guide to the Bodhisattva Way of Life*. Translated by Vesna A. Wallace and B. Alan Wallace. Ithaca, NY: Snow Lion Publications.

Schaeffer, Kurtis R. 2005. *Dreaming the Great Brahmin: Tibetan Traditions of the Buddhist Poet-Saint Saraha*. Oxford: Oxford University Press.

Senge, Tri Gyaltsen. 1995. *Yamāntaka Cycle Texts.* Vol. 1, *Part 1 & 2*. Translated by Sharpa Tulku and Richard Guard. New Delhi: Tibet House.

Shankman, Richard. 2008. *The Experience of Samādhi: An In-Depth Exploration of Buddhist Meditation*. Boston: Shambhala Publications.

Sharma, Parmananda. 1997. *Bhāvanākrama of Kamaśila*. New Delhi: Aditya Prakashan.

Sherburne, Richard S. J. 2000. *The Complete Works of Atiśa Śri Dīpaṁkara Jñāna, Jo-bo-rje*. New Delhi: Aditya Prakashan.

Sprung, Mervyn. 1979. *Lucid Exposition of the Middle Way*. Boulder, CO: Prajna Press.

Stewart, Jampa Mackenzie. 1995. *The Life of Gampopa: The Incomparable Dharma Lord of Tibet*. Ithaca, NY: Snow Lion Publications.

Thanissaro Bhikkhu. 2012. *Right Mindfulness*. Available from The Abbot, Metta Forest Monastery, PO Box 1409, Valley Center, CA 92082, USA.

Tharchin, Sermey Khensur Lobsang. 1999. *Six-Session Guru Yoga*. Howell, NJ: Mahayana Sutra and Tantra Press.

Thrangu Rinpoché. 1994. *King of Samadhi*. Hong Kong: Rangjung Yeshe Publications.

———. 2006. *A Song for the King: Saraha on Mahamudra Meditation*. Translated by Michele Martin. Somerville, MA: Wisdom Publications.

———. 2015. *Advice from a Yogi: An Explanation of a Tibetan Classic on What Is Most Important*. Translated by the Thrangu Dharmakara Translation Committee. Boston: Shambhala Publications.

Thuken Losang Chökyi Nyima. 2009. *The Crystal Mirror of Philosophical Systems*. Translated by Geshe Lhundub Sopa. Somerville, MA: Wisdom Publications.

Tibet House. 2015. *Prayer and Meditation Manual.* New Delhi: Tibet House, Cultural Center of His Holiness the Dalai Lama. Available for download at http://bodhiwisdom.org/wp-content/uploads/2017/03/PrayerBook.pdf.

Tillemans, Tom J. F. 1990. *Materials for the Study of Āryadeva, Dharmapāla and Candrakīrti,* Vol. 1. Vienna: Arbeitskreis für Tibetische und Buddhistische Studien.

Treasury of Lives: Biographies of Himalayan Religious Masters. n.d. Accessed December 2, 2018. http://www.treasuryoflives.org.

Tsering, Geshé Tashi. 2008. *Relative Truth, Ultimate Truth*. Somerville, MA: Wisdom Publications.

Tsering, Geshé Tashi. 2016. *Tantra*. Somerville, MA: Wisdom Publications.

Tsongkhapa. 1996. *A Book of Three Inspirations*. Translation in *Tsongkhapa's Six Yogas of Naropa*. Translated, edited, and introduced by Glenn H. Mullin. Ithaca, NY: Snow Lion Publications.

———. 2000. *The Great Treatise on the Stages of the Path to Enlightenment,* Vols. 1–3. Translated by the Lamrim Chenmo Translation Committee. Ithaca, NY: Snow Lion Publications.

———, and Gareth Sparham. 2008–13. *Golden Garland of Eloquence*. Vols. 1–4. Fremont, CA: Jain Publishing.

———. 2012. *Middle-Length Lam-Rim*. FPMT Basic Program. Translated by Philip Quarcoo. https://www.jangchuplamrim.org/wp-content/uploads/Archive-Texts/JCLR-ENGLISH-03-20120710-MiddleLengthLamRim-PhilipQuarcoo-FinalDraft.pdf

Wangchen Rinpoché. 2009. *Buddhist Fasting Practice: The Nyungne Method of Thousand-Armed Chenrezig*. Ithaca, NY: Snow Lion Publications.

Westerhoff, Jan. 2010. *Dispeller of Disputes: Nāgārjuna's Vigravyavartani*. Oxford: Oxford University Press.

———. 2018. *Crushing the Categories: Vaidalyaprakaraṇa by Nāgārjuna*. Somerville, MA: Wisdom Publications.

Willis, Janice. 1995. *Enlightened Beings: Life Stories from the Ganden Oral Tradition*. Boston: Wisdom Publications.

Yangchen Gawai Lodoe. 1995. *Paths and Grounds of Guhyasamaja According to Arya Nagarjuna*. Translated by Tenzin Dorjee. Dharamsala, India: Library of Tibetan Works and Archives.

Yeshe, Lama. 2014. *Becoming Vajrasattva: The Tantric Path of Purification*. Boston: Wisdom Publications.

Zimmermann, Michael. 2002. *A Buddha Within: The Tathāgatagarbhasūtra – The Earliest Exposition of the Buddha Nature Teaching in India*. Bibliotheca Philologica et Philosophica Buddhica VI. Tokyo: The International Research Institute for Advanced Buddhology, Soka University.

Zopa Rinpoche, Lama. 2000a. *A Chat About Heruka*. Boston: Lama Yeshe Wisdom Archive.

———. 2000b. *A Chat About Yamantaka*. Boston: Lama Yeshe Wisdom Archive.

———. 2001. *The Preliminary Practice of Vajrasattva*. Portland, OR: FPMT.

———. 2010. *Kadampa Teachings*. Boston: Lama Yeshe Wisdom Archive.

———. 2017. *Abiding in the Retreat*. Boston: Lama Yeshe Wisdom Archive.

Index

About the Author

His Eminence Chöden Rinpoché was born in eastern Tibet on the fifteenth day of Saka Dawa in 1930 and was recognized as a young boy as the reincarnation of the previous Chöden Rinpoché. When he was fifteen, he enrolled at Sera Jé monastic college, where he excelled; he completed all the study necessary for the highest degree of geshé lharampa and was chosen as a debate partner for the Fourteenth Dalai Lama when His Holiness was taking his geshé exams. After the Chinese takeover of Tibet, Rinpoché entered solitary retreat, in which he stayed for nineteen years. In 1985 the Dalai Lama asked him to leave Tibet to teach in India and Nepal. He taught students in the geshé program at Sera Jé for many years, as well as offering teachings all over the world. He passed away in 2015.

Tenzin Gache (Brian Roiter) grew up in the Boston area, attending Milton Academy and Tufts University, graduating summa cum laude in 2005 with a BA. In his first years of college he resolved to ordain as a Buddhist monk. In 2004 he met Chöden Rinpoché, who invited him to join Lhopa Khangtsen, Rinpoché's house group at Sera Jé. At the end of 2005, he traveled to India, where several months later he received monastic ordination from His Holiness the Dalai Lama. In August of 2006 he moved to Sera Jé, where he has lived and studied since. Currently he is slightly over halfway through the long course of study for the degree of geshé and aspires to attend the six-year round of Geluk examinations qualifying for the degree of lharampa.

What to Read Next from Wisdom Publications

Stilling the Mind
Shamatha Teachings from Düdjom Lingpa's Vajra Essence
B. Alan Wallace

"A much needed, very welcome book." —Jetsun Khandro Rinpoche

Meditation on the Nature of the Mind
His Holiness the Dalai Lama
Khöntön Peljor Lhündrub
José I. Cabezón

"We all have the same human mind—each and every one of us has the same potential. Our surroundings and so forth are important, but the nature of mind itself is more important . . . To live a happy and joyful life, we must take care of our minds." —His Holiness the Dalai Lama

Mind Seeing Mind
Mahāmudrā and the Geluk Tradition of Tibetan Buddhism
Roger Jackson

"*Mind Seeing Mind* is a model study of the historical and doctrinal literature of Buddhism in Tibet." —Matthew T. Kapstein, École Pratique des Hautes Études, Paris, and the University of Chicago

Liberation in the Palm of Your Hand
A Concise Discourse on the Path to Enlightenment
Pabongka Rinpoche

"The richest and most enjoyable volume from the lamrim tradition . . . published to date." —*Golden Drum*

Tsongkhapa's Praise for Dependent Relativity
Lobsang Gyatso and Geshe Graham Woodhouse

"In this elegant text, the venerable Geshe Graham Woodhouse translates Tsongkhapa's jewel-like masterpiece. The radiance of Tsongkhapa's poetry is refracted and enhanced by the brilliant and lucid commentary of the late Gen Losang Gyatso." —Dr. Jay Garfield, Dorris Silbert Professor in Humanities and Professor of Philosophy at Smith College

The Easy Path
Illuminating the First Panchen Lama's Secret Instructions
Gyumed Khensur Lobsang Jampa
Edited by Lorne Ladner

"A marvel." —Jan Willis, author of *Dreaming Me: Black, Baptist, and Buddhist*

Meditation on Emptiness
Jeffrey Hopkins

"An essential book for anyone interested in Madhyamika philosophy." —*Buddhist Studies Review*

About Wisdom Publications

Wisdom Publications is the leading publisher of classic and contemporary Buddhist books and practical works on mindfulness. To learn more about us or to explore our other books, please visit our website at wisdomexperience.org or contact us at the address below.

Wisdom Publications
199 Elm Street
Somerville, MA 02144 USA

We are a 501(c)(3) organization, and donations in support of our mission are tax deductible.

Wisdom Publications is affiliated with the Foundation for the Preservation of the Mahayana Tradition (FPMT).

Thank you for buying this book!

Visit wisdomexperience.org
/mastering-meditation-recitation/
to hear Ven. Gache recite his translation of
Highway of the Conquerors.